THE

OHIO SCHOOL SYSTEM

AND

SCHOOL LAWS IN FORCE.

A MANUAL

OF THE

OHIO SCHOOL SYSTEM;

CONSISTING OF

AN HISTORICAL VIEW OF ITS PROGRESS,

AND A REPUBLICATION OF

THE SCHOOL LAWS IN FORCE.

By JAMES W. TAYLOR,
AUTHOR OF THE "EARLY HISTORY OF OHIO."

CINCINNATI:
H. W. DERBY & Co.
1857.

INTRODUCTION.

The Common School System of Ohio* has attained such proportions, and has assumed such features, as render it not only an object of vital importance to citizens of this State, but of interest scarcely inferior to the intelligent friends of education in other States.

An investment of upward of three millions of dollars in permanent structures, and an annual expenditure of nearly three millions of dollars — nine tenths of which sum last named is produced by taxation — is a financial fact of great significance; while the application of so munificent a provision, under the administration of thirty thousand school officers and twenty thousand teachers, to the education of eight hundred thousand youth, is a fact transcending all material considerations by its relation to the moral and political welfare of the people.

Ohio, on the subject of education, is, in a peculiar sense, a Middle State — holding a golden mean between the prejudices which incumber and obstruct the progress of the Atlantic States and the unavoidable privation or postponement of school advantages which the more Western States must sustain. Thus, while

---

*For the following introductory and explanatory remarks the Publishers are indebted to the late active and efficient Commissioner of Common Schools, at whose suggestion the work was undertaken.

the attempt in New York to establish schools exclusively free, nearly produced a civil convulsion, Ohio, under the Constitution of 1851 and the Revised Act of 1853, quietly and without apparent opposition, abolished the collection of tuition fees, and rendered free every public school of the State—a reform from which no step backward need be apprehended.

The following pages from the pen of the State Librarian, purport to trace from its feeble beginnings, the successive steps of this imposing crusade against ignorance, whose host of directors, teachers and pupils are now marshaled within the limits of Ohio. Our legislation has been voluminous—presenting a proof of the solicitude of the people to frame the best system of measures for the great object of popular instruction. In its progress, a great variety of methods have been tried; and it is desirable that the present generation should be informed, not only of what the law is, but of the nature and results of former experiments. The latter are often brought forward, as proposed amendments, and consume the time and distract the attention of the General Assembly, when the fact of a previous trial and abandonment, if known, would be promptly decisive of their fate. The Historical Outline of School Legislation, now presented, will probably prove advantageous in the future discussion of the School Act—and, if so, it will be in the manner above indicated.

An attempt has also been made to preserve the recollection of those services to the cause of education by the early men of the State, which, in the natural course of events, have become unfamiliar to the younger portion of the community. It is high time that some effort was made to redeem our Ohio Biography, especially of the founders of our State institutions, from the obscurity of neglect.

A republication, in a separate form, of all the general laws relating to education, follows the Historical Narrative. This embraces every statute, which controls the organization of Special

School Districts in cities, towns, etc. The people have been furnished with the General Act of 1853, but not with those enactments "for the better regulation of schools in cities and incorporated villages," which powerfully influence the School System of the State — constituting, as they do, the models for the imitation and emulation of the townships.

It is hoped that this history of the origin, progress and present condition of the School System of Ohio, may serve the two-fold purpose of preventing hasty and inconsiderate legislation, effecting radical changes in the system, and of indicating the educational spirit and tendency of the age. By exhibiting, in a condensed form, those enactments in relation to schools which have been fully and fairly tried and then repealed because they failed to accomplish what was designed, this compilation, it is believed, will tend to prevent the re-enactment of those provisions in former school laws, which, for the want of efficiency, have been thus rejected.

It will also tend to satisfy the public mind that the idea of universal, free education, is fast becoming the grand central idea of the age; that our System of Common Schools, to succeed in accomplishing its full and perfect mission, must be open and free to all the youth of the State, without distinction or discrimination; and that wherever an individual exists with capacities and faculties to be developed, trained, improved and directed, the avenues to knowledge should be freely opened, and every facility afforded to an unrestricted entrance.

Formerly, it was believed that the cost of education should be regarded as a personal expense, to be defrayed by rate bills assessed upon those whose children attended school. This principle virtually excluded the children of the poor. To obviate this defect, the education of the children of those whose pecuniary means did not enable them to incur the expense of it themselves, was made to depend either upon public charity, or upon the power of school officers to exempt the indigent from the payment of tuition fees. Such exemptions, rendered the Common Schools, to some extent, *charity schools*, or schools for the *poor*, a feature which will disparage every system of public instruction, into which it is incorporated, because it is repugnant to the feelings of American citizens. Experience has abundantly demonstrated the fact, that a System of Common Schools, with the charity principle engrafted upon it, will prove inefficient, and fail to accomplish the object at which it aims, because it tends to create distinctions hostile to the character and spirit of our institutions.

Every where, the conviction seems to be settling down upon the public mind, that the free school principle should be engrafted upon our educational systems, and that the funds necessary for their purpose, should be provided by a combination of State and county, or township tax, to be equitably levied on real and personal property, according to a fixed and uniform standard of valuation; and distributed, in both cases, according to the enumeration of youth of school age.

In short, the modern educational doctrine is: "*That the property of the State ought to educate the youth of the State.*" This is regarded as a sound principle, having the value of a *golden maxim.*

It is a principle which the people have, in effect, incorporated into the Constitution of the State. In Art. VI, Sec. 2, it is expressly required, that "the General Assembly shall make such provisions by taxation or otherwise, as, with the interest arising from the the School Trust Fund, will secure a *thorough* and *efficient* system of Common Schools throughout the State."

This language is too plain to be misunderstood. No feeble system, or half-way work, will comply with this wise and noble requisition. But how is such a system to be maintained? The constitution replies, by "taxation," to be levied by "uniform rule." The Legislature has, therefore, enacted a school law establishing a general system of free schools, and imposing for their support, upon all the taxable property of the State, a State School Tax, on the broad principle, that the property of the State should be charged with the responsibility of educating the youth of the State. This system is based upon the principle, that there is no security for a Republic, but in the intelligence, wisdom, and virtue of the people; that "the power of self-defense, and self-protection, the power to cultivate and strengthen the powers of its own being, to improve its own nature, belongs as much to every government as to every man," and that the State is even more deeply and permanently interested in the education of its children than their parents.

But it is sometimes urged by those who do not seem inclined to take a very comprehensive view of this matter, that the property of the State ought to be no more bound to educate the youth of the State than to clothe and feed them. This assertion embraces a sentiment, which, if not traceable to selfishness or an unphilanthrophic disposition, is, at least, as unpatriotic as it is inconsistent with the best interests of the State, and the rising generation. *It is mind that makes the man, and not dollars.* And hence there is a wide difference between the mental and physical wants of our children. They have not the ability to judge of their mental needs, nor have they the power or the disposition, if left to themselves, to provide for such needs.

It is not denied that every parent is under obligation to provide, according to his means, for the education of his children; but since all have not the means, and some have not the disposition, the State should provide a system of free Common Schools, and declare that the expense of it shall be borne by the aggre gate of taxable property within its limits.

In many instances, parents regard the mental culture of their children as a matter of but secondary importance, if they do not treat it with total neglect. What would soon be the mental and moral condition of our population, were the State to discontinue her parental care and guardianship of our free Common Schools? This question is sufficiently answered by referring to the benighted condition of the masses in those States and countries where no system of free schools has, as yet, been established.

The truth is, the State, as such, has a vital interest in this matter of popular education; and is bound in her sovereign capacity, to look to it. All her youth have a *God-given right to an education*—to such an education, moral, and mental, as constitutes a perfect manhood; and, therefore, they have a claim, not only upon their parents, and the State, but upon the entire property of the State, to furnish them with all the requisite facilities for attaining to such a degree of intellectual culture as will enable them rightly to comprehend their duties and relations to God, to the State, and to their fellow-men.

It is not territory, or wealth, that constitutes a great and powerful State. It is *well educated men*; a population, honest, industrious, intelligent. Is it not, then, as much the duty of the State to establish a general system of free schools, as it is to establish courts of justice? As a matter of public policy, the one is as necessary as the other. Yet, it is not contended that free schools should be made a branch of the government; but it is maintained that a republican form of government can not long be sustained without them. This important fact has been, within a few years, sufficiently illustrated in France. All true patriotism, and all true civil and religious liberty, must be based upon popular intelligence and virtue.

Ignorance, superstition, and oppression, whose elements of power enable the few to "lord it over the many," are old associates, and the *implacable enemies* of free institutions. But in this country, as long as the *governed* are their own *governors*, and free Common Schools are maintained by State authority, and rendered accessible to the children of the poor as well as of the rich, there can be no danger of a concentration of power in the hands of irresponsible persons, nor will corrupt influences creep into the Republic and control its destinies. Let our Common Schools be free, and the people will be free.

What is the object of government, but the benefit of the governed? What is the true, legitimate motive for imposing taxes of any kind, but the security, the prosperity, and the happiness of the people? Why should a State School Tax, then, be regarded as burdensome?

Will not a thorough and efficient system of Free Schools subserve these important ends? Who pays this tax? Those who reap the benefit of it. Who reap the benefit of it? Those whose lives are protected by the virtue and regard to law which a good education always inspires,—those whose property is rendered more valuable by the industry and skill which a good education always imparts,—those who sleep in peace, because education and the virtues of which it is the handmaid, have extinguished the torch of the incendiary,—those who enjoy quiet and security, because education has disarmed the robber and assassin.

And who are those that are thus protected in the peaceable enjoyments of their possessions? ALL. The benefits of education are not confined, like the waters of our rivers, within certain narrow channels; but they are like those waters changed into vapors, which a Beneficient Power diffuses far and wide. The objection sometimes urged against a State School Tax seems to arise from the narrow view taken of Education, and of the relation which educated men sustain to the State. The important fact is too often overlooked, that disorder and misery in one part bring disorder and misery upon every part; that the prosperity of *one* communicates itself to *all;* that the strength, wealth, intelligence and happiness of *each,* are entwined with the vigor, and prosperity and security of *all.* In a Republic, *all* are elevated in the elevation of *one,* and *all* are depressed in the depression of *one.*

Surely no tax should be regarded as burdensome which yields a greater and more substantial return than the tax itself. And what branch of the public revenue is there whose disbursement yields so many, so certain, and such invaluable returns as this? Or in what department of the public service does the amount of labor for the same amount of money compare with that in our Common Schools? What has produced the remarkable development of power and activity exhibited within the last twenty years? The answer is, that better and more efficient systems of Education have exerted an important agency in producing these grand results. The mind of the masses has been stimulated by the animating power of Education, and the benefits are hourly being unfolded before us. Good schools not only increase the value of property, but the value of human life. And although their agency in enhancing the value of property and in developing the physical resources of the country may not be so visible as that of turnpikes, plank-roads, and canals, yet it is even greater and far more certain.

Their influence is like that of the dew, and the shower, and the sunshine, quiet and almost imperceptible; but let them cease to diffuse their benefits and their blessings, and devouring famine would not more surely come in the one case, than would a deadly blight upon our prosperity and happiness follow in the other. To abandon, then, the idea of *free schools*, is to turn back half a century to that crude system of education which every step of modern progress, and every result of modern improvement unite in condemning as unsuited to the times in which we live. We might almost as well recall from the past its obsolete system of finance, its iron forms of government, its slow modes of commerce, and its bloody superstitions.

H. H. BARNEY.

CONTENTS.

SCHOOL LAWS IN FORCE.

THE

OHIO SCHOOL SYSTEM.

CHAPTER I.

A GENERAL VIEW OF EUROPEAN SYSTEMS OF PUBLIC INSTRUCTION.

No SYSTEM of public instruction was recognized by the ancients. Common schools are of comparatively recent date, and their benefits are mostly confined to Europeans and their descendants. Prior to Grecian civilization, education was the privilege of those who were designed for official or ecclesiastical stations. Moses was educated in a priestly school in Egypt; Cyrus at a seminary connected with the Persian court; the Indian Brahmins imparted instruction in secret schools; in Palestine, those conversant with the Scriptures taught in the schools of the prophets; at later periods in the synagogues, and in the schools of the rabbis. The advantages of these schools were accessible to few; the means of learning were limited to conversation, reading, committing to memory, and hearing explanations of the sacred books.

Sparta may be regarded as an exception to the invariable practice among the ancients, to leave the education of children exclusively to parents or special classes; but the system of Lycurgus was more intended for the development of the physical powers than the intellect. Still, the Greeks were not without conceptions of the great value to a commonwealth of

2

education. The philosophers were surrounded by ardent disciples; and the popular discussions of the people afforded a superior culture. Nevertheless, even at the most enlightened period of Greece, the mass of freemen were enveloped in profound ignorance.

The Romans, also, from 300 B. C., had schools for boys in the cities, and from the age of Cæsar, who conferred the rights of citizenship on teachers, possessed the higher institutions of the grammarians. In these, Latin and Greek were taught scientifically, and young men of talent went from the grammarians to the rhetoricians, who, like Quintilian, prepared them, by exercises in declamation, for speaking in public. But a regular school system had no existence among the Romans. Schools were institutions confined to particular classes, or were the fruit of private enterprise. Many of these, under the patronage of the emperors, were well adapted to train young men for the public service.

Christianity, by degrees, succeeded to the entire control of education. During the middle ages, the monastic orders sustained schools, whose chief merit consisted in the preservation, to our times, of what survived of ancient literature; but while these conventual schools rivaled the episcopal and cathedral schools of an earlier epoch, yet they were always directed more to the advantage of the priesthood than to purposes of general instruction. That such was the fact is apparent from the traditional designation of the "Dark Ages," which has not been misapplied to that period.

Charlemagne had in view a system of national instruction, when he issued, in 789, his decree for the improvement of the schools of his empire. Not only every bishop's see, and every convent, but every parish was to have its schools; the two former, for the instruction of clergymen and public officers, the latter for the commonalty. At his court, Charlemagne established an academy of distinguished scholars, to whom he himself resorted for instruction, and whom he employed to educate his children, and capable boys belonging to the nobility and other classes, in the court school. The ladies of his court also partook in the benefits of instruction; and some nunneries, in their institutions for female education, rivaled the seminaries in the monasteries. The ladies learned Latin, which was then the common medium of communication between persons of different countries, as French is at present. Charlemagne took upon himself the superintendence of the schools in his empire, had reports sent to him, made examinations, and delivered addresses to the pupils of the school at his court. These schools often enabled him to discover the talents of young men, whom he appointed to high offices in the Church and State. It is one of the noblest traits in his character, that, in that age of gross ignorance, he labored with zeal for the instruction of the nations under his sway. But Charlemagne's decrees were forgotten during the disputes of his grandsons about the government, under whom, also, the above-mentioned court school was abandoned; and his great establishment declined, like the school establishment of the great Alfred, in England, which was begun with equal zeal and on an equal scale, in the ninth century, and was destroyed by the invasions of the Danes; though Edward the Confessor, endeavored to restore it.

Meanwhile the influence of Arabian civilization became apparent in southern Europe, by the cultivation of mathematical and medical science. Institutions, for the purpose of qualifying men for the different professions, sprung up—first, for medicine, and afterward in the learning and practice of the canon law. It was not long, however, before these fell under clerical influence.

About the beginning of the sixteenth century—full eight hundred years after the enlightened but fruitless measures of Charlemagne and Alfred—some improvement is observable. A pious fraternity of the Jeronymites was organized, consisting of clergymen and laymen, who lived together, occupied partly with mechanical arts, partly with the instruction of girls and boys, to whom they taught reading, writing, and the useful arts. For boys of talent and diligence, there were Latin classes. On the model of these schools, others were established in the Netherlands, on the Rhine, and in northern Germany. These soon came into communication with the Greeks who had fled to Italy; and thus the study of the classics became more cultivated. Through the efforts of men like Thomas-a-Kempis, Hegius, Erasmus, Agricola, Renchlin, and Melancthon, a liberal study of the remains of classic antiquity was commenced. From such a beginning we may date that vast intellectual progress, and that effective system of popular instruction, which constitute the crowning glory of modern Germany.

The Reformation gave a forward impulse to education, in Catholic as well as Protestant States. The Jesuit schools became prominent about the close of the sixteenth century, and for a long period rivaled those of Germany. But a variety of circumstances contributed to produce degeneracy in these Catholic schools, as well as in those of the Protestants. The former became again confined to a fixed routine; the latter passed from the strictness of the conventual schools to licentiousness, through the influence of the privileged universities. To this was added, in Germany, the Thirty Years' War, in which fanaticism on both sides destroyed what had been judiciously established.

It is within one hundred years, however, that the agency of government in the education of the people has become a powerful element of modern society; although, in some instances, the germ of a system of public instruction was deposited long previously.

Germany—comprising under that designation the heart of Europe, from the Alps to the Baltic[a]—Germany holds the

---

(a) The German States, although under different governments, are noted for a common nationality. This community of sentiment is doubtless produced by a common origin and language—a fact finely illustrated by a popular song of M. Arndt, in which occurs the following passage:

> "What country does a German claim?
> His Fatherland; know'st thou its name?
> Is it Bavaria—Saxony?
> An inland state, or on the sea?

foremost rank in educational progress. Prussia, Saxony, Wirtemberg, Hanover, Bavaria, Baden, Switzerland, even Austria—each has established an effective system of public instruction, although, in some of these States, many provisions and features exist which are inapplicable to our republican institutions. A volume would be insufficient for such details; but the example of Prussia may be briefly cited as an illustration of the general plan.

Prussia has, indeed, taken the lead of Europe (although, since 1833, the republic of Switzerland holds an equal rank) in the establishment of a complete system of national education. With rare exceptions, every individual in the kingdom can both read and write. This happy result has been obtained, first, by establishing an adequate number of schools in all parts of the monarchy, and then enforcing attendance by a law, which provides that every child, from the age of five years, unless certified to be receiving a suitable education at home, or in a private seminary, must be in attendance at a national school, until such time as the course of instruction therein provided has been completed. This course occupies about eight years, so that it may be regarded as a general rule, that all Prussian children between the ages of six and fourteen are at school. The different classes of schools are, 1. The elementary school, at which the great majority of the people receive their education; 2. The city school, which is always attached to a gymnasium; 3. The gymnasium, in

---

There, on the Baltic's plains of sand?
Or 'mid the Alps of Switzerland?
Austria, the Adriatic shores?
Or where the Prussian eagle soars?
Or where hills covered by the vine
Adorn the landscape of the Rhine?
O no, O no! not these, alone,
The land, with pride, we call our own—
Not these. A German heart or mind
Is to no narrow realm confined:
Where'er he hears his native tongue
When hymns of praise to God are sung,
There is his Fatherland, and he
Has but one country—Germany!"

which Latin and Greek are taught. In most of the small towns are normal schools for the training of teachers. Prussia also possesses the celebrated universities of Berlin, Halle, and Bonn, besides those of Breslau, Greifwald, and Konigsberg, and numerous literary and learned societies. The universities are all under the control of the Government.

The following table shows the number of schools of various kinds, and of teachers and pupils in 1849:

	Number.	Teachers.	Pupils.
Elementary schools,	24,201	30,865	2,453,062.
Middle and higher schools,	505	2,269	69,302.
Upper female schools,	385	1,118	53,570.
Gymnasia,	117	1,664	29,474.
			2,605,408.
Normal seminaries,	46	——	2,411.
Universities,	7	——	4,306.

In 1849 the number of children between six and fourteen years of age, was 3,223,362, of whom, as seen in the above table, 2,605,408 were at school, leaving a balance of 617,954 to be accounted for, partly by private teaching, partly by the fact that many do not enter school until they are above six years old, and many leave before they are fourteen; and many, doubtless, received no education during the year in question.

France, prior to the revolution of 1789, had been as regardless of the intellectual welfare of the mass of her people as of their political rights. The convulsion of 1789, was an inevitable result of that neglect—so obviously, indeed, that by various orders of the Convention, a system of public schools was projected, in which primary education was to be free to all at the expense of the State. Out of these ordinances sprung the first normal school in France, and the Polytechnic School, in 1794.

But the promise of good primary schools was not realized, and the normal school was abolished in the following year. In 1802 the promise was renewed in a new ordinance; but it was silent and inoperative in the midst of universal war.

In 1808 Napoleon organized the Imperial University, embracing under that designation the governmental control of all the educational institutions of France; primary, secondary, and superior. In one of his decrees, primary instruction (intended for the masses of society) was limited to reading, writing, and arithmetic; and the legal authorities were enjoined "to watch that the teachers did not carry their instructions beyond these limits." Under the organization established by Napoleon, and with views of primary education but little expanded beyond the imperial ordinance referred to, and with even these limited views unrealized, the Government continued to administer the system of public education until the revolution of 1830. Then some amelioration occurred under the administration of Louis Phillippe. Steps were taken to increase the number and efficiency of the schools already established, by additional appropriations for their support, and a Department of Public Instruction was re-organized. M. Victor Cousin, whose metaphysical writings are so well known to both continents, was directed to examine and report on the "condition of public instruction in Germany, and particularly in Prussia;" and did so, demonstrating the immense superiority of all the German States, even the most insignificant duchy, over any and every department of France in all that concerned institutions of primary and secondary education. On the experience of Prussia as a basis, a great and comprehensive measure of elementary education was framed, in 1832, by M. Guizot, and the following year it became a law. Besides the University of France, composed of twenty-six academies dispersed over the departments, with ample faculties of Theology, Law, Medicine, Science, and Letters, or Literature, the law ordains at least one elementary school in each of the 39,381 communes into which France is divided; and these communes, where the population exceeds 6,000, are required to support one superior primary school, and are aided in opening infant primary schools, evening schools, classes for adults, and high schools. Attendance, by a law of 1841, is made obligatory;

efficient supervision and inspection are provided, and normal schools to supply the annual demand for teachers of primary schools, are required to be established. In 1846 there were ninety-two normal schools, seventy-six of which were for the education of school masters, and sixteen for the education of school mistresses; and to fifty-two of them enough land is attached to teach Agriculture and Horticulture.

Though Russia still ranks among the more imperfectly educated countries of Europe, the Government has long taken a distinguished lead in the cause of education, and promulgated a complete national system, which, though not yet carried into full effect, has made great progress. The basis of this system was laid by Peter the Great, and promoted by Catherine II; but it is indebted for its fuller developments to Alexander and Nicholas. Since 1848, however, the Russian youth have been considerably restricted in their range of studies, by the measures taken by the Government to prevent its subjects coming in contact with the opinions that have extended over the other countries of Europe. In many institutions Theology has taken the place of Philosophy; and the official report of 1851 assumes as its basis the Emperor's own idea, that "religious teaching constitutes the only solid foundation of useful instruction." The system recognizes military schools of three classes; army, naval, and the children of the soldiery; ecclesiastical, mining, and commercial; and a large variety of establishments under the Minister of the Interior, including those devoted to charity and benevolence. The total number of pupils instructed in the above classes of schools is about 600,000, besides whom it is estimated that about as many more receive a home education, making an aggregate of 1,200,000 under instruction. To give unity and vigor to the school system, a special Ministry of Public Instruction has been appointed, and now forms one of the great departments of the State.

Few countries, in proportion to their size, have done so much for education as Denmark. At the head of the educational institutions stands the University of Copenhagen, and the Holberg Academy, at Soroe. In the sixty-four provincial towns, are twenty schools, in which the learned languages are taught, and one hundred and thirty town, free, and upper general schools, besides a number of private establishments; in the country there are 2,504 common schools, or *volks-schulen*, and five normal schools. Denmark has the greatest number of pupils in school, in proportion to the total population, of any country in the world.

Norway, although politically connected with Sweden, has an interesting school system of her own. Gratuitous instruction, of an elementary kind, is placed within the reach of all capable of receiving it; and all children of seven years complete, in town, and eight years in the country, are required to be in attendance at school until confirmation, which usually takes place between the ages of fourteen and seventeen. The law forbids the marriage of any one who can not procure a certificate of confirmation, and this is only given to those who can read. Every individual of the age of twenty, not confirmed, is liable to be sent to a house of correction to receive the necessary instruction. The schools designated by the name of *almue skoler*, or people's schools, are located in all towns and parishes. In towns, the instruction is not only elementary; in certain cases it is superior. In the country, the instruction is only elementary; but in the schools themselves, an important distinction is made, some being what is called *fast skoler*, or stationary schools, and others *omgangs-skoler*, or ambulatory schools. The latter, as the name implies, shift about at certain periods of the year from place to place, in the more thinly-peopled and isolated districts, and thus have the effect of bringing education to those who, but for this wise and benevolent arrangement, would be doomed to live without it. The towns possess, in addition to these people's schools, what are called middle schools, middle and royal schools, burgher schools, and Latin or learned schools; in all of which superior instruction is given. There are, also, four cathedral schools; one each in the towns of Christiana, Bergen, Frondhjem and Christiansand. There is a military school at Christiana, and a school of marine at Fredericksham. Six normal schools are supported by the State. At the head of all the educational establishments is the University of Christiana, at which, complete courses of lectures are delivered, to qualify for the different learned professions and the higher grades of official employments.

The people of Sweden, in point of intelligence and education, are scarcely surpassed by any country in Europe. This is partly owing to the enlightened spirit of the Government, in endeavoring to provide schools in every important locality; but it derives great additional aid from the parents, who, in many parts of the country, where regular schools, owing to the scantiness of the population, can not be maintained, are careful to give a substantial education to their children at their own firesides. The system comprises Universities at Upsala and Lund, two secondary and grammar schools, (classical and practical schools), and three primary schools, or schools for the people, the whole under the inspection of the bishop and chapter of the cathedral. In 1800 there were 143,526 pupils in the stationary, and 126,178 in the ambulatory primary schools, 6,223 in the secondary schools, 17,464 in private institutions, 128,996 educated at home, and 25,718 in Sunday schools. All children between the ages of nine and fifteen must attend school or receive instruction at home. A normal school was established in 1842.

England, in regard to this momentous interest, compares unfavorably with the lesser powers of northern Europe. For the aristocratic and wealthy classes, and the clergy of the Established Church, England possesses, in the Universities of Oxford and Cambridge, two of the most celebrated institutions in the world. For what her public men style the middle classes, a much more scanty provision has been made. The deficiency, however, has, in some measure, been supplied by the erection, within comparatively recent times, of a great number of colleges and endowed schools, in which instruction in the various branches, both of general and professional education is furnished at a moderate expense. But the education which, in a national point of view, is the most important of all—that suited to the great mass of the population—was for a long time greatly neglected. The public mind, however, has finally, in a measure, been awakened to the necessities of the case; accurate statistics of the educational state of the most important districts of the kingdom have been obtained, proving both the lamentable extent to which ignorance prevails, and its decided tendency to foster pauperism, immorality, and crime; and all classes of the community are now making commendable exertions to extend the blessings of education. The great work of popular instruction is materially clogged by the pertinacity of the Established Church, in seeking the control of the national schools; although an organization exists, known as the British and Foreign School Society, the constitution of which is so framed as to receive the support of all denominations. In no respect is the union of Church and State more disastrous, than by its influence upon the efforts to organize an educational system in England. The support which popular education receives from the Government, through the board organized for that purpose, consists only of an original grant of £30,000, now raised to £125,000 per annum; while from the reports of the French Minister of Public Instruction, for 1843, it appeared that for ten years prior to that year, France expended the sum of £2,565,883 (about $11,000,000) in the erection of school-houses and residences of teachers; and in 1843 the expenditure for the current expenses of her educational establishments was a little short of $4,000,000, independent of the sum paid by the communes, individuals, and parents, in school fees, which amounted to near $5,000,000. In England, the proportion of the population under instruction—both public and private—is one to eleven, while in some of the Swiss cantons it is as one to five. To this fact—the scanty provision made for the education of the masses—is to be traced one of the most prolific sources of crime; and it has been ascertained that out of 335,429 persons committed for offenses, in England and Wales, between 1836 and 1848, not fewer than 304,772, or more than 90 per cent., were uninstructed.

Passing Ireland—another monument of the evil effect of a Church establishment upon public instruction—Scotland affords a very satisfactory illustration of the benefits afforded by general education. Her parochial schools are justly distinguished. The foundation of the system was laid in 1494, when it was enacted, by the Scotch Parliament, that all barons and substantial freeholders throughout the realm should send their children to school from the age of six to nine years, and then to other seminaries to be instructed in the laws; that the country might be possessed of persons properly qualified to discharge the duties of sheriffs, and to fill other civil offices. Those who neglected to comply with the provisions of this statute were subjected to a penalty of £20. In 1560, John Knox and his compeers held the following memorable language, in the "First Book of Discipline," presented to the nobility:

"Seeing that God has determined that his kirk here on earth shall be taught, not by angels, but by men; and seeing that men are born ignorant of God and of godliness; and seeing, also, that he ceaseth to illuminate men miraculously, of necessity it is, that your honors be most careful for the virtuous education and godly bringing up of the youth of this realm. For as they must succeed to us, so we ought to be careful that they have knowledge and education to profit and comfort that which ought to be most dear to us, to wit, the kirk and spouse of our Lord Jesus Christ. Of necessity, therefore, we judge it, that every several kirk have one schoolmaster appointed; such an one, at least, as is able to teach Grammar and the Latin tongue, if the town be of any reputation. And further, we think it expedient that in every notable town, there should be erected a *college*, in which the arts at least of Rhetoric and Logic, together with the tongues, be read by sufficient masters, for whom honest stipends must be appointed; as also that provision be made for those that are poor, and not able by themselves or their friends to be sustained at letters.

"The rich and potent may not be permitted to suffer their children to spend their youth in a vain idleness, as heretofore they have done; but they must be exhorted, and by the censure of the kirk, compelled to dedicate their sons by good exercises to the profit of the kirk and commonwealth; and this they must do because they are able. The children of the poor must be supported and sustained on the charge of the kirk, trial being taken whether the spirit of docility be in them found or not. If they be found apt to learning and letters, then may they not be permitted to reject learning, but must be charged to continue their study, so that the commonwealth may have some comfort by them; and for this purpose, must discreet, grave, and learned men be appointed to visit schools, for the trial of their exercise, profit, and continuance; to wit, the ministers and elders, with the best learned men in every town. A certain time must be appointed to reading and learning the Catechism, and a certain time to Grammar and the Latin tongue, and a certain time to the arts of Philosophy and the other tongues, and a certain time to that study in which they intend chiefly to travel for the profit of the commonwealth; which time being expired, the children shall either proceed to further knowledge, or else they must be set to some handicraft, or to some other profitable exercise."

In 1615 the bishops were empowered to establish a school in every parish; and in 1696 the defects of this law were supplied by another, which provides for the means of support. The landlords of each parish were required to build a school-house and a dwelling-house for the master, and to pay him a given salary, at first from £5 to £11, and subsequently, as the value of money diminished, from £16 to £22 per annum. In addition to this, the teacher receives fees from the pupils, from 2s. 6d. to 7s. 6d. per quarter. It has been usually expected that a Scotch parish schoolmaster, besides being a person of unexceptionable character, should be able to instruct his pupils in the reading of English, in the arts of Writing and Arithmetic, the more common and useful branches of practical Mathematics, and that he should be possessed of such classical attainments as might qualify him for teaching Latin and the rudiments of Greek.

It would be no easy matter to exaggerate the beneficial effects of the elementary instruction obtained at parish schools, on the habits and industry of the people of Scotland.

It has given to that part of the British Empire an importance to which it has no claim, either from fertility of soil or amount of population. The universal diffusion of schools, and the consequent education of the people, have opened, to all classes, paths to wealth, honor, and distinction. Persons of the humblest origin have raised themselves to the highest eminence in every walk of ambition, and a spirit of forethought and energy has been widely disseminated.

At the period when the act of 1696 for establishing parish schools was passed, Scotland, which had suffered greatly from misgovernment and religious persecutions, under the reign of Charles II, and his brother James II, was in the most unprosperous condition. "There are," wrote Fletcher of Saltoun, a celebrated Scotch patriot, in 1698, "at this day in Scotland *two hundred thousand people begging from door to door*. Many murders have been discovered amongst them, and they are a most unspeakable oppression to poor tenants. There are such outrageous disorders, that it would be better for the nation that they were sold for the gallies or the West Indies, than they should continue any longer to be a burden and a curse upon us."

No country ever rose so rapidly from so frightful an abyss. In the autumn circuits or assizes, for the year 1757, no one was found guilty, in any part of the country, of a capital crime. And now there are very few beggars in the country, nor has any assessment been imposed for the support of the poor, except in some of the large towns, and in the counties adjoining England; and even that is so light as scarcely to be felt. In a large part of the country, nearly the whole population is able to read and write; but in some parts, chiefly in the Highlands, the parishes are so extensive that there are many who have no means of education within reach. Latterly, also, the population has advanced so rapidly, that the parochial system, though it continues tolerably effective in rural parishes, became almost powerless in large towns, and Scotland began to descend rapidly from her foremost place among educated nations. Fortunately, however, a happy rivalry has been excited among the different religious bodies, urging them to strenuous exertion in erecting schools by means of voluntary subscriptions, supplemented by Parliamentary grants. If sectarian influences could cease altogether, instead of being strengthened by rivalry, nothing would be wanting to restore the proud position of Scotland in the cause of education. Her example, as she stands, is of great value.

The remote and bleak island of Iceland illustrates what has been observed among the Norwegians and Swedes, namely: the prevalence of family instruction, when schools are difficult of access. Although Iceland has its college, with eight professors and eighty pupils, and sustains a few public schools, yet domestic education is universal, and the people are intelligent. Their intellectual capacity is of a superior order. Peasants often are masters of the Greek and Latin languages; many of the most valuable works of European literature have been translated into the native tongue; and even the poems of Milton are read and appreciated at many of the cottage firesides.*

The foregoing review of the career and condition of education in Europe, exhibits one interesting fact, that wherever the family is most firmly rooted in the affections of the people—the predominant institution of society—there is precisely where the school is most prosperous and influential. There is entire harmony, therefore—not the antagonism sometimes asserted to exist—between the rights of the parent and the duties of the teacher. Their earnest and cordial co-operation is the crowning excellence of the most successful systems of public instruction in Europe, especially those of Germany and northern Europe.

---

* In this rapid outline of the educational condition of the European States, Spain, Portugal and Italy have been omitted, so meagre and inadequate is their provision for that purpose. Sardinia and Tuscany are not entirely inactive, while Turkey, by an edict of 1847, has established a system quite on the plan of northern Europe. It includes elementary schools, attendance at which is compulsory on all Mohammedan children

CHAPTER II.

EDUCATIONAL SYSTEMS OF THE ATLANTIC STATES AND BRITISH POSSESSIONS.

The high distinction belongs to New England, and prominently to Massachusetts, of first proclaiming and establishing the principle, that it is the right and duty of government to provide, by means of fair and just taxation, for the instruction of all the youth of the community.

This common school system is one of the most ancient institutions of Massachusetts. Indeed, it is only since the period of Independence, that any other schools have been known to her laws; the earliest incorporation of an establishment for instruction, below the rank of the university, being that of Phillips Academy, at Andover, in 1780. The first free school of the colony was that of Boston, where in 1635, five years from the settlement of that peninsula, the inhabitants voted in town meeting, "on the thirteenth of the second month," "that our brother, Philemon Permont, shall be entreated to become schoolmaster for the teaching and nurturing of youth among us." That he served only a short

---

who have attained their sixth year; middle schools, in which among other branches, Geography, History, Geometry, and Composition are taught, and colleges, arranged under the different heads of Military, Naval, Medical, Veterinary, Agricultural, etc. Most of the medressehs and colleges have libraries attached to them, containing a respectable list of works in various branches of literature. The authorities relied upon for the foregoing summary are, American Annals of Education, I, 244; North American Review, XLVII, 274; Barnard on Normal Schools; Encyclopedia Americana; Blackie's Imperial Gazetteer.

time, if at all, is probable, because at the end of the same volume of Record, with the date of August, 1636, is a curious memorandum of subscription "toward the maintenance of a free school master, Mr. Daniel Mande being now also chosen thereto." So that within five years from the first peopling of the peninsula of Boston, where the modest wants of its inhabitants were yet very imperfectly satisfied, a school was established among them, apparently under the auspices of John Winthrop, the first Governor of the colony, for the purpose of promoting universal instruction. And this is the foundation of the free schools, and the popular education of New England.

In 1647, free schools became a matter of legislation in the colony of Massachusetts Bay, and by a law then passed "to the end," as the preamble sets forth, "that learning may not be buried in the graves of our forefathers," it was ordered that every township with fifty families should provide a school where children might be taught to read and write; and that every township of one hundred families should provide a *Grammar* school, where youth could be fitted for the university; to which another law was added, in 1683, providing that every township with more than five hundred families, should maintain two Grammar schools and two Writing schools; a burden which, considering the feeble means of the colony, and the dark period when it was assumed, was, no doubt, vastly greater than any similar burden that has been borne since. It is a singular fact, too, that no legal requisitions made since have, even in name and form, come up to this noble standard, established by the founders of Massachusetts, in the middle of the seventeenth century. The Charter of William and Mary, having rendered a new law expedient, an act was passed by the province in 1692, containing provisions similar to that of 1647, but omitting the requisition made, in 1683, on towns of five hundred families, to maintain two Grammar schools and two Writing schools. A still greater falling off followed the settlement of the Constitution of 1780, though that Constitution solemnly recognized the duty of cherishing the Grammar schools; for by the act of 1789, towns of five hundred families were required to support a Reading and Writing school six months in the year, instead of twelve, as before, and towns of two hundred families were required to have a Grammar school, instead of towns of one hundred, as before; and by the act of February 18, 1824, any town might refuse to have a Grammar school whose inhabitants fell short of five thousand.

Massachusetts, in 1827, revised her school legislation, and required that every town or district, containing fifty families, shall be provided with a school or schools, equivalent, in time, to six months for one school in a year; if containing one hundred families, twelve months; one hundred and fifty families, eighteen months; and the towns are required to raise the sums of money necessary for the support of the schools in the same manner as other town taxes. In 1834 was established the Massachusetts school fund, in which were invested, by the act, the proceeds of the Massachusetts claim upon the General Government for services during the war of 1812, to the amount of $280,000, and one half the net proceeds of the sale of Maine lands, until the sum amounted to $1,000,000. Subsequently, in the discharge of his duties as Secretary of the State Board of Education, Horace Mann gave a remarkable impulse to the cause of education. According to the census of 1850, Massachusetts had 3,679 public schools, with 176,475 pupils, and $1,006,795 income; of which $37,341 was from public funds, $16,906 from endowments, and $935,141 from taxation; and 381 academies, and other schools, with 12,774 pupils, and $310,177 income, of which $19,470 was from endowments. In 1854, according to the American Almanac, the towns raised by taxation, for the support of schools, $1,013,472.26; the aggregate expended—including State fund—$1,140,132.79; number of children from five to fifteen years, 206,625. The amount of State school fund on December 31, 1854, had reached $1,602,-597.42. The value of the public school-houses in 1848 was $2,750,000, of which $2,200,000 had been expended since 1838. There are four normal schools supported by the State, at an annual cost of about $11,000; one at Westfield, one at Farmingham, one at Bridgewater, and one at Salem, for girls; averaging annually, in all, about 260 pupils. Teachers' institutes are frequently held; and State Agents have been employed, under the direction of the Board of Education, in visiting the different parts of the State to awaken the people to the cause of education, and instruct them in relation thereto.

The Board of Education consists of the Governor and Lieutenant Governor, and eight members, one being appointed each year, by the Governor and Council, for eight years. There is a Secretary of the Board, who has an assistant, and is the executive officer of the Board. Provision is made, by law, for the education and training of young men to be principal teachers in the high schools in the commonwealth, by establishing forty-eight State scholarships in the colleges of the State, and paying $100 annually to each.

The annual reports of the Massachusetts Board of Education indicate very clearly that the greatest obstacle to the efficiency of the school system, consists in the organization of independent districts, and the fact that the schools ordinarily maintained by them are no longer capable of giving the education required by the character of the times.

Maine has derived the leading features of her school policy from Massachusetts. By act of April 17, 1854, provision is made for the appointment of a Superintendent of Common Schools. His duty is to "devote his time to the improvement of common schools and the promotion of the general interests of education in the State." He is to hold annually, in each county, a teacher's convention, for one week at least, of which he has the charge, and he is to employ suitable instructors and teachers to assist him therein. To defray the expenses of these conventions, $2,000 are to be appropriated annually. The permanent school fund is $125,281,01. The amount apportioned for the year 1854, was $55,860,53. Towns are obliged, by law, to raise annually an amount of school money equal to 40 cents for each inhabitant. The number of scholars, in 1853, was 238,736.

The direction of the schools of New Hampshire is intrusted to County School Commissioners, who form a State Board of Education. The whole amount raised for district schools, during 1855, was $231,434,92.

According to the American Almanac, Vermont had, in 1851, 90,110 pupils attending her public schools, at a cost of $217,402, of which $90,893 was from the public funds. The office of Public School Superintendent having been abolished, and the school fund applied to pay the State debt, no returns have been received since that year.

In Rhode Island, great attention has been paid to education. The school fund, invested in bank stock, amounted, in 1854, to $61,386. About $50,000 is annually paid from the State treasury for public instruction. In 1854, the towns raised $61,013. A State Normal School was established by the Legislature in May, 1854, on the recommendation of E. R. Potter, Commissioner of Public Schools, and $3,000 a year appropriated therefor. Teachers' institutes are annually held in different localities, supported by the State.

The school system of Connecticut has attracted great attention, from its ample endowment. The foundation of this fund was laid in 1795, by a legislative dedication of the proceeds from the sale of the Ohio Western Reserve, amounting to $1,200,000. This endowment has been increased, reaching a capital, in 1855, of $2,049,953,05; revenue for the year, $144,137,73, or $1,25 to each scholar. It has been often observed, that the effect of such bounty, dispensing with the necessity for local taxation and effort, was rather deleterious than otherwise. The state of education in Connecticut is not superior to what it was before the creation of the fund. The means of instruction had previously been so excellent, that it was very rarely that a person could be found who was unable to read and write; but more recently such instances are less infrequent. General apathy reigned, until, in 1839, Henry Barnard infused new life into the system. His report, as second Secretary of the Board of Education, constituted, of itself, an epoch. It is characterized by Chancellor Kent, in the notes to the last edition of his Commentaries, as a bold and startling document, founded on the most pains-taking and critical inquiry, and containing a minute and instructive exhibition of the practical condition and operation of the common school system of education. He proposed that one-half of the dividends of the school fund should be proportioned to the amount of money raised by the school societies, (as the township organization for school purposes is styled,) or to the number of children, and the actual attendance for any given period. He further proposed that the expenses of the schools should be made to fall, not exclusively upon those who send their children, but upon the property of the school society or town; he stated that the great instrumentality in the prosperity of the common school system, was *good teachers*, and they could be procured only by education for the very employment, and by higher wages; he urged that a seminary for teachers, especially for females, with a model school annexed, ought to be endowed by the State and private contributions, and he pressed, in an animated manner, the necessity of the establishment of normal schools for the education of teachers, male and female, qualified to conduct the schools.

The Legislature of the State has responded to the zeal of its school officer. A Superintendency of Public Instruction has been established; high schools authorized and encouraged. The Legislature appropriated $10,000, in 1849, for the formation of a State normal school, which, in 1850, was attended by 154 pupils. These are educated gratis; but the number, at one time, must not exceed 220. There are schools connected with this for exercising the pupils in the practice of teaching, which had 400 pupils in 1851. An active zeal is manifested for improvement in the modes of instruction; and to promote this end, societies of teachers are formed, and State and county conventions held. By the revised statutes of 1849, it is made obligatory upon parents, etc., to cause their children to be instructed "in Reading, Writing, English Grammar, Geography, and the elements of Arithmetic," and to be brought up to some honest calling; and in case of their neglect, the selectmen of the town, with the advice of a justice of the peace, may take the children from their parents or guardians, and bind them to some proper master. "Stubborn children, refusing to obey their parents or masters, may be committed by justices of the peace, on complaint and due inquiry, to the house of correction for a time not exceeding thirty days." Another section provides that no child, under fifteen years, shall be employed to labor in any business, unless he shall have attended a competent school during three months of the preceding year. Massachusetts and New Hampshire adopt this last provision, the latter State making a special application of it to manufacturing establishments.

The State of NEW YORK has so powerfully influenced the school organizations of other States, that a detailed sketch, mostly compiled from an article by S. S. Randall, Superintendent of Schools for the City of New York, and published in the American Journal of Education for April, 1856, is here presented.

At the opening of the session of the Legislature in 1795—more than sixty years since—GEORGE CLINTON, the first Governor of New York, in his annual message, urgently and earnestly recommended "the establishment of common schools throughout the State."

On the 11th of January of that year, the Assembly appointed a committee upon that portion of the Governor's message, who reported a bill "for the encouragement of schools," which became a law on the 9th of April, 1795. By this act, the sum of $20,000 or $50,000 was annually appropriated, for five years, "for the purpose of encouraging and maintaining schools in the several cities and towns in this State, in which the children of the inhabitants residing in the State shall be instructed in the English language, or be taught

English Grammar, Arithmetic, Mathematics, and such other branches of knowledge as are most useful and necessary to complete a good English education." The amount thus appropriated was apportioned among the several towns, according to the number of taxable inhabitants in each; and the Boards of Supervisors of the respective counties were required to raise, by a tax upon each town, a sum equal to one-half of that apportioned by the State, to be applied in like manner. Under this act, common schools were organized in the several counties of the State, (then numbering only twenty-three,) and from the returns made in 1798, it appeared that the whole number of districts in which schools were taught, and from which reports were received in accordance with law, was 1352, in which 59,660 children had been taught during the preceding year.

On the expiration of the five years with which the appropriation terminated, several ineffectual attempts were made, by the friends of education in the Legislature, to continue the system; but, notwithstanding the repeated and eloquent appeals of Governors George Clinton, Jay, and Lewis, and the earnest efforts of other eminent statesmen and philanthropists, the organization was abandoned in 1800, and no efficient steps were taken for its renewal until after the lapse of more than ten years. In 1811 a commission was appointed by Governor Tompkins, in pursuance of an act of the Legislature, "to report a system for the organization and establishment of common schools." On the 14th of February, 1812, a bill was reported, comprising substantially the main features of the New York common school system, as it existed up to the year 1849. Fifty thousand dollars were apportioned by the State, from a fund specifically set apart for the purpose, among the several counties and towns, in proportion to the population in each, and an equal amount was required to be raised by the Board of Supervisors of the respective counties, and applied to the same object. The aggregate amount thus received was distributed annually among the several school districts, according to the number of children of suitable age to attend school residing in each, to be expended exclusively in the payment of the wages of duly qualified teachers. Three Commissioners and three Inspectors of Common Schools were annually to be elected in each town, and three Trustees, a Clerk, and Collector, in each district. A State Superintendent was required to be appointed by the Legislative Council, upon which should devolve the general supervision, direction, and control of the system. This office was conferred upon Gideon Hawley, Esq., who continued to hold it until 1821, when he was displaced, from political considerations, and a successor appointed, whose incompetence was so glaringly obvious that the Legislature promptly abolished the office, and devolved its duties on the Secretary of State, to which office they continued to appertain until a very recent period.

The number of districts organized under the new system, prior to the 1st of January, 1816, was about 5,000, in which about 200,000 children were instructed. Under the administration of De Witt Clinton, the public interest was promptly directed, by that eminent statesman, to the condition and advancement of the common schools; and the impulse thus given to the cause of elementary education was energetically followed up by his successors. The enlightened and vigorous supervision of the several Secretaries—Yates, Flagg, Dix, Spencer, Young, Benton, Morgan, and H. S. Randall—gave animation and life to the entire organization, and has enabled it, in the face of many formidable obstacles, to attain to its present pre-eminence. The library system was engrafted upon it in 1838, through the efforts and exertions of Secretary Dix, the Rev. Dr. Alonzo Potter, now Bishop of Pennsylvania, and the venerable James Wadsworth, of Genessee.

In 1841, the plan of county supervision was adopted, in accordance with the recommendation of Secretary Spencer, and County Superintendents were appointed for each county of the State. In the midst, however, of the rich harvest of beneficial results which this system was effecting, the law was, in 1847, repealed. In 1843, on the recommendation of Col. Young, the offices of Town Commissioner and Inspector of Common Schools were abolished, and that of Town Superintendent substituted in its stead. In 1844, the State Normal School, for the education and preparation of teachers, was established. In 1849, the "act for the establishment of free schools throughout the State" was passed, by the provisions of which the inhabitants of each district were authorized and required to provide annually, by a distinct tax, for all the expenses of supporting and maintaining their schools, beyond the amount contributed by the State, an equal amount levied by the Board of Supervisors on the county, and an additional equal sum levied upon the taxable property of each town. This act, which passed the Legislature by a nearly unanimous vote, was submitted to the people, for their approval, at the ensuing general election, and sustained by a majority of upwards of 150,000 votes. In consequence, however, of the neglect on the part of the local Boards of Supervisors to provide the requisite funds to be raised for the support of the schools, the burden of taxation fell, with an insupportable weight, upon the districts; and before any opportunity had been afforded for testing its value, public sentiment in the rural districts declared decidedly for the repeal of the obnoxious law. The question was again submitted to the electors of the State, by the Legislature, and at the general election in the fall of 1850, heavy majorities were given for repeal in forty-two of the forty-nine counties. These majorities were, however, overcome by the unprecedentedly heavy vote against the repeal, cast in the several cities and large towns of the State, and especially in the city of New York. The Legislature of 1851, not feeling at liberty under the vote thus taken, to repeal the act entirely, passed a new bill, transferring the burden of taxation, for the support of schools, from the districts, towns, and counties, to the State at large—

requiring the sum of $800,000 to be annually levied and collected on the taxable property of the State, and applied, together with the annual revenue from the common school and United States deposit funds, to the payment of teachers' wages, the replenishment of the district libraries and the purchase of necessary school apparatus. In case the share of this combined fund, apportioned to the respective districts, and applicable to the payment of teachers' wages, failed to meet the charge upon it, such deficiency was required to be met by a rate-bill against those sending to school, as heretofore had been usual. This act of 1851 is still in force.

The unproductive capital of the common school fund of New York consists of about 400,000 acres of land, owned by the State, chiefly in the northern section of the State, the value of which may be estimated, in round numbers, at $2,000,000.

The productive capital of the fund is at this time about..	$2,400,000.
The capital of that portion of the United States deposit fund, the interest of which is annually appropriated to the support of common schools, is............	2,750,000.
To which may be added a sum that will annually produce an income of $25,000, reserved by the Constitution from the income of the last-named fund, to be added to the capital of the school fund..................	41,666 67.
Making an aggregate of............................	$5,566,666 67.

The annual interest on this sum, at 6 per cent. is $344,000; of which $300,000 is annually appropriated and paid over for the support of schools—including $55,000 for the purchase of books for district libraries and for school apparatus generally.

According to this amount, the $800,000 required to be raised upon all the real and personal property of the State, we have the sum of $1,100,000 as the aggregate sum now annually apportioned, by the State Superintendent, among the several school districts, of which $1,045,000 is applicable exclusively to the payment of teachers' wages, and the remaining $55,000 to the purchase of books and school apparatus. One-third of this aggregate amount is required, by law, to be divided equally among the several districts, and the remaining two-thirds to be distributed among the several towns and counties, on the basis of population.

In addition to this, the inhabitants of each town, in annual town meeting assembled, are *authorized*, if they deem it expedient, to raise, by tax, an additional amount equal to their share of the State fund, to be appropriated to the same purposes; and many of the towns are in possession of local funds applicable to this object, derived from the sale of lands, originally set apart by the State, in each township, for this purpose. These local funds amount, in the aggregate, to about $20,000. As a still farther resource against deficiency of funds, a rate-bill may be imposed.

The officers of the system, as already intimated, consist of three Trustees in each district, elected for three years, and a District Clerk, Collector, and Librarian, who are annually chosen; a Town Superintendent, the County Clerk, who transmits the reports of the Town Superintendents to the seat of Government, and a State Superintendent of Public Instruction. Their respective duties can be readily anticipated.

Provision is also made for a State normal school at the capital; teachers' institutes in the counties, for periods varying from two to four weeks in the spring and fall; and union, or graded schools, by a consolidation of contiguous districts.

The grand result is 12,000 schools, taught for an average period of eight months during each year, by teachers of both sexes, in which 900,000 children are annually gathered, under the general and special supervision of sixty thousand officers of various grades, with an annual expenditure of two and a half millions of dollars.

The exemplary founder of PENNSYLVANIA took care to incorporate with the frame of government, prepared for that province in 1682, the important truth "that men of wisdom and virtue were requisite to preserve a good constitution, and that these qualities did not descend with worldly inheritance, but were to be carefully propagated by a virtuous education of youth." A law was passed a very few years after the colonists, under William Penn, first landed upon the soil, declaring that "instruction in good and commendable learning is to be preferred before wealth." And the law enjoined it as a duty upon the several county courts, to see that all the children in the province were instructed in Reading and Writing, so that they might be able, at least to read the Scriptures; and it imposed a penalty of £5 upon every parent, guardian, or overseer, of sufficient estate and ability, for every child not thus educated; but this compulsory provision ceased to be enforced. The present Constitution of Pennsylvania enjoins it upon the Legislature, as a duty, to provide by law for the establishment of schools throughout the State. Under this injunction, a general free school system was adopted in Pennsylvania as late as 1834, which has since been remodeled and improved; but still much room is left for amendment before it can fully meet the requirements of the age. To the latter, Philadelphia has long and fully adapted her educational arrangements.

By the act of May 8, 1854, the school laws of Pennsylvania were carefully revised. The Secretary of State is continued to be, *ex officio*, the Superintendent of Common Schools, with the authority to appoint a deputy. The office of County Superintendent is established; and it is made the duty of that officer, who is elected by the School Directors of the several districts in the county, for three years, to attend specially to the schools in the county, and to examine and give certificates to teachers. The school districts are put under the immediate care of the School Directors, who report to the County Superintendent. Teachers are required to report monthly to the Directors, and can have no pay until such report is made. The districts, for school purposes, are made bodies corporate, with power to sue and be sued; to borrow money, to an amount not exceeding one-half of one per cent. of the assessed value of the real estate of the district, to purchase ground, or build school-houses. The Directors are required to establish, in their districts, separate schools for mulatto and negro children, when they can be so located as to accommodate twenty pupils; and when so established, and kept open four months in any year, the Directors shall not be compelled to admit such pupils into other schools of the district. No district can receive its share of the State appropriation for any year, until the schools have been kept four months in such year. The Directors and teachers in each district meet annually before the schools are opened, and determine the school-books to be used during the coming year; and no others but those thus selected, can be used. The County Superintendents are to report to the State Superintendent in June of each year. In 1853, the amount of local taxation, for school purposes, was $1,021,337.34; while the State appropriation has averaged $200,000 since 1844.

The school system of New Jersey is under the direction of a Superintendent and a Committee, in each township; but the organization is not unlike that of New York. The amount raised in 1854 by tax, to support schools, was $210,023.44; received from the State, $85,250.

Maryland has a school fund, arising out of advances made on account of the war of 1812, and repaid by Congress, together with the avails of a tax on the capital of every bank created by the Legislature. This fund, in 1854 amounted to about $160,000. Its income is distributed to the several counties; and by the County Commissioners is paid over, in some cases, to primary schools, and in others to one or more academies. There is no uniform system of public schools, each county being left at liberty to adopt its own system; in consequence of which there is the most gross inequality of school privileges, and an entire absence of reliable returns as to the condition of such schools as are established. The public schools of Baltimore are in a good condition.

Delaware has a permanent school fund of $435,505, which yielded, in 1854, the sum of $33,829 which was increased by a tax, levied on the several districts, of $24,000. The system provides a free school within reach of every family. The education of 10,236 children—in a white population of 71,169—is amply provided for.

Virginia has grievously disappointed the hopes of Jefferson, whose scheme of popular education was at least one hundred years in advance of his generation.* Little has been done except to encourage the University of Virginia—a head without body or members. There is no general free school system; but an appropriation is made for the instruction of the poor, amounting, in 1854, to $75,000. Of the free adult population 88,520 were ascertained, by the census of 1850, to be unable to read and write.

North Carolina, in 1850, had 2,657 public schools, with 104,095 pupils, and $158,564 income, of which $42,936 was from taxation, and $97,378 from public funds. The attendance reached 120,000 in 1855.

South Carolina, in 1849, sustained 1,023 free schools, with 1,019 teachers, and 9,122 scholars. The Legislature appropriates $75,000 annually to free schools. Governor Manning, in his message of November 28, 1853, says that "under the present mode of applying it, that liberality is really the profusion of the prodigal, rather than the judicious generosity which confers real benefit." He recommended "the establishment of a Board of Education, and the appointment of a Commissioner of Public Instruction, whose duty it shall be to gather facts with regard to the State, and thoroughly inform himself upon the systems of such other Governments as educate their people the best, and report the result of his labors to the Board, who together shall digest a

* See Appendix to the report, for 1854, of H. H. Barney, Ohio School Commissioner, for a summary of Jefferson's plan of graded republican schools.

plan to be submitted to the Legislature for ratification or rejection." Academies are established, called the Arsenal and Citadel Academies, in which the youth are practically educated in Military Tactics, and in Engineering and Surveying. The State provides annually for the education, at the South Carolina College, of one youth from the Charleston Orphan House, to be selected as a reward of merit by the Commissioners.

GEORGIA appropriated, in 1783, 1,000 acres of land to each county, and in 1792, £1,000 were appropriated for the endowment of an academy in each county, which was increased, in 1817, by the further grant of $250,000. The former is designated as the free school fund, and the latter the academic fund. The University of Georgia was originally endowed in 1784, by a grant of 40,000 acres of land, not all of which became available. The University has realized about $130,000 out of the grant. The avails of the free school fund ($23,000) are paid out to teachers, in each county, in favor of certain scholars who are reported, by the magistrate, as proper recipients of it, on account of poverty. The number thus aided, in 1854, was 20,000.

The educational statistics of the new States, as distinguished from the original thirteen, are reserved for separate consideration, inasmuch as all the former—except Kentucky and Tennessee—are included in the surveys of the General Government, and have been the recipients of Congressional donations for the purpose of education.

As in Europe, the system of public instruction seems to flourish in northern latitudes. The southern States, with their sparse population and slave tenure of labor, are disposed to encourage colleges and academies for the dominant class, but regard the free school system as a charity to the indigent, and not an obligation to the people. The contrast between the different sections of the Union is very apparent from the following tabular statement of the census of 1850; and which, so far as the States westward of the Alleghanies are concerned, anticipates the contents of the subsequent chapters:

STATISTICS OF THE WHITE POPULATION OF THE UNITED STATES ACCORDING TO THE CENSUS OF 1850.

STATES, ETC.	Total Pop.	Under 20 years.	Over 20 years.				Number attending School.
			Whole No.	Unable to read & write	Per cent. of.	Rank of State	
Alabama	426,514	248,097	178,417	33,757	7.91	23	62,778
Arkansas	162,189	97,402	64,787	16,819	10.37	30	23,350
California	91,635	11,378	80,257	5,118	5.58	17	992
Connecticut	363,099	153,862	209,237	4,739	1.30	3	82,433
Delaware	71,169	36,873	34,296	4,536	6.37	21	14,216
Florida	47,203	25,898	21,305	3,859	8.17	24	4,746
Georgia	521.572	303,798	217,774	41,200	8.99	28	77,015
Illinois	846,034	476,823	369,213	40,054	4.85	15	181,969
Indiana	977,154	565,179	411,975	70,540	7.22	22	220,034
Iowa	191,881	110,609	81,273	8,120	4.23	13	35,456
Kentucky	761,413	429,043	332,370	66.687	8.74	27	130,917
Louisiana	255,491	121,458	134,033	21,221	8.30	25	32,838
Maine	581,813	288,396	293,417	6,147	1.05	2	185,941
Maryland	417,943	208,084	209,859	20,815	4 98	16	60.447
Massachusetts	985,450	416,917	568,533	27,513	2.79	9	220,781
Michigan	395,071	210,831	184,240	7,912	2.00	5	105,754
Mississippi	295,718	172,469	123,222	13,405	4.53	14	48,803
Missouri	594,004	334,936	257,068	36,281	6.12	19	95,245
New Hampshire	317,456	137,224	180,232	2,957	.93	1	88,148
New Jersey	465,509	230,849	234,660	14,248	3.06	11	89,775
New York	3,048,325	1.436,113	1,612,212	91,293	2.99	10	687,874
North Carolina	553,028	301,106	251,922	73,566	13.30	31	100,591
Ohio	1,955.050	1,064,212	890,838	61,030	3.12	12	512,278
Pennsylvania	2,258,160	1,162,874	1,095,286	66,928	2.50	8	498,111
Rhode Island	143.875	62,270	81,605	3,340	2.32	7	28,359
South Carolina	274,563	149,322	125,241	15,684	5.71	18	40,293
Tennessee	756,836	440,627	316,209	77,522	10.21	29	146,130
Texas	154,034	85,869	68,165	10,525	6.18	20	19,369
Vermont	313,402	145,989	167,413	6,189	1.97	4	92,152
Virginia	894,800	481,372	413,428	77,005	8.60	26	109,711
Wisconsin	304,756	156,175	148,581	6,361	2.08	6	56,354
District Columbia	37,941	18,400	19,541	1,457	3.84	..	6,103
Minnesota	6,038	2,656	3,382	649	10.74	..	207
New Mexico	61,525	31,572	29,953	25,085	40.77	..	466
Oregon	13,087	6,499	6,588	157	1.38	..	1,875
Utah	11,330	6,223	5,107	153	.25	..	2,035
Totals	19,553,068	8,692,184	10,860,884	962,869	......	..	4,063,046
Native	17,312,487	....	9,516,538	767,784	4.55	..	....
Foreign	2,240,581	....	1,344,346	195,114	8.71	..	....

In speaking of the facts exhibited above, the Superintendent of the census remarks: "In New England so admirable is the school system, and so deserving of all imitation, that only one person in every four hundred of the native whites over twenty years, is incapable of reading and writing. In the south and south-west, the number is one in about twelve; in the territories, one in about six; in the slaveholding States, one in twelve; in the non-slaveholding, one in forty; and in the whole Union, one in about twenty-two."

"The proportion of pupils to the whole population, has increased largely (since the census of 1840) in the several sections. The proportion for the Union has increased from

13,189 to 20.14 per cent. In consequence of the large influx of foreigners, the whites over twenty, who can not read and write, have increased, in every section, and in the United States, from 3.77 to 5.03 per cent. The proportion of foreign illiterate is twice that of the native."

Within a comparatively recent period, the British provinces, on this continent, have become distinguished for their liberal and effective measures of popular instruction.

In Nova Scotia, the system of Grammar and common schools is established and supported by funds from the treasury, and by parents, and sums raised in the parishes. The system has, by several statutes, in 1832, 1836, and 1841, been placed under the management of a Board of Commissioners; but it is not sufficiently vigorous, and a great number of children are left without education. The same remark will apply to New Brunswick. A valuable work on "Colonial Literature, Science, and Education," by George R. Young, Esq., of Halifax, Nova Scotia, exhibits a favorable condition of public sentiment. He urges, as the elements of a perfect and modern system of education, 1. Infant schools for the training of children; 2. Normal schools for the education of teachers; 3. Common schools; 4. Academies; 5. Useful knowledge institutions; 6. Itinerating libraries; 7. Colleges for the higher branches of learning and science; and, again, he says education ought to be conducted under the superintendence of the government, and regulated by law, and supported by legislative funds or local taxation, and the funds made permanent, certain, and compulsive.

In regard to East Canada, there has not been any legislative provision, until lately, for popular education. Its educational endowments, for colleges and seminaries, were owing to the liberality and zeal of the Catholic Church; and they have been munificent, and the course of education in them has been well conducted, under accomplished teachers. Though they are Catholic institutions, Catholics and Protestants are admitted into the best of them, indiscriminately, and no attempts are made to convert the youth. But a general system of education has not been so successful as in West

Canada, owing to the inextinguishable jealousies of the French and English populations.

The western province, or Upper Canada, has suddenly assumed rank with New York, Ohio, and Michigan—situated adjacent to these States, geographically, it has fully succeeded to their educational impulses.

In 1841, a provincial statute was enacted, granting money to each county, to be expended in the support of common schools, on the condition that the county should raise, for educational purposes, an equal amount by local taxation. Several laws, altering and improving the details of this system, were subsequently passed; and in 1850, all the provisions of former laws, which experience had sanctioned, and others which it had shown to be necessary, were incorporated in one statute.

Before the provisions of this law are stated, it should be premised that, by other laws, Canada West is divided into counties, townships, incorporated cities, and villages; each of which has a Council, which manages its affairs; and by an act of the provincial Legislature, the sum of £25,000, equal to $125,000, is set apart as a school fund, to be applied anually to purposes of education.

The school act empowers each township Council to divide the township into school sections, answering to our school districts, and also, to establish a township model school. These sections are authorized to choose, at first, three Trustees, to remain in office, respectively, one, two and three years, and every subsequent year to choose one to take the place of the Trustee retiring; and also to decide in what manner they will procure the funds necessary to defray their school expenses; whether by voluntary subscriptions, by rate-bills on parents sending children to the schools, or by rates on the property of all.

The Trustees are empowered to employ a teacher or teachers, male or female, or both, and give such compensation as they may think proper; to appoint a Collector, to estimate the sum necessary to defray all expenses to issue their warrants, to collect the amount, and to exercise a general supervision over all the schools in the section. Analogous provisions, to accomplish the same purposes, are made with regard to incorporated cities and villages.

The school fund before mentioned is apportioned annually, by the chief Superintendent, among the several townships, according to the population of each; and by the local Superintendents among the sections, according to the average attendance of the scholars; and each section is required to raise a sum, at least as large as that received from the treasury. Should it fail to do so, the county Council is required to assess and levy the whole sum, or the amount deficient, to be expended for the benefit of the section.

The county Council appoints a local Superintendent of Schools for the whole county, or for any one or more townships, not giving to any one Superintendent the oversight of more than one hundred schools. He is entitled to at least four dollars each year, for every school placed under his charge, and may be, and often is, allowed additional compensation. He is required to visit every school once a quarter, to deliver a public lecture in each school section, once a year, and to report annually to the chief Superintendent. And it is provided, that no section shall be entitled to any portion of the school fund, from which a satisfactory report was not received the preceding year.

All the local Superintendents, and the Trustees of all the Grammar schools in the county, are constituted a Board of Instruction for the county. To this Board is entrusted the duty of examining all persons who desire to be employed as teachers. Those whom they deem qualified they arrange in three classes, according to their qualifications, and state, in the certificate given, the class to which he who receives it belongs. No person is entitled to receive compensation as a teacher unless he has such a certificate, and no section can receive any portion of the fund unless a school has been kept in it six months during the year, by a qualified teacher.

Besides the local Superintendents, who are required, all clergymen recognised by law, the members of the Legislature, and all magistrates, are authorized to visit the schools within their parishes, towns or counties, and are desired to attend especially the quarterly examinations. The county and township Councils are authorized to raise such sums as they think proper, for public school libraries; and general regulations in regard to them are prescribed.

A Council of Public Instruction, and a chief Superintendent of Schools, both appointed by the crown, are placed at the head of the whole system. To the Council is entrusted the management of the provincial normal and model schools, for the establishment of which provision is made by law; it recommends text-books and books for the school libraries; prescribes regulations for the organization, government, and discipline of common schools, the examination and classification of teachers, and the establishment and care of libraries. To the chief Superintendent are assigned other duties than have already been mentioned, similar to those usually performed by the same officer in the States.

Such is a very brief sketch of the system of public instruction in Upper Canada. It is now in active operation, and the intelligence and zeal with which it is administered justify the highest anticipations of its success and future usefulness. In July, 1851, a normal and model school was founded at Toronto, capable of accommodating two hundred teachers in training, and six hundred pupils in the model school, to which eight acres of land are attached; two of which are occupied as a botanical garden, three for agricultural experiments, and the remainder by the buildings of the institution, and as grounds for the gymnastic exercises of students and pupils. Thus, lectures on Vegetable Physiology and Agricultural Chemistry are practically illustrated on the adjoining grounds, in the culture of which the students are employed during a portion of their hours of recreation.

The educational history of Canada West, from 1853 to

1855, was even more distinguished. A system of free public libraries was put into successful operation; the Grammar schools were re-organized, and salutary regulations for their government, and for the government of common schools, were adopted; a fund for the support of superannuated common school teachers was created; and a special grant made by the Legislature, to enable the Superintendent to supply the public schools with suitable maps, charts, diagrams, and those other useful and appropriate adjuncts in the process of education, whose value has been tested by experience. The annual report, for 1854, enumerates 3,311 public schools, for the maintenance and support of which nearly a million of dollars is appropriated, with an attendance of 208,455 pupils. At the close of 1855, 150 libraries were reported, containing 120,000 books. Lord Elgin, under whose administration the Canadian system reached its present excellence, claimed, in a recent speech at Glasgow, that "the means of obtaining elementary education, free of cost, and upon condition that can do violence to no rights of conscience, are placed within the reach of every child in the community; and every child, who manifests superior intelligence or industry, may ascend from the elementary school to the higher, in which a superior education is given upon the same terms, and from the superior school to the university." The claim is just. Canada is a fine illustration of the American system of general education.

Having thus passed hastily in review the general features of the systems of public instruction in the older States, an imperfect impression of their utility would be received, if the remarkable development of their practical operation in some of the Atlantic cities remained unnoticed. Boston, New York, and Philadelphia may well claim pre-eminence on this continent, and are unsurpassed by the most advanced capitals of central Europe. It is well, before limiting our attention to the western slope of the Alleghanies, to select the school arrangements of the city of New York, for instance, as an instructive example of the adaptation of free schools to the highest educational wants of the community.*

There are, in the city of New York, twenty-two wards, in each of which there are two Commissioners, two Inspectors, and eight Trustees of Common Schools, elected by the people; the two former classes of officers for two years, and the latter for four years each—one Commissioner, one Inspector, and two Trustees being annually elected. These officers constitute the local administrative board of their respective wards. The two Commissioners of each ward compose the Board of Education, one-half of which is annually replenished by the election of new members, and which has power to organize and establish schools in any locality where their necessity is certified to by the local Boards, to make the necessary provision for their maintenance and support, as well as of those already established, in the manner prescribed by law, and generally to exercise supervisory powers over the administration of the system in all its parts. The several local Boards have the immediate charge of all the schools established in their respective wards, and, under such general rules and regulations as the Board of Education may see fit to adopt, contract with and employ teachers, furnish supplies, procure text-books, and make all needful regulations for the good order and general discipline and management of the schools under their charge. A city Superintendent of Schools, and two assistants, are biennially appointed by the Board of Education, whose general duty it is to visit every school as often as may be practicable, to inquire into all matters relating to their government, course of instruction, books, studies, discipline, and conduct; to advise and counsel with the Trustees; to examine and license teachers; to report monthly on the condition of the schools to the Board, and "generally, by all

---

* See an article in the American Journal of Education and College Review, for March, 1856, by Hon. S. S. Randall, Superintendent of Schools for the city of New York.

the means in their power, to promote sound education, elevate the character and qualifications of teachers, improve the means of instruction, and advance the interest of the schools committed to their charge." The Inspectors of each ward are required to inspect and examine their respective schools, at least twice in each year, and annually to report to the Board of Education as to the condition of the several school buildings in their wards; whether any, and if any, what repairs, alterations, or modifications are necessary or desirable; their general cleanliness and order; the mode and results of heating and ventilation; the studies pursued; the progress of the pupils; punctuality of attendance on the part, as well of teachers as of scholars; the order, attention, and general appearance of the schools; the number and qualifications of the teachers; and such other facts as, in their opinion, are important to insure the discipline or extend the usefulness of the schools under their charge. The services of all these various officers and agents, with the exception of the city Superintendent and his assistants, are entirely gratuitous.

The funds authorized and required, by law, for the support of the system, including all expenses for the purchase of sites; the erection and repairs of school-houses; furniture, fuel, books, and apparatus; payment of teachers' wages, and salaries of officers of the Board are derived from the following sources:

1. The distributive share, belonging to the city, of the income of the State common school fund, and of the annual State tax of $800,000 for the support of schools.

2. An equal amount, raised by tax upon the city, with the addition of a sum equal to one-twentieth of one per cent. of the value of real and personal estate in the city.

3. Such additional sum as the Board of Education shall certify to be necessary to meet the current annual expenses of public instruction, not exceeding four dollars for each pupil who shall have been under instruction during the preceding year.

Under these provisions, fifty ward schools have been organized and established, with three separate and distinct departments in each—male, female, and primary—and upward of one hundred primary schools. In these schools, about one hundred and thirty thousand pupils are annually instructed, for a longer or shorter period, with an average attendance, during the whole term of eleven months, of some 60,000. The whole number of teachers employed exceeds 1,000, of whom 800 are females; and the aggregate annual expenses of the system, over and above the amount contributed by the State, considerably exceed $1,000,000, of which $450,000 is paid for teachers' wages, and the residue for the erection of new school buildings, the purchase of sites, and the incidental expenses of education.

The ward schools are divided, as before observed, into Grammar schools for girls, Grammar schools for boys, and primary departments, each occupying a separate story. The buildings are, for the most part, especially those recently erected, spacious, tasteful, and commodious—costing, including the sites, from $30,000 to $60,000 each—well-arranged and suitably furnished. Each story is provided with a large hall, or assembling room; that in the primary is capable of accommodating from five hundred to a thousand children, according to the size of the building and the number of pupils in ordinary attendance; and that in the upper departments, from three to five hundred each; also several large and convenient class-rooms, suitable playgrounds, and separate front and rear entrances for both sexes. The seats and furniture generally are of the most modern and improved structure; and in most of the schools, pianos are furnished for the instruction of the classes in music, in one or both of the upper departments.

The primary schools occupy a more humble, but equally convenient grade of building—adapted to the accommodation of from three to five hundred children each; and generally consist of two stories, one for each sex. One or two of those, recently erected, are on a larger and more extensive scale, capable of accommodating a thousand pupils; while, on the other hand, several of the older structures are antiquated and inconvenient, and some still continue to occupy the basements of churches and other public buildings, where they were originally located at an early period. From these schools, promotions are semi-annually made to the ward schools in their vicinity, and from the primary to the upper departments of the ward schools themselves. The girls' Grammar schools, the primary departments, and primary schools, are under the exclusive charge of female teachers.

In these schools, all the elementary branches of instruction are thoroughly and systematically taught, and carefully and frequently reviewed; and, in the upper departments, many of the higher branches, including Algebra, Physical Astronomy, Natural History and Philosophy, Physiology, General History, and Book-keeping, form portions of the course. Vocal Music, Composition, Declamation, and Drawing, are also universally practised. Each department is divided into five general classes, with as many sub-divisions as are required by the number of pupils in each—thirty or forty being considered as many as can profitably be taught by any one instructor. The hours of instruction are from 9, A. M., to 3, P. M., with two recesses of half an hour each.

The order and discipline of the schools are uniform and admirable. Precisely at nine o'clock, each department is assembled, in a quiet and regular manner, in its respective hall; and, amid profound stillness and attention, a select portion of the holy Scriptures is read by the Principal; after which, the Lord's Prayer is reverently repeated by the children, in conjunction with their teachers, and an appropriate hymn of praise and thanksgiving sung by the whole school. The classes are then dismissed to their respective recitation-rooms, and the lessons of the day entered upon. Previous to, and immediately after, each recess, the school is again assembled, and a short interval is devoted to singing, music, and such general exercises as are interesting and instructive to all. Noise and confusion are almost entirely unknown; and cheerfulness and enjoyment, regularity and order, pervade the entire group.

One of the most striking and peculiar features of the New

York system of public schools, consists in the general interest which is felt and manifested in their behalf, as well on the part of the numerous officers engaged in their administration and supervision, as on that of the community. Scarcely a day passes in any of the schools without the official visits of one or more of the school officers, and in many of the most advanced as well as primary departments, one day in each month is specially set apart for the reception of visitors. These occasions are regarded as holydays by the schools. The regular exercises are suspended. The pupils, in their holyday attire, are assembled, and the spacious halls are crowded with parents, friends, and visitors. After the usual opening ceremonies are concluded, a few of the highest class are examined in the various branches of study in which they are engaged. Compositions are read and premiums awarded for good conduct and scholarship; specimens of Drawing, Penmanship, Book-keeping, and Embroidery are displayed, and the exercises are agreeably diversified by music and singing, and appropriate addresses. A favorable opportunity is thus afforded to all who are interested, to observe the condition and progress of the schools, while both pupils and teachers are encouraged in their efforts for advancement and excellence. There can be no doubt that these frequent and periodical receptions exert a most favorable influence on the prosperity and welfare of the schools; enabling, as they do, the public to appreciate their value and to witness the results they are producing.

A thorough and complete public examination of the several pupils, by classes, is, also, semi-annually made by the Superintendents, in the presence of the school officers of the respective wards, and such others as choose to attend; and in addition to this, the officers of the wards themselves hold periodical examinations.

In the opinion of competent judges, no class of schools of a similar grade, which the city affords, are superior, in point of scholarship, general appearance, good order and discipline, and moral training, to those under the charge of the

Board of Education. Composed, as they are, of the children of all classes of the population, rich and poor, high and low, humble and exalted in station, the standard of intellect and of virtue is conspicuous in all, and all the influences which surround and pervade them are eminently favorable to the acquisition of correct habits, sound and useful knowledge, and Christian principles.

Having thus passed in review the principal features of the system, and of the public schools themselves, the incidental and auxiliary provisions which so essentially contribute to their advancement and success, remain to be considered. These are:

1. The normal schools, of which there are three in number—one for male teachers, one for female, and one for teachers of the several colored schools. These consist of all those teachers in the employ of the Board of Education who do not already hold certificates of qualifications of the highest grade, entitling them to fill the place of Principals or Vice-Principals of any of the schools. The female normal school assembles in the hall of the Board of Education, on Saturday of each week, and remains in session for six hours. It numbers between five and six hundred teachers, all of whom are actively engaged in teaching during the other five days of the week, and is under the immediate charge of a Principal, Vice-Principal, and twelve assistants, selected by the Executive Committee of the Board, and acting under their general supervision. The course of instruction comprises all the branches of a complete English education. The male normal school consists, in like manner, of all the male teachers of the several public schools, not holding full certificates, and assembles at the same place, on the afternoon of Tuesday and Friday of each week. The colored normal school assembles, on Saturday of each week, at one of the ward schools appropriated to their use. Hitherto, no institution has been organized for the special instruction and preparation of those designing to become teachers, but who have not

yet entered upon the active duties of the profession. The Board, however, have taken the necessary preliminary measures for the establishment of such an institution at the earliest practicable period.

2. The evening schools. These are thirty in number, comprising an attendance of nearly thirteen thousand pupils, and are in session for a period of five months, from the first of October in each year, to the first of March succeeding. They are designed exclusively for the benefit of those whose avocations and pursuits prevent attendance in any of the day schools. The range of instruction includes most of the branches ordinarily taught in the ward schools, with the addition of specific instruction in such of the practical applications of science, as are specially adapted to the peculiar wants of the class of pupils generally in attendance. The attendance in these schools is rapidly increasing, as their benefits and advantages become more generally and extensively known and appreciated; and they are unquestionably destined, at no distant day, to become an important and prominent feature of the general system. They are also under the special charge of an Executive Committee of the Board of Education, and the teachers employed are chiefly drawn from those on daily duty in the ward schools.

3. The schools for the instruction of colored children. These are chiefly included in the enumeration, above given, of the ward and primary schools and departments; and, although occupying separate buildings, are, in all other respects, on the same footing, and enjoy all the benefits and advantages of those schools. There are three large ward schools, divided into male, female, and primary departments, and five smaller and primary schools; comprising, in the whole, about three thousand pupils. The general standard of scholarship and deportment, in these schools, is of a very high order, and the qualifications of the teachers, and their success in the management and discipline of the schools under their charge, is worthy of all commendation.

4. Corporate schools, participating in the annual distribution of the school moneys. There are twelve of these institutions, numbering in the aggregate about five thousand pupils, with an average attendance of about half that number, under the immediate charge of teachers appointed by the institutions themselves. Their sole responsibility to the Board of Education, consists in the proper expenditure of the funds which they derive from this source. They are subject to the visitation and inspection of its officers, and the general course of instruction corresponds essentially with that of the several primary departments and schools. Among these institutions may be enumerated the House of Refuge, the several Protestant and Catholic orphan asylums, the Leake and Watts Orphan House, the House of Industry, and the juvenile asylums.

5. The free academy for boys. This is, to all intents and purposes, a collegiate institution, designed to carry its pupils through the entire course of studies requisite to complete a full collegiate education. Any male pupil of one year's standing in the ward schools, and who has attained the age of twelve years, is entitled to admission to the Preparatory department of the academy, provided, on examination, he shall have been found to possess the requisite qualifications—a thorough and accurate acquaintance with all the branches ordinarily pursued in the public schools. The full course of instruction in the academy occupies five years, at the expiration of which the pupil is graduated, with all the usual collegiate honors and degrees.

The institution is under the general supervision of a special committee of the Board, and the immediate charge of a Principal, (Horace Webster, L. L. D.,) twelve professors, and seven tutors. The number of pupils at present somewhat exceeds five hundred. An active and vigorous competition exists, among the several schools, for the honor of furnishing the greatest number of pupils generally to this institution; and the high inducements of a finished education, free from charge, operate as a powerful stimulant to all who are eligible to admission. A similar institution for the complete education of the female graduates of the ward schools will, doubtless, speedily be established under the authority conferred on the Board for that purpose.

CHAPTER III.

SCHOOL SYSTEMS OF THE WESTERN STATES.

The provision for public education in the western States, is intimately connected with the munificence of the Congress of the Confederation. In 1785, by the cessions of the original States, whose conflicting claims to the western wilderness had endangered the revolutionary cause, the region north-west of the river Ohio had become a domain, with the exception of the Connecticut Reservation, and some indefinite stipulations in behalf of Virginia military claimants. These western lands were regarded as a great resource for revenue; the right of Congress to dispose of them was unclogged by conditions; and yet the Congress of the Confederation determined to recognise, in the earliest legislation for their survey and sale, the paramount interest of public education.

On the 20th of May, 1785, "an ordinance for ascertaining the mode of disposing of lands in the western territory," was perfected by Congress, and became the foundation of the existing land system of the United States; and, by one of its provisions, a thirty-sixth of every township was expressly reserved from sale, "for the maintenance of public schools within the said township."

A township of land, under the surveys of the United States, contains 23,040 acres. This area is six miles square, and is subdivided into thirty-six equal divisions, called sections. Each section contains 640 acres, and every sixteenth section was reserved, as above stated, for the support of schools. In 1787, the ordinance for the government of the territory north-west of the river Ohio, was passed, which confirmed the provisions of the land ordinance of 1785; and further declared, that "RELIGION, MORALITY, and KNOWLEDGE, being necessary to good government, and the happiness of mankind, SCHOOLS, and the means of EDUCATION, shall forever be encouraged."

The negotiations which led to the first appropriations for university purposes in the North-West Territory, were commenced in the year 1786, by the Ohio Company, and concluded the following year by a contract for the purchase of one and a half millions of acres of the public lands. In this contract, in addition to reservations for school and religious purposes, was a provision for the grant of two outline townships as an endowment for a university. These two townships were selected together at Athens, in Ohio, and the university located upon them. The year after, John Cleves Symmes, of New Jersey, and his associates, made application for the purchase of another large tract of land between the Miami rivers. The school reservation in Symmes' Purchase was thus expressed: "Of lot No. 16, for the purpose mentioned in the land ordinance of the 20th of May 1785;" and one entire township was granted perpetually for the purpose of an academy or college, finally resulting in the endowment of Miami University.

The intention of Congress unquestionably was, that these donations for academies, colleges, and universities, should be inseparably connected with the provision for public schools in the townships; and such has been the result in Michigan and Wisconsin, thus furnishing a higher gradation of common or free schools. That community is fortunate where no institutions superior to the seminaries of the people—the latter being the best possible—are regarded as a public necessity.

A long series of acts have confirmed and extended the policy of these grants; although, in some instances, Congress has relaxed its early condition, namely, "to *each township respectively* for the use of schools;" simply granting section sixteen, etc., "for the use of schools in the State." By this means greater equality of benefit is secured; and the administration of a State school department is much facilitated. The elevated policy of the General Government, in this respect, has been well characterized by an American statesman, (Mr. Cushing,) as "a noble and beautiful idea of providing wise institutions for the unborn millions of the west; of anticipating their good by a sort of parental providence; and of associating together the social and the territorial development of the people, by incorporating these provisions with the land titles derived from the public domain, and making school reservations and road reservations essential parts of that policy."

In the organization of the territory of Oregon, in 1848, two sections of land in each township were set apart for school purposes. The grant of an additional school section to the new territories, was recommended by Mr. Robert J. Walker, while Secretary of the Treasury of the United States; and has recently been made to Utah, New Mexico, Minnesota, Kansas, and Nebraska, as well as to the Pacific organizations.

The amount of lands thus appropriated by the federal Government, up to January 1, 1854, is exhibited in the subjoined table:

States.	Acres.	States.	Acres.
Florida,	908,530.	Missouri,	1,199,139.
Alabama,	902,774.	Iowa,	905,144.
Mississippi,	837,584.	Wisconsin,	958,648.
Louisiana,	786,044.	California,	6,719,324.
Arkansas,	886,460.	Minnesota,	5,089,224.
Ohio,	704,488.	Oregon,	12,140,907.
Michigan,	1,067,397.	New Mexico,	7,493,120.
Indiana,	650,317.	Utah,	6,681,707.
Illinois,	978,755.		
			48,909,535.

The General Government has also appropriated 4,060,707 acres of land in the above States and territories for the support of universities.

Postponing the detailed narrative of educational progress

in Ohio, the remainder of this chapter will be occupied with a survey of the western States, similar to the summaries already given of the Atlantic States.

MICHIGAN was the first State in the Union that established a "Superintendent of Public Instruction" as a constitutional officer. The system contemplated by the framers of the first Constitution and laws, embraced a wide field. It consisted of a head of the department, designated as above, with general supervision; a university, in which education was free, governed by a Board of Regents, now elected by the people, with a local Faculty; branches of the university, and a system of primary schools, under the management of township officers, designated Inspectors of Primary Schools; and district officers, known as Moderator, Director, and Assessor of the School District. To these have been added, by the Legislature of 1850, a State normal school, the exclusive purposes of which are defined in the organic law, to be "the instruction of all persons, both male and female, in the art of teaching, and in all of the various branches that pertain to a good common school education; also, to give instruction in the arts of Husbandry and Agricultural Chemistry; in the fundamental laws of the United States, and in what regards the rights and duties of citizens." This school is under the government of a Board of Education, consisting of three members and the Superintendent of Public Instruction, who are elected by the people. It went into operation in April, 1853.

The school statistics for Michigan, for 1854, exhibit 129,517 children in attendance upon the schools; $130,996.69 apportioned by the State for their support; $156,916.90 raised by districts; 63,763.43 raised by rate-bills; 121,201 volumes in the township libraries, and $67,179.55 collected by a two mill tax for their increase; a primary school fund, derived from sales of lands, of $1,384,288.03; a university fund of $452,-423.07, and $56,503.71 from the net sales of normal school lands. A model farm and agricultural school has also been established at Lansing, during 1855

Wisconsin has adopted the policy of Michigan. Public instruction is under the charge of a State Superintendent, by whose report of December 31, 1854, it appears that the capital of the school fund was $1,160,258.77, at seven per cent., and which will probably reach $5,000,000 by the sale of lands. The university fund is $161,146.61. Wisconsin has also instituted a library system.

Indiana has a school fund derived from several sources. Governor Wright, who is distinguished for the leading interest he has taken in the subject of education, in his able message of December, 1853, estimates this fund at $4,988,988. It is made up of the Congressional township fund, surplus revenue, saline and bank tax funds, forfeitures, and the profits of the sinking fund; more than $1,000,000 is not at present available. The receipts from the university fund, for 1852, were $15,528, and from the common school fund, $73,839. There were expended for the Indiana University, in the same year, $16,361. The Constitution provides for the election, by the people, of a Superintendent of Public Schools, to hold office for two years.

By an act of 1855, a State Board of Education is established, consisting of the Governor, Secretary of State, State Treasurer, the Auditor, the Attorney General, and the Superintendent of Public Instruction, who meet annually for conference, discussion, and the determination of questions arising under the school law. The Superintendent has the general oversight of the schools, and must spend at least one day a year, in each county. The Board of Trustees of each township have the general custody and management of the school property and lands, a limited power to lay taxes for building school-houses, and the authority to employ teachers, when the inhabitants do not designate them. The inhabitants of each school district elect, for one year, a School Director, who takes care of the school-house, provides fuel, etc., and reports to the Trustees.

There is to be assessed each year the sum of ten cents on each $100 worth of property, and fifty cents on each poll (except upon the property and polls of negroes and mulattoes, who have none of the benefits of the act) for the use of the common schools; and one quarter of a mill on each dollar, and twenty-five cents on each poll, for the purchase of township libraries—such libraries to be purchased under the direction of the State Board of Education.

The State school fund of ILLINOIS, derived from the public lands, the surplus revenue of the United States, and from county and township funds, yields an income of $299,047. The whole amount expended for schools in 1854, as returned by seventy-nine counties, was $308,385.52, educating 136,371 children six months.

It is provided, by the Constitution of IOWA, that a Superintendent of Public Instruction shall be chosen by the people, for three years; and that all lands granted by Congress, all escheated estates, and such per cent. as may be granted by Congress, on the sale of the public lands in Iowa, shall constitute a perpetual fund, the interest of which, with the rents on the unsold lands, shall be applied to the support of common schools. The Assembly shall provide for a school in each school district, for at least three months in each year; and all moneys received for exemption from military duty, and for fines imposed by the courts, shall be appropriated to support such schools, or for the establishment of school libraries. The money arising from the lease or sale of public lands, granted for the support of a university, shall remain a perpetual fund to maintain such an institution.

The school fund, being the proceeds of lands sold, amounted, December 4, 1854, to nearly $1,000,000. It was under the management of the School Fund Commissioners, and loaned at ten per cent. interest. A considerable amount of school lands remains unsold. There have been sold university lands to the amount of $58,571.31. The entire value of the lands is estimated at $200,000. The law provides for the establishment of three normal schools, and public libraries.

MISSOURI has a school fund of $575,668, and another fund of $100,000, called the seminary fund. The State also appropriates one-fourth of its revenue to the support of schools; making an annual income of about $200,000, which is distributed among the counties.* The State University, located at Columbia, in Boone county, is endowed with six townships of land by the General Government. From the report of the Superintendent, made to the Legislature, in January, 1855, it appears there were reported, in 1853, 233,327 scholars between the ages of five and twenty, of whom 80,605 were in organized school townships. In 1844, 67,974 children, from an aggregate of 202,658, were taught within the year. There were 1,117 district libraries.

The school fund in KENTUCKY amounted, in 1854, to $1,400,270.01, consisting of State bonds and bank stocks, besides an annual tax on property, amounting to about $78,000. The number of children reported in that year was 207,210—average number at school, 76,429. The distribution for school purposes, in 1854, was $146,047.

The year 1855 indicates a new impulse to the cause of education in Kentucky. The people, by a majority of 57,526 (all the counties but five contributing to that immense aggregate,) voted an additional tax of three cents on each $100 of taxable property, in aid of common schools. At the present time there are 3,374 common schools in the State, in which about 5,000 teachers are engaged in the instruction of 113,763 youth. Transylvania University has recently offered property and funds, exceeding in value $100,000, for the establishment of a normal school at Lexington, of which the Legislature will unquestionably avail itself.

The school fund of TENNESSEE, in 1851, was $1,321,655. The expenditure for schools during the two years, ending October 3, 1853, was $244,884.

In MISSISSIPPI, there is no uniform common school system for all the counties. Each township has a school fund from

* The Superintendent of Common Schools, under date of April 26, 1856, announces that the apportionment of school moneys for 1856 distributes $217,674 to 272,093 children, or eighty cents per head.

the lease of lands granted by Congress, mostly for ninety-nine years. The money thence arising is loaned annually, at not less than eight nor more than ten per cent., which income is applied annually to tuition. There is also a county fund, arising from fines, forfeitures, licenses, etc., which is distributed in those townships that are destitute, or have but a small school fund. In all larger towns, public schools have been established, and there are many flourishing high schools.

ALABAMA has a common school fund of $2,300,970, the income of which is $237,515. The State University at Tuscaloosa receives annually $30,000 from the State, most of which is the proceeds of an university fund. In 1854, the Legislature provided for the appointment of a Superintendent of Common Schools, as preliminary to a thorough revision of the system. According to the returns made to him, in 1855, there were 145,518 children, between the ages of five and eighteen years, and about 1,000 schools in operation.

FLORIDA, although an Atlantic State, is here mentioned, because she was the recipient of Congressional donations—908,503 acres of land having been appropriated for common schools, and 46,080 acres for a university. By an act of the Legislature of 1849, the proceeds of the sales of the school lands, or sixteenth section, and five per centum of the net proceeds of other lands granted by Congress for purposes of education, of all escheated property, and all salvages, shall constitute a school fund, for the support of common schools in the State. According to the census of 1850, there were but 69 public schools, with 1,878 pupils, and $22,386 income.

In ARKANSAS, the Secretary of State is *ex officio* Commissioner of Common Schools. His last report is dated 13th of November, 1854. The returns to him from the School Commissioners are exceedingly imperfect. Only 40 schools are reported in the entire State. The sale of the school lands would make a large fund. The Commissioner says, "The great obstacle in the organization of common schools is not so mnch a deficiency to maintain them" as it is "the indifference that pervades the public mind on the subject of education."

LOUISIANA has received 786,044 acres of land for common school purposes, and 46,080 acres for a higher seminary. The Constitution provides for a State Superintendent, and that free public schools shall be established throughout the State; the proceeds of land granted for the purpose, and of lands escheated to the State, shall be held as a permanent fund, on which six per cent. interest shall be paid by the State for the support of these schools. The yearly sum of $250,000 is appropriated for the support of the free schools of the State, and is derived from the levy of a tax of one mill on the dollar, and from the imposition of a poll-tax of one dollar on each white male inhabitant of the State. The school fund, January 1, 1855, amounted to $461,269.65. There is, besides, the seminary fund, which, at the same date, was $151,539.66. But these now are funds of account only, and consist of a debt of the State to the fund. The number of school districts in the State, January 1, 1855, was 681; average attendance, for the year 1854, estimated at 36,000. The amount apportioned to the several parishes, for the year, was $250,524.56. The report of the Superintendent of Public Instruction contains but few statistics. The Governor in his message speaks of the "educational system" as in an unsatisfactory condition, and as "almost a failure."

In TEXAS, according to the census of 1850, there were 349 public schools, with 7,946 pupils, and $44,008 income, with two colleges, and ninety-seven academies.

The Constitution of CALIFORNIA provides for the election of a Superintendent of Public Instruction, to hold office for three years, and that the Legislature shall establish a system of common schools, to be taught at least three months in each year. By the same instrument, the proceeds of the public lands granted to the State for schools, the 500,000 acres granted to new States under the act of Congress of 1841, the estates of persons dying without heirs, and such per cent. as

Congress shall grant on the sale of lands within the State, shall be a fund, the interest of which, and unsold lands, are to be inviolably appropriated to the support of common schools. The estimated amount of lands to which the school fund is entitled, from the sixteenth and thirty-sixth sections in each township reserved for the use of schools, is stated by the United States Surveyor-General, in California, to be 5,201,244 acres. The price per acre, by existing laws, is two dollars, which would give $11,402,488 for the school fund. On the 1st of January, 1856, $28,269.60 was apportioned by the State Board of Education, being the entire income to the State school fund for the previous half year; of the 26,170 resident children reported, 6,422 form the daily average attendance of the common schools.

The munificent donations to the territories, when fully secured and applied, will constitute satisfactory endowments for schools. Minnesota has already organized a territorial university, and entrusted to a Superintendent of Public Instruction the responsibility of putting the school system into practical operation. Oregon and Washington have taken similar measures; and Kansas, Nebraska, and New Mexico will doubtless, at no distant day, imitate their examples. With a donation of lands double that enjoyed by the older western States, and with the benefit of their experience, the communities hereafter to be organized between the Mississippi and the Pacific will be very culpable, if they do not husband effectually their educational resources.

CHAPTER IV.

ADMINISTRATION OF ARTHUR ST. CLAIR—1788-1802.

On the 13th of July, 1787, Congress passed the "Ordinance for the Government of the Territory of the United States, north-west of the river Ohio." On the 5th of October, Arthur St. Clair was appointed Governor of the Territory, Winthrop Sargent, Secretary, and Samuel Holden Parsons, James Mitchell Barmim, and John Cleves Symmes, Judges. The 7th of April, 1788, is the memorable date of the settlement of Marietta; and on the 9th of July, Governor St. Clair arrived, and entered upon the duties of his office.

The first allusion to the interests of education in Ohio, is found in an Oration, pronounced at Marietta, the following year, April 7th, 1789, in commemoration of the commencement of the settlement formed by the Ohio Company, by Dr. Solomon Drown, and printed at Worcester, Massachusetts, by Isaiah Thomas. The following paragraph is less ambitious, but more worthy of quotation than the bulk of the production in question:

"This country," he observes, "will afford noble opportunity for advancing knowledge of every kind. A communication with all nations will enable you to introduce the most useful and excellent scientific improvements, which are to be found in every kingdom and empire on earth. Effectual measures have been taken by Congress, for cultivating and diffusing literature among the people, in appropriating large tracts of land for the establishment of schools and a university. The institution of a public library would be of great benefit to the community, not only by affording rational amusement, and ameliorating the disposition, but by giving those who have not a liberal education, an opportunity of gaining that knowledge which will qualify them for usefulness."

It was not until the population of the territory had reached 5,000, when the people were entitled, under the ordinance, to a representative government, that any measures were taken in regard to education. The first session of the territorial Legislature, was held at Cincinnati, beginning on the 17th of September, 1799; and Governor St. Clair, in his address to that body, held this language: "The benefits that result from early education, and due instruction in the principles of religion, are of immense value to every country, and are too obvious that an attention to them, for the rising generation, should be pressed upon you."

We have the authority of Judge Jacob Burnet, that "the subject of education occupied the serious attention of the territorial Legislature; and, among other measures, they instructed the delegate in Congress, (William Henry Harrison,) to use his influence to induce that body to pass laws which were considered necessary, to secure to the territory the title of the lands that had been promised for the support of schools and colleges, including section No. 16 in every township, by the ordinance of May, 1785, and confirmed by another in July 1787.*

By a resolution, at this session, December 18, 1799, Rufus Putnam, Benjamin Ives Gilman, and Jonathan Stone, were requested to lay off, within the two townships donated for the endowment of a university, a town plat, containing "a square for the colleges; also, lots suitable for house-lots and gardens for a president, professors, tutors, etc., bordering on, or encircled by, spacious commons; and such a number of town-lots, adjoining the said commons and out-lots, as they should deem for the advantage of the university;" and they were instructed to report the same to the Legislature, at its next session.

At the second session of the General Assembly, held at Chillicothe, on the 3d of November, 1800, an act was passed, incorporating Griffin Green, Robert Oliver, Benjamin Ives

* Burnet's Notes on the North-West Territory, p. 305.

Gilman, Isaac Pierce, Jonathan Stone, and Ephraim Cutler, as Trustees, with authority "to lease all lots of lands granted for religious purposes, and *the support of schools*, in the county of Washington, or the Ohio Company's Purchase, for any term not exceeding seven years; and to require such improvements to be made thereon, as they might think reasonable." This Legislature indicated a disposition to protect the school lands from sacrifice.

At the third session of the General Assembly, January 9, 1802, an act was passed, establishing a university in the town of Athens, in the ninth township of the fourteenth range within the Ohio Company's Purchase, by the name and style of the "American Western University," for "the instruction of youth, in all the various branches of the liberal arts and sciences; for the promotion of good education, virtue, religion, and morality; and for conferring all the degrees and literary honors, granted in similar institutions."

The preamble asserted that "institutions for the liberal education of youth, are essential to the progress of arts and sciences, important to morality, virtue, and religion; friendly to the peace, order, and prosperity of society; and honorable to the government that encourages and patronizes them." The corporators were to consist of the President, *ex officio*, and not more than seventeen, nor less than eleven Trustees—Rufus Putnam, Joseph Gilman, Return Jonathan Meigs, jr., Paul Fearing, Rev. Daniel Story, Griffin Green, Robert Oliver, Ebenezer Sproat, Dudley Woodbridge, and Isaac Pierce, being designated in this act, as the first organization. They were empowered to appoint a Faculty, and other officers and servants of the institution, to make needful rules; to fix salaries; to remove either Trustees or Faculty, and servants, for cause; to fill vacancies in their own body, until the next session of the Legislature should supply the same; to keep a seal; to execute deeds and instruments in writing, by the signature under seal of their Treasurer; to sue and be sued, provided that the process against the corporation should be, by summons, served upon the Treasurer, at least twenty days before its return; to have power to divide and lease the two townships donated by Congress, provided, "that no lease be made for a longer term of time than twenty-one years," and that the tenants or lessees "should enjoy and exercise all the rights and privileges of citizens, as if they held the same lands in fee simple;" to apply the clear annual rents and profits, as directed by the act; to accept donations, if for a suitable purpose; to lease, for a small annual rent, on condition of a capital sum being paid in hand, the whole, or any part, of the house-lots and out-lots of five acres, in the town of Athens, as laid out under the resolution of December 18, 1799, by Rufus Putnam, Benjamin Ives Gilman, and Jonathan Stone, and apply said capital sum, or a part thereof, in the erection of necessary buildings; to elect a president of the University; and, until such election, and in all cases of vacancy or absence of the president, then the Trustees were authorized to appoint one of their number to preside in their meetings. The Legislature reserved the power to modify or change the act in all respects; and Rufus Putnam was authorized to fix the time and place, of the first meeting of the corporation. Section 14 provided, that the lands in the two townships, appropriated and vested in said Trustees, with the buildings which might be erected thereon, for the accommodation of the president, professors, and other officers, students, and servants of the University, and any buildings appertaining thereto, and also, the dwelling-houses and out-houses, or other buildings of the tenants or lessees, then erected and built, or which might thereafter be built and erected on the lands within the said townships, should forever be exempted from all territorial and State taxes; provided, that no exemption from the payment of county taxes, or upon personal estates, should be asserted under the act. The Treasurer of the University was required to execute a bond, to the acceptance of the president and Trustees; and it was probably intended that he should not be of their number.

Before dismissing the administration of Governor St. Clair, justice to him requires some allusion to his efforts to secure the township reserved from Symmes's Purchase, for an academy or college. In doing so, some legislation, which occurred after the organization of the State and the retirement of Governor St. Clair, will require recapitulation. The whole subject has been presented lucidly, by Judge Jacob Burnet, in his "Notes on the North-West Territory," and free use is, therefore, made of the testimony of so competent a witness.

The ordinance under which the early sales of the public domain were made, did not authorize a grant of college lands to purchasers of a less quantity than two millions of acres. The original proposition of Mr. Symmes, being for that quantity, would have entitled him to the benefit of the grant, had it been carried into effect. It was therefore stated in his pamphlet, containing the terms of sale and settlement, that a college township had been given and located as nearly opposite the mouth of the Licking river, as an entire township could be found eligible, in point of soil and situation. The selection of that township was made in good faith, on one of the best tracts in the Purchase; and was marked on his map as the college township. It was situated opposite the mouth of the Licking, and was reserved from sale for the purpose intended, until it was ascertained, that the agents appointed to close the contract with Government, under the powers given in the letter of attorney, had relinquished one half of the quantity proposed to be purchased by Mr. Symmes; and, as a matter of course, had relinquished, also, his claim to a college township. After that relinquishment, he erased the entry made on that township, on his map, as he had a right to do; and offered it for sale. As it was one of the best in the Purchase, it was soon entirely disposed of. The matter remained in that situation, until 1792, when the Judge applied to Congress, as is stated above, to change the boundaries of his Purchase, and grant him a patent, for as much land as he was then able to pay for. When the bill for that purpose was before Congress, General Dayton, the agent of Mr. Symmes, and then a very influential member of the House, introduced a section, authorizing the President to convey to Mr. Symmes and his associates, one entire township, in trust, for the purpose of establishing an academy and other schools of learning, conformably to the ordinance of Congress, of October 2, 1787; to be located, with the approbation of the Governor, for the time being, of the the territory north-west of the river Ohio, (within the term of five years, as nearly as may be,) in the center of the tract of land granted by the patent.

The fact was, that under that ordinance, the right to the township had been lost, by relinquishing half the quantity of his proposed purchase; yet from some cause, either from a want of correct information, or a disposition to be generous, the provision was retained, and became a part of the law. At that time there was not an entire township in the Purchase, undisposed of; portions of each and all of them had been sold by Mr. Symmes, after his right to college lands had been lost, and before the law of 1792 had renewed the claim. He could not, therefore, make the appropriation required.

The matter remained in that situation until the first Territorial Legislature was elected, in 1799. Mr. Symmes, then feeling the embarrassment of his situation, and aware that the subject would be taken up by that body, made a written proposition to the Governor of the territory, offering the second township of the second fractional range, for the purposes of a college. The Governor, on examination, found that Mr. Symmes had sold an undivided moiety of that township, for a valuable consideration, in 1788, four years before the right to a college township existed; that the purchaser had filed a bill, in the Circuit Court of the United States, for the district of Pennsylvania, to obtain a specific performance of his contract; and that the Judge had also sold small portions of the same township to other persons, who then held written contracts for the same, in the form of deeds. As a matter of course the township was rejected by the Governor.

Soon after that occurrence, the subject was brought before the territorial Legislature, at the instance of Mr. Symmes, who repeated the same offer to them. They also refused to receive it, for the same reasons which had been assigned by the Governor, as appears from the Journal of that body. A similar refusal, for the same reasons, was subsequently made by the State Legislature, to whom it was again offered by the Judge. Not satisfied with these repeated refusals, in 1802-3 he offered the same township to Congress, for the same purpose. His proposition was referred to a committee of that body, who, after hearing his own *ex parte* statement of the facts relating to the township, were fully satisfied that it could not be held for the purpose for which it was offered; and, therefore, they also refused to receive it.

It was affirmed in the written communication of Judge Symmes to Congress, very correctly, that the Miami Purchase did not obtain a right to college lands, until the law of 1792 was passed; that prior to that time, he had sold large portions of every township, in his Purchase, as he had a right to do; that the township he then offered, *had not been reserved for a college, but to be sold and disposed of, for his own benefit; and that he had sold large portions of it, as early as* 1788, *but that those sales, in his opinion, were void.*

Some persons had the charity to believe, that when he first proposed that township, for the use of a college, it was his intention to purchase out the claimants, which he probably might have done, at the time the law passed making the grant, on fair and reasonable terms; but he omitted to do so, until that arrangement became impracticable, and until his embarrassments rendered it impossible for him to make any remuneration to Congress, or to the people of the Miami Purchase.

The delegates representing the territory in Congress, were instructed, from time to time, to exert their influence to induce the Government to grant a township, in lieu of the one which had been lost, but nothing effectual was accomplished, until the establishment of a State Government, in 1802-3, when a law was passed by Congress, vesting in the Legislature of Ohio a quantity of land, equal to one entire township, to be located under their direction, for the purpose of establishing a college or an academy, in lieu of the township already granted for the same purpose, by the act entitled, "An act authorizing the grant and conveyance of certain lands to John C. Symmes, and his associates."

In April, 1803, the Legislature of Ohio passed an act, appointing Jacob White, Jeremiah Morrow, and William Ludlow, Commissioners, to locate the college lands, amounting to thirty-six sections; by virtue of which they selected and located them, as they are now held by the Miami University. In consequence of the numerous sales that had been made in the Miami Purchase, the college lands were, from necessity, located west of the Big Miami river, without the limits of the Miami Purchase.

In February, 1809, the Legislature passed a law, containing the following provision, to-wit: "There shall be a University established and instituted, in manner hereafter to be directed, within that part of the country known by the name of John Cleves Symmes's Purchase; which university shall be designated by the name and style of the Miami University." The act then proceeded to describe the powers and duties of the corporation, and to appoint Trustees, etc.; it then made a formal grant of all the land vested in them by Congress, for the use of the Miami Purchase, to the corporation created by that act, and their successors forever, for the sole use and benefit of the said University.

The 17th section appointed Alexander Campbell, the Rev. James Killburn, and the Rev. Robert Wilson, Commissioners, to fix on the place for the permanent seat of the University, *in such part of* John C. Symmes's Purchase, as an eligible place could be found, paying regard to health, etc.

The 19th section directed the first meeting of the corporation to be at Lebanon, in the county of Warren. At the time appointed for the meeting of the Commissioners, the Rev. Dr. Wilson was detained at home by sickness in his family. The other Commissioners, his colleagues, attended, and after having examined all the places presented for their consideration, including Cincinnati, Dayton, and Lebanon, they selected the town of Lebanon, in the county of Warren, as the seat of the university, and made their report accordingly to the Legislature.

It was then generally understood, that the seat of the institution was unalterably fixed, although the citizens of other places, who had failed in their applications, were greatly disappointed. But at the next session of the Legislature, a proposition was made by Mr. Cooper, of Dayton, to establish the university on the college lands, without the limits of Symmes's Purchase. This proposition was objected to, on various grounds. It was contended that the donation was originally made to the people of the Miami Purchase, for their exclusive benefit; that the patent of 1792 granted the township for the sole intent and purpose of erecting and establishing, *within that Purchase*, an academy, etc.; that the law, subsequently passed in 1803, vested the land in the Legislature, for the purpose of an academy, in lieu of the township already granted for the same purpose.

It was further contended, that, by the law of 1809, the Legislature had established a university *within the limits of John C. Symmes's Purchase*, and had granted the fee of the land, to the trustees of that institution, for its sole and exclusive benefit; that they had thus executed their trust, and exhausted their power, and that they could not revoke that grant, or apply the fund to another institution, established *without* the Miami Purchase. The Legislature, however, thought differently, and passed an act, establishing the university on the land, without the limits of John C. Symmes's Purchase. That institution is now in a very flourishing state, and although the original beneficiaries of the grant have been wrongfully deprived of their rights, yet it is now too late to relieve them, without great temporary injury to the cause of science, and on that account it is desirable that no effort be made to disturb the institution, or to check its advancement.

CHAPTER V.

THE ORGANIZATION OF THE STATE OF OHIO—EDUCATIONAL COMPACTS.

By the act of April 30, 1802, Congress authorized the organization of the State of Ohio, and, among other inducements for a provision exempting lands sold by the United States from taxation for a period of five years, proposed, "that the section number sixteen, in every township, and where such sections had been sold, granted, or disposed of, other lands equivalent thereto, and most contiguous to the same, shall be granted to such township for the use of schools."

The Ohio Convention accepted the proposition of Congress, but with an important condition, as follows: "*Provided*, The following addition to, and modification of, the said propositions shall be agreed to by the Congress of the United States, namely: that, in addition to the first propositions securing the said section number sixteen, in every township within certain tracts, to the inhabitants thereof, for the use of schools, a like donation equal to the one-thirty-sixth part of the amount of the lands in the United States Military Tract, shall be made for the support of schools in that tract; and that the like provision shall be made for the support of schools in the Virginia Reservation, so far as the unlocated lands in that tract will supply the provision aforesaid, after the warrants issued from said State have been satisfied; and, also, that a donation of the same kind, or such provision as Congress shall deem expedient, shall be made to the inhabitants of the Connecticut Reserve; that of all the lands which may hereafter be purchased of the Indian tribes, by the United

States, and lying within the State of Ohio, the one-thirty-sixth part shall be given, as aforesaid, for the support of public schools; that all lands before mentioned, to be appropriated by the United States, for the support of schools, shall be vested in the Legislature of said State, in trust for said purpose."

Congress, by act of March 3, 1803, assented, enacting (section 1,) that the tracts therein described were "appropriated for the use of schools in the State, and shall, together with all the tracts of land heretofore appropriated for that purpose, be vested in the Legislature of the State, in trust, for the use aforesaid, and for no other use, intent, or purpose whatever." The same section proceeds to grant eighteen quarter townships, or one-thirty-sixth of the lands in the United States Military District, "for the use of schools within the same;" secondly, fourteen quarter townships, also situated in the United States Military District, "for the use of schools in that tract commonly called the Connecticut Reserve;" thirdly, "so much of the Virginia Military Reservation, to be selected by the Ohio Legislature from unlocated lands therein, as would amount to one-thirty-sixth of the whole tract;" and, fourthly, (which is the last clause of the first section,) "one-thirty-sixth part of all the lands of the United States lying in the State of Ohio, to which the Indian title is not extinguished, which may hereafter be purchased of the Indian tribes by the United States, which thirty-sixth part shall consist of section sixteen, in each township, if the same shall be surveyed in townships of six miles square; and shall, if the lands be surveyed in a different manner, be designated by lots." The second section declared, "that the several appropriations for schools, made by the preceding section," were "in conformity to, and in consideration of, the conditions agreed on by the State of Ohio, by the ordinance of the Convention of the State, bearing date the 29th day of November, 1802."

In order that the territorial divisions, above alluded to, may be fully understood, the Ohio State School Commissioner,

Hon. H. H. Barney, in his first annual report, presented a synopsis on this subject, which is no less minute than instructive. In what follows, an acknowledgment of indebtedness to his sketch of the irreducible funds of the States, is freely tendered.

By act of March 2, 1807, Congress appropriated eighteen quarter townships, and three sections, to be selected by lot, from lands lying between the United States Military Tract and the Western Reserve, for the use of schools in the Virginia Military Reservation—thus removing a restriction contained in the act of 1803, which confined their selection to the Virginia Military District. In return, the State of Ohio released to the United States the thirty-sixth part of the tract first designated, accepting the above grant in lieu thereof. It may be well to add that the Virginia Military District, (or the tract between the Scioto and Little Miami, reserved by Virginia from her cession of the territory north-west of the Ohio river, for the satisfaction of land bounties issued to her troops upon Continental establishment,) may be traced upon a township map of Ohio, as follows: It includes the whole of Adams, Brown, Clermont, Clinton, Fayette, Highland, Madison, and Union Counties; half of Hardin, or Taylorsville, Hale, and Dodley townships, and a large portion of Roundhead; part of a single township (Goshen) in Auglaize; one half of Logan, or Rush Creek, Bokengehelas Creek, Jefferson, Perry, Zane, and Goshen townships, with large fractions of McArthur, Monroe, and Lake, and a smaller portion of Stokes; one quarter of Champaign, or Wayne, Rush, and Goshen townships, with a large part of Union, and a less fraction of Salem; the north-east and south-east extremities of Clark, being the eastern portions of Pleasant and Harmony, and the southern portions of Madison and Greene townships; three-fourths of Greene, or all of the county except Bath and Beaver's Creek townships, and those portions of Miami and Xenia which lie west of the Little Miami river; two-fifths of Warren, or Hamilton, Salem, Washington, and part of Wayne townships; a single township, (Anderson,) at the south-east angle of Hamilton; two-fifths of Scioto, namely: Nile, Washington, Union, Brush Creek, and Morgan townships; three-fifths of Pike, namely: Camp Creek, Sunfish, Mifflin, Perry, Preble, Benton, Peepee, and the west half of Jackson townships; two-thirds of Ross, namely: Franklin, Huntington, Paxton, Scioto, Twin, Paint, Buckskin, Concord, Union, and Deerfield townships; two-thirds of Pickaway, namely: Wayne, Deer Creek, Perry, Jackson, Monroe, Muhlenberg, Darby, and Scioto; seven of the nineteen townships of Franklin, namely: Jackson, Pleasant, Prairie, Franklin, Norwich, Brown, and Washington; a narrow belt along the west line of Delaware, to-wit: the townships of Thompson and Scioto, and a fraction of Concord; and, finally, the two south-western townships of Marion, namely: Green Camp and Bowling Green—to the place of beginning, "in a large, wet prairie, or swamp," whence flow, in opposite directions, the Scioto and Great Miami toward the Gulf of Mexico, and the Auglaize northwardly to its junction with the Maumee or Miami of Lake Erie. The sale of the school lands allotted to the inhabitants of the Virginia Military District, occurred in pursuance of acts passed by the General Assembly, in 1827 and 1828.

The United States Military District, so frequently mentioned in the present connection, was appropriated, by an act of Congress, in 1796, to satisfy the land bounties granted by the Continental Congress to the officers and soldiers of the revolution. It was bounded as follows: "Beginning at the north-west corner of the original seven ranges of townships,*

* The ordinance of the Continental Congress which first provided for the disposition of lands north-west of the river Ohio, passed May 20, 1785, resulted in the survey of the Seven Ranges, which are bounded on the north by a line drawn due west from the Pennsylvania State line, where it crosses the Ohio river, for the distance of forty-two miles; thence south to the Ohio river at the south-east corner of Marietta township, and thence up the river to the place of beginning. This tract comprises all of Jefferson, Harrison, Belmont, and Monroe counties, most of Carroll, and small portions of Columbia, Tuscarawas, Guernsey, Noble, and Washington, along their eastern boundaries.

and running thence fifty miles due south, along the western boundaries of the said range; thence due west, with [*to?*] the main branch of the Scioto river; thence up the main branch of the said river, to the place where the Indian boundary line crosses the same; thence along the said boundary line, to the Tuscarawas branch of the Muskingum river, at the crossing place above Fort Laurens; thence up said river, to a point where a line run due west from the place of beginning, will intersect the said river; thence along the said line to place of beginning." The language here quoted, is from the act of June 1, 1796, and is, geographically, inaccurate; for when the old Greenville line (the Indian boundary mentioned) reaches the site of Fort Laurens, (near the villages of Calcutta, on the southern border of Stark, and of Bolivar, in Tuscarawas counties,) there is no need of ascending the Muskingum to reach a point due west from the place of beginning. A few miles from the site of Fort Laurens, directly east, connects with the north-east corner of the seventh range of townships. The act further directed this tract to be surveyed into townships of five miles square; and these were afterward surveyed into quarter townships of two and a half miles square, containing 4,000 acres each. Consequently, the grant to the United States Military District of eighteen of these quarter townships, contained in the act of 1803, amounted to 72,000 acres, or about one-thirty-fourth of the whole extent of the District. The appropriation to the Connecticut Reserve, by the same act, of fourteen quarter townships, or 56,000 acres, was, of course, inadequate; while the subsequent allotment of eighteen quarter townships, and three sections within this tract, for the benefit of the Virginia Military District, may have amounted, together with other locations made between the Scioto and Little Miami, from 1803 to 1807, to the proportion of one-thirty-sixth of the lands in the latter tract.

The school lands originally granted to the United States Military District, remained under lease until 1827–8, when the inhabitants were authorized to vote their consent to sell them, which was done, and their proceeds now constitute a portion of the irreducible fund. The district entitled to a uniform division of their yearly income, may thus be designated on the map of Ohio: The whole of Coshocton county, and the following fractions, greater or less, of the adjacent counties of Tuscarawas, all except most of Warren and Union, and smaller portions of Will and Rush townships; of Guernsey, all except Londonderry and Oxford on the eastern, and Spencer on the southern border; of Noble, sections 10, 20, 21, and 22, in township one, range one, west of the seven ranges; of Muskingum, whatever lies north of the latitude of Zanesville, namely: Union, Perry, Washington, Falls, Hopewell, Highland, Salem, Muskingum, Licking, Monroe, Adams, Madison, Jefferson, and Jackson; of Holmes, all but Washington and Ripley, and portions of Prairie, Salt Creek, Paint, Knox, and Monroe; of Licking, all but Etna and Bowling Green, and parts of Union and Licking, which constitute its southern border; of Knox, all but a narrow wedge extending from west to east, along the northern line of Middlebury and Berlin; about half of Morrow, namely: Chester, Bloomfield, Harmony, Bennington, Penn, Lincoln, Westfield, and part of Franklin townships; most of Delaware, all except the narrow belt west of the Scioto; and of Franklin, the north-eastern townships of Jefferson, Mifflin, Clinton, Plain, Blendon, Sharon, and Perry.

The donation of 56,000 acres, for the use of schools on the Western Reserve, was probably one-thirty-sixth of the land east of the Cuyahoga river; but when, in 1805, the Indian title was extinguished by the treaty of "Fort Industry, on the Miami of the Lake," east of the meridian line drawn from Lake Erie along the western limit of the Connecticut Reserve, and thence south to the Greenville line, it became the duty of Congress to furnish a due proportion of school land for the remainder of the Reserve, which was estimated by a memorial of the Ohio Legislature, dated January 21, 1827, to be 43,000 acres. It was not, however, until June 19, 1834, that an act of Congress was passed, directing the

President of the United States to reserve from sale, public lands in Ohio, sufficient, in addition to the grant of 1803, to constitute one-thirty-sixth of the area of the Western Reserve, for the use of schools. Under this act, it was ascertained that the State of Ohio became entitled to 37,758 acres, most of which was located in the counties of Defiance, Henry, Williams, Paulding, Vanwert, and Putnam; in 1848, the people of the Western Reserve, by a vote authorized by the General Assembly, decided in favor of their sale; in 1850, provision was made for their appraisement and sale, and the lands in question are now generally disposed of. An income of six per cent. upon their net proceeds, is paid to the counties of Ashtabula, Trumbull, Lake, Geauga, Portage, Cuyahoga, Medina, Lorain, Huron, and Erie; to ten townships of Mahoning, namely: Berlin, Ellsworth, Canfield, Boardman, Poland, Milton, Jackson, Austintown, Youngstown, and Coitsville; to all of Summit, except Franklin and Greene townships; to three townships of Ashland, namely: Ruggles, Troy, and Sullivan; and the eastern extremity of Ottawa, consisting of Danbury township, and a portion of the Bass islands in Lake Erie.

The Moravian school fund also requires some explanation. Congress, at an early day, granted three tracts of 4,000 acres each, to the Society of United Brethren, for propagating the Gospel among the heathen, in trust for the Christian Indians of the Muskingum. These tracts included the missionary stations of Schœnbrunn, Gnattenhutten, and Salem, in Tuscarawas county, and were re-conveyed in 1824, to the United States, in consideration of certain provisions for the benefit of the Society, and the remnant of Indians then surviving. By an act of Congress, passed the same year, the Secretary of the Treasury was allowed to set apart, from the sale of these lands, one lot, not exceeding one-thirty-sixth part of each tract, the title being vested in the Legislature of Ohio, in trust for the use of schools, in the same manner that other lands have been granted for that purpose.

By a communication from Hon. F. M. Wright, the Auditor

of State, it appears that the total amount of payments into the State treasury on the sum constituting the school trust fund, or the bulk of the "irreducible debt of Ohio," was as follows:

Virginia military school fund	$152,495 54.
United States " "	120,532 41.
Western Reserve " "	254,027 64.
Section sixteen	1,722,241 92.
Moravian	3,160 58.
	$2,252,458 09.

The State receives these funds as a perpetual loan, and pays an annual interest of six per cent. thereon, for distribution in the localities entitled to the proceeds.

In order fully to understand the concurrent legislation by Congress and the State of Ohio, in 1802, subsequent enactments have been anticipated, thereby relieving a merely chronological summary; but the latter form of narrative has its advantages; and it is now proposed to continue, in the ensuing chapters, the educational annals of the State of Ohio during its earliest periods.

CHAPTER VI.

ADMINISTRATION OF EDWARD TIFFIN—1803–1807.

The earliest State Legislature, as well as that of the territory, indicated sanguine expectations that the land donations of Congress would be adequate to sustain schools, including a higher grade of institutions. This is apparent from the Bill of Rights, article viii, section 25, of the Constitution of 1802:

"That no law shall be passed to prevent the poor, in the several counties and townships within this State, from an equal participation in the schools, academies, colleges, and universities within this State, which are endowed, in whole or in part, from the revenue arising from donations made by the United States, for the support of schools and colleges; and the doors of the said schools, academies, and universities, shall be open for the reception of scholars, students, and teachers, of every grade, without any distinction or preference whatever, contrary to the intent for which said donations were made."

A prior clause of the same article, (section 3,) had declared, in language made familiar by frequent citation, that "religion, morality, and knowledge, being essentially necessary to good government and the happiness of mankind, schools, and the means of instruction, shall forever be encouraged, by legislative provisions, not inconsistent with the rights of conscience."

In the first message of Governor EDWARD TIFFIN, March 4, 1803, he congratulates the General Assembly, that "the liberal grants of land made by the United States, for the purpose of erecting and endowing universities and other seminaries of learning, and for the support of religion, are advantages, in these respects, superior to those which, perhaps, any other country can boast of."

Legislation speedily followed; and, as a contrast to the subsequent disposition of school lands, it may be well to reproduce the first law enacted by the General Assembly of Ohio, in regard to the fund arising from the proceeds of section sixteen, (see Ohio Laws, vol. I, p. 61, chapter xix):

"AN ACT *to provide for the leasing of certain lands therein named.*

"SECTION 1. *Be it enacted by the General Assembly of the State of Ohio*, That the lands granted for the support of schools, in the several parts of the State, shall be let, on lease, for the purpose of improving the same, and thereby rendering them productive, that the profits arising therefrom may be applied to the support of schools, according to the true intent and meaning of the original donation, and the several laws of the United States, reserving, granting, and appropriating the same.

"SEC. 2. That all the lands lying within the United States Military Tract, which have been appropriated for the use of schools, shall be let to lease for any term not exceeding fifteen years; and, that section number sixteen, in all other parts of the State, (except such as have been heretofore leased by persons legally qualified to lease the same,) and the sections that shall be located in lieu of such as have been sold or otherwise disposed of, by the United States, so soon as they shall be selected by the Secretary of the Treasury, shall be let to lease, for any term not exceeding seven years.

"SEC. 3. That on each tract of land, consisting of one hundred and sixty acres, or more, there shall be required the following improvements, to-wit: Fifteen acres cleared, and fenced in separate fields or parcels, one parcel or lot of which to consist of five acres, with all the timber and other wood cut and cleared off, and sowed down in timothy or red clover seed, and another lot, of three acres, cut and cleared in the same manner, and planted with one hundred thrifty and growing apple-trees, and the remaining tract, of seven acres, cleared and prepared for cultivation, in the ordinary manner of improving arable land: *Provided always*, That the person or persons to whom any of the said lands are leased, shall be obliged to complete the same improvements on all lands leased for fifteen years, within the time of the first twelve years of the same, and on all lands leased for seven years, within the time of the first five years of the said lease.

"SEC. 4. That it shall be the duty of the Governor, and he is hereby required, to appoint suitable persons in the several counties or districts in the State, with full power and authority to lease the several tracts of land within his county or district, conformably to the terms and provisions of this act: *Provided always*, That the Agents or Commissioners, appointed as aforesaid, shall not lease out any of the said lands in tracts less than one hundred and sixty acres, nor larger than three hundred and twenty acres, except in cases of fractional sections: *And provided also*, That it shall be the duty of said Agents or Commissioners, before they proceed to lease any of the said lands, to make application to the Surveyor General, for a list of such part or parts of the same as have been leased under the authority of the United States, in their respective districts or counties.

"SEC. 5. That each of the said Agents shall be, and is hereby, entitled to receive, for each lease, the sum of two dollars; to be paid by the said lessees respectively.

"SEC. 6. That it shall be the duty of the several Agents, within sixty days after being notified of their appointments, to give notice, in one or more newspapers, printed, or in circulation in the county, or by advertisement set up in three or more public places, expressing the terms for which the lands within his county or district are to be leased; and he shall, moreover, enter in a book, to be by him provided and kept for that purpose, the name of each person that shall apply for a lease; designating at the same time, the number, and part of the section applied for, and the term of years for which the applicant proposes to make the improvements required by the third section of this act; and in forty-two days after such application, if no other person shall apply for the same, and propose to take a lease on a shorter term, the said Agent shall proceed to make out a duplicate lease, to the said first applicant, one part of which shall be retained in the hands of the Agent; but if any succeeding applicant shall propose to take the same for a shorter space of time, then, and in that case, the lease shall be made to the person proposing to take the same on the shortest term: *Provided always*, That if two or more persons shall apply at the same time, and on the same terms, for any one tract, then the said Agent shall determine, by lot, in their presence, the priority of claim: *And provided also*, That leases shall be given to persons living on the land, if such persons shall apply for the same, on as short term as any other applicant, at any time within the forty-two days, notwithstanding such persons shall not be the first applicants.

"SEC. 7. That it shall be the special duty of the said Agent to inspect and inquire into any waste or trespass that may be committed on any of the aforesaid lands, by cutting and carrying away timber or stone, or any other damage that may be done to the same, whether by persons residing thereon, or others; and the said Agent is hereby authorized and required, where, in his opinion, any waste or trespass has been committed, to proceed against the person or persons committing said waste or trespass, according to law: *Provided always*, That no person residing on any of the said lands shall be liable to damages for cutting timber or removing stone for any necessary or useful improvement made on the same.

"SEC. 8. That actions for waste or trespass, shall be sustained by the Agent, and the damages recovered shall be, one-half to the use of such Agent, and the other half to be applied to the same purposes as the net proceeds of the land on which the damage was sustained; and the Agent for these lands in the United States Military Tract, which are appropriated to the use of schools in the county of Trumbull, shall receive such compensation for his services rendered, in pursuance of the seventh section of this act, as the Court of Common Pleas for said county of Trumbull shall allow, to be paid out of the county treasury.

"SEC. 9. That section number twenty-nine, in the several townships within Judge Symmes's patent shall be let to lease by the same persons, on the same terms, and under the regulations and restrictions of the aforesaid sections number sixteen.

MICHAEL BALDWIN,
Speaker of the House of Representatives.
NATH. MASSIE,
Speaker of the Senate.

April 15, 1803.

Of the same date with the foregoing, was an act incorporating David Hudson, Eliphalet Austin, Henry Champion, John Leavitt, Martin Smith, Ephraim Root, Herman Canfield, John Walworth, John S. Edwards, William Hart, Turhand Cutland, Solomon Griswold, and the Rev. Joseph Badger, and their successors, as Trustees of the "Erie Literary Society;" a representation having been made to the General Assembly, as stated in the preamble, "by certain persons associated under the name of 'Erie Literary Society,' that a number of proprietors of land, within the county of Trumbull, (then embracing the whole Western Reserve), are desirous to appropriate a part thereof to the support of a seminary of learning, within said county," etc. Subsequent sections defined the powers of the Trustees, in accepting such grants, leasing the same, erecting buildings, appointing "a president and instructors," naming a Treasurer, and receiving a bond from him ; and how process should be served on said Corporation, namely: "by summons, leaving an attested copy thereof, at least twenty days before the return, with the Treasurer." The president, professors, trustees, and instructors of said seminary were empowered to direct the mode and course of education to be pursued therein, to establish rules for the government of the students, which should be in force until disapproved of by the Corporation, and to confer all the degrees and honors usually granted by similar institutions. David Hudson was authorized to summon the first meeting of the Corporation. The seventh and last section was adopted from the territorial act organizing the University at Athens, to-wit: "That the Legislature of this State may grant any further and greater powers to alter, limit, or restrain, any of the powers by this act vested in the said Corporation, as shall be judged necessary to promote the best interest and prosperity of the said seminary."

The General Assembly still, on the 16th of April, 1803, by joint resolution, appointed Samuel Carpenter, James Wells, and Henry Abrams, Commissioners, to "appraise the land included within the two college townships, in the county of Washington, (Ohio Company's Purchase,) at its real value in its original and unimproved state; to divide and value said land into four different qualities, or rates, and make return of the quantity contained in each division, as near as may be, and the value thereof, to the next General Assembly, on oath." They were also required to return the present value of the land, including houses and clearings. By another resolution, the Trustees under the territorial act "establishing a university in the town of Athens," were required to report what measures they had taken to carry its provisions into operation.

At the second session of the General Assembly, commencing December 5, 1803, the only enactment of educational interest was a revision of the "act establishing a university in the town of Athens." Its name was changed from the "American Western University" to the "Ohio University." The persons designated as Trustees, who were to be not more than fifteen, nor less than ten in number—were Elijah Backus, Rufus Putnam, Benjamin Tappan, Bazaleel Wells, Nathaniel Massie, Daniel Symmes, Daniel Story, Samuel Carpenter, Rev. James Kilbourne, Griffin Green, and the Governor of the State, *ex officio;* the territorial act was repealed, but all its provisions, except those directing the disposition of the lands, were retained in the new act; and the Governor was instructed to summon the re-organized

Corporation to their first meeting. The two sections relating to the disposition of the land endowment, were as follows:

"Section 12. *And be it further enacted*, That one or more of the aforesaid Trustees (to be appointed by the Board for that purpose) shall, within six months from the passage of this act, proceed (by the oath of three disinterested and judicious freeholders) to lay off the lands in said townships, (those included in the town of Athens excepted,) or such part thereof as they may deem expedient, into tracts of not less than eighty nor more than two hundred and forty acres, and to estimate and value the same as in their original and unimproved state, (for which service such compensation shall be allowed as the Trustees shall think reasonable, to be paid out of the funds of the university,) and having thus laid off and estimated said lands, the Trustees after giving four weeks notice in the newspaper printed at Marietta, shall proceed to make out leases of the said tracts to such of the present occupants as shall apply for the same, within three months after such notice given, and to all persons that shall apply hereafter, for the term of ninety years, renewable forever, on a yearly rent of six per centum on the amount of the valuation so made by the said freeholders; and the land so leased shall be subject to a re-valuation, at the expiration of thirty-five years, and to another at the expiration of sixty years, from the commencement of the term of each lease; which re-valuation shall be conducted and made on the principles of the first, and the lessee shall pay a yearly rent of six per centum, on the amount of the re-valuation so to be made, and forever thereafter, or a yearly rent equal to, and not exceeding, six per centum of the amount of a valuation to be made, as aforesaid, at the expiration of the term of ninety years aforesaid, (which valuation the Trustees and their successors are hereby authorized and directed to make:) *Provided, however*, That such last-mentioned rent shall be subject to the following regulations, to-wit: at the expiration of the aforesaid period of ninety years, three referees shall be appointed, the first by the Corporation of the university; the second by the lessees, under the provisions of this section of this act, and the third by the two referees thus chosen, or (in case either or both of the parties shall neglect to choose an umpire,) the General Assembly, at its next session, shall appoint such number of referees, not exceeding three, as the case may require; which referees shall meet within a reasonable time, to be agreed on between them, at the town of Athens, and then and there determine on and declare the medium price, per bushel, of the article of wheat; which determination shall be grounded on a calculation of the average price of said article, at the town of Marietta, for the five preceding years; which declaration shall be made in writing, and entered of record on the books of the Corporation; and at the commencement of each and every succeeding period of twenty years thereafter, the amount of rent of such period shall be fixed on and determined by referees, to be chosen upon the principles herein-before directed, from a comparison of the aforesaid recorded price of wheat, with its average price at Marietta, for the five years which shall have been then last past; in which leases shall be reserved a right of distress, and of re-entry, for non-payment of rent, at any time after it shall have been due two months: *Provided always*, That the said Corporation shall have power to demand a further yearly rent on the said lands and tenements, not exceeding the amount of the tax imposed on property of like description by the State, which rents shall be paid at such time and place to such person, and collected in such manner, as the Corporation shall direct.

"SEC. 13. That the Trustees shall lay off the aforesaid town of Athens, conformably to a plan made out by Rufus Putnam and others, in pursuance of a resolution of the territorial Legislature, of the eighteenth of December, one thousand seven hundred and ninety-nine, with such variations, however, as they may find it expedient to make; and the same being thus laid off, and a plat of the same, with a designation of the uses of the several parts, recorded in the office of the Recorder of the proper county, and six weeks previous notice given in at least two of the newspapers of this State, may proceed to sell, from time to time, at public auction, such of the house and out lots as they may think proper, for which lots, on payment being made, or satisfactory security given, according to the conditions of such sale, they shall execute to the purchasers, respectively, leases for the term of ninety years, renewable forever on an annual rent, equal to and not exceeding, six per cent. of the amount of the purchase money, which lots, with the improvements which may be made on the same, shall be subject to such further yearly rent as may be equal to the tax imposed, from time to time, on property of like value and description, by the State; and they are likewise authorized to deliver a reasonable compensation for the improvements which have been made on lands within the town of Athens, to be paid out of the funds of the university."

The subject of schools was a prominent topic of Governor Tiffin's message, at the opening of the third session of the General Assembly, December 4, 1804. His suggestions anticipated so distinctly the future policy of the State, that this part of his message is given in his own words:

"The acknowledged maxim, 'that knowledge is, in every country, the surest basis of public happiness,' is strikingly exemplified by contrasting the situation of the people of these United States with those of other governments, where its diffusion is neglected, or is beyond the reach of the lower classes of the people; for, however just the observation may be, that governments are instituted for the benefit of the governed, yet, if they have not the means of acquiring a knowledge of their rights, they will never feel their value, and, consequently, not be careful to guard against their invasion. They can not discern between oppression and the exercise of lawful authority—between burdens imposed from a regard to the public wants, and those which might be imposed insidiously, and under color thereof, to accomplish the means of wresting from them every vestige of liberty. The great resources of lands, which this State possesses for the support of schools and other seminaries of learning, afford the Legislature a sublime employment, inasmuch as the benefits, which may result therefrom, will have their effects in the continued support of the best government in the world, truly styled, 'its best hope;' and which, while correctly administered, is eminently calculated to promote public and individual happiness, as well as extending the civil and religious blessings we enjoy, to future generations.

"These observations will naturally lead you to inquire whether any, and if any, what improvements are necessary to the act entitled, 'an act establishing a university in the town of Athens.' Under this act, a quorum of the Trustees met in June last, and so far as their powers extended, carried it into effect; a committee of two members of the Board was appointed to superintend the surveying of such part of the two townships of land, which were appropriated for the university, as might be applied for by those willing to become lessees; also, to superintend the sales of a small part of the town and out lots, which were designated by the Board to be sold as an experiment; and in exhibit No. 1, I lay before you a communication from Gen. Putnam,* one of the committee, which shows that the prospects are flattering; but it is necessary to observe, from actual observation, when there, and from information derived from intelligent characters since, that the settlers on these lands were induced to apply for leases, under an impression that the Legislature would review the law, and be governed by a more liberal policy. Should it be thought that these lands ought to be valued at a generous price, once for all, and leases be authorized to issue upon the payment of the legal interest yearly, there can be no doubt but that they would soon be all occupied, and from the sales of the town and out lots, a sufficient sum would be raised to erect such public buildings as may be immediately wanted; and that the rents of the lands and lots would be sufficient to support the university, answer every purpose for which the donation was originally made, and the State be immediately benefited by the institution.

"It is further thought, that it would greatly enhance the demand for those lands and town lots, as well as prepare the way for the accommodations and comforts of the youths who may be sent to the university, if a new county was erected, and its seat established at Athens, which may conveniently be done, without injury to those adjacent, and which the convenience of that part of the country imperiously requires.

"But few of the school sections are yet leased under the 'act to provide for the leasing of certain lands therein named,' and it is presumed for want of observing a more liberal policy; for where the means of acquiring a fee simple to lands are so easy, and almost within the reach of all, but few will be induced to improve lands not their own, without sufficient compensation; and these lands, which ought to be brought into a state of productiveness as soon as possible, will be suffered to lie either in a state of nature, or be pillaged of their timber, to the great injury of the public."

On the 20th of February an act passed, to take effect June 1, 1805, which repealed the provisions for leasing section sixteen contained in the act of April 16, 1803. The Trustees

---

* Gen. Rufus Putnam and Col. Samuel Carpenter, were the committee referred to. The former wrote to Gov. Tiffin, Nov. 6, 1804, that the sales of the house and out lots of the town of Athens, amounted to $2,223.50; average of house lots, $43.33½; of out lots $39. In the south township, seventy-five tracts, or 11,000 acres, were applied for. In the north township, under the superintendence of Col. Carpenter, Gen. Putnam was not informed fully; but in August previous, seventy-five applications for leases, covering 8,670 acres, had been made.

of the townships, severally, were required to apply the net proceeds "to the education of youths within the particular surveyed township or fractional township wherein the section was situated, in such manner that all the citizens resident therein might be equal partakers of the benefit thereof." They were directed to lease lots of not less than eighty, or more than two hundred acres to those making the most advantageous proposals after a prescribed notice of thirty days; but no lease was to be granted for a longer time than fifteen years. They were not to lease more than one lot to any one person, and the lessee was bound not to waste or destroy the timber or sugar-camps thereon, and to make such improvements as might be prescribed. As yet no power of sale was given, but only to lease.

At this session, February 22d, William Creighton, jr., Joseph Buell, Benjamin Tupper, Jacob Linley, and Michael Baldwin, were appointed Trustees of Ohio University; and, in accordance with Governor Tiffin's recommendation, by an act passed February 21, 1805, James Denny, Emanuel Carpenter, jr., Isaac Dawson, Relotiah White, and Ezekiel Denning, were appointed to appraise the two university townships, "at the present real value as in its original and uncultivated state, and make report thereof to the Board of Trustees of the said University;" and the said Trustees were directed to lease the same to any persons who had or might apply, agreeable to law, for the term of ninety-nine years, renewable forever, with a fixed annual rent of six per centum on the appraised valuation, but in no case below one dollar and seventy-five cents per acre. Whatever legislation of the previous session was contrary to this, was repealed.

In the year 1805, February 21st, occurred the first library incorporation. Rev. William Robertson, John Elliott, and William Miller, were recognized as the first Directors, Benjamin Van Cleve, Librarian, and John Fulkirth, Treasurer, of the "Dayton Library Society."

At the fourth session of the General Assembly, an act was passed, January 2, 1806, "to incorporate the original surveyed townships." The county Commissioners were required, as soon as there were twenty electors in any original surveyed township, or fraction, on their application, to appoint an election of three Trustees and a Treasurer, who, when chosen, were incorporated, and succeeded to all the powers and duties in respect to school lands, which had previously been imposed upon the Trustees of civil townships. These officers were elected for two years; the Treasurer was prohibited from paying any of the rents and profits arising from section sixteen, "but upon the order of the Trustees;" and was directed to "keep a book, with fair and accurate entries of all moneys received, together with a list of the disbursements, and carefully file the vouchers in relation thereto;" but if the rents and profits were in produce, the Trustees were to direct how they should be disposed of; and, in the following section is found the first legislative reference to the sub-district, now so prominent a feature of the school organization of the State.

"The Trustees are hereby authorized, so soon as they may think necessary, to lay off said townships into proper divisions, and the same to alter, from time to time, as they shall think proper, for the purpose of establishing schools therein; which divisions shall be laid off in such manner as shall best suit the interest and convenience of the inhabitants; and each division thus laid off shall receive a fair and equitable dividend of the profits arising from their reserved section, according to the number of inhabitants contained therein."

The following section was new and important:

"Every surveyed township and fractional township aforesaid, in this State, that has a county line running through the same, shall be considered, as it respects number sixteen, in the same situation as though no such interference had taken place; and any suits or actions, that may take place between the Trustees of such townships in their corporate capacity, and individual or individuals, or body corporate, shall be tried and determined in the county where the reserved section lies; and the officer appointed to serve process in such cases, shall have full power to go any where throughout the township, in execution of his official duty, in the same manner as though no such division line had ever existed."

This corporate organization exists to this day; but at the date of the above enactment, the Trustees had no greater power of disposition than their predecessors, namely, to lease tracts of from eighty to two hundred acres for fifteen years.

At the fifth session of the General Assembly, January 26, 1807, Timothy Rose, Timothy Spelman, Elias Gilman, Samuel Thrall, Jacob Case, Samuel Rose, Samuel Bancroft, John Duke, Hiram Rose, and Jeremiah R. Munson, and their successors, were incorporated as the "Granville Alexandrian Society," (denominated, in the title of the bill, a "Library Society,") with power to hold any estate, real or personal; and the same to sell, grant, or dispose of, or bind by mortgage, or in such other manner as they shall deem most proper for the best interest of the Corporation." The manner in which this act was subsequently perverted, belongs to the financial history of the State.

At this session, the "Cincinnati University" was incorporated, (January 23, 1807,) with the following list of Corporators: John S. Gano, Joseph Van Horn, Matthew Nimmo, William Stratton, Jacob Burnet, James Ewing, Thomas Ramsay, Ethan Stone, Elmore Williams, David E. Wade, John Riddle, Stephen Wood, William McFarland, Joseph Delaplaine, Elias Glover, Isaac Anderson, Charles Kilgore, James Ferguson, Joel Craig, Henry Disbrow, Jacob Williams, William Betts, David Christy, Martin Baum, Edward H. Stall, William Ramsay, David L. Carny, Thomas Dugan, John O. Ferrill, Nehemiah Hunt, Ezekiel Hall, Thomas Stanberry, Joseph Prince, Daniel Symmes, Hugh Moore, Hugh McClelland, Robert Caldwell, John Bradburn, Alexander King, John W. Browne, Simon Stockdill, Samuel Patterson, John Smith, Isaac Dexter, Philip Rice, William Wallace, Joel Williams, and their associates.*

* The motive for preserving these lists of names, is the fact that they generally furnish a memorial of citizens prominent as literary men in their respective localities.

By act of January 23, 1807, the Trustees of the Ohio University were authorized to lease lands at their appraised value, although that might be below $1.75 per acre.

Governor Tiffin having been elected United States Senator, resigned the office of Governor; and Thomas Kirker, Speaker of the Senate, was acting Governor, from March 4, 1807, to December 12, 1808.

At the fifth session of the General Assembly, the town Council of Marietta, were authorized to lay out section sixteen "into such lots or parcels, as in their opinion [should] be most convenient, and tend best to accomplish the object of the donation;" they were to be appraised, taking into view the improvements thereon, (buildings excepted,) and the town Council might then lease the same, "for the term of ninety-nine years, renewable forever, subject to an annual rent of six per cent. on the valuation, and subject also to a re-valuation at the expiration of every ten years, chargeable with the same per centage on each succeeding valuation. Effective remedies for the recovery of rent, etc., were also provided.

At this session, acts were passed: 1. Recognizing the lessees of the Ohio University lands as freeholders; giving the Treasurer the right to distrain for rent, and appointing Eliphas Perkins, Sylvanus Adams, Jehiel Gregory, Abel Miller, Leonard Jewett, and Moses Hewitt, additional Trustees of said University; 2. Incorporating James Kilbourne, Isaac Case, Moses Maynard, Ezra Griswold, Alexander Morrison, Thomas Palmer, and Noah Andrews, and their associates, as the "Worthington Academy;" 3. Incorporating James Welsh, Daniel E. Cooper, William McClure, David Read, Benjamin Van Cleve, George F. Tennery, John Filkirth, and James Hannah, and their associates, as the "Dayton Academy;" 4. Incorporating Robert Wilson, Thomas Worthington, Edward Tiffin, William Sprigg, William Creighton, Henry Massil, Duncan McArthur, William McFarland, and Samuel Finley, as the "Chillicothe Academy;" and, 5. Incorporating Michael Debolt, Jacob Frazey, William Webb, Clayton Webb, James Grimes, John Webb,

Arthur Morrison, John Irvin, Griffith Thompson, John Tobias, John Barnes, William Highland, Samuel Earhart, Resin Newell, John Newell, Levin Hardisty, John Day, George Campbell, Josiah Frazey, John Campbell, Philip Crockfield, Alexander Morrison, James Clark, John Carbrey, Josiah Hally, Samuel Hally, Joshua H. Brown, Leonard Armstrong, Timothy Day, Nathaniel Armstrong, Samuel Dunseth, Nathan Sutton, Robert Hurley, Ichabod R. Miller, Philip Turpin, Luther Ross, John Ross, and Daniel Day, and their successors, as the "Newtown Library Company, in the county of Hamilton."

CHAPTER VII.

ADMINISTRATION OF SAMUEL HUNTINGTON—1808–10.

At the seventh session of the General Assembly, by an act passed February 15, 1809, Robert G. Wilson, Jessup N. Couch, John P. R. Bureau, Elijah Hatch, jr., and Henry Abrams, were appointed Trustees of Ohio University; the Board of Trustees were authorized to receive produce in payment of rent, until 1811; nine of them were recognized as a quorum; and the tracts of lessees were authorized to be divided and sub-let, upon certain conditions; the sub-lessees receiving from the Treasurer of the institution separate leases, in their own names. By another act, February 9, 1809, the inhabitants of every fractional township, within the Ohio Company's Purchase—although the number of electors might fall below twenty—were authorized to lease section sixteen, pursuant to law; and by an act of January 24th, a special organization of fractional township, number four, in the second fractional range of townships, was authorized to appraise section sixteen, at not less than two dollars per acre, subject to re-valuation every fifteen years, and to lease the same for ninety-nine years, renewable forever, in such lots as the Trustees might direct, at rents not less than six per cent. on such valuation.

At this session, the first measures were taken for the creation of a fund from the proceeds of the lands granted for the use of schools in the Virginia Military District. The first section of the act of February 16, 1809, directed the legislative appointment of a Surveyor, Register, and Treasurer, for terms of three years, under bond, respectively, of $10,000; the Surveyor to run off the lands into quarter sections, receiving the compensation allowed by the United States for similar services; the Register, as soon as the plat of said surveys was deposited with him, to give public notice of sale, for at least six weeks, in newspapers at Pittsburg and Brownsville, Pennsylvania, and Wheeling, Virginia, to attend said sales, offering first the north-east quarter section, thence west, on the same parallel, and so on, with successive tiers of quarter sections; provided that no part thereof was sold for less than two dollars per acre, besides its proportion of the cost of surveying, advertising, and offering for sale; to require as conditions of sale, a first payment of the sum chargeable on each quarter section, for the expenses of survey and sale, and yearly payments thereafter, forever, at the rate of six per cent. per year, subject to such commutation as future Legislatures might prescribe; to execute deeds of lease for ninety-nine years, renewable forever, to the purchasers, recording the same in a book provided for that purpose; to audit and settle Surveyor's and other accounts; to renew sales, as aforesaid, from year to year; and to hold his office at Mansfield, Richland county, (in the vicinity of the lands granted by Congress, in 1807, for the use of schools in the Virginia District,) with a salary of $150, payable out of the avails of lands sold, and one and a half per cent. on the amount of sales; while it was made the duty of the Treasurer to attend said sales, receive and keep the payments of money, collect rents due, and re-enter and sell the same for non-payment, keeping his office likewise at Mansfield, and receiving the same compensation as the Register.

This legislation was important, as a title was conveyed, as fully advantageous to the permanent lessee as a fee-simple, unincumbered by a condition of re-valuation, and with a prospect of commutation by the Legislature. Indeed, at the ensuing session, the act of February 16, 1810, fixed the first or contingent payment at ten dollars for each quarter section, and instead of yearly payments, immediately thereafter, of six per cent., such payments were postponed for five years; but in consideration of this indulgence, purchasers were required, within three years, to "build a good, comfortable cabin, and clear at least three acres of ground on each quarter section," with the usual penalties for non-compliance with said amendatory act, of re-entry and forced sale.

In his second annual message, December, 1809, Governor Huntington held the following language:

"Suffer me, in this place, to call your attention to the state of our seminaries and schools of education, and to recommend them to the patronage and encouragement of the State; it is in a public as well as in a private point of view that the State is interested in the diffusion of learning and useful knowledge; where the means of education are extended, and the great body of the people are enlightened, the arts of designing and ambitious characters can never succeed in undermining the liberties of the country."

At the eighth session of the General Assembly, 1809–10, besides the act amendatory to the act for the disposition of Virginia Military School lands, already cited, a series of local acts were passed: 1. Appointing Eleazer Hickcox and Peter Hitchcock, Trustees of the "Erie Literary Society." 2. Incorporating Clement Vallandigham, John Stough, Resin Beall, John Thompson, Thomas Rowland, Alexander Snodgrass, Rudolph Blair, Joseph Stibbs, David Hostetter, and John Hindman, of Columbiana county, John Sloan of Stark county, and Thomas G. Jones, of Trumbull county, as the "New Lisbon Academy." 3. Incorporating the shareholders of the "Poland Library Society," and appointing Thirkand

Kirtland, James Duncan and John Strothers its first directors. 4. Incorporating Edmund Munger, Daniel Bradstreet, Noah Tibbals, John Harris, Israel Harris, Benjamin Maltbie, Amoni Maltbie, Ethal Kellogg, Jeremiah Hole, Elihu Kellogg, Freeman Munger, Edmund K. Munger, Reuben Munger, Ezra Kellogg, Jonathan Munger, and Henry Munger, and their successors, as the "Washington Social Library Company," in Montgomery county.

Governor Huntington, in his last annual message to the General Assembly, December 3, 1810, thus alluded to the subject of education:

"The utility of institutions for the promotion of education is too obvious to need illustration. In a free government, where the rights of the people are in their own keeping, it is peculiarly necessary they should have a correct knowledge of their rights, to guard, on the one hand, against the encroachment of power, and on the other hand, against the evils of anarchy; and no means are so well adapted to this purpose, as a general diffusion of knowledge and information, the foundation of which must be laid in schools, and seminaries of learning.

"I am well aware that the state of our funds will not permit much assistance to be given them, in the way that would be most effectual; but if any legislative aid can be devised, within the resources of the State, it would undoubtedly be a measure of sound policy to extend it to so useful an object. Nor will it be an unimportant inquiry, whether the most effectual measures have been taken, to render the lands appropriated by Congress, for the use of schools, in this State, subservient to the purposes for which they were granted."

CHAPTER VIII.

ADMINISTRATION OF RETURN J. MEIGS—1810–14.

In the inaugural address, December 8, 1810, of Governor Meigs, he thus expressed himself:

"The Constitution of the State has wisely declared, that 'religion, morality, and knowledge, being essentially necessary to a good government and the happiness of mankind, schools and the means of instruction shall forever be encouraged by legislative provision.'

"Correct education is the auxiliary of virtue—moral science will exalt the mind, while ignorance, the badge of mental slavery, debases it.

"Where the structure of government rests on public opinion, knowledge is of vital interest; public opinion, to be correct, must be enlightened, and the culture of the understanding is the preserver of republican principles. Man informed of his political rights becomes reluctant to renounce them. Tyrants govern the ignorant. Intelligence alone is capable of self-government.

"Respect for religion, purity of morals, and love of country, comprise the substance of civic obligations.

"As with individuals, so is it with nations, that vice is the precursor of ruin; and taken in its extensive sense, it is permanently true, 'that righteousness exalteth a nation.'

"Public excellence ascends from domestic purity; and just principles, extending from families to communities, enlarge the sphere of utility, and give to patriotism its proudest devotion.

"A fervent attachment to our country and its free institutions, is a principal of predominant obligation. Foreign influence is the harbinger of destruction to States which are free. It was the gold-dividing influence of Macedon which demolished the fairest temples of Grecian freedom; and Rome saw, in the corruption of her citizens, her liberties entombed forever. With us, were every good citizen to cast his mite into the stock of public virtue, the fund would be inexhaustible.

"Happily for us, our State is endowed with liberal grants and reservations of land for the use of schools, and universities, and we should be unfaithful to ourselves, and unjust to posterity, were we to fail to regulate them in a manner most beneficial to these important objects. Our schools and academies are advancing in improvement, and promise to sanction the hopes entertained of their utility."

The legislation of the ninth session of the General Assembly, 1810–11, upon educational subjects, was mostly local. It consisted, 1. Of the incorporation of Elias Gilman, Timothy Rose, Silas Winchel, Daniel Baker, and Grove Case, as Trustees of the "Granville Religious and Literary Society," with power to dispose of two lots in the town of Granville, Licking county, donated by the New England Licking Land Company, for the support of a school in the town of Granville; 2. Of the incorporation of Lyman Potter, James Snodgrass, John Rea, Bazaleel Wells, John McDowell, Benjamin Tappan, David Hoge, Obadiah Jennings, Thomas McKean Thompson, James Larrimore, John C. Bayless, Thomas Henderson, Thomas Scott, Samuel Hunter, and Jesse Edginton, of Jefferson county, as President and Trustees of "Steubenville Academy;" 3. Of two acts transferring from the town Council of Marietta, and the Trustees and Treasurer elected in fractional township, number four, second fractional range of the townships in the Miami Purchase, under an act of January 24, 1809, the powers possessed by those bodies respectively to the Trustees and Treasurer, elected under the act of February 6, 1810, incorporating original surveyed townships; and, 4. Incorporating the following persons as the "Gallia Academy" in Gallipolis, to-wit: Claud R. Menager, Henry Due, Joseph W. V. Vacht, Edward W. Tupper, Thomas Rodgers, John Miller, Luther Shepard, Calvin Shepard, Elnathan Barlow, Gustavus Keys, Francis Leclerc, William Harvey, Phineas Mathews, Adam Long, Lewis V. Vonschrittz, Lewis Newsom, Stephen Monnat, Peter Ferrard, John B. Le Tailleur, John Cantrell,

Charles Clendinen, Francis Larquilhon, John Entsminger, Andrew Johnson, John P. R. Bureau, Levi Mercer, James Wilson, Andrew Lewis, Spencer E. Gibson, William Clendinen, Benjamin Burrage, John Bing, Tobias Ruffner, David Ridgeway, Thomas Northup, Christopher Etienne, Edward Farler, Edward McMullen, Samuel Logue, Joseph Fletcher, Orasha Strong, David Reese, Samuel Blagg, Robert Safford, David Irwin, Rene Carel, Lewis Leclerc, William Sterrett, Peregrine Foster, Allen Pryor, Nathaniel Gates, Robert Herriford, Charles Drinnen, James Callison, John B. Ferard, Jos. McMullen, Toussaint Shouman, John Atchison, Lewis Summers, and Henry Cushing.

The legislation at the tenth session of the General Assembly, 1811–1812, was as follows: 1. Nathaniel Hamilton, Simeon Deming, William Ford, and their associates, were incorporated as the "Wooster Library Society;" 2. John McLean, Joseph Canby, and Joshua Collett, directors, Rev. William Robertson, Librarian, and Silas Hurin, Treasurer, and their successors, were incorporated as the "Lebanon Library Society;" 3. Benjamin Carpenter, Ezekiel Brown, Solomon Jones, Thomas Brown, (of the towns of Sunbury and Berkshire, in the county of Delaware,) and their successors, were incorporated as the "Platonic Library Society;" 4. Samuel P. Hildreth and Seth Adams were appointed Trustees of the "Ohio University," and the Board of Trustees were authorized to loan their funds collected from rents, at six per cent., and to anticipate their collections by the issue of orders, not to exceed in amount the whole amount of rents payable in a succeeding year; 5. Permanent leases for mill-sites, with eighty acres adjoining, from sections 16, in township one, range two, and in township two, range three, between the Miami rivers, were authorized, without a clause of re-valuation; and 6. In an act transferring the powers of the Trustees and Treasurer of fractional townships four, fractional range two, of Miami Purchase, to the officers of the incorporated original surveyed townships, is found the following provision, which seems the first direction to report school statistics.

"That the schoolmasters in said fractional township shall each keep a daily account of each and every scholar sent to his school, and the name of the person sending them, and transmit a certified copy of the same to the said Trustees, on or before the first day of April, annually; and the Trustees shall make out a fair and equal dividend of the net proceeds of said school section, to each person resident in said township, sending to school, according to the number of scholars sent by them respectively, and the time for which they have attended; and the teacher's receipt as to any of the lessees of the school section, shall be received by the Trustees in payment of any rents due from them respectively, as far as may then be due to the said lessee or lessees."

The war of 1812, with its preparation and events, diverted public attention from educational activity. During the three years of its progress, the following laws were enacted: 1. January 2, 1813, Jacob Burnet, James Findlay, Daniel Symmes, Nicholas Longworth, Ethan Stone, Ethan A. Brown, and William Barr, were organized as "The Circulating Library Society of Cincinnati;" 2. Provision was made, January 12th, to enlarge the college green of Ohio University; 3. February 4th, Samuel Sharpless, John Kinsey, and George Sharpless were allowed, after due appraisement, to lease permanently 204 acres of section sixteen in township six, range three, in Belmont county, for the purpose of erecting a fulling mill thereon, paying six per cent. upon said valuation, but subject to re-valuation every thirty years; 4. February 9th, in consideration that many of the lessees of school lands in the Virginia Military Tract, leased at Mansfield, had been driven from their possessions by the savage enemies of our country, it was enacted, that any person or persons who had purchased or leased any tract, or tracts, of the Virginia Military school lands, and had not improved the same, should have one year further time for that purpose; 5. February 6th, William Wilson was appointed Trustee of Ohio University; 6. January 17, 1814, another year's indulgence was allowed to the lessees of Virginia school lands, and the Register required to report to the General Assembly an annual statement of sales; 7. January 19th, John Northrop, David

Noble, Samuel Swan, John Davidson, Asa Baldwin, Samuel Clark, Joseph Platt, Abner Webb, Joseph Merchant, Charles A. Boardman, Nathaniel Blakely, Daniel Fairchild, George Stilson, Eliakim Stodard, and Richard I. Elliot, were incorporated as the "Boardman Library Company;" but the property so held (other than books, maps, and charts) was limited to $2,000, and the corporation was prohibited from applying their funds to any other purpose than that of establishing and supporting a library; 8. January 19th, James Youart, George S. Houston, Asa Coleman, Cornelius Westfall, and Alexander Telford, were incorporated as the "Troy Library Society," in the county of Miami; 9. February 10th, Lewis Dille, David Hendershot, Alexander McElrath, Amos Palmer, Asa Dille, Andrew McElrath, Thomas McElrath, Thomas Thomas, Thomas Barr, Samuel Dodge, John Shaw, Daniel S. Judd, jr., Timothy Doane, Elias Cazad, and William Coleman, were incorporated as "The Euclid Library Society," in the county of Cuyahoga; 10. February 11th, original surveyed township three, range eight, in Washington county, and township six, range fourteen, in Gallia, were authorized to lease, permanently, subject to re-valuation every thirty-three years, their school lands; 11. December 22d, the act incorporating the "Circulating Library Society of Cincinnati" was revised; 12. December 22d, Bill Kennedy, Gideon Finch, John Ford, Eleazer Hickcox, Uri Hickcox, Lyman Benton, Jedediah Beard, Selah Bradley, Andrew Durand, Simeon Rose, and others, were incorporated as the "Village Library Society of Burton," in the county of Geauga; 13. January 13, 1815, James A. Nisbet, Alexander C. Lamer, Philip Helm, James Crawford, and their associates, were incorporated as the "Eaton Library Society," in the county of Preble; 14. January 30th, original township six, range ten, in Champaign county, authorized to lease section sixteen permanently, with thirty-three years re-valuation; 15. February 4, William Lytle, Martin Baum, Oliver M. Spencer, Solomon Langdon, William Burke, Joshua L. Wilson, John S. Gano, John H. Piatt, Daniel Symmes, John Kid, Ezekiel Hall, Jacob Wheeler,

Jesse Hunt, James Findlay, William Henry Harrison, Thomas Graham, William Lyne, David E. Wade, William Barr, Joseph Raffrer, etc., were incorporated as the "Cincinnati Lancaster Seminary;" 16. February 16th, the "Northern Social Library Company," with its present shareholders, was incorporated at Harpersfield, in Ashtabula county; 17. February 16th, John Lawrence Lewes and Joseph Wood, of Washington county, Rev. James Culbertson, of Muskingum county, and Charles R. Sherman, of Fairfield, were appointed Trustees of Ohio University.

CHAPTER IX.

ADMINISTRATION OF THOMAS WORTHINGTON—1814–18.

The summary of legislation during the war, has anticipated one year of Governor Worthington's administration. Othniel Looker, Speaker of the Senate, acted as Governor from April 14 to December 8, 1814, Governor Meigs having resigned, and accepted the Post-Office department at Washington.

At the fourteenth session of the General Assembly, 1815–16, permanent leases were authorized, of section sixteen, in township 8, range 8, in Green county, in township 2, range 1, east of a meridian drawn from the mouth of the Great Miami; in township 9, range 21, in Ross county; in town ship 2, range 12, in Gallia county; in township 1, range 4, in United States Military Tract, in Guernsey county. Charters were granted for the "Fearing Library Society," in Washington county; for the "Social Library Company of Salem," in Ashtabula county; and for the "Dayton Academy," in Montgomery county.

At this session, the law, directing the manner of leasing

the Virginia school lands, was revised. It differed from the act of 1809, in appointing a Register for three years, and in requiring a re-valuation of the premises, exclusive of improvements. After 1820, the Register was directed to lease lands undisposed of, to the highest bidder above the appraised value, who should annually pay six per cent. on the amount thus bid and accepted. The office of Treasurer was merged into that of Register; but the latter was required to account to the State Treasurer, reserving a salary of $150, and two per cent. on the amount received and paid over to the State Treasurer.

At the fifteenth session, (the first held at the present seat of government,) Governor Worthington, in his message of December 3, 1816, held the following language:

"Among the objects which claim your particular attention, are the public schools, and the means of improving the mind of the rising generation, the navigable rivers, and public roads of the State.

"The opportunity of acquiring an education in Ohio, has hitherto, been confined to the few, and as a general dissemination of learning necessarily conduces to the improvement of morals and behaviour, while in effect it gives to the people a more extensive knowledge of their rights, it becomes the Legislature of a free State, to adopt measures co-extensive with their means to accomplish these objects."

An act was passed, January 24, 1817, for the incorporation of schools and library companies. Its first section was as follows:

"That at any time when six or more persons shall have associated themselves together for the purpose of establishing a school and building a school-house, or for the purpose of establishing a library, and shall have given themselves a name, it shall, and may be lawful for such associations to obtain letters of incorporation in the following manner: Such persons shall make out and subscribe their articles of association, in which shall be set forth the name of the association, the time and manner of electing their officers, to consist of a President and four Trustees, and such officer to serve as Treasurer, Clerk, or Librarian, as may be proper and necessary; the time for the stated meetings of the President and

Trustees, and the method of convening a special meeting. Such articles shall make provision for the acquisition and disposition of property, real and personal, by the association, and shall prescribe the manner of enacting by-laws for the good government of the school or library, and for the proper management and preservation of the estate and funds of the association, the property to be owned by such association, except philosophical and mathematical apparatus, books, maps, and charts, shall at no one time exceed the value of ten thousand dollars, no part of which shall at any time be applied to any other purpose than the establishment and support of a school or a library, as the case may be."

The articles of incorporation were then required to be approved by the President, Judge of Common Pleas, and two Judges of the Supreme Court, and recorded in the county; the corporate powers were granted in the usual form, and all existing associations, for schools and libraries, allowed to organize under this act; and it was further provided, that if any association so incorporated, used their funds for banking purposes, or in any way deviated from the purposes of their charter, the penalty of forfeiture should be enforced.

A general method of leasing school lands was also established. The supervision of section sixteen, especially in the unorganized surveyed townships of the State, was entrusted to the Commissioners of counties. Three freeholders, when an original surveyed township was unorganized, were to be appointed by the Commissioners, to lay off the school section thereof into convenient lots of not less than forty nor more than one hundred and seventy acres, and appraise the same; their proceedings being recorded by the clerk of the Trustees of the township, if organized, otherwise by the clerk of the county Commissioners. Leases might then be executed, or re-issued to former lessees, for an annual rent of six per cent. on the appraised value; but the premises were subjected to re-valuation every thirty-three years by three freeholders, as aforesaid. The Trustees, or Commissioners, as the case might be, were clothed with ample remedies for the collection of rents—the same, however, as those provided by the various special acts for which this general law was substituted. If lots could not be leased at the appraised value within twelve months, then they were to be sold, after usual notice, to the highest bidder, for annual rent. The fact that the school lands lay in a different county from a fractional township, for whose benefit they had been assigned, was declared immaterial, and jurisdiction given to the Court of Common Pleas to make partition, with the aid of appraisers and a surveyor, if two fractional townships held their school lands in the same section, and could not agree on the division and leasing of the same.

The Court of Common Pleas was authorized to lease school lands in the United States Military District, except those granted for the use of schools in the Western Reserve, after their survey, division into one hundred and sixty acre tracts, and appraisement by three freeholders, whom the Court appointed, on the same conditions as above, of permanent lease and re-valuation every thirty-three years. Whenever lessees had failed to improve their tracts as required by law, they forfeited their right to receive a permanent lease; but original improvement lessees, who had fulfilled their stipulations, were entitled to an exclusive privilege of receiving a lease for the tracts so held by them.

It was made the duty of the Clerk of the Court to return a copy of all leases so granted, to the county Commissioners; and rents were to be paid into the county treasury subject to legislative disposition, in conformity with the original grant. If rents were in arrears, the county Treasurer, by the direction of the county Commissioners, might re-enter and re-sell the permanent lease. Other provisions of the law fixed a tariff of fees for the services of the officers.

Notwithstanding this general law, the school sections of township 3, range 2, in the Miami Purchase, and township 3 or 8, in the county of Gallia, were directed, by special laws, to be leased permanently without a clause of re-valuation, in consideration of the erection of mills thereon.

It is deemed unnecessary to notice the special enactments

in respect to school lands or school incorporations, as from this session, general acts on those subjects are found on the statute books. Some curiosities of legislation may be occasionally noticed, as a lottery for the benefit of the Ohio University, but local legislation thenceforth becomes too voluminous for continuous citation.

At the sixteenth session, we ascertained the locality of the "Erie Literary Society," the first organization of the kind by State legislation, it will be remembered. An act was passed January 23, 1818, exempting from taxation all lands donated to said Society, "for the purpose of erecting a college *at Burton*," Geauga county.

Hamilton county was released from the operation of the general law of the preceding session, "for leasing school lands," and remitted to the operation of the "act to incorporate the original surveyed townships."

The State Library was founded by Governor Worthington, who made an appropriation to that object of a portion of his contingent fund. The Legislature, by a joint resolution of January 29, 1818, first recognized the existence of the State Library. This resolution was as follows:

Resolved, By the General Assembly of the State of Ohio, that the following rules and regulations be observed in the library of the State of Ohio:

1. The library shall be kept in one of the chambers of the public offices.
2. The library shall be opened every day during the session of the General Assembly, Sundays excepted, from eight o'clock in the morning, to one o'clock in the afternoon, and from four o'clock, until eight in the evening.
3. It shall be the duty of the Librarian to label and number the books, and make and preserve due catalogues of the same; he shall also keep an accurate account of all issues and returns of books, as the same shall be made.
4. Books issued by the Librarian shall be returned as follows: A folio, within three weeks; a quarto, within two weeks; an octavo, or duodecimo, within one week; and no member shall receive more than one folio, one quarto, or two octavos or duodecimos, at one time, unless when so connected as to be otherwise useless.

5. The Librarian shall open an account with the Governor, Secretary, Treasurer, and Auditor of State, the Judges of the Supreme Court, and the members of the General Assembly, and their respective clerks, in which he shall charge them respectively with all books issued, and credit them with all books returned; and in case any person entitled to books shall detain one beyond the limited time, he shall forfeit, and be charged as follows: For a folio, twenty-five cents per day; a quarto, octavo, or duodecimo, twelve and a-half cents per day; which forfeiture may, for good cause shown, be remitted by the Speaker of the Senate or House of Representatives, for the time being. And in case any person entitled to the use of the library shall neglect or refuse to pay any penalty incurred by not returning any book or books within the time above specified, unless the same shall be remitted as aforesaid, his rights, from the time of such neglect or refusal, shall cease, and until he shall comply with these rules and regulations.

6. All books shall be returned two days before the close of a session, whether the time allowed for the use thereof be expired or not.

7. If a book be returned damaged, the person returning it shall not be entitled to another, until the damage for the first shall be satisfied, and the Librarian shall charge the person therewith.

8. The Librarian shall, two days before the termination of every session of the Legislature, furnish the Speakers of both Houses with a list of members who have been delinquent, particularly specifying the nature of the delinquency; and it shall be the duty of the Speaker of each House, in settling the accounts of any such member, to retain a sum equal to double the value of the book or books detained; and if a part of a set shall be detained, then double the value of the whole set, and also a sum equal to the fines and damages with which such member may stand charged.

9. That before any Senator or Representative shall obtain leave of absence for the remaining part of the session, it shall be the duty of the Speaker of either House to ascertain, from the Librarian, the state of such member's account, and in case such Senator or Representative shall be delinquent, a sum shall be retained to cover the value of books or sets of books detained, and penalties incurred.

"*And be it further resolved*, That the Governor have charge of the State library until the next session of the General Assembly."

Governor Worthington opened his communication to the General Assembly, at its sixteenth session, by the expression of sentiments which, aside from other evidences of his sagacity, would have been a sufficient warrant for his high rank among the early statesmen of Ohio. He foreshadowed, at a period so remote as the year 1817, the great necessity of a normal school, and we doubt whether any public man of the country has recorded an earlier recommendation of the kind. The discussion in Connecticut and Massachusetts was long subsequent. This portion of his message is annexed:

"While in the enjoyment of these extraordinary blessings, we should not forget that we are accountable for their abuse, and that it is our duty to use all the means in our power to perpetuate the blessings of a free government to those who may come after us. This is the duty of all, but more especially of those to whom the people delegate the power of government.

"With a view to the fulfillment of the duties assigned me, I shall recommend for your consideration such subjects as are deemed most important for the promotion of this great object, as well as the present comfort and convenience of our fellow citizens; and first, as I consider it most important, I recommend to your particular attention, the education of the rising generation. Without information and knowledge, the blessings of a free government can not be long continued. The wisest and best men in all ages have agreed on this important point; and so thoroughly convinced of it, and so anxious that it should be attended to, were our forefathers, the patriots, who, under Providence, gave us the fair heritage we enjoy, that in the instrument which contains the fundamental principles of our government, for our admonition, they have declared, that 'religion, morality, and knowledge, being necessary to good government, schools and the means of education shall forever be encouraged.'

"In conformity with this admirable sentiment, we have received from the United States, means, to a very considerable extent, which, if rightly used, would go great lengths toward the general diffusion of knowledge. To bring these means, with others, if necessary, into action; to devise, organize, and to put in practice a system, of education for the rising generation, which will dispel ignorance, and diffuse light and knowledge throughout the State, while it would be one among the greatest benefits which could be conferred on posterity, would, I am persuaded, gentlemen, be the most pleasing duty you could perform. The propriety of the measure proposed, and the means of effecting it, are subjects which should be examined; of the propriety of the measure, no rational mind friendly to liberty can doubt; and that we possess the means, if earnestly disposed to effect the object, I have as little doubt. It is true it must be a work of time; hence the necessity of commencing it.

"The great difficulty of procuring teachers whose moral character and other qualifications fit them to enlighten the minds, and shape the morals of the rising generation, even when suitable compensation can be made, is evident. Indeed, it but too often happens that persons of the most profligate morals, and the least qualified, seek this employment as a cover for idleness. It can not be expected that any thing good can proceed from so corrupt a source. In the formation of a superstructure, the foundation must be solid, to make it lasting and useful. If we expect in our youth 'religion, morality, and knowledge,' suitable teachers must be employed to produce this effect. With a view to aid in effecting this desirable object, I recommend to the consideration of the General Assembly the propriety of establishing, at the seat of government, a free school, at which shall be taught the different branches of an English education, at the expense of the State, to such number of boys, the children of parents unable to educate them, and no others, as the Legislature may deem proper; that whenever young men thus educated shall become qualified for that purpose, they shall, when proper salaries are furnished them, have the preference of employment in the public schools of the State, and shall be obliged to serve as teachers of schools until they are twenty-one years of age, and afterward, so long as they conduct themselves well, shall have the preference of employment. The whole to be under such regulations as the Legislature may from time to time adopt."

It is proper, also, to preserve Governor Worthington's own allusion to the foundation of the State library, toward the close of the same message:

"The fund made subject to my control by the last General Assembly, besides paying the ordinary demands upon it, and for the articles mentioned in a resolution of the Legislature, of the 28th of January, 1817, has enabled me to purchase a small but valuable collection of books, which are intended as the commencement of a library for the State. In the performance of this act I was guided by what I conceived the best interest of the State, by placing within the reach of the representatives of the people, such information as will aid them in the discharge of the important duties they are delegated to perform."

At the seventeenth session of the General Assembly, 1818–19, Governor Worthington, in his last communication, thus further expressed himself upon the subject of education:

"Among the measures which I have heretofore recommended to the Legislature, for their consideration, and on which they have not acted, a good plan for the education of the rising generation, has been considered first in importance.

"Time, and further reflection, have confirmed me in the opinions I have before communicated; and from a sense of duty to the State, I must again recommend the subject to your attention. Surely, nothing can be more important than information, to the citizens of a government free as ours is. Indeed, I feel convinced, a perpetuation of that freedom we now possess, greatly depends on the means which may be used, under Providence, to produce that state of general information which will enable the people to appreciate the liberty they enjoy. From my own observation, I am fully convinced it is the first duty of the Legislature to adopt, with as little delay as possible, a system for the establishment of elementary schools throughout the State. In the first settlement of a country like ours, the labors necessary to clear the lands and produce the means of subsistence, prevent, in a great measure, those who are thus employed, from giving to their children even a common education. The more wealthy citizens, who possess the means, will educate their children, while those of the poorer class, whose parents have not the means, yet by their labor are greatly promoting the prosperity of the State, will be brought up in a state of comparative ignorance, unable to manage, with propriety, their private concerns, much less to take any part in the management of public affairs; and what is still more to be lamented, unacquainted with those religious and moral precepts and principles, without which they can not be good citizens; I am fully aware that all can not be learned, nor receive the advantages of an education of the highest order; nor is this necessary; yet, I am as fully convinced it is within the power of the State to disseminate a general state of information, which will be productive of the best effects. The wealthy are deeply interested in such a state of things. Information, and the practice of moral and religious principles, never fail to produce order, and secure the rights of property in society; they, therefore, should feel a willingness to contribute toward effecting objects of so much importance. Information is common stock, or national wealth; and in proportion as it is increased, are our means enlarged and national liberty secured. I avail myself of this last opportunity offered me, of recommending to your serious attention a subject of so much importance, and propose for your consideration, gentlemen, the propriety of appointing one person from each judicial circuit of this State, who, together, shall form a Board for school purposes, and who, in the recess of the Legislature, shall collect such information, relative to the school funds of the State, and who shall lay before the next Legislature such a system for the establishment of elementary schools throughout the State, as they may be enabled to devise from all the information to be obtained on the subject."

The valuable suggestion here made, was not immediately acted upon, although the messages of Governor Worthington gave a great impulse to the legislation of a few years later. At this session, Philander Chase, James Kilbourne, Thomas S. Webb, Chester Griswold, Recompence Stansbury, Chauncey Barker, Stephen Maynard, Ezra Griswold, Benjamin Gardiner, Orris Parish, Lucas Sullivant, and Leonard H. Cowles, were incorporated as "the President and Trustees of the Worthington College."

By an act passed January 16, 1819, the purchasers of Virginia Military school lands were authorized to assign their lands; but their assignments were directed to be recorded by the Register.

CHAPTER X.

ADMINISTRATION OF ETHAN A. BROWN—1818–1822.

All the memorials of the period comprised by the administration of Governor Brown, show great financial distress among the people of the State. There was much political excitement, also, in the General Government, by the question of the admission of Missouri, and in the home Government, growing out of the struggle between the State of Ohio and the Bank of the United States. The want of accessible markets, bore disastrously upon the people. The lessees of the Virginia military school lands obtained a further remission of their first payment of six per cent.; and neither Legislature nor people, in the general gloom, were prepared for much expenditure in behalf of schools. Governor Brown, in his message of December 5, 1820, presented a very unfavorable view of the school fund, arising from the rents of section sixteen. He said:

"You can not fail to be sensible of the confidence reposed in your disposition to encourage the pursuit of useful knowledge, by the best application of the means in your power, of which you shall believe them capable. So far as my information extends, the appropriation of the school lands in this State has produced, hitherto, (with few exceptions,) no very material advantage in the dissemination of instruction—none commensurate with their presumable value. Whether this be owing to the comparatively new state of the country, and the low rate of rents; whether the property has been let too low, or durable leases given at unpropitious periods; or whether the fault, if any, be attributable to an injudicious application of the proceeds, or expense of the management, is difficult to decide, from defect of official returns to Government on the subject. If an inquisition were made, especially where no account is rendered to you, to ascertain the value, the proceeds and their expenditure, and the condition of these lands, it might assist the Legislature in forming systematic regulations, to prevent the useless dissipation of this fund, and direct its application, effectually, to the purpose intended."

Nevertheless, under these depressing circumstances, the foundation was laid of the present school system of Ohio. On the 22d of January, 1821, an "act to provide for the regulation and support of common schools," was passed in the following terms:

"SECTION 1. *Be it enacted by the General Assembly of the State of Ohio*, That the Trustees of the several townships in this State, shall give public notice in writing, set up at three of the most public places within their respective townships, before the elections in March, notifying the electors within said township, to vote at the next township election, for or against organizing said township into school districts; and if a majority of all the votes given by householders, should be in favor of such organization, the Trustees shall, within twenty days thereafter, lay off the same, or any part thereof, into school districts; which districts when so laid off, shall not contain less than twelve, nor more than forty householders: *Provided always*, That the Trustees shall not allow themselves, or receive any compensation for their services under the provisions of this act.

"SEC. 2. That if the Trustees of any township should be of opinion, that the interest of the inhabitants of any neighborhood would be better subserved by laying off school districts from parts of one or more of the adjoining townships, and it should appear to be the wish of the inhabitants of such neighborhood so situated, they shall notify the Trustees of such adjoining township or townships, to meet at such time as they may appoint, at some place within the district to be laid off; and when so met, if a majority of them think expedient, they may lay off such district.

"SEC. 3. That whenever the inhabitants of any neighborhood may wish to be laid off into a school district, the Trustees having previously omitted to lay off said neighborhood into school districts, they may, on petition signed by two-thirds of such householders, be entitled to be laid off into a school district, for the purposes contemplated in this act, if the Trustees of such township or townships shall deem it expedient, and the petitioners shall be bound to pay the expenses thereof; and on petitions as aforesaid, the Trustees may proceed to lay off new districts from parts of one or more contiguous districts, if it shall appear to them that the petitioners aforesaid are situated at an inconvenient distance from the school-house or houses of their district or districts, (as the case may be,) or that the interest of such neighborhood would be promoted thereby, so that in no case shall the number of householders in such district, or either of the old districts from which it may have been laid off, be less than twelve, such petitioners paying the expense as aforesaid.

"SEC. 4. *Be it further enacted*, That the Trustees shall, in all cases, cause the township Clerk to make a record of each district so laid off; and when such district shall consist of parts of two or more townships, the Clerks of the several townships in which such district may be situated, shall record the same.

"SEC. 5. That the Trustees, in laying off school districts, shall have regard to any school company incorporated under the provisions of the act, entitled 'an act to provide for the incorporation of school and library companies,' or under any other law for the incorporation of school companies; so far as to include the members of such incorporation within one district, and not to affect their corporate rights.

"SEC. 6. That the householders in each of the school districts, shall meet at such places as may be agreed upon in said district on the first Monday of May, in each year; and when so met, to the number of ten or more, they may proceed to elect three of said householders, as a School Committee for said district; and also some suitable person as Collector, who, by virtue of his office, shall be Treasurer for said district; and said Committee shall appoint a Clerk, whose duty it shall be to keep a record of such meetings, and to make out such tax bills and keep such accounts as the Committee may direct; and said Committee, Collector, and Clerk, shall hold their appointments until their successors are elected and qualified.

"SEC. 7. That the Committee aforesaid be, and they are hereby authorized to cause the erection of a school-house in some convenient place in each district; and for that purpose, they are hereby authorized to receive, by donation or purchase, any quantity of land not exceeding two acres that they may think expedient; and the title of the same shall be vested in said School Committee and their successors in office, to and for the use of said district, for the purposes as aforesaid;

two-thirds of such householders having previously at their meeting, agreed upon the erection of such school-house.

"SEC. 8. That, for the purpose of purchasing land on which to erect such school-house, the Committee may apply any donation or subscription which may be made for that purpose, together with the taxes which they are authorized to raise by the provisions of this act.

"SEC. 9. That the property of all persons residing in said district, and which property may be situated therein, and liable to taxation for State or county purposes, shall be liable to be taxed for the purpose of erecting a school-house as aforesaid, and also for the purpose of making up the deficiency that may accrue by the schooling of children, where parents or guardians are unable to pay for the same; and said Committee is hereby authorized to assess taxes for these purposes, on property as aforesaid, not exceeding, in any one year, one-half of the amount of taxes which might, by law, have been levied on the same objects for State or county purposes; and said Collector shall have power to collect the same, in such manner as county taxes are collected.

"SEC. 10. That the Committee aforesaid are hereby authorized to employ a competent teacher or teachers, for such term of time as they may judge for the interest of the district, in each year; and such school shall be open to all the scholars of a suitable age within said district, and the Committee are hereby authorized, quarterly, or at such other times as they may deem expedient, to cause the expenses of said school to be assessed on the parents or guardians of all the scholars, in proportion to the number of scholars who may have been schooled, being residents in such district, and the collection shall be made by the Collector as aforesaid: *Provided, however*, That said Committee may remit the whole or any part of said assessment, which, in their opinion, may have been assessed on parents or guardians who are unable to pay the same, and such deficiency, if any such there should be, shall be paid from the fund raised by taxes, as are, in the ninth section of this act, authorized to be raised for that purpose.

"SEC. 11. That the Committee may require of the Collector acting as Treasurer for the proper district, such bonds as they may think sufficient, for the punctual paying over all moneys by him received, on the orders of the Committee, attested by the Clerk, for the purposes aforesaid, excepting the amount of two per cent. which he may be allowed to retain, as a compensation for his services; and the Clerk shall keep an account with the Treasurer, which shall be adjusted and settled under direction of said Committee, from time to time, as said Committee may deem expedient; and on failure of such Treasurer to pay over the money he may have in his hands, on the order of the Committee, he shall be liable on the suit of such Committee, in any court having competent jurisdiction, to pay the same without stay of execution, together with ten per cent. damages; and said Committee are hereby authorized to sue for, and recover the same: *Provided, however*, That no person except the Collector, shall be allowed any fees or compensation for his services under this act.

"SEC. 12. That in such townships as, by law, are entitled to public moneys from the rent of section number sixteen, or other school lands, the Trustees of such township shall allow said district its proportion of such money, to be ascertained and proportioned under such laws as may be in force at the time application may be made, regulating the application and division of such school fund; and the Treasurers of the several school districts are hereby authorized to receive the same, for which they shall be accountable to said Committee, in the same manner as they are accountable for the other moneys coming into their hands by the provisions of this act."

At the same session the law was revised which provided for leasing the school lands within the United States Military District, retaining the jurisdiction of the Court of Common Pleas, but separating the fund thus accumulated, from the State treasury, and directing its custody and distribution by the Treasurers of the respective counties interested therein.

By the following extract from Governor Brown's annual message, delivered December 4, 1821, it appears that the Congressional land endowment for schools was, at that time, the subject of very earnest discussion throughout the Union. His observations are full of historical interest:

"I have possessed no means of acquiring information for the Legislature of the success that has followed the act 'to provide for the regulation and support of common schools;' you must, of course, judge of its operation in your respective neighborhoods, from your own observation. In this state of things, new suggestions from me on this head would probably be premature. I will, therefore, barely repeat the remark, that in devising and improving a plan for the establishment of common schools, accounts of the value and revenue of the section number sixteen, may be of some consequence.

"Notwithstanding that the appropriations of lands in the western country, for the support of schools, have hitherto been very little productive, as a literary fund, their advantage and value have been very highly appreciated by a part of our brethren in the eastern States. A report and resolutions adopted by the Legislature of the State of Maryland, and now laid before you, will show that a claim is advanced to a portion of the public lands in the new States and the territories, equal to one-thirty-sixth part of the area of each old State, with the addition of one-fifth of that amount, to equalize, as is pretended, a participation of endowment for schools, from this fund, among the States having common property in the national possessions. The pretensions therein set forth, and supported by the State of New Hampshire, I respectfully advise, should meet the remonstrance of this Assembly, to prevent a scheme, founded on principles believed to be mistaken and erroneous, and fraught with serious wrong to this, with the other new States, and the territories.

"Among the grounds urged in support of the claim, much apparent confidence is placed in the 'regal' ownership of the provinces before the war of the revolution, and the joint conquest of all the public land embraced by the treaty of 1783; which principle, if extended, would include the public lands within the present limits of the original States.

"As the discussion of the right of property, in that portion ceded to the Union by some of its members, was supposed to be terminated by the cession, and the destination of the lands is no longer a question—as the property of particular States in public domains retained in their respective jurisdictions, for their own purposes, has been long acquiesced in by common consent, and as it is not even pretended that the share of any claimant, in the proposed distribution, can now be augmented, on account of the public land so retained—it is not easy to perceive why we should be called to renew an inquisition into the motives and consideration of the accommodation. If those States shall consent to revive the question, justice will award to us possessions far more extensive than those which have been heretofore allowed. It is, therefore, believed, with all due respect for the Legislatures and the revolutionary merits of the two States before mentioned, that neither justice nor policy countenance, *on this occasion*, a recurrence to the topic of 'regal or proprietary ownership;' which may serve to embarrass, but not to elucidate the question proposed to be triumphantly carried by a majority formed of 'ONE HUNDRED AND SIXTY-NINE VOTES against SEVENTEEN!' An intimation of power you may be surprised to see introduced into an argumentative, official document, by a sister State, from whom we should have expected a more magnanimous sentiment, in discussing a question of relative and distributive justice.

"The new States include their school lands; but a different basis of computation is proposed for the old. No particular mention is made of our contribution, to acquire the Indian title; no plan promulgated, as an equipoise to the condition of settlement; no allusion made in our favor to the fact, that Louisiana and the Yazoo lands were not purchased by the treasure of the sixteen enumerated States alone; nor that the receipts for public land would have been less had not the inhabitants north of the Ohio stood the brunt of frontier wars. Respect prevents an imputation of these errors and omissions to any other than accidental causes, and solicitude of the claimants for their own interest; but an equal vigilance for that of their western brethren could hardly have excluded us *totally* from the benefit of the uncontested argument, that 'the common property ought to enure to the common use.'

"Presuming that the disquisition of relative merit in the acquisition might well have been avoided in these reports, I trust you will support me in controverting the position that 'the literary appropriations, heretofore made, have been granted for *State*, and not for *national purposes;* and appropriated, *exclusively*, to the use of the western citizen;' and I rely on your assent, in contending that no part of the grants, treated throughout the reports as pure and simple donations, has been ceded to us, nor probably to any western State, without a consideration to the full value.

"In tracing the financial history of the Union, it will be found, that so early as May, 1805, Congress devised a plan for the disposal of the western lands, of which the reservation of section number sixteen, for schools, forms a feature which has been, ever since, preserved. We shall be far from denying the meritorial destination of the concession; but it seems sufficiently apparent, although it may not be found 'in the preambles of acts,' that in the embarrassment of the treasury attending that period, when the nation was too poor to be generous, Congress must have been actuated by other motives than the mere encouragement of literature in a country destitute of white people. The raising of money, and the value of their possessions by sale and population, were more pressing considerations, when the inducement of a school section was proposed, *on condition of settlement;* which has continued to be offered and accepted; the object being marked, by its inuring to the benefit of the inhabitants, within each surveyed township. Those school lands within the purchases of the 'Ohio Company,' and in John Cleves Symmes's, were clearly a stipulation for valuable consideration. The three college townships, there contracted for, are all the grants in Ohio for seminaries of a higher grade than common schools; and their amount comports but ill with the arithmetic of the equalizing design. In ordinary transactions, a measure, analogous to this pursued by Congress, could not be mistaken; it is every day's practice, without being thought to lay the purchaser under obligation. The same reasoning will apply to the three per cent. fund, for the making of roads.

"It is not to be denied, that some distinction may be drawn, in this respect, between those settlers in the military tracts on Connecticut Reserve, and our other inhabitants; yet the case of the former constitutes but a part of the system to induce settlement, and receives, besides, some counter-balance from the actual sale in the purchases aforesaid. Even a gratuity to the revolutionary soldier can surely form no item of bounty to the State, in prejudice to other members of the confederacy; nor can the question of "*exclusive benefit*" be affected by the circumstance that the grants were *secured* to us by compact.

"But I beg leave to observe, that, beside the consideration thus paid by our citizens, the State, as a body politic, has abundantly remunerated the old members of the Union for the school lands, and all other grants made to her on her admission.

"The act of cession by Virginia, conforming with the ordinance of 1787, required that States should be formed in the ceded territory, and 'admitted into the Union *on an equal footing with the original States*, IN ALL RESPECTS WHATEVER.' It will be recollected, that in construing this provision, there were not wanting politicians, who maintained, that if this were 'admitted a member of the Union, having the same rights of freedom, *sovereignty*, and independence, as the other States,' the United States would be placed in the situation of other proprietors here, as respects the liability of their lands to be taxed. No such claim was insisted on at the time of our admission, and the compact exempted their property, to the presumed amount of 14,500,000 acres, from taxation, for five years after it should be sold. The exemption was not for the exclusive benefit of individual proprietors; its effect upon the price of public and of other land is obvious—it added to the domestic taxes, and retarded public improvement. This immunity, at the medium rate of taxation, imposed by acts of the State Legislature, amounts in five years, to more than $900,000. In return for which the State of Ohio has received,

1. The school lands, (if admitted,) which should be rejected from this account, as otherwise paid for. Their amount for the whole State, including the college township, is estimated at about 750,000 acres.

It is probably incorrect to estimate these lands to us, by the average of receipts for many years, during which our population had received a prodigious increase, and the country became considerably cultivated. The inhabitants should not be charged with the increased value derived from their labor. Congress, after twenty years experience, has reduced the price fixed in 1800. It should not be forgotten that the price of the public land, sold before the opening of the land offices, was payable in evidences of the public debt; and the value of these securities, at the time of the contracts, should be calculated. Choice, too, was offered of a large region of country; the goodness of No. 16 depending upon chance, and the enjoyment of it remote. The true method would have been, to have estimated the value of the literary appropriations of Ohio in 1802; and they would then have been rated high at thirty cents per acre.

2. Three per cent. on the nett proceeds from the sale of lands in the State, for roads; the amount received, and estimate of that expected, when the land shall be sold, amounting to $600,000.

So far as the application of this fund should serve to enhance the value of land, the benefit the United States might have calculated to derive from it, is supposed to have been (to that of the State,) as 14½ to 9½. If we admit its immediate convenience to the people, to balance the advantages accruing to both parties from the expenditure of the fund, it might obviate objections to charging the United States with one-half.

3. The thirty-six sections including certain salt springs—unalienable—the grant clogged with conditions that prevent their being made available, and if placed in the market at the time of their highest and overrated estimation, not worth the lowest cash price of public land under the late system.

Allowing the whole of these items, we are left creditors to a large amount.

But the more correct statement of this account, will probably be as follows:

Five years taxes, ...		$906,250.
School lands, ...	$000,000.	
One-half three per cent. fund, ...	300,000.	
Salt spring sections, never productive to the State, and never likely to be so, under existing regulations, ...	000,000.	
		$300,000.
In order to meet various views on the subject, we may make a copious allowance from this difference, ...		606,250.

And still exhibit a balance of half a million of dollars, devoted to *national*, and not to *State* purposes.

"I think it is, therefore, plain, that in every point of view in which the framers of the reports have thought proper to place the subject, their claim can not be sustained without disturbing the principles of harmony on which the cessions to the Union were adjusted—without a breach of equity towards the adopted members of the political family, nor, in the language of the reports, 'without a violation of the spirit of our national compact,' as well as the principles of justice and sound policy.

These facts are not adduced by way of complaint that Ohio has yielded for a poor equivalent, rights and privileges necessary to place her emphatically *on an equal footing*. We have asked no favors from the United States, on the score of a hard bargain. We are even less querulous than some of our eastern brothers, who, in order to raise money and the value of their land, offered a premium to their citizens to settle in the west, and now *officially* complain they suffer by the emigration. The complaint, on our part, is against a scheme that treats our school lands as a gratuitous bounty, entitling the claimants to a donation without our participation—against this agrarian project, which might, with the same propriety, embrace a three per cent. road fund, graduated on the same scale.

"I have endeavored to show that the grants to the new States are not favors, and the case the report supposes, of a grant made to New York, and refused to Virginia, will not apply to our situation. In the supposition of an appropriation of the revenue arising from commerce, to education in a favored State, *exclusively*, the analogy equally fails. A more parallel hypothesis would have been, in supposing a

State to have relinquished a large amount of her internal taxes, and her citizens to have paid large sums, in consideration of a grant for their benefit.

"If land in Ohio should be specially granted to the original States, and they should retain it, to derive revenue from the cultivation, (which, however, may not be intended,) you are too familiar with the consequences of expending, in the Atlantic States, the public money raised here, not to be sensible of the impoverishing effect, to be caused by an additional drain of the annual rents from a large district of country.

"Though the appropriations now claimed should be refused, it can not thence be inferred, that this State will remain indebted for her future rank in the scale of literature, or her children, for the rudiments of education, to the generosity of the old States, by reason of the liberality of the grants heretofore made to her; since it should be remembered that, in 1802, the few inhabitants of our still young, though proud State of Ohio, just breathing from the hardships of their new settlements, under the numerous disadvantages described, without public treasure or domain, concluded an arrangement with Congress, whereby they made a sacrifice to the general prosperity, of an offering so great, as I have attempted to explain."

Allen Trimble, Speaker of the Senate, was acting Governor from January 4, 1822, to December 8, 1822, Governor Brown having resigned at the former date.

Governor Trimble, in pursuance of a resolution of the General Assembly, announced in his message of December 4, 1822, that he had appointed Messrs. Caleb Atwater, John Collins, James Hoge, Nathan Guilford, Ephraim Cutler, Josiah Barber, and James M. Bell, Commissioners, to report a system of education adapted to common schools.

At this period, a strong disposition in favor of unconditional sales of the school land, was manifested in the Legislature; but doubts were entertained whether the assent of Congress was not requisite. An act was passed January 27, 1823, that whenever leases of school lands were surrendered, no lease should afterward be granted for a longer term than one year, with a condition against waste; and the Registers of the Virginia and United States military fund were required to make a detailed report to the ensuing General Assembly.

CHAPTER XI.

ADMINISTRATION OF JEREMIAH MORROW—1822–26.

Governor Morrow added to his other claims to grateful remembrance by the people of Ohio, a deep interest in common school education. This is apparent from the following passage of his message, delivered on the 2d of December, 1823, at the twenty-second session of the General Assembly:

"Provisions for the encouragement of learning, and the support of schools, have been the frequent topic of executive recommendation, and of legislative discussion. Difference of opinion can not well exist as to the advantages to society from the general diffusion of education throughout the community. Indeed, no sentiment is more generally held to be incontrovertible, among enlightened freemen, than that morality and knowledge are necessary to good government. The necessary dependence which civil liberty and free institutions in government have on the moral qualities and intelligence of the people, give importance to the provisions for the encouragement and support of common schools. An interest so important to the welfare of society, and to the future respectability of the State, should not be left on the insecure ground of the force of moral sentiment in each member of the community, for its regulation and protection. However universal the agreement in sentiment may be, as to these views of the subject, there is still ground for difference of opinion as to the measure of support to be given, and the mode in which it shall be administered. In this State there are causes, extensive in their nature, for difference of opinion on the subject. The population is composed principally of emigrants from the different States of the Union, with habits and modes of thinking on the subject, as different as are the regulations of the States from whence they came. It will, then, require concessions of opinion, and the abandonment of early prepossessions to be made, before we arrive at a favorable result. The systems of regulation for common schools, which have been adopted in the several States where any regulations have been made, may be reduced, in their essential features, to two classes. The mode in the one, is that of collecting the whole means for the purpose into a common fund, and from thence distributing to the several school districts throughout the State. The other is the organization of the particular townships or districts for the purpose, and the vesting in the township officers the power to provide for the support and regulation of schools within each several township. These systems have each, when carried into effect, been found efficient, and have, perhaps, equally recommended themselves by their salutary effects. The latter system is unquestionably the most simple, and least expensive in its operation. It was that which was in use when the first reservations of lands for the support of schools were made by Congress, and appears to have been in view, by the terms in which they were made. They are made in the townships severally, and for the support of schools within the same specially. This circumstance of the speciality of the appropriation of the school lands, to the use of the several townships and districts within a large portion of the State, would appear to recommend that system as the best adapted to the situation of the State. No benefit, it is believed, commensurate to the expense of the operation, would arise, from the collection of the proceeds of the school lands in the several townships and districts, into a general fund, when distribution shall be made in proportion to the receipts from each. The act of the 22nd of January, 1821, "for the regulation and support of common schools," contains the general features of a system calculated for that purpose. But, however well the provisions may be adapted to the purpose, they are rendered nugatory by the option given to the electors in the several townships, to give them effect or not, as they shall by their votes determine. Was this act made positive, and in some other respects modified, we should have a system in force—perhaps not perfect—for the regulation of common schools, which could be further improved, as experience under it should point out its defects."

At the previous session, the House of Representatives adopted the draft of a memorial to Congress, but which was not acted upon by the Senate, asking the passage of a law declaring the authority of the State of Ohio to sell the school lands, and invest the proceeds with a State guarantee of an income of six per cent. upon the amount, to be applied to the use of schools, pursuant to the original grants. At the next session, however, both branches, by their resolution of February 26, 1824, concurred in a very elaborate memorial to the above purport. Although many of the statements of this document have been anticipated, yet as a clear review of the history of an intricate question, for more than a quarter of a century, it is deemed advisable to reproduce it.

"The memorial of the State of Ohio, in General Assembly, respectfully represents, That by the act of the Congress, of the United States, passed the thirtieth day of April, in the year one thousand eight hundred and two, the following, among other propositions, were offered to the Convention, to be assembled for the formation of a State government for the people of the eastern division of the territory north-west of the Ohio, including the State of Ohio; that is to say, that the section number sixteen in every township, and where such section had been sold, other lands equivalent thereto, should be granted to the inhabitants of such township for the use of schools.

"Secondly, that the six miles reservation, including the Salt Springs, commonly called the Scioto Salt Springs, the Salt Spring near the Muskingum river, and in the Military Tract, with the sections of land which include the same, should be granted to the said State, for the use of the people thereof: *Provided*, the said Legislature should never sell, nor lease the same for a longer period than ten years.

"That the foregoing propositions, when acted upon and considered in Convention of Ohio, and by an ordinance passed the twenty-ninth day of November, in the year one thousand eight hundred and two, the aforesaid propositions were accepted: *Provided*, That the following modifications should be made thereto, that is to say, that in addition to the first propositions securing the section number sixteen in every township within certain tracts to the inhabitants thereof, for the use of schools, a like donation, equal to the one-thirty-sixth part of the amount of the lands in the United States Military Tract, should be made for the support of schools within that tract, and also, that the like provision should be made for the support of schools in the Virginia Reservation, so far as the unlocated lands in that tract would supply the proportion, after warrants issued from said State should have been satisfied, and also, that a donation of the same kind, or such provision as Congress should deem expedient, should be made to the inhabitants of the Connecticut Reserve, and that out of all the lands which might thereafter be purchased of the Indian tribes by the United States, and lying within the State of Ohio, the one-thirty-sixth part should be given as aforesaid, for the support of public schools, and that all lands before mentioned, to be appropriated for the use of schools, should be vested in the Legislature of said State of Ohio, in trust for said purposes.

"That a certain proportion of the lands lying within the State of Ohio, had already been disposed of by the United States, and by patent, dated on the thirtieth day of September, in the year one thousand seven hundred and ninety-four, certain lands therein described were granted unto John Cleves Symmes, reserving to the United States out of each township within the same, lot numbered sixteen, for the use of schools, being one-thirty-sixth part of the whole tract granted as aforesaid.

"That a certain tract had also been granted unto Manassah Cutter, and others, under the name of the Ohio Company, in which, lot number sixteen, being one-thirty-sixth part, was also reserved for the use of schools, in addition to which are the appropriations for the Ohio and Miami Universities, but to which last appropriations to the Ohio and Miami Universities, your memorialists have only adverted, as not being intended to be embraced in the prayer of the memorial, herewith submitted.

"That the ordinances of the Convention of Ohio, of November, one thousand eight hundred and two, gave rise to the act of the Congress of the United States, of the third day of March, in the year one thousand eight hundred and three, by which it was enacted more specifically:

"1. That certain quarter townships in the tract commonly called the United States Military Tract, and in said act, particularly described, amounting to the one-thirty-sixth part of the estimated whole amount of lands within that tract.

"2. That certain other quarter townships in the same United States Military Tract, and in said act particularly described for the use of the tract of country commonly called the Connecticut Reserve, were also by said act granted or reserved.

"3. So much of that tract within this State, commonly called the Virginia Military Reservation, as would amount to one-thirty-sixth part of the whole tract, was also granted, to be selected by the Legislature of the State of Ohio, out of the unlocated lands in that tract, after the warrants issued from the State of Virginia should have been satisfied.

"4. There was also granted and secured by the same act, one-thirty-sixth part of all the lands of the United States, lying in the State of Ohio, to which the Indian title had not been extinguished, which might thereafter be purchased of the Indian tribes, by the United States, which thirty-sixth part should consist of the sections number sixteen, in each township, the specified and declared object of the aforesaid grants and reservations, were for the use of common schools, within the several districts of country therein specified, and were, as your memorialists conceive, granted upon full consideration arising from the increased value of the remaining lands belonging to the United States, and also from the relinquishment, on the part of the State of Ohio, of the right to tax the lands of the United States, within the State of Ohio, until five years after the sale thereof; and that it was, by the aforesaid act, expressly declared that the several appropriations for schools made therein were in conformity with, and in consideration of, the conditions agreed on by the State of Ohio, by the ordinance of the Convention of said State, bearing date the twenty-ninth day of November, in the year one thousand eight hundred and two, and hereinbefore particularly referred to.

"That your memorialists conceive that it was the intention of the parties to the compact aforesaid, that one-thirty-sixth part of all the lands within the State of Ohio should be granted to the people thereof, for the use of common schools, and should be placed under the control of the *Legislature* thereof; and that this construction is warranted by the spirit, and even by the letter of the different acts of the Congress of the United States, when considered in relation to the ordinance of the State of Ohio above referred to, and to which a direct reference is had by the aforesaid last recited act of the Congress of the United States.

"That when it was afterward ascertained that the grant aforesaid, in relation to the tract of country commonly called the Virginia Military Reservation, would be rendered wholly inoperative, in consequence of the limitation and condition thereunto annexed, by reason of the great and uncertain amount of warrants which had been issued by the State of Virginia, together with the extended period for locating the same, the Congress of the United States, in pursuance of the stipulations of the compact aforesaid, by the act passed the second day of March, in the year one thousand eight hundred and seven, appropriated eighteen quarter townships, and three sections, as are in said act described, for the use of schools in that tract of land, in the State of Ohio, commonly called the Virginia Military Reservation, which were, by the said act, also vested in the Legislature, in trust for the use aforesaid.

"That at the period when the act aforesaid, making an appropriation for the tract commonly called the Connecticut Reserve, was passed, the Indian title had been extinguished to that part only which lies east of the Cuyahoga river, and the appropriation was made only in relation to that part to which the Indian title had been extinguished, and consisted of a tract equal to one-thirty-sixth part of the Reserve, to which the Indian title had been so extinguished; since which time the Indian title to that part of the Reserve lying west of the Cuyahoga river has been extinguished by the United States, for, and on account of the State of Connecticut, who made the necessary appropriations for that purpose.

"That, as your memorialists conceive, it was in conformity with the spirit and intention of the compact aforesaid, and formed a material item of the consideration which induced the State of Ohio to make the concessions they did make under that compact, that they should receive, in return, lands equal to one-thirty-sixth part of all the lands within the State of Ohio, to be appropriated for the use of common schools within said State.

"The Legislature of the State of Ohio, construing the terms and spirit of the compact in the manner above set forth, do not hesitate to represent to the United States that when the Indian title was extinguished to the tract of country lying in the Connecticut Reserve, west of the Cuyahoga, the terms aforesaid required of the United States that a law should be passed, appropriating, from their unlocated lands within the State of Ohio, a tract equal to one-thirty-sixth part of the Connecticut Reserve, lying west of the Cuyahoga river, and that they, relying on the justice and good faith of the government of the United States, confidently anticipated the passage of such an act, in aid of the exertions of the State of Ohio, in establishing a system of common free schools throughout the State.

"That in relation to the lands already appropriated, as above described, the Legislature of the State of Ohio, in pursuance of the trust aforesaid, and in aid of the great and important objects contemplated, have resorted to various methods of rendering them productive, and in particular, that of leasing them to such individuals as have applied therefor; that experience, however, has fully demonstrated that this fund will be wholly unavailing in their hands, in its present shape. That, in order that the beneficial and laudable objects contemplated by the grants aforesaid may be secured to the people of the State of Ohio, it will, as your memorialists conceive, be necessary that the Legislature should possess the unlimited control over the lands aforesaid, with the power of disposing of them in fee.

"The objections which are urged against the present mode of administering that fund, are, in the first place, that by reason of the facilities which the State of Ohio affords for acquiring a property in real estate, a necessity exists of leasing the lands in question to persons almost wholly destitute of pecuniary means, whereby the avails of those lands are rendered, at least, uncertain; in consequence, also, that, as these lands are detached over the whole State of Ohio, the expense which must necessarily be incurred by creating a superintendence over them, renders them much less productive than your memorialists conceive they might be rendered, if the lands were sold, and the proceeds concentrated in one fund.

"The fact, also, before adverted to, that these lands must necessarily be entrusted to the possession of those of the lowest class of the community, and who possess no permanent interest in the soil, has produced a waste upon these lands of their timber, and otherwise, equal, perhaps, to the whole revenue which may have been derived from them. The fact, also, that, by holding them under the present tenure, your memorialists are compelled to offer upon lease so great a proportion of their soil, as will invite and retain a population within her boundaries, of a character not to be desired, and in amount so great as to create an evil which can only be conceived of, in a country where every individual, possessing a very moderate portion of industry and economy, may, within a single year, appropriate to himself, in fee, a quantity of land sufficient to furnish means of support for an ordinary family, is also a circumstance which your memorialists conceive is not undeserving of consideration.

"While the State of Ohio, in common with her sister States, shall have her ordinary proportion of idle and unprofitable members, this great proportion of land, which must be held by lease, must of necessity produce a corresponding feature in her population. Although many industrious and valuable citizens may be found among the lessees of school lands, yet it must be admitted, that the great body of those who constitute the strength and basis of every government, and who are to be considered as the friends of good order and public improvement, are among those who are the owners as well as occupiers of the soil. Those evils, as your memorialists conceive, arise wholly from the system of granting these lands upon leases, and are such as can not be remedied by any course of legislation whatever, if, as some have supposed, the State have not the power, under the terms of the original grant, of disposing of these lands in fee. Notwithstanding your memorialists may be of opinion that they already possess this right; yet so long as the question shall admit of any doubt, it must of necessity have the effect to restrain its exercise: it is true, that if the forms of proceedings established by States as the rules of action for its members, shall or can, be brought to operate upon the States themselves, this question might, perhaps, be rendered still more uncertain; but your memorialists conceive that the grants aforesaid, being made to the people of the State of Ohio, through the medium of the Legislature for the use of the people, that no limitations can have any operation, further than as it shall furnish an argument against diverting this fund from its original and legitimate object. The Legislature of the State of Ohio being in all respects sovereign, within the Constitution, their capacity to do any and every act in relation to property which its citizens, hold in common is, as they conceive, necessarily implied, nor can they acknowledge that any rule, other than the Constitution, can operate with any obligatory effect, upon the power which has created the rule itself, except upon considerations of justice and policy toward those who may be affected by their acts. It may, it is true, be said these grants partake of the nature of a compact between the United States and the State of Ohio, and that, therefore, they are to be limited to their particular terms in relation to the State of Ohio. It is admitted that the grant exists in consequence of a compact; but, inasmuch as the United States have received a full and valuable consideration, which formed the inducement of the grant, and inasmuch as they have not reserved to themselves any beneficial interest in the land aforesaid, or possibility of reversion or any title whatever; it can not be supposed that they can possess any controlling power. It may be urged, also, that inasmuch as there has been no method pointed out in respect to the manner in which this trust should be executed, the Legislature of the State of Ohio have an unlimited discretion in this respect, and may avail themselves of every possible method of producing the greatest advantage to those whom they represent. This argument, they conceive, is powerfully supported by the fact, that the same act grants to the State, as well as the school, the lands in question, as the six miles reservation, including the Scioto Salt Springs; in respect of which latter the Legislature are expressly restrained from selling the same or leasing them for a longer period than ten years; and that the inference from this circumstance is direct, that it was the intention of the parties to that compact, that no such restraint should exist in relation to the other lands which did not come within this provision. While your memorialists have been thus particular in endeavoring to give the proper definition of the powers they possess, in order that no conclusions may hereafter be drawn unfavorable to their claim from having made this application, and have thereby perhaps shown, that, in a particular point of view, this application is wholly unnecessary, they are of opinion that an act of the Congress of the United States declaratory of the extent of the grants aforesaid, will be productive of much benefit, in case the Legislature of the State should hereafter determine to dispose of the same. That it will have the full effect of removing every doubt in the minds of the purchasers, and thereby enhance the price which will be obtained for the same.

"Therefore, your memorialists represent that it would be of advantage, and conduce to the future prosperity of the State of Ohio, that a law of the United States be passed, declaring the authority of the State of Ohio to dispose of the said lands granted for the use of schools within said State, in fee; and that the proceeds thereof be invested in some permanent fund, the proceeds of which shall be applied under the direction of the Legislature for the use of common schools within the townships or districts to which they were originally granted in said State, and for no other use and purpose whatever: *Provided*, That the sections numbered sixteen, granted as aforesaid for the use of schools, shall not be sold without the consent of the inhabitants of such original surveyed townships, and that they may be authorized and empowered to sell and dispose of the aforesaid six miles reservation, including the Scioto Salt Springs, the Salt Springs near Muskingum river, and in the Military Tract, with the sections of land which include the same, and apply the proceeds thereof to such literary purposes as the Legislature of the State of Ohio may hereafter direct.

"*Resolved further*, That the Governor be requested to forward the foregoing memorial to the Government of the

United States, and take such order and disposition of the funds as shall seem to him proper."

February 26, 1824.

The twenty-third session of the General Assembly, 1824–5, has the distinction of having established a tax of one-half a mill for school purposes in the respective counties. The discussion had been warm, and a measure for supporting free schools by taxation, it is quite probable, only prevailed at this time because the friends of a canal system could not otherwise obtain the co-operation of sections of the State not directly interested in their construction. The strongest friends of free schools were from the east and north-east, while the canal interest was predominant in the central and western districts. Both measures have since become prominent features of State administration.

Nathan Guilford deserves the honor of having secured the passage of the act of February 5, 1825, "to provide for the support and better regulation of common schools." Former commissions had been discordant on the subject: but early in the session, a joint committee on Governor Morrow's recommendation in respect to schools, had been appointed, consisting, from the Senate, of Nathan Guilford, Robert Young, Daniel Harbaugh, and David H. Beardsley; and from the House, of James W. Lathrop, Homer Hire, George B. Holt, and John Colton; and their draft of a bill became a law, with scarcely a verbal alteration, although opposed with great bitterness. The bill was accompanied by a report, both being understood to be from the pen of Mr. GUILFORD; most of the report was occupied with a review of the legislation and condition of other States. One paragraph earnestly advocating free schools, should be quoted in honor of its author:

"The system of free schools has always been found the most general and efficacious in its effects. It extends the means of common education to the door of every man, and among all ranks and conditions. It is particularly favorable to the education of youth in the country, where the population is scattered and difficult to be united without some general system for the purpose. In towns, cities, and villages, schools always exist, and when left to itself, education is always much better attended to in these places than in the country. Nothing but free schools has ever succeeded in diffusing education among the mass of the people who cultivate the soil. This system scatters schools in every neighborhood, is within the reach of every farmer, and freely offers to the poor tenants of every cabin the means of instruction. The yeomanry of every country constitute its sinews and strength; and it is among them that those wholesome, honest, and home-bred principles are preserved, which constitute the safety and honor of a nation. How doubly important is it, then, that they should be well informed! In New England, where this system has prevailed ever since the first settlement of the country, it is extremely rare to meet with a person of either sex who can not read and write. A taste for reading, and a desire for further information is thus created; and in almost every town and village, a respectable circulating library is to be found. These common schools are the nurseries of the academies and classical seminaries which exist in almost every populous county, and which are the natural consequence of the common schools."

The act of February 5, 1825, was as follows:

"Whereas, it is provided by the Constitution of this State, that schools, and the means of instruction, shall forever be encouraged by legislative provision. Therefore,

"SECTION 1. *Be it enacted by the General Assembly of the State of Ohio*, That a fund shall hereafter be annually raised among the several counties in this State, in the manner pointed out by this act, for the use of common schools, for the instruction of youth of every class and grade, without distinction, in Reading, Writing, Arithmetic, and other necessary branches of a common education.

"SEC. 2. That the Commissioners of the several counties in this State, at their appointed meeting, in June, eighteen hundred and twenty-six, for the purpose of determining the per centum to be levied upon the general list, or grand levy, in their respective counties; and at every such annual meeting thereafter, shall levy and assess upon the *ad valorem* amount of said general list, one-twentieth of one per centum, or one-half of a mill upon the dollar, to be appropriated for the use of common schools in their respective counties, in the manner hereinafter provided; which said assessment shall be apportioned among the several townships, levied and collected in the same manner as all other taxes for county and State purposes, and paid into the county treasury.

"SEC. 3. That it shall be the duty of the county Auditor, immediately after his annual settlement with the county Collector, to make out, and deliver to the Treasurer of said county, a certificate of the amount collected for the use of schools, upon the duplicate of each township; and also to open an account in a book, to be by him kept for that purpose, with each of said townships, in which each township shall be credited with the amount collected as aforesaid, upon its duplicate for the use of schools. And the amount so collected, in each township, shall remain in the county treasury for the use of the schools in such township.

"SEC. 4. That it shall be the duty of the Trustees of each incorporated township in this State, to lay off the same into one or more school districts, in such manner as they shall think most suitable and convenient for the population, and different neighborhoods of the township, always paying a due regard, in forming such districts, to any school-house already erected, or district already formed, and to any incorporated school company, and to schools in villages or populous towns.

"SEC. 5. That when two or more townships adjoin, and the line of such townships divide a population which can most conveniently be formed into a school district, it shall, and may be lawful for a majority of the Trustees of each of the townships so adjoining, to meet and lay off such school district in such manner as will best suit the population of their respective townships. And each township from which such district is formed, shall contribute toward the support of schools therein, in proportion to the number of families belonging to the parts of said township included in such district.

"SEC. 6. That it shall be the duty of said Trustees, immediately after laying off, and forming or altering any such district in their respective townships, to describe and number the same, and to deliver the number and description thereof, in writing, to the clerk of the township, who shall record the same in the township records: and when a district shall be formed out of two or more adjoining townships, or shall be altered, a description of a part thereof in each township, or any such alteration shall in like manner be delivered by the Trustees of the several townships to the clerks of their respective townships, to be by them recorded as aforesaid; and it shall be the further duty of said Trustees to take, or cause to be taken, a list or enumeration in writing, of all the householders residing in each of said districts, and to deliver the same to the township Clerk, who shall record the same;

and said Trustees shall have power to correct said list, by taking a new enumeration, or inserting therein any changes which shall increase or decrease the number of householders, in said district, from time to time, when they shall think proper.

"SEC. 7. That it shall be the duty of said township Clerks, as soon as they shall have recorded the same, to deliver to the county Auditor the number and description of each school district, and part of district, in their respective townships, and, also, the list or enumeration of the householders residing in each, and all alterations which shall from time to time be made.

"SEC. 8. That it shall be the duty of the county Auditor to receive and file in his office the description and number of all such districts, with the name of the householders in each; also, all alterations which shall from time to time be returned to him as aforesaid.

"SEC. 9. That whenever any school district shall be formed as aforesaid, any one or more inhabitants of such district may call a district meeting, by notifying all the householders residing within said district, of the time and place of holding such meeting. And the *householders*, or inhabitants, of such district shall assemble together, in pursuance of such notice, and when so assembled in district meeting, if one-third of all the householders of said district be present, shall be a legal meeting, for the transaction of business, with power to adjourn from time to time. It shall be the duty of said meeting to organize and to choose a clerk, who shall keep a record of their proceedings: they shall then proceed to elect three school Directors, to manage the concerns of said district, who shall hold their offices for one year, and until their successors are chosen: the said district meeting shall also have power to designate and determine upon the site of a school-house, and to provide the means of building the same; also, to provide the necessary funds, and to do all other things necessary for organizing a school in said district.

"SEC. 10. That it shall be the duty of said school Directors to employ a teacher, and to manage and superintend the concerns of said school; it shall also be their duty, when necessary, to call district meetings, by giving due notice thereof to the householders of said district; they shall also receive and faithfully expend all funds, subscriptions, donations, or dividends of school funds; and they, or any two of them, may make any lawful agreement for such purpose, or maintain any action at law, to recover any money due said district, or any damage done to the property belonging to the same.

"SEC. 11. That the Court of Common Pleas of each county shall annually appoint three suitable persons, to be called Examiners of Common Schools, to serve for the term of one year, and until their successors shall be appointed, and fill any vacancy which may happen, whose duty it shall be to examine every person wishing to be employed as a teacher; and if they find such person qualified and of good moral character, to give a certificate to that effect; and any one or more of said Examiners may visit the schools in the county, and examine the same, and give such advice relative to discipline, mode of instruction, and management of said schools, as they may think beneficial.

"SEC. 12. That no person shall be allowed to teach any district school until such person be examined and approved by one or more of the Examiners of Common Schools, and receive a certificate of approbation from said Examiner o Examiners; and no teacher of any district school, who shall not have obtained such certificate, shall recover at law any wages or compensation for teaching such school.

"SEC. 13. That the Trustees of each and every original surveyed township in this State, wherein there is the reserved section number sixteen for the use of schools, or to which township any such section, or other lands in lieu thereof, appertains, shall pay over to the school Directors of the several school districts, and parts of districts, within their respective townships, a dividend of all rents or monies received on account of said section, in proportion to the number of families in each district or part of district.

"SEC. 14. That it shall be the duty of the school Directors to pay the wages of the teachers, who shall have been by them employed, out of any money which shall come into their hands, from the revenues arising from donations made by Congress for the support of schools, or otherwise, so far as such money shall be sufficient for the purpose; and for the residue of the wages of any such teacher, the said school Directors shall give to such teacher a certificate, particularly stating the length of time which said teacher has been employed in teaching the school of said district, and the amount or balance due him on account of wages thereof. And it shall be the duty of the county Auditor, upon the presentment of any such certificate, to draw an order upon the county Treasurer in favor of such teacher, in payment of the amount so certified to be due, out of the dividend belonging to such district, provided such order shall not exceed the amount of said dividend; which said dividend shall be struck and apportioned by said county Auditor, among the several districts of said township, in proportion to the number of families in each.

"SEC. 15. That no township shall be entitled to receive any part of the moneys collected for school purposes, until the same shall be laid off into districts, and a list of the householders in each district taken and delivered to the county Auditor as provided by this act; and no school district shall be entitled to receive its dividend of the money so collected, except in payment of the wages of a teacher duly employed and certified, as provided by this act; and if the Trustees of any township shall not, within five years from the passage of this act, lay off the same into one or more districts, and take a list of the householders as aforesaid, it shall be the duty of the county Auditor to divide and apportion all the moneys collected upon the duplicate of taxes from such township among the other townships of the county, which shall have been laid off into districts according to the number of families in each; and if any school district in any township which may be laid off according to this act, shall neglect to employ a teacher and to keep a school therein at any one time for the space of three years, it shall be the duty of the county Auditor to divide and apportion the dividend among the other districts in said township which shall employ teachers, and keep schools, according to the number of families in each.

M. T. WILLIAMS,
Speaker of the House of Representatives.
ALLEN TRIMBLE,
Speaker of the Senate."

February 5, 1825.

Governor Morrow congratulated the General Assembly, at the commencement of the twenty-fourth session, upon the legislation of the preceding winter, in the following terms:

"The state of education, and means for mental improvement among us, can not be viewed with the same satisfaction as that of the other important interests of our country. Measures for improvement in this regard have been a standing theme of executive communication ever since the commencement of our government. Much has been said, and nothing effectually done, until at the last session of the General Assembly. Then, the incipient steps were wisely taken for the introduction of a system of common schools. From the institutions then authorized, if duly supported and cherished by the Legislature, the most beneficial effects to society must result. The necessity of such support is obvious; because it is a palpable fact, that science and intellectual improvement have fallen far behind, in their pace, the progress of population, wealth, and general improvements, on the face of the country; and equally unquestionable that the cultivation of these are essential to the well-being of society. No interest, it is believed, confided to the Legislature is of more importance than this, whether we regard it in its influence on human happiness, or on the permanency of our republican system."

In his last message to the Legislature, December 6, 1826, Governor Morrow again referred to the school question, as follows:

"It is conceived that, on an investigation, such as is proposed, into the public concerns, and on a view of the state of society at present, it will be found that the situation of this State is in many respects peculiar, and be discovered that the present period forms an interesting crisis in her destinies. The State has grown up almost to maturity, with a rapidity unexampled; her population is composed principally of emigrants from the several States of the Union, with the share of education common to the several States from whence they came: they have brought with them habits, manners, customs, peculiar to the countries of their nativity and former residence, and which, for want of general intercourse, and a common system of education, remain fixed and unassimilated. With that tide of emigration which so copiously flowed, were had a full supply of those qualified for the liberal professions. We have heretofore had the advantages of all the provisions made for education in the original States; but now, from the comparative density of population, and the wider range of settlement toward an extended frontier, that flow of emigration has ceased. The society is placed on its own ground, with its own means to cultivate native resources, physical, mental, and moral. The inquiry is interesting—are we prepared, from the present state of the public institutions of learning, to become independent in that respect of the older States in the Union? And is the present state of common school education such as to warrant the belief, that we shall establish and sustain a character to society of being respectable, moral, and intelligent? Or must we, in the neglect of improving our own means, supply the defect by a dependence on others.

"To remedy the evils, and avert the consequences, which must result from the present state of things, if they are not misconceived, will require a liberal spirit of enterprize and united exertion on the part of the community, as well as energy, with an enlightened zeal, on the part of the Legislature. It is true that much has been done for general education, by the law for the regulation of common schools; that system, however, is defective, and the hope can scarcely be indulged that, with its present provisions, it can be brought into general use. It contains not sufficiently the principle of either compulsion or inducement, to insure its general operation; and experience has shown, that without one or the other of these, the chance of its being carried into effect, is, in the inverse ratio to the necessity of its use. Should this system be improved by more perfect provisions, and the fostering care of the Legislature be extended to our seminaries of learning, giving them support as they shall have means; and the plans for internal commercial intercourse, which are now in successful progress, be steadily persisted in, the flattering prospect is presented, and the hope may be indulged, that this State will rise to the exalted station, and continue to sustain that rank among the other States of the American Union, which by extent of territory, exuberance of soil, and salubrity of climate, she is entitled to hold, and that our country will soon become the seat of useful knowledge, where the arts and sciences will be firmly planted, and that in it will be found whatever can exalt and adorn society, and administer to the real happiness of man."

CHAPTER XII.

ADMINISTRATION OF ALLEN TRIMBLE.—1826-30.

Governor Trimble was inaugurated on the 19th of December, 1826, and in the address delivered on that occasion remarked as follows:

"Education is of such vital importance in its effects upon

all the various relations of society, that it may justly be ranked among those subjects which should first claim the attention of a free and enlightened people. The diffusion of useful knowledge, is a theme on which the philanthropist, statesman, and divine, have long dwelt with enthusiasm. And to afford to youth the means of instruction, and to facilitate their march in pursuit of useful knowledge, has been the anxious care of the wise and good in every age and country; nor can the political condition of that country long continue prosperous and happy, where the progress of intellectual and moral improvement is not commensurate with the development of its resources of wealth and power. The framers of our Constitution, in penning the charter of our rights, were not unmindful of the great importance of universal education, in a Government deriving all its powers from the people, nor of their duty to posterity, when in strong and imperative language, they required 'that schools, and the means of instruction shall forever be encouraged by legislative provision.' The different executive officers of the State, impressed with similar views, have not failed to recommend the subject to the consideration of the Legislature; yet, strange as it may seem, the subject was not acted upon until the year 1821, when, by virtue of a resolution of the General Assembly, a committee was appointed to report a system for the establishment of common schools, though no effectual measures were adopted to complete the system of education, until the session of 1824–5. To what extent the law has been carried into effect, and the estimation in which it is held by the people, must be best understood by their representatives; it is fair however, to conclude, that an enlightened community, appreciating the value of knowledge, virtue, and morality, will approve a measure, upon the success of which, more than any other, depends the future fame and happiness of their country. The system is now in its infancy, but if approved by the people, and cherished by their representatives, it will prosper, and insure a general diffusion of useful knowledge throughout the various classes of society; and many of our indigent youth, who would otherwise be deprived of a participation in the means of instruction, will be reclaimed from ignorance, folly, and vice, and become useful members, and many of them ornaments, of society. Then may we indulge the animating hope, that general intelligence, virtue, and morality, will be the characteristics of the sons and daughters of Ohio. No wise Government should afford the means of instruction to a few, in exclusion of the many; but should extend a liberal and equitable patronage, shedding its benign and salutary influence through the medium of common schools, in which all may participate, and with a fostering and parental care, endow liberally its colleges and universities, where learning may pursue her march, and unfold to her sons those sublime lights and immortal treasures which science alone can boast. The policy heretofore pursued by the State, has been to commit the highest branches exclusively to the patronage of that part of the community who have felt the greatest interest in its success. But however munificent or devoted to the cause of literature, few of our citizens have been successful in raising funds to endow, even moderately, their favorite institutions. The Ohio and Miami Universities, endowed by grants of land from the General Government, from the proceeds of their domain, have supported reputable schools; and it is gratifying to learn, that they, with a few other seminaries, are enabled to extend their usefulness to the community. Yet it is a melancholy fact, that many of our young men have been, and now are, abroad, for want of the adequate means of instruction at home; the consequence of which is a constant drain upon the resources of the State, of a large amount annually; which, if judiciously applied, would contribute salutary aid to some one of our home institutions, and enable the parent who sends one son abroad, to educate at least two at home. Nor is this the only evil—our young men, by resorting to colleges in or near to populous cities of the Atlantic States, to pursue their studies, may, and frequently do, suffer losses more to be regretted, and much more fatal to themselves and their country, than the sacrifice of fortune.

"The youth of our State, generally, partake of those habits of temperance, industry, and economy, and have imbibed those principles of virtue and morality, which characterize the great mass of our population. To place them in large cities, free from the guidance of their parents or guardians, where the allurements of pleasure, vice and folly are presented in their most fascinating forms, is a test too severe for youthful minds. There are some, whose experience and fortitude may preserve them from danger; but may we not fear that there are many who fall victims to dissipated habits and vicious principles? And such is the high estimate set on whatsoever is of foreign growth, or acquired from abroad, that it is to be feared that, on the return of our young friends, even their vices and profligate habits, with the gloss of an eastern polish, will be considered by our unsuspecting youth, as accomplishments essential to the gentleman and scholar. If then, by sending them abroad, the sacrifice of wealth is certain, and the danger great, of demoralizing our most promising sons, and disappointing the brightest hopes of their friends and their country, the duty of providing for their education at home becomes imperative."

The legislation at the twenty-fifth session was of much practical importance. Congress had not responded in accordance with the legislative memorial, asking a declaration in favor of the construction that the State might sell, instead of lease, section sixteen; but on the 29th of January, 1827, an act passed the Legislature to that effect. It directed the county Assessors to record the votes in the original surveyed townships, for and against a sale, and deliver the book containing the votes, to the county Auditor, who might receive legal votes until the third Tuesday of October following said April canvass of the townships. The county Auditor and two associate Justices were made triers of any contest as to the right to vote on such proposition of sale; and even if the first decision by a township was adverse, still, on the petition of twelve white male inhabitants, of twenty-one years of age, (there being twenty or more such residents in a township) the county Auditor might direct a further canvass on the subject. He was required to certify such proceedings to the Auditor of State.

It was made the duty of the Auditor of State to report to the Legislature annually, on the first Monday of December, a statement of the votes given in every such township, or fractional part thereof, for and against a sale of section sixteen, or any part thereof, belonging to the same, and also a summary statement of the valuation of such lands by the assessors. It was then provided, that they should be offered for sale, in such year as the Legislature might direct by joint resolution, or otherwise, by the county Auditor, under the direction of the State Auditor. The premises were to be appraised, and could not be sold below the appraisement; but the title would be in fee simple, to be conveyed by the

Governor when four payments of equal amount, one at the sale and three deferred, were completed. A certificate of sale issued first, and finally a deed, under the seal of the State. Of course, if the conditions of sale were not complied with, the premises were forfeited, and might be re-offered. The proceeds of sales were to be first received by the county Treasurer, but were required, on or before the fifteenth of January, in each year, to be paid into the State Treasury. The usual directions for notices of sale and officers' fees were added.

Two sections of the act, providing for the disposition of outstanding, permanent leases, were in the following terms:

"SECTION 6. That in all cases where the county Auditor shall be instructed by the Auditor of State, as hereinbefore provided, to sell any of the sections sixteen, or fractional parts thereof, or other sections in lieu thereof, whereof leases may have been heretofore granted for ninety years, or for any other number of years, and renewable forever, it shall be lawful for the lessee thereof, or other person or persons being the lawful assignee or assignees, or owner or owners of such lease, to return such lease to the county Auditor of the proper county, and it shall be the duty of such Auditor to endorse on the back of such lease, that the lessee, or the owner or owners thereof, does release to the State of Ohio, in trust, for the use of the township to which the land belongs, all the right, title, interest and estate, which was originally granted by such lease; which said endorsement shall be signed and sealed by the lessee, or the owner or owners thereof, in the presence of said Auditor, whose duty it shall be to enter in a book, to be by him provided for that purpose, the date of such lease, the name of the original lessee, the name of the owner or owners who surrendered the same, the range, township, section, quarter section, or part thereof, the number of acres or other smaller quantity specified in such lease, the rate per acre, or value of the smaller quantity, at which the land was appraised prior to granting the same, and if such lease has been recorded, the number of the book and page in which the same may be found, and also the date when such lease was surrendered: *Provided*, That where any such leased land shall have been re-appraised after any such lease shall have been granted, according to any special law for that purpose, the appraisement last made shall be deemed and taken as the true value of such land, to all intents and purposes as if the same had been inserted in such lease.

"SEC. 7. That on the surrendering any permanent lease as aforesaid, such lessee, or the owner or owners of such lease, as the case may be, shall be entitled to receive from such county Auditor a certificate of purchase for the land contained in such lease, by paying therefor the appraised value of said land, as herein before specified, together with all rents which may be due upon such lease, up to the time of surrendering the same, if any such rent be unpaid, in manner following, namely: all the rent due as aforesaid (if any) except as herein after excepted, together with one-eighth part of the appraised value of the land as aforesaid, shall be paid at the time of such surrender; and the residue of such appraised value shall be divided into seven equal instalments, one of which said instalments, together with interest at six per cent. on the whole amount of such appraised value remaining unpaid, shall be paid annually, from and after the date of the surrender of such lease, until the whole be paid."

An act supplementary to the school act of 1825, created the office of school district Treasurer, and defined his duties; authorized the School Directors to levy a special tax for building or repairing a school-house, not exceeding $300, provided three-fifths of the householders present at a meeting, called according to the act by the Directors, should agree thereto: all fines imposed and collected by any Justice of the Peace, for any offense or immoral conduct, were required to be paid to the district Treasurer for the use of schools; and it was declared lawful for the Court of Common Pleas to increase the number of School Examiners, but not to exceed the number of organized townships in their respective counties.

Another act was passed, January 30, 1827, establishing a fund for the support of the common schools. The proceeds of section sixteen were funded, and an income of six per cent. appropriated to the townships or district of country, (as the Virginia, and United States Military,) with a pledge of the faith of the State for its annual payment. In addition, a State fund for the support of common schools was established, consisting of the net proceeds from the sales of salt lands, and such donations, legacies, devises, etc., as might be made to such fund, or to any person or persons in trust for the same, the interest thereof to be funded annually, until January 1, 1832, and then distributed annually to the several counties in the State for school purposes, in proportion to the number of free male inhabitants above the age of twenty-one years, as by law should be ascertained for the apportionment of representatives.

Ten years after the enactment of the law above referred to for the sale of section sixteen, the operation of sections six and seven was thus explained in a report by Samuel Lewis, State Superintendent, to the General Assembly.*

"Thus a school section in an improving settlement was leased at an early day—say from 1810 to 1820—at the very low price at which lands in the country were then held, say from one to ten dollars per acre, for the term of ninety-nine years, renewable forever, subject to re-valuation every twenty or thirty years, as the case may be, for they vary in time; the interest on the valuation was paid annually. In the meantime, the land had, when the law was passed, increased in value two or three hundred per cent., and, since its passage, has risen as much more; so that land only paying an interest of four dollars per acre is worth, in some cases, from twenty to thirty dollars per acre, and generally in that proportion at least.

"By the operation of this law, the tenant may surrender his lease, and, on paying the former appraisement, take a deed in fee simple for land sometimes worth six times as much as he pays. Cases have come to my knowledge where land has thus been taken at six dollars per acre, worth, at the time, fifty dollars. Thus, the township which was, in fact, well provided with school lands, is deprived of almost the whole value, by a law which can in no case operate for their benefit, but always against them; none but good lands are taken on those leases, and they are not surrendered unless they have greatly increased in value; the tenants, to be sure, make their fortunes, but the schools are sacrificed. In this way a large quantity of land has been conveyed, and a large quantity of valuable land is now exposed to the like operation. The whole loss can not be estimated now, though it

* These sections were repealed by an act passed March 16, 1838.

must be immense—in some single townships more than fifteen thousand dollars. A great number of citizens have urged the repeal of those two sections, or modifying them so as to avoid the present difficulties.

"It is suggested, that the voters in townships where these lands lie were called on to vote, in many cases, without having seen the law, and without being informed that the lands sold must go at the former valuation; there was no opportunity of publicly discussing the question; the whole depended, in a great measure, on the influence of the person taking the vote, if he chose to exercise it; and, in one very aggravated case, the assessor was a lessee on the land. No public vote could be got now to dispose of these lands at these terms; and some complain that votes taken ten years since, before the lands had become valuable, and before they were advised of all the consequences, should be binding still where the leases have not been surrendered; they say individuals would not consent to take for their property now the same price they had fixed even five years since."

Governor Trimble addressed the twenty-sixth session of the General Assembly as follows, upon the school policy of the State:

"The experiment of educating *all* the youth of a community, has been successfully made by several of the American States; and it is a well attested fact, that under a well regulated system of common schools, the expense of imparting instruction is diminished, and the entire population may participate in advantages which otherwise would be limited to comparatively few. It is equally true, and a circumstance not to be lightly estimated, that of the many thousand children taught in the free schools in one of the most commercial and populous districts in the Union, not an instance had occurred in 1825, of one of them being convicted of a crime.

"This circumstance alone carries with it an irresistible argument in favor of universal instruction, and should induce our fellow citizens, who are opposed to the introduction of the system of common schools, to adopt from motives of economy, a measure, which would expel ignorance and vice, rather than be taxed a large sum to punish crime. If the first should be neglected, the latter will be inevitable; for no nation is 'permitted to be in ignorance with impunity.'

"A school should be planted and supported in every neighborhood; it would prove, if cherished and invigorated, a 'tree of useful knowledge, producing good without evil, and help to make a paradise, as that of forbidden use occasioned the loss of one.' Impressed with the belief that a wise application of public money, for the purpose of education will contribute largely, as well to the present prosperity as to the future fame and happiness of the country; I respectfully recommend an increase of the tax for common schools, and that such aid be given to our universities as will enable them to extend their means of usefulness, commensurate with the increasing requisitions for learning and literature throughout the country."

By the legislation of 1827–8, the recent policy of the State in regard to the disposition of section sixteen, was extended, in all particulars, to the Virginia and United States Military Districts; but leases of school lands were only authorized for not less than three nor more than seven years, unless the inhabitants had declared in favor of a sale, when leases were required to be from year to year only.

At the twenty-seventh session, by the act of February 10, 1829, three-fourths of a mill, instead of one mill, was levied for school purposes within the counties; provision was made for forming a school district from parts of two or more townships; minute directions for holding district meetings were given; the powers and duties of School Directors, district Treasurer, and district Clerk, defined; the number of county Examiners (still to be appointed by the Court of Common Pleas) fixed at not less than five nor more than the townships of the county; rate-bills authorized, after failure of school fund; and unless townships were districted and organized into schools within three years, then a forfeiture of school funds, etc. The first section of this act qualified its assurance of the "instruction of youth of every class and grade without distinction," by providing "that nothing in this act contained shall be so construed as to permit black or mulatto persons to attend the schools hereby established, or compel them to pay any tax for the support of such schools; but all taxes assessed on their property, for school purposes in the several counties of this State, shall be appropriated as the Trustees of the several townships may direct, for the education of said black and mulatto persons therein, and for no other purpose whatever." Suits on behalf of a district were to be brought in the name of the district Treasurer.

In his message to the twenty-eighth session of the General Assembly, Governor Morrow said:

"If there is any one subject which, more than another, claims your attention, as possessing within itself, in a greater degree, the means of preserving our free institutions, of increasing our happiness, and advancing our prosperity, it is education—a system of general instruction, that shall diffuse its blessings to every class, and shed its enlightening influence on every mind. History is full of examples where popular liberty has degenerated into licentiousness and anarchy—where powerful factions have grown up to oppress the few; and the people, incapable of governing themselves, to avoid the turbulent rules of many, have submitted to the tyranny of one. All men have the right, but the wise and the good *only* have the power, to remain free.

"Should the subject of educating youth receive the attention due to its importance, intelligence will become common, public virtue will accompany it, and united, they will form a basis upon which the freedom, future fame, and happiness of the country will rest secure. The system of common schools which has been adopted by the State, like seed sown in good soil, is taking deep root, and promises a continued harvest of the first fruits of virtue as well as letters, which we hope, in many instances, to see ripened and refined in our higher institutions of learning. It is regretted that the number taught in our common schools is not known. In the Universities of Athens and Oxford, and Kenyon College, which also deserve to be classed with the institutions of the State, there are about four hundred young men annually taught; and with but small additional expense, instruction might be imparted to double that number."

In an amendatory school act, passed February, 22, 1830, first occurred a provision, afterward often repeated in successive revisions, which exhibits a remarkable deference to non-resident proprietors. The tax for school-house construction was limited as follows:

"*Be it enacted by the General Assembly of the State of Ohio*, That no tax exceeding fifty dollars, in any one year, shall be levied by any school district, under the provisions of the tenth section of the act to which this is an amendment; unless at least one-third of the property subject to taxation, within such district, be owned by persons residing therein; and when one-third, or more, but less than half of the taxable property within any district, be owned by persons residing therein, such tax shall not exceed one hundred dollars, in any one year; and where half, or more, but less than two-thirds of such property, be owned by persons residing in such district, such tax shall not exceed two hundred dollars in any one year."

By former legislation each householder was required to pay at least one dollar building tax; this act reduced the minimum to fifty cents, and allowed a delinquent district tax to be paid without penalty. District school officers were required to take an oath of office, and were subjected to a penalty for refusal to serve. Governor Trimble retired from the office of Governor with the following statement, contained in his message of December 8, 1830:

"Our common schools have gradually increased under the law for their regulation and support. From calculation, founded upon the enumeration of children between the ages of four and sixteen years, in the Virginia Military District, it is believed that not less than 350,000 children within the State, receive, or are entitled to receive, instruction in these primary schools. Our numerous academies and colleges are in a flourishing condition, and are all receiving a gradual accession of students. Our female academies are increasing; and a deeper interest is felt throughout the State for the instruction of this most interesting part of our population."

At this period the system of schools had assumed a form which, with the exception of the superintendence of Samuel Lewis for three years, was not materially modified, until the constitutional revision of 1851, and the legislation subsequent thereto. That period, therefore, instead of the separate consideration of each political administration, will constitute the next division of this historical outline.

CHAPTER XIII.

EXECUTIVE RECOMMENDATIONS—1831–51.

The testimony of those distinguished citizens, who have been honored by the people of Ohio with elections to the chief magistracy of the State, although uniform in its character, affords a guarantee of the value and usefulness of the school system, which it is deemed expedient to retain in these annals. During the twenty years under consideration, the office in question was filled more frequently by popular election than in the preceding thirty years; consequently, the opportunity for unfavorable expression, if such had been the direction of public opinion, was very fully afforded.

Gov. Duncan McArthur, in his message of December 6, 1831, observed:

"Having myself experienced much inconvenience, and frequent embarrassment, from the want of a more liberal education, I feel more sensibly the great importance of securing to the rising generation the benefits of instruction; and I most earnestly recommend to you, gentlemen, a continuation of those laudable efforts which have hitherto characterized our Legislature for the promotion of education. Our schools and colleges, from that valuable institution, the Sunday schools, up to those of the highest grade, should always claim the most favorable consideration of our Legislators. A well educated and enlightened people only are capable of *self-government*, the greatest temporal blessing which *Heaven* has bestowed upon man."

Gov. Robert Lucas, in his inaugural, of December 7, 1832, said:

"The Constitution declares 'that schools and the means of instruction shall forever be encouraged by legislative provision.' This is a subject that can not be too forcibly impressed upon our minds; it has been urged by executive communication, from the organization of our government, but never, until the session of 1824 and '25, could the Legislature be brought to give their assent to the passage of a bill to regulate common schools. The first act met with serious opposition in some parts of the State, and petitions were presented for its repeal, but without success, the law having been continued so that the people have become acquainted with its objects, and are now generally in favor of the system. Subsequently to the passage of the first school law, an act was passed appropriating the avails arising from the sales of the salt reservations, as a foundation upon which to build a permanent fund, for the support of common schools within the State. This fund is, at this time, insufficient to answer any valuable purpose; but I trust the time is not far distant when public opinion will be concentrated in favor of supplying the means of instruction, and that, by an increase of that fund, a system of common schools will be established upon a permanent basis, sufficiently enlarged to extend its benefits to every child in the State; and that the higher branches will receive sufficient encouragement to enable them to extend their benefits in a proportionate degree. All that is wanting to accomplish this desirable object, is to have public opinion in its favor; with this, under Providence, we can accomplish any thing—without it, we can do nothing."

Again, December 3, 1833:

"The establishment of a well-regulated system for the education of the rising generation, is among the most important subjects presented for legislative consideration; for nothing can be more important than general information to the citizens of a government, where the sovereign power is lodged with the people, and whose will, through their constituted agents, controls its operations. And as knowledge is power, in a government where every member has equal rights, its general diffusion must strengthen the bonds of society, and add to the durability of our institutions. A system of common schools that will impart to our whole population the benefit of a competent business education, would vastly promote the happiness of individuals, and the prosperity of the State.

"The importance of perfecting such a system can not be too firmly impressed upon your consideration. And while we consider common schools as the foundation of a well-regulated system of education, and entitled to the first consideration yet we are duly sensible of the benefits and importance of supporting, with all the means under our control, those institutions of a higher order that diffuse their benefits in a more eminent degree, none of which are more entitled to our commendation than those that have attached to them systematic manual labor, where, in addition to the disciplining and cultivation of the mind, the pupil is carefully trained to habits of industry and morality, and thereby doubly prepared for usefulness in life."

Governor Lucas, in his message of December 8, 1835, thus alludes to the European methods of instruction, and especially to M. Cousin's celebrated report to the French Government:

"The subject of education has been frequently pressed upon the consideration of the General Assembly, and numerous acts have been passed on the subject of schools, academies, colleges, and universities; and, in addition to those institutions erected by law, many other means have been resorted to, by the pious and philanthropic classes of the community, to diffuse intelligence, improve the mind, and reform the morals of the people. Yet our system of education is languishing, in proportion to our other improvements. The question may be asked, Why is it so? It is admitted by all intelligent statesmen, that in knowledge consists the strength of all liberal governments; that the prosperity and happiness of every people are in proportion to their virtue and intelligence. Notwithstanding this admission, but few nations in the world have established regular systems of elementary schools. This subject, however, has, of late, excited the attention of some of the most enlightened nations of Europe, and the various systems of public instruction in operation in the different governments, have been examined by men of the highest literary acquirements; and according to the report of M. Victor Cousin to the Minister of Public Instruction in France, the Prussian system has been thought superior to any heretofore established in any government in Europe. Though many parts of this system of public instruction are not adapted to the spirit and feelings of the American people, nor to our form of government, yet, from the results of this great experiment in giving the whole people that kind and degree of instruction which they need, some of the most useful, practical lessons may be obtained. The nature and operations of the human mind are the same in all countries; and the relation which exists between knowledge and the intellectual and moral faculties, remains unchanged. M. Cousin has in his report made a full and faithful statement of the workings, and practical application of the well-tried school system of Prussia. A copy of an American edition of this work has been forwarded to me by the publishers in New York. This system appears to be the result of a constant accumulation of practical knowledge for fifty years. The evils of either teaching or legislating which appeared, have received a remedy; and the highest point of excellence of one age has been made the starting point of improvement by the age succeeding. This experimental knowledge is what we want. The reason why we legislate for the education of the people so badly is, that there is little instruction to be derived from past experience. In the preface to this work, the school systems adopted by the several States in the Union are examined, and whatever is deemed their defects are pointed out. The report of M. Cousin is divided into four sections, to-wit: general organization of public instruction; primary schools; instruction of the second degree; and higher instruction in universities. This book I have placed in the State library, and respectfully recommend it to the consideration of the General Assembly and to the School Committee, as a work containing much important information on the subject of education generally, and from which much useful knowledge may be obtained with regard to the establishment and regulation of common schools."

Governor Lucas signalized his retirement from the gubernatorial chair, by exerting his influence in favor of an application of the United States surplus revenue fund to school purposes, as well as by other practical suggestions of much value. In his message of December 6, 1836, he observes:

"The first and most important subject to which your attention is directed, is a communication from the Secretary of the Treasury of the United States, dated June 27, 1836; together with an act of Congress transmitted therewith, entitled 'an act to regulate the deposits of the public money.' A copy of the communication of the Secretary of the Treasury, together with a copy of the act of Congress referred to in the same, are herewith transmitted, to which I solicit your immediate consideration.

"You will perceive that the thirteenth section of the act of Congress aforesaid, declares, 'that the money which shall be in the treasury of the United States, on the first day of January, 1837, reserving the sum of five millions of dollars, shall be deposited with such of the several States, in proportion to their respective representation in the Senate and House of Representatives of the United States, as shall by law, authorize their Treasurers, or the competent authorities, to receive the same on the terms hereinafter specified; and the Secretary of the Treasury shall deliver the same to such Treasurer, or other competent authorities, on receiving certificates of deposit thereafter, signed by such competent authorities, in such form as may be prescribed by the Secretary aforesaid; which certificates shall express the usual and legal obligations, and pledge the faith of the State for the safe keeping and re-payment thereof, and shall pledge the faith of the States receiving the same, to pay the said moneys and every part thereof, from time to time, whenever the same shall be required by the Secretary of the Treasury, for the purpose of defraying any wants of the public treasury, beyond the amount of five millions aforesaid: *Provided*, That if any State declines to receive its proportion of the surplus aforesaid, on the terms before named, the same shall be deposited with the other States agreeing to accept the same on deposit, in the proportion aforesaid.

"I presume there can be but one opinion on the propriety and expediency of receiving our proportion of the surplus revenue, upon the terms specified in the act of Congress. The condition on which a re-payment can be required by the Secretary of the Treasury of the United States is for the purpose of defraying the wants of the public treasury. These wants would have to be supplied if this surplus fund had no existence. By the regular operation of our revenue laws, there is little probability that such wants of the public treasury will ever become sufficient to justify a demand upon the States, for the re-payment of their several proportions, deposited with them under the act of Congress aforesaid.

"With this view of the subject, I can perceive no impropriety in receiving our portion of the surplus revenue, and making immediate application of it, to permanent purposes within the State. The precise sum that may fall to our portion, can not at present be ascertained; but from the late report of the Secretary of the Treasury of the United States, it will probably exceed THREE MILLIONS OF DOLLARS. This sum being providentially placed under our control, through the operation of our revenue laws, after the entire extinguishment of the national debt, is truly a cause of gratulation, and if judiciously applied within the State, to purposes of a permanent character, can not fail to extend its benefits to the latest posterity.

"This money is emphatically the property of the people, in which the poor and the rich have an equal right, and in its application special regard should be had to an equal distribution of the benefits to be derived therefrom.

"On this subject I have thought much, and can devise no plan for the application of this money, that would be likely to diffuse its benefits to every class of community, more than its application to the support of common schools; I would, therefore, recommend to your consideration, in the most express manner, the propriety of constituting it at once a common school fund, to be *irrevocable;* the State to become the trustee of said fund, with authority to invest the principal, either to the extinguishment of the canal debt—to fill the loans authorized by law, for the purpose of extending our canals within the State, or for other public improvements—or to vest it in such stocks within the State, as may be deemed most safe and profitable; the interest or dividends accruing therefrom to be distributed annually among the several counties in the State, for the support of common schools therein, in proportion to the number of children in each county respectively. This would enable us to exalt the character of our common schools, and lay the foundation for a superstructure of intelligence sufficiently spacious to extend, to every child in the State, a common school education, and to open the way, for those who may possess talents and an inclination to obtain a higher degree of education, to progress from step to step, to the highest degree of universal science.

"This, gentlemen, is one of the most important subjects that has been presented for legislative consideration. Our system of public instruction has hitherto languished for want of the means of support; the means now under your control, if applied to the purposes of education, can not fail to exalt the character of the State in an eminent degree.

"It has been wisely said, that 'knowledge is power,' and that 'virtue and intelligence constitute the strength of republics.' The truth of these maxims has been tested by all past experience.

"To perfect a system of public instruction, I am convinced that we must begin with common schools, and that the most, effectual support that can be given to our academies, colleges, and universities, will be to raise the standard of *common schools*, to that of preparatory schools, where the scholar can be prepared, under the immediate eye of the parent, for an entrance into a seminary of a higher degree.

"The application of this fund in the manner suggested, will be attended with a double benefit; the State will enjoy all the advantages to be derived from an immediate application and circulation of the principal, while the accruing benefits may extend to the latest generations.

"The foregoing suggestions are respectfully submitted to your consideration, with an ardent solicitation that you will give to the whole subject that prompt and serious attention to which it is justly entitled.

"The resolution of the 11th of March last, 'providing for a School District Manual,' made it the duty of the Governor to appoint a committee of two persons, to prepare and report to the next General Assembly, a School District Manual, explaining the duties of all officers under the 'act regulating common schools,' 'with proper forms of proceedings, in levying taxes, holding school meetings, conducting suits, and in all other matters relating to district schools, etc.' In compliance with the duty required by said resolution, the Honorable John H. James, of Urbana, and the Honorable Joseph R. Swan, of Columbus, were appointed said committee, and severally accepted the appointment. The character of these gentlemen, is a sufficient guarantee that an able and explicit report on the subject referred to them will be made in due time.

"A copy of the resolutions of the 14th of March, 'in relation to public instruction and education,' requesting the Rev. C. E. Stowe, Professor in one of the literary institutions in this State, to collect, during the progress of his contemplated tour in Europe, such facts and information as he might deem useful to the State, in relation to the various systems of public instruction and education, which have been adopted in the several countries through which he may pass, and to make report thereof, with such practical observations as he might think proper, to the next General Assembly,' was transmitted under the seal of the State, to Professor Stowe, a few days after its passage, who acknowledged its receipt, and accepted the trust therein reposed.

"He proceeded to Europe shortly afterward; and his return to the United States (as I have been informed) was expected in November. I have not yet heard of his arrival. When he returns to Ohio, we may anticipate a lucid report on the systems of public instruction and education, in some of the most enlightened nations in Europe, from which much benefit to the cause of education in Ohio may be derived."

These views were enforced by Governor Joseph Vance, in his Inaugural Address of December 13, 1836, who remarked:

"Gentlemen, there is one other subject I feel it to be my duty to bring to your consideration:

"Under a law of Congress, that portion of the surplus revenue of the country belonging to Ohio, is about to be placed at your disposal. Various plans have been proposed for its application—some for applying it to the payment of the State debt, some for appropriating it to new objects of improvement, some for dividing it among the counties, and others in favor of its application to the establishment of a State bank. All these objects may be worthy of your consideration; but it would be well for you in the first place, to inquire what is the character of this fund, and to whom it properly belongs, and see whether there is not a portion of society that have not that direct interest in the payment of the debt, the further improvement of the State, the building up of county interests, or the establishment of a bank, who have at least an equal, if not a paramount, claim upon a portion of this fund, and who can not agree that its application shall be made to these objects, without palpable injustice to their own immediate wants.

"I can not say, with certainty, what portion of this fund belongs to this particular class of society; but, from the best computation I have been able to make, at least one third of it is theirs, and should be applied to their exclusive benefit, and to no other use or purpose whatever.

"This fund has been commonly, but erroneously, called the *surplus revenue*. It is, in reality, the avails of our great land capital converted into money, and not *revenue*, which is the ordinary income of a country from imposts and taxes on her property, her trade, and her business. Thirty-five millions of the balance now in the treasury of the United States has arisen from the sales of the public lands, since the payment of the national debt for which these lands were pledged. This sum, at least, is the inheritance of the people, originally gained by the toil, and suffering, and blood of their revolutionary fathers.

"It is a sacred gift to us, now freed from incumbrance, and belongs alike to the whole body of our people—'the humblest and the proudest, the wealthiest and the most destitute.' That which we have received by the uncompromising fidelity of those in whom the guardianship and trust was reposed, it is our duty to invest and preserve for ourselves and for our posterity.

"Then, gentlemen, it is your duty to make the computation, and see what portion of it belongs to the poor and destitute. Remember that you are now about to become their trustees and guardians, and that a heavy responsibility rests upon you to make such application of their means as will enable them to become worthy members of society, and enlightened and useful citizens of the State. This can only be done by building up our common schools; and when we reflect that the very foundations of our political system rest upon the virtue and intelligence of our people, and that the interest at stake is no less than the perpetuation of our free institutions, you can not falter in your exertions to accomplish the great object in view.

"Read our Constitution, and there learn what were the feelings of our fathers upon this subject. The twenty-fifth section of the eighth article reads thus: 'No law shall be passed to prevent the poor in the several counties and townships in this State from an equal participation in the schools, academies, colleges, and universities of this State, endowed in whole or in part from the revenues arising from donations made by the United States.'

"How has this injunction been regarded? We, to be sure, have not passed a law to prohibit the poor from entering our colleges and universities, but from a want of that system and organization necessary to give efficacy to our common schools, they are as much excluded as if they were prohibited by positive statute.

"Our school system has had great difficulties to encounter; it has been met by the combined force of avarice, wealth and ignorance; but I now congratulate its early advocates that their labors are about to be crowned with success. A fund is now within their reach that avarice has no claim to, wealth can not control, and which will make ignorance itself acknowledge its fatal error, and bow in perfect submission. Then let the grumbler no more talk about his heavy contributions for the education of the poor; if the poor and the destitute get their rights, they will no longer be quartered upon his bounty; but rather let it be our ambition to vie with each other in our exertions to bring into form a system of education which will insure a faithful and impartial application of the means now at our command, with those in prospect, so that a diffusion of the benefits and blessings of a thorough common school education shall reach every child throughout every section of our State.

"No person can appreciate more sensibly than myself the want of an early education: even in the place in which I now stand, it is felt with a pungency and force more easily understood than explained. This whole matter is now about to be committed to your care; and I have a strong confidence that it will meet with that favor that its high claims upon your consideration so loudly calls for."

In his message of December 5, 1837, Governor Vance enlarged upon the preceding views, urging as a permanent national policy the distribution of the public lands for school purposes.

Governor Wilson Shannon, in his Inaugural Address of December 13, 1838, said:

"In a republican government like ours, where the sovereign power is vested in the people, and where virtue, intelligence, and patriotism are indispensably necessary to the maintenance and perpetuity of our free institutions, the subject of education should be one of the first importance. No people, in an organized state of society, can be either free or happy without virtue and intelligence; and, to secure both, a well digested and liberal system of education is indispensable.

"The framers of our Constitution, convened for the purpose of creating the organic law of our State, were so deeply impressed with the primary importance of education, that they declared in the constitution itself, that 'religion, morality, and knowledge, being essentially necessary to good government and the happiness of mankind, schools and the means of instruction shall forever be encouraged by legislative provision.' So universal and wide-spread is the opinion that education is indispensable to the perpetuity of our institutions, and the well-being and happiness of the people, that we find similar declarations in the Constitution of every State, perhaps, in the Union. The European communities are also alive to the importance of this subject; and the persons in power, yielding to the strong current of public opinion, or actuated by an enlightened and patriotic sense of public duty, have established some of the best systems of education with which I am acquainted. I trust that we will not disappoint the just expectations of the framers of the Constitution, or fall behind the spirit of the age, by neglecting to foster and cherish a broad and liberal system of education, which will furnish the means of instruction to all the rising youth of the State. It is not by the erection of academies, colleges, and universities, that a people are to become educated; these, it is true, are highly useful, and justly considered indispensable in every well organized system of education; but their benefits and advantages, from necessity, must be limited to a few individuals, and those generally of the more wealthy portion of the people. It is only by the system of free common schools that the means of education are furnished to every one—that the rich and the poor are alike able to avail themselves of the advantages of instruction, and the whole community enlightened and improved.

"Our common school system, which was commenced in 1825, and which, since then, has undergone various modifications and changes, has no doubt been the means of doing some good; but it is to be regretted that our legislation on this subject has been so unstable, that it has been difficult for those whose duty it was to carry out the law, and put the system into practical operation, to keep pace with the continually changing provisions of the statute. This has no doubt been owing to a laudable desire, on the part of the Legislature, to improve and perfect the system; but it has prevented the people from becoming acquainted with the mode of doing business under it, and, in some cases, excited objections which would not otherwise have existed.

"It is to be hoped that the light which has recently been shed upon this subject, and our past experience, will render our legislation in reference to common schools, less changeable than heretofore. From the various sources provided by law, there will, hereafter, be annually applicable to the object of common school education near half a million of dollars. This fund, if judiciously applied, will do much to promote the cause of common school education in our State, and diffuse among the youth of the country that universal intelligence so essential to the happiness of mankind, and so indispensable in the preservation of our republican institutions.

"Under the present act, for the support and better regula tion of common schools, our German population are, in some degree, excluded from its benefits. The present law requires that Reading, Writing, and Arithmetic, shall be taught in the English language: *Provided, however*, That any other language may be taught in addition to the English, at the discretion of the Directors. Although the German may be taught in connection with the English language, if the School Directors so order, yet it is impossible, in many places, to procure a teacher capable of teaching both German and English, or to procure an English teacher capable of teaching German children. The consequence is, that in German settlements, they are unable to sustain any other than German schools, by which they are entirely excluded from the benefit of the school fund. This is not justice, to say the least. The Germans contribute their equal proportion toward the school fund, with other citizens; they have the same interest in it with others, and no portion of the community more cheerfully comply with all the laws of the country than they do. They constitute a large portion of our population, and are increasing annually. They are industrious, frugal, intelligent and virtuous, and devotedly attached to our free institutions. Their rights and interests should not, therefore, be disregarded. Why not leave it discretionary with each district, whether the English, or German or both, shall be taught? It is true it may be desirable that all our population should be capable of understanding the English language, but this can not be brought about in a day; it will require time, and must, and no doubt will, take place gradually, by the necessary and continual intercourse between the German and English population. But it can not be produced by an arbitrary act of legislation, requiring that to be done which is impracticable, either on account of the feelings and education of parents, or the impossibility of procuring suitable teachers.

"Our German population should be furnished with the school, and all other important laws of the State, printed in their own language. A large portion of them, from their avocations and advanced age of life, are prevented from learning the English language. They are required to obey the law, and comply with its various provisions; and if they fail to do so, they must abide the consequences. The means, therefore, of becoming acquainted with it should be placed within their reach."

Again, in his annual message of December 3, 1839.

"Education, and moral and intellectual improvement among our citizens, are steadily and rapidly advancing under our liberal system of instruction. That general intelligence which is, and must ever continue to be, the great bulwark of our republican institutions, and which is the result, in a great degree, of our liberal system of education, and the inquiring spirit of the age, is rapidly increasing throughout the whole country. It is a duty which we owe to ourselves, as well as to posterity, to adopt all the necessary means, which prudence may suggest and wisdom devise, to preserve and perpetuate our free institutions. From the history of the past we may learn something of the future; and it is a fact worthy to be remarked, that no other people have long been able to preserve their freedom, when the mass of the community were uneducated and uninformed. The great and unprecedented success which has marked our free institutions, and the wisdom and prudence which has generally characterized the administration of our public affairs, are mainly to be attributed to the force of enlightened public opinion, emanating from an intelligent and well educated community. If we expect to avoid the fate of other republics in times past, and preserve our free institutions from the inroads of despotism and the selfish ambition of the designing few, we must foster and cherish the means of general instruction. An enlightened system of education, by which the rising youth in each succeeding generation will be prepared and qualified to act the part assigned them by the theory and fundamental principles of our government, as they take their position on the stage of human action, is the strongest barrier that can be presented against anti-republican principles. We may with confidence anticipate, that so long as we maintain a liberal, enlightened, and general system of instruction in our State, our free institutions will be maintained, liberty and a love of order and good government will be cherished, and, under Providence, we will continue to be a prosperous and happy people.

"There is some opposition still existing to our system of common schools; nor is it to be presumed that the system is without some objections, or that any general law could at once be put in operation that would meet with universal approbation. The system established by the present school law is, comparatively speaking, new, and we have not become familiar with the mode of doing business under it; but it is doubtful whether a better system, as to its general features, could be adopted; or one that would give more universal satisfaction to the people. Time and experience will suggest the defects in the present school law, and they will, no doubt, be gradually removed by legislative action, until it is rendered as perfect, and as satisfactory to the public as any system which could be devised. Any great and radical change, unless for very obvious and weighty reasons is to be deprecated; new experiments should be avoided; and our legislation on this subject should assume a stable character. The law of last session, by removing the just causes of complaint, has had the effect of reconciling, in a great degree, our German population to the present school law. I have not heard of any complaints from this valuable and patriotic portion of our fellow citizens, since they have been permitted to an equal participation with other citizens in the benefits of the system.

"I would respectfully call your attention to the very able and satisfactory report of the Superintendent of Common Schools, made at the last session of the Legislature, on the subject of school lands, and the proceeds of school lands. It will be perceived, upon an examination of that report, that several townships in this State have been deprived of school section sixteen, and have never received any section in lieu thereof; and that they are entitled, either from the State or General Government, to an equivalent for the land of which they have been deprived. Also, that there is a deficiency in one of the quarter townships, in the United States Military school land, of four hundred and eight acres, as found on actual survey, which Congress would, no doubt, make good upon a proper application. There were a large number of fractional townships in this State having no section sixteen, and unprovided with school land under the original law. In eighteen hundred and twenty-seven, Congress passed a law, giving to each township and fractional township, for which no previous provision had been made, school lands in proportion to the size of the township, to be selected in the respective land districts, where the townships unprovided for were situated. The amount of school lands due this State under this act, was about thirty thousand acres. What proportion of this has been selected, I am unable to state, but no selections have been made, as I am informed, in the Chillicothe land district, where a great number of these fractional townships are situated, on the ground, that there is no suitable land within the district subject to be selected. In all cases where suitable selections can not be made, under the law, within the land districts, Congress should permit the selections to be made from other government lands out of the district. This is so obviously just, that upon a proper application to Congress, I presume they would not hesitate to authorize selections to be made from any government lands within the State. I would respectfully suggest the policy of submitting the whole subject to Congress, at the present session, and asking that body to pass a law, providing for those fractional townships which have been deprived of school section sixteen, and to authorize selections to be made under the act of Congress of eighteen hundred and twenty-seven, from any lands belonging to the general government in the State. The only lands owned by the United States, within the limits of Ohio, that are considered of much value, are the reserved sections embraced within the limits of the Wabash and Erie, and Miami Canal grants. These lands, it is expected, will be brought into market, and sold the ensuing year; and unless Congress can be induced to act immediately on the subject, their interference hereafter can be of little use to the State. Our school fund, and the means of education, have been permanently impaired by that improvident system of legislation which authorizes, under certain circumstances, the sale of our school lands. It seems to me our true policy is, to retain these lands for the benevolent and wise purposes for which they were intended, and to authorize their sale in no case unless under very peculiar circumstances, and when the interest of our school fund would be obviously promoted."

Also, in the message of December 8, 1840:

"The cause of education and intellectual improvement has continued to advance under our liberal and enlightened system of instruction. At no period heretofore have our colleges, academies, and common schools been in a more flourishing and prosperous condition than they are at the present time. The deep solicitude felt by parents generally to have their children receive a good education, and the noble ambition that characterizes so many of our youth to attain this desirable object, can not fail to excite, in the bosom of every patriot and friend to our democratic institutions, well-grounded hopes that they will long continue to shed their blessings and benefits on a great, prosperous, and intelligent people.

"It is a fact that can not be too often repeated, or too deeply impressed on the minds of the present and rising generation, that our free institutions can only be preserved and perpetuated by a virtuous, intelligent and uncorrupted people. The history of all free governments admonishes us of the danger to which public liberty is most exposed. We are differently and more favorably situated, it is true, than any of the republics of ancient or modern times. Our population are scattered over a wide surface; engaged on their farms and in their work-shops; pursuits well calculated to promote and encourage the growth of that virtue and love of liberty, the want of which has been so fatal to the cause of free government in other countries and other times. It is on the great producing classes, which constitute and ever must constitute a large majority of our population, that we must mainly rely for the preservation of our free institutions. They are honest, patriotic, and intelligent, and will so continue unless the means of education are neglected, and the onward march of intellectual improvement, which so pre-eminently characterizes the age in which we live, should receive some great and unexpected check. Notwithstanding, however, our circumstances and population are so auspicious to the growth and perpetuation of public liberty and free government, we should not be unmindful of the means by which they are to be preserved and best secured. It is the duty of every citizen of the State to promote the cause of virtue and encourage the diffusion of intelligence. But it is peculiarly the province of those who have been selected by the people to discharge the important and highly responsible trust of legislating for the country, to guard against the growth of vice, ignorance, and corruption, by encouraging, by all proper means, the education of the rising generation, and thereby enable them to enter upon the important duty which, in the rapid course of time, will devolve upon them of preserving our free institutions in their original simplicity and purity, and handing them down, unimpaired, to posterity."

Governor Thomas Corwin, in his first annual message of December 7, 1841, (he was inaugurated at the close of 1840,) thus expressed himself:

"It is in times of profound tranquillity, when the people are undisturbed by the tumults of war, that the duties of enlightened patriotism invite us to the grateful task of giving depth and permanency to our free institutions. It is only at such periods that a commonwealth can hope to deliberate calmly and successfully upon systems of polity, calculated to stimulate industry, by giving it legal assurance that it shall be protected in the enjoyment of its acquisitions; to strengthen general morality, by laws which shall tend to suppress vice and crime in all their forms; to give energy and independence of character to all classes, by measures which will promote, as far as practicable, equality of condition, and thus establish rational liberty for ourselves, and give hope of its continuance for ages to come.

"Of measures which contribute to these ends, education, comprehending moral as well as intellectual instruction, is of the first importance. Under a Constitution like ours, which imparts to every citizen the same civil rights, education must ever remain a subject of vital interest, in reference to the general welfare of the State. If we are to trust the lessons of history, we are brought to the conclusion that government is, and always has been, the most efficient of all the causes which operate in forming the character and shaping the destinies of nations. Where the right of suffrage is so unrestricted as with us, government is necessarily the offspring of all the people, and will reflect the moral and intellectual features of its parent, with unvarying fidelity.

"If the speculations of the most profound thinkers had left us in doubt upon this interesting subject, the familiar history of the last century alone has furnished numerous and melancholy proofs, that no people to whom moral and intellectual culture have been denied, are capable of achieving or enjoying the blessings of rational liberty, founded upon any system which tolerates popular agency in the conduct of public affairs. So profoundly impressed with this great truth were the framers of our Constitution, that they did not leave it to the judgment of the future to decide. They did not allow the subject of education to remain in that class which might be, in after times, adopted or rejected upon the doubtful test of expediency. They incorporated it into the Constitution. In the third section of the eighth article of the Constitution, it is expressly declared that 'religion, morality, and knowledge, being essentially necessary to good government and the happiness of mankind, *schools and the means of instruction shall forever be encouraged by legislative provision*, not inconsistent with the rights of conscience.' In the schools, the encouragement of which is thus enjoined as a proper subject of legislative provision, it is apparent that the makers of the Constitution intended to combine moral with intellectual instruction. All experience and observation of man's nature have shown that merely intellectual improvement is but a small advance in the accomplishment of a proper civilization. Without morals, civilization only displays energy, and that the more fearful in its powers and purposes as it wants the restraining and softening influences which alone give it a direction to objects of utility or benevolence.

"The object in view, when our present system of common schools was established by law, was, doubtless, the same embraced by the provisions of the Constitution. As the habits and opinions of our population touching the subject, were exceedingly diverse, the system worked its way to favor in the public mind, under auspices by no means favorable. Hitherto, however, it has met with little opposition in any quarter, and may be considered as a part of the permanent policy of the State. While, therefore, it would be both unwise and impracticable to attempt any radical change, it is obvious that experience will, from time to time, suggest improvements. The law formerly provided a Superintendent, with powers of general supervision of the schools throughout the State. This officer has been dispensed with, and his duties transferred to the Secretary of State. The time of this officer and his attention, it is obvious, will generally be mainly employed in the proper duties of Secretary of State. I submit to the Legislature whether it is not proper, even in a pecuniary view, to devolve the duties of general Superintendent of Common Schools upon one, whose exclusive business it shall be to discharge them. This officer should be at liberty to visit the schools at different points in the State, to collect and report, to each successive Legislature, ample and accurate statistical facts, by which the system can be thoroughly understood and vigorously enforced. The reports from the county Auditors, required by the present law, in some instances, are not made at all; and in those instances where there has been an effort to comply with the law, the information given generally embraces only a small portion of those facts, which it is most necessary should be known to the Superintendent as well as to the Legislature. I earnestly recommend legislative provision, by which this branch of the system may be more satisfactorily administered in future."

On retiring from office, Governor Corwin, in his message of December 6, 1842, observed:

"Speculative writers on the nature and proper elements of free government, have agreed that civil rights and political power can only be safely extended to the masses of any people, when general intelligence and pure morality have been widely diffused and exert a controlling influence. The unsuccessful efforts of men in past ages, to assert and maintain equal rights, all concur in furnishing evidence of the truth of this great principle in the science of government. In Ohio, every citizen who has attained to majority, after a short residence in the State, and who has been charged with, or paid taxes, is armed with the right of suffrage. Our fundamental law, therefore, and the general legislation of the State, have all been made to wear the same aspect; they each regard all men as equal, and seek to extend to all an equal amount of power in the conduct of public affairs. In such a system it must be obvious, that education, combining both moral and intellectual culture, is a matter of primary public interest. It is with us not merely the ornament of our political edifice, it is the foundation on which it stands, and without which it must crumble into ruins, and crush in its fall those who, in a false and fatal security, have taken up their abode within it.

"In a former communication I have had occasion to urge upon the Legislature the necessity of maintaining, in full vigor, the school system now in force, and of improving it by every means which experience may from time to time suggest. Any act which wears the appearance of weakening, or looks to the future abandonment of it, must be considered as a blow aimed at a system of policy, which all enlightened men of modern times regard as of vital importance. By an act of the last session, the school fund was reduced by an amount of about fifty thousand dollars. The necessity, real or imagined, for the reduction of such a fund, is greatly to be deplored. Heavy as the taxes now are, I can not doubt but the people of the State would have cheerfully paid the amount thus taken off, knowing that their children were thereby to be fitted for the proper exercise of the great powers and privileges of American freemen. If the present rates of taxation should be reduced, I earnestly recommend that such reduction may be made to fall on other objects, many of which will readily suggest themselves to the wisdom of the Legislature, as interests which may safely be postponed to that of general education. It is by educating poor children, wherever they may be found, that we place them, to some extent, at least, upon a footing of equality with the fortunate inheritors of rich estates. It is, of all agencies yet discovered, the most efficient in producing that perfect and just equality among men, which brings harmony into the social system, and gives permanency to free government."

Governor Wilson Shannon, in his annual message of December 5, 1843, said:

"Our common school system has taken a strong, and, I trust, a permanent hold on the public mind. Its advantages and blessings are beginning to be duly appreciated by all our citizens. Opposition to it has, in a great measure, ceased. Time has given to it form and permanency, and its existence, as a part of the settled policy of the State, we confidently believe, will continue so long as our republican institutions are cherished and held up by a free people.

"It is not, however, all we should desire it to be. We should aim to improve our common schools, and give to them the capacity of imparting a more enlarged and liberal education; we should seek to elevate the grade of public instruction so as to be in unison with the progressive spirit which is now animating the civilized world. The education of the rising youth of our country, thus qualifying them for self-government and the maintenance of free institutions, is an object which commends itself to the fostering care of every American statesman and patriot."

Governor Shannon having resigned on the 15th of April, 1844, was succeeded by the Speaker of the Senate, Thomas W. Bartley. Governor Bartley, in his message of December 3d, said:

"The most certain reliance for the security and permanency of our civil institutions, is to be found in an efficient and well conducted system of common schools, by which the benefits of education can, upon liberal terms, be placed within the reach of every person of suitable age in the State. Every citizen is entitled to a voice in the management of our public affairs. Our laws are but the emanation of popular opinion. It is a matter, therefore, of vital importance, that popular opinion should be aided and enlightened by intellectual culture, and molded and directed by a pure and elevated tone of moral feeling. The European systems of education confine the means of instruction chiefly to the favored and fortunate classes, to the exclusion of the mass of the people, and thus keep up and augment those artificial and arbitrary distinctions in society which constitute one great source of the oppression and degradation of the great body of the people. The youth of this country are born to nobler privileges and higher responsibilities. The very genius and spirit of our institutions require that a public system of instruction should be kept open and free to all; placing those in the most humble walks of life upon the same platform and equal footing with those who are in more fortunate circumstances; elevating the intellectual, moral and social condition of the mass of the people, and perpetuating that degree of moral, intellectual and social equality, which is essential alike to the permanency of our government, and the happiness of our people.

"The great conservative influence of a public system of education on the future destiny of our country, was fully appreciated by the eminent statesman who framed the first elements of our civil institutions. It was provided in the ordinance of 1787, for the government of the territory northwest of the Ohio river, that 'religion, morality, and knowledge, being necessary to good government and the happiness of mankind, schools, and the means of education, shall forever be encouraged.' In the organization of our State government, this provision was, in substance, copied into the bill of rights, and now constitutes a part of the Constitution of the State, imperatively enjoining upon the Representatives of the people, that 'schools, and the means of instruction should forever be encouraged by *legislative provision*, where not inconsistent with the rights of conscience.' The subject of education has been urged upon the consideration of the Legislature in almost every annual message of the Governor since the origin of the State Government. The solemn injunctions of the fundamental laws of the State, which it is our sworn duty to support, and the warning voice of every successive supreme executive officer of the State, ought not to be treated as mere ceremonious formula, entitled to but slight and superficial attention. They are the authoritative and living promulgations of public sentiment, expressed in characters as visible and impressive as if written in stars on the arch of the firmament.

"To the mode of instruction, discipline, and training, given to the juvenile portion of our population, we are to look for the model of the future character of our people, and the elements which will control the future destiny of our republic. It is to this source that we are to look for the formation of that elevated standard of intellectual superiority, moral excellence, and public virtue, which shall preserve our country from ignorance and superstition, stay the tide of corruption usually flowing from a dense population, and rescue our posterity from the intellectual and physical degeneracy so commonly produced by luxury and its enervations, after a continuance of national prosperity.

"The system of common schools in this State, although productive of much benefit, and in its general provisions well adapted to the accomplishment of its objects, is yet susceptible of very great improvements. The fact can not escape the most superficial observation, that great inefficiency and want of energy exist in its execution and management, and that during the last two or three years it has been retrograding, instead of progressing toward a higher degree of perfection. I have no hesitation in saying, that if our system of common school instruction were conducted with proper efficiency, and under the improved regulations and modes of teaching at this time in use in some other places, greater benefits would be derived from half the present expenditure of time and money. The Secretary of State, and several county Auditors, to whom the general superintendence of our common school system is at present intrusted, have doubtless performed their respective duties with fidelity, and done all which could reasonably be expected from them; but their time and attention has been chiefly occupied by the other and more appropriate duties of their offices. I submit to your consideration the propriety of appointing a State Superintendent of Common Schools, and of authorizing the election of a county Superintendent, by the people of each county, for the purpose of giving greater efficiency to the system, by having the exclusive attention of the Superintendents devoted to the management and improvement of this important branch of the public service. I entertain no doubt but that the appointment of these officers, and the payment of competent salaries for them out of the school funds, will prove a matter of economy in the management of the school funds, for the cause of education. A great want of punctuality has existed in the reports of information required by law to be made from the several school districts and townships. This neglect of duty might be effectually remedied, by a provision requiring the necessary reports to be made, before a school district or township should be permitted to draw its proportion of the public money.

"The subject of normal schools or seminaries for the education of teachers, is attracting much attention in several of the States of the Union, and in other countries; and by the pre-eminent advantages afforded by this means for advancing the cause of education, it commends itself to your favorable consideration. Departments for the education of professional teachers, in the Ohio and Miami Universities, could be established under the authority of the State, and by a part of the means derived from the large endowments which these institutions have received from the government.

"The following statement will show the product of the State common school fund, for the year ending 15th November, 1844:

Balance on the 15th November, 1843,	$40,132 47.
Amount received arising from interest on surplus revenue, grand levy, tax on banks, etc.	195,600 69.
Total,	235,733 16.
Amount apportioned and paid the several counties,	200,000 00.
Remaining balance in treasury,	35,733 16.
In addition to the above, there has been paid to counties entitled to the following funds :	
Virginia Military school fund,	11,718 67.
United States military school fund,	7,149 76.
Connecticut Western Reserve school fund,	9,519 54.
Section sixteen,	56,133 90.
	$84,521 89.

'This amount has been drawn from the canal fund, being the interest on the principal of each fund."

Governor Mordecai Bartley, in his Inaugural Address of December 3, 1844, observed:

"The first and most important of all political measures of a republican government, is to quicken, strengthen, and educate the youthful public mind. Where the elective franchise is almost universal, it is indispensable that the mass of the people be instructed in moral and political science.

"On this point, argument is unnecessary, since it is universally admitted, that the perpetuity of our political institutions depends, under God, upon the diffusion of sound education. An uninformed people, with the best constitution, are as unstable as the sea, and utterly incapable of fixing any safe and settled policy, but are destined to be the dupes of the reckless and designing, and after unsuccessful efforts at self-government, to surrender their liberties.

"The wise framers of our excellent Constitution were careful to lay in that instrument the basis of a system of public instruction; and ever since the organization of the State Government, the Legislature has given more or less attention to the subject. Although I would propose no radical change in the present school law, yet I humbly conceive that experience has shown that it is not incapable of improvement; and I submit to the consideration of the Legislature, whether it ought not at this time to undergo revision; whether alterations are not demanded, to elevate the character of the school-teacher; to secure such a uniformity of school-books as is not incompatible with the progress of improvement in the art of instruction; to widen the sphere of common school education, so that it may embrace, not only the elements of that knowledge which is essential to the ordinary intercourse and business of the humblest walks of civilized life, but also the rudiments of moral and political science; to provide for a more strict accountability of Directors, Examiners, and all other officers acting under the law; and for the appointment of a General Superintendent of Instruction."

In his first annual message, December 2, 1845, Governor Bartley said:

"The subject of education has been so often brought to the consideration of the Legislature, that I need scarcely do more than call your attention to former Executive communications. The importance of a liberal and thorough system of education can not be too highly estimated. The future character of our people, and the future destiny of our free institutions, are in no small degree dependent upon it. It is, perhaps, a matter of no little surprise, that hitherto subjects of mere temporary and comparatively inconsiderable interest, have occupied the attention of the Legislature, to the great neglect of a subject of such immense importance as this, not only to the great body of the people at the present period, but also to future generations. It is true that much has already been effected, by our present system of common schools. But even a superficial observer must admit that it is very deficient, and, for want of energy and efficiency, has utterly failed to meet the expectations of its friends. The example of other States has taught us, that it is within the power of the Legislature to adopt measures which will bring the system of common schools to a high degree of perfection.

"I respectfully commend to your consideration the expediency of establishing a State Board of Education, and the appointment of a competent and suitable person as a State Superintendent of Common Schools; and also, the adoption of measures that will give more energy and efficiency to the county and school district supervision, and management of the system. Among the liberal and enlightened persons in Ohio, who entertain enlarged views, and are eminent for their benevolence and their regard for the cause of education, can be easily found persons who will faithfully discharge all the duties which can appropriately be enjoined upon a State Board, without any charge for their services. In a matter, however, of such magnitude and enduring public interest, as that of improving the means of common school education, neither pecuniary considerations, nor party feelings, nor local or sectional views, should be permitted to interfere. While thousands and millions are annually expended to minister to the taste, vanity and pride of mankind, the appropriation of the comparatively small sum requisite for improving and perfecting the means of cultivating the intellect, and training the virtues of the youth of the State, can certainly be no obstacle in the way. By the means suggested, I humbly conceive that great public interest can be awakened among the people of the State on the subject of education, the necessary discipline adopted and put into practice, information on the subject of the best and most improved methods of instruction procured and furnished to every school district, the competency of instructors greatly improved, and the system brought to a high degree of perfection.

"The Miami University, at Oxford, and the Ohio University, at Athens, are institutions which have been in a manner placed under the guardianship of the State, and richly endowed by extensive donations of land from the General Government. The former is in a prosperous condition, and is accomplishing the useful purposes of its institution. But the Ohio University, on account of pecuniary embarrassment and other causes, not, perhaps, very well understood, has partially suspended operations. The difficulties in the management of this institution are of some standing; and for some years it has been failing to accomplish the high objects of its creation. It is not improbable that the difficulties which have blighted its prosperity, have had their origin in the fact, that the interests of the lessees of the college lands in the midst of which the University is located, have conflicted with the prosperity of the institution. I earnestly commend the condition of this institution to your consideration, in order that you may inquire into the causes of its failure, and devise a remedy for the evil."

In his last annual message, December 8, 1846, Governor Bartley said:

"The cause of education, combining both moral and intellectual culture, has been a matter of primary interest in Ohio since the first foundation of the State Government; and no subject can be of more lasting and vital importance to a free people. A system of education has been very properly looked upon as not merely an ornament of our political edifice, but also as the foundation on which it rests, and the rock of its future safety. The importance of the subject, however, and the zeal with which it has been espoused, have not fully overcome, as yet, the deep-rooted prejudices of some portions of our people against the measures necessary for the improvement of the system. It is to be lamented that our school system is yet so inefficient in its operations, and that our common school fund, that source of just pride to the people of the State, is expended every year with less than half the advantages to the youth of the State which ought to be derived from it. There is a general want of energy, efficiency, and discipline in the system. In a former communication I had occasion to urge upon the General Assembly the means deemed essential for the further improvement of this system of education, to which I respectfully refer you.

"The following statement shows the condition of the school fund for the year 1846:

Common school fund received, being proceeds of taxes	$69,582 39.
Auction duties and peddlers' licenses	5,812 11.
Tax on lawyers and physicians	4,909 21.
Banks, insurance, and bridge companies	28,844 15.
Surplus revenue interest, five per cent	91,268 81½.
Whole amount received during the year	$200,516 67½.
Balance in the treasury on the 15th Nov., 1846	31,775 56½.
Total	$232,292 24.
Balance of common school fund in the treasury, Nov. 15, 1846	32,292 24.
Paid out and distributed among the counties of the State	200,000 00.
Interest paid upon the Virginia and United States military school fund, Western Reserve school fund, ministerial fund, and other trust funds	88,450 00.
Total amount paid out of State treasury for support of schools and religious purposes, etc.	$288,450 79.

Governor Wm. Bebb, in his Inaugural Address of December 12, 1846, invoked the General Assembly as follows:

"Let her colleges, asylums, and schools continue to receive at your hands such consideration and support as their great importance demands, and I especially recommend the appointment of a Superintendent of Common Schools."

Governor Bebb, in his annual message of December 6, 1847, after stating that the disbursement by the State, for the support of common schools was $201,319.31, added:

"It is a matter of rejoicing to every lover of enlightenment and freedom, that the cause of education, in all its departments, was never more prosperous than during the past year. The common school system is firmly established in the habits and affections of the people, and though falling, in many things, short of the hopes of the patriot and philanthropist, fully partakes of the progressive spirit of the age, and will not, in the end, fall short of its high destiny, the universal diffusion of useful knowledge. It needs no recommendation of mine to command your cordial and continued support."

Governor Seabury Ford, in his Inaugural Address of January 22, 1849, remarked:

"History and example teach that a republican government, depending as it does upon the will of the people, can only be maintained where information and knowledge are generally diffused. Impressed with this truth, the framers of the Constitution declare in that instrument, that 'schools, and the means of instruction shall forever be encouraged by legislative provision.'

"Considering the age of our State, much has been already done in obedience to this requirement of the Constitution. But much more remains to be done before our system of education will become as perfect as its importance demands. In the administration of our school law, a greater number of persons are engaged than in the administration of any other law upon our statute book; it should, therefore, be plain, explicit, and easy to be understood. The acts now constituting our system of common schools, are scattered through the different volumes of the statutes; sections and parts of sections changed, altered, and repealed, until it is no easy matter, even for a skillful lawyer, to ascertain what the law is. I would, therefore, recommend to the Legislature a revision of these laws, so that the whole subject of common school education may be embraced in a single statute."

The foregoing suggestion was renewed by Governor Ford, in his annual message of December 31, 1849:

"It is unnecessary for me to present arguments to the Representatives of the people of the State of Ohio, to show the necessity of sustaining and encouraging a uniform and general system of common school education. Its paramount importance is uniformly felt and acknowledged by all our citizens. Upon the right education of the rising generation, and the universal dissemination of knowledge, mainly depends the permanent existence of our free institutions.

"It is nearly twelve years since the principal law now in force on that subject, was enacted. It, like most important laws, had its defects, and has since gone through such a variety of changes and amendments, that it requires more than ordinary skill to ascertain what the law is upon any point which may be brought in question. Many portions of it, and more particularly that portion relating to the raising of taxes for various purposes, and the supporting of schools beyond the means supplied by the various school funds, is a fruitful source of trouble in the districts, and a general cause of complaint against the system. I would recommend to your consideration, the propriety of a thorough revision of all the laws upon the subject."

In his last annual message, Governor Ford reiterated his recommendation of a revision of the school system:

"History and experience will attest the fact, that where science, general knowledge, and moral cultivation are most universally diffused among the people, there liberty is the most cherished, the rights of persons and property are the most safe. Virtue and religion, and whatever else can adorn society and render mankind prosperous and happy, are held most sacred. To extend and secure to coming generations the benefits of liberty and well regulated free institutions, it is necessary for the statesman to look with earnest care to the means of instruction for the youth of the country; for by them he may shape the destinies of the State and the nation for good or for evil through succeeding ages.

"An efficient system of common schools, thoroughly executed, is the only means of attaining this desirable object. Under our present law on this subject, much has been done; but the law is imperfect. The law which now professes to regulate this system has been in force for many years. It has undergone many alterations, is printed in many different volumes of the statutes, and is thus made difficult to be found, and still more difficult to be understood by the great majority of persons whose duty it professes to point out. That portion which relates to forming and altering districts from two or more townships, and the portion providing for fixing sites and levying taxes for building and repairing school-houses, and the supporting of schools beyond the means supplied by the various school funds, is obscure and of uncertain import, the cause of much serious complaint and trouble, and begets much dislike to the whole system. I would recommend to your consideration the propriety of a thorough revision of all the statutes on the subject, so as to make them plain to all, and effectual to the accomplishment of the objects desired."

The new Constitution took effect September 1, 1851. The provisions of that instrument, and the legislation under it, are reserved for consideration in a subsequent chapter.

CHAPTER XIV.

ABSTRACT OF SCHOOL LEGISLATION FROM 1831 TO 1851.

The struggle with the wilderness, and the exposures of a remote frontier, engrossed the first generation of the people of Ohio, although the incorporation of libraries and schools, from time to time, indicated the intellectual bias of the rising community; but the legislation of 1821, providing for the erection of school districts, the election of school committees, and local taxation for school purposes, and that of 1825, imposing a general tax of half a mill, which was raised to three-fourths of a mill in 1829, introduced a new era in the history of the State. During the next twenty years, legislation accumulated with great rapidity, often producing no slight degree of confusion. For the purpose of clearness, these laws will not be considered, except in connection with the general features of the system, as established by their provisions:

SUPERINTENDENCE.

The office of Superintendent of Common Schools was created by an act passed March 27, 1837—at first for the term of one year, but afterward by the act of March 7, 1838, for the term of five years. Samuel Lewis was the incumbent for three years when he declined further service, and by the act of March 23, 1840, the office was abolished, and its duties devolved upon the Secretary of State.

The duties of Superintendent, as fully defined in the law of 1838, were,

1. To collect and report annually to the Legislature, information upon the common schools of the State, especially the whole number of children and their attendance at school; the number, quality, and duration of schools; the qualifications of teachers, and the amount paid for their wages; the number of school-houses and the expenditure therefor; the sources and condition of school funds; and whatever else he might suppose the public interest required.

2. To ascertain and report the condition and value of all the school lands in the State, with the amount of the different school funds due to each township from lands or interest; and to secure the immediate location of school lands as authorized by an act of Congress, passed May 20, 1826, entitled "an act to appropriate lands for the support of schools in certain townships and fractional townships not before provided for."

3. To furnish suitable forms to school officers and teachers for all returns and registers required by law, and to deliver, on the 15th of December annually, to the Auditor of State, an enumeration of all the white children between the age of four and twenty-one years, to serve as the basis of the apportionment of school funds according to law.

4. To take an account of all funds and property given in any way for the support of education, and report the same annually to the Legislature; and for this purpose, to exercise all needful rights of visitation, and to summon the interposition of the Prosecuting Attorneys of the counties.

5. To publish bi-monthly during the year 1838–9, an official school journal, called the "Ohio Common School Director."

The salary of the Superintendent was fixed at $1,200, with the use of an office, etc., and the right to employ a clerk, when the business of his office required it.

The activity and zeal of Mr. Lewis, enforced by a remarkable eloquence, were very instrumental in arousing public interest in the cause of education. By his influence the sacrifice of section sixteen under the legislation of 1827, for the surrender of permanent leases, subject to re-valuation, was arrested, thereby saving to the school funds of the State, one hundred-fold the expense of the office of Superintendent. During his administration, a very efficient revision of the school law was effected, and the act of March 7, 1838, constituted the main body of legislation prior to the law of 1853.

The three annual reports of Mr. Lewis were an auspicious commencement of that series of documents. They were followed during the period in question, by the report of William Trevitt, Secretary of State, in 1841; by three reports from J. Sloane; by six from Samuel Galloway, and two from Henry W. King. Of these communications, that of Mr. Trevitt, among other valuable suggestions, urged a system of normal schools. Mr. Sloane advocated earnestly a system of school libraries, as did all his predecessors and successors; Mr. Galloway contributed a succession of powerful and eloquent appeals in behalf of all the educational reforms of the day; and Mr. King aided materially the revision of the school laws by his clear and laborious summons of the Legislature of the State in regard to schools. None of them failed, however, to urge the organization of an Executive Department of Public Instruction, distinct from the office of Secretary of State.

At one period the necessity for some further supervision was recognized by the General Assembly. An act for the appointment of a State Board of Public Instruction was passed on the 22d of March, 1850, but so late in the session, that no appointments were made by the Legislature at that session, as prescribed by the act; and hence it became inoperative. This act provided for a Board, to consist of five members, to hold their offices for one, two, three, four, and five years respectively; one to be styled the State Superintendent of Common Schools, to act as Chairman of the Board, reside, and keep his office at the seat of Government, and perform the usual duties of such an officer; the others to be styled district Superintendents, and one each year to act as State Superintendent by rotation. The Board was to hold semi-annual meetings; each district Superintendent to report to the State Superintendent annually, and the latter to report to the Legislature; the signature of the district Superintendent to be necessary to give validity to certificates of all teachers in his district; each teacher to pay to the county Board of Examiners one dollar on receiving his certificate, which certificate entitled him to teach in any county of the State for the period named therein, and for the same period to receive the "Ohio School Teacher," (a monthly paper to be published at Columbus, by the State Board,) and attend Teachers' Institutes, and normal classes, all free of charge. The fund thus raised was to pay the salaries and expenses of the Board; and to that end the Clerk of each county Board of Examiners was required to pay over the whole amount received from teachers, at the end of the year, to the district Superintendent, and forward receipt therefor to the Treasurer of State; but in no event were these salaries and expenses to be a charge on the State treasury.

Although no effort was made to render this system efficient, as a legislative enactment, yet it is very apparent that the Ohio State Teachers' Association, with its "Journal of Education," and very effective organization, is the practical sequel of the foregoing proposition.

TAXATION FOR THE SUPPORT OF SCHOOLS.

By the act of 1821, each district determined its own taxation for school purposes; but the law of 1825 contained the first uniform rule on this subject. The county Commissioners were directed to levy half a mill on the dollar "to be appropriated for the use of common schools in their respective counties." This assessment fluctuated under successive acts as follows: In 1829, raised to three-fourths of a mill; in 1831, power given to county Commissioners, at their option, to add one-fourth of a mill; in 1834, raised one mill, and an additional half of a mill at the option of the county Commissioners; in 1836, raised to one and a half mills, with an additional half mill, at the option of the Commissioners, or not exceeding a mill and a half by a vote of a township, in case the Commissioners refused to levy half a mill; in 1838, raised to two mills; in 1839, discretion given to county Commissioners to reduce from two mills to one; in 1847, reduced to two-fifths of a mill; in 1848, the county Commissioners authorized, but not required, to levy one mill; while in 1851, the Commissioners were required, not merely authorized, to levy a county school tax of *not less* than one mill. This was the state of the law when, by the act of 1853, the county taxation for schools was superseded entirely by a State levy of two mills, since reduced to a mill and a half on the dollar valuation.

STATE COMMON SCHOOL FUND.

By the act of March 2, 1831, as has already been stated, the net proceeds from the sales of salt lands, and all donations, legacies, and devises to that object, were "constituted a fund for the support of common schools, to belong in common to the people of the State," the interest thereon to be funded until 1835, and the income then distributed to the counties in proportion to the number of white male inhabitants above the age of twenty-one years.

The act of March 7, 1838, established a State common school fund "consisting of the interest on the surplus revenue at five per centum, the interest on the proceeds of salt lands, the revenue from banks, insurance and bridge companies, and other funds, to be annually provided by the State, to the amount of two hundred thousand dollars;" and directed its annual distribution to the counties "according to the number of white youths (unmarried) between the ages of four and twenty years." The above amount was reduced, March 7, 1842, to $150,000, and raised, March 24, 1851, to $300,000.

By the act last named, the basis of the fund was slightly

modified. In 1843, the surplus revenue had been pledged to the payment of a canal stock, and only the balance after that payment was pledged to schools. In addition to the above sources of revenue, (salt lands, etc.,) the act of 1851 added "all moneys paid into the State treasury for licenses to peddlers, for auction duties, and for taxes upon lawyers and physicians."

At present, the State common school fund for general distribution, is defined by the act of 1853, which repealed the above provisions, leaving these sources of revenue to other disposition. As a substitute therefor, as well as for the county levy already described, the present school law directs a tax of a mill and a half for distribution to the counties, and thence to the townships, in proportion to the number of youths between the ages of five and twenty-one; but authorizes a township tax not exceeding two mills, in the discretion of Boards of Education, to prolong the schools after the State fund is exhausted.

SCHOOL-HOUSE STRUCTURES.

The legislation in this behalf is greatly diversified, and has resulted in an investment, estimated by the State School Commissioner, in 1855, at $3,090,306. In 1821, two-thirds of the householders in any district established under the act of that year, were authorized to instruct the School Committee of the district, to purchase a site and erect a school-house, by means of a district tax, "not exceeding, in any one year, one-half of the amount of taxes which might, by law, have been levied for State or county purposes."

By the act of 1825, the householders or inhabitants of a district, provided one-third of all the householders of said district were present, were empowered to "designate and determine upon the site of a school-house, and to provide means for building the same."

In 1831, the provisions on this subject became quite complicated. If the number of householders in a district did not exceed thirty, one-third of their number, otherwise, ten householders, was considered a quorum; a meeting to determine whether a tax should be levied for erecting, repairing, or furnishing a school-house, or improving a school-house lot, was required to be special, after thirty days' notice; and at such meeting, all residents liable to taxation, were allowed to vote, but no such tax could be assessed, except by a vote of three-fifths of those present. It was further provided, that the amount of such tax should not exceed fifty dollars in any one year, unless at least one-third of the property subject to taxation within the district, was owned by persons residing therein; and in case one-third or more, but less than half, was thus owned, then not to exceed $100; if one-half, but less than two-thirds, not to exceed $150; but such tax in no case should exceed $250 in one year. Prior to the assessment of a tax, the district meeting must agree upon and designate a site; land lying more than three miles from the school-house was exempted from taxation therefor; nor could the land of a non-resident proprietor, once taxed for school-house construction, be again taxed for such a purpose within three years. The tax, though assessed by the county Auditor, was collected by the district Treasurer.

The act of 1834 repeated these provisions, except that it was silent upon what constituted a quorum; the notice for a special district meeting was to be twenty days instead of thirty, and the maximum of school-house tax was raised from $250 to $275 in any one year.

In 1836, the assent of two-thirds, not three-fifths, of those present, was made requisite, and the maximum of school-house tax was fixed at $300.

The elaborate school act of 1838 changed materially the law regulating school-house construction. At the annual district meeting, on the third Friday of September, or at a special meeting after twenty days' notice, stating an intention to propose a school-house tax, *a majority* of the voters present, being householders, were authorized to "determine by vote, upon the erection and purchase of a school-house, or the purchase of a lot or lots, on which to erect such house, and how much money [should] be raised for such purchase, and the purchase of fuel, and for building, repairing, or furnishing any school-house or school-houses in their district." The manner of collection was unchanged.

The Directors were also authorized to sell or exchange a school-house or site, and re-invest the proceeds in a new site or structure.

Under the act of 1853, the power of taxation for school-house construction, is vested in Boards of Education, and is unrestricted.

LOCAL SCHOOL OFFICERS.

The subdivision of a township into districts, under the former system, was the duty of the township Trustees. Maps of the same were deposited with the township Clerk and county Auditor. Alterations might be made at an annual meeting, but public notice of the contemplated change, thirty days previously, and posted in three public places, was requisite, together with new maps.

Three Directors were annually chosen in each district, who appointed from their own number a Clerk, who was also Treasurer. The Directors were a body corporate, capable of suing and being sued; and of receiving any gift, grant or devise, for the use of the district. In them was vested the title and control of the school-house; they might divide their district into sub-districts; select sites for school-houses, and purchase the same; repair and keep in order the school-houses; provide fuel for the schools, and for this purpose assess a tax not exceeding ten dollars; superintend the construction of school-houses, and furnish the same, when duly authorized; establish schools; employ teachers; make all needful rules and regulations; and report to the annual district meeting an account of their official proceedings for the preceding year, showing the amount of school funds apportioned to the district, and how it had been expended; how many schools had been taught, for what time, and the amount of the salaries paid to the teachers; the number of pupils in each school; the branches taught; the amount of money raised by district tax, for purchasing lots, building or repairing school-houses, or any other purpose; with an account of all the disbursements.

The township Clerk was required to keep copies of all district maps, and deposit them with the county Auditor; approve bonds of district Treasurers; be township Superintendent; return to county Auditor annually, by November 15th, an enumeration of youths; fill vacancies in the Board of School Directors, and where no elections were held, appoint Directors; make and transmit to county Auditor, annual abstracts of statistics returned by districts; visit the schools, and estimate expense of supporting them six months; post notices for levying township school tax, to defray that expense; and report the vote of the township to the county Auditor; and be responsible for all losses sustained by the township by reason of his neglect of duty.

Township Treasurers were treasurers of the school fund, under bond, etc.; they received and paid out all school moneys on the order of the Directors; annually, in December, they settled with the county Auditor; they sued for all moneys belonging to the several districts in their townships, in the name of the State of Ohio; and were allowed fees for their services by township Trustees.

The county Auditor gave a general direction to the collection of taxes for school purposes; was county Superintendent; made annual apportionments of school moneys to the districts; collected all fines and other funds applicable to school purposes; and made an annual report of all information received at his office, to the State Superintendent.

The above outline was slightly modified by an act which was passed March 24, 1851, and remained in force until repealed in 1853. It directed the election of a district Treasurer and Clerk; authorized the School Directors to levy a tax of fifty dollars for necessary repairs, fuel, etc.; permitted the purchase of a district library with the assent of a district meeting; and very clearly digested the mass of existing laws, in respect to local school officers.

TOWNSHIP TAXATION.

A very important duty of the township Clerk, as Superintendent of Common Schools, deserves to be separated from the routine of his ministerial functions. He was required to make an annual estimate of the amount of money required in his township, in addition to the State and county taxation, to provide at least six months' good tuition to all the white unmarried youth in the township, during the year ensuing; and to cause public notice to be given of the amount required, by posting the same in writing on the door of every common schoolhouse in the township, and at the usual place of holding the election, at least fifteen days before the annual township election, at which the electors proceeded to vote for "school tax," or "no school tax." If affirmatively, the amount was certified to the county Auditor, and added to the current taxation of the township.

SCHOOL EXAMINERS.

A county system for the examination and certification of teachers, has generally existed in Ohio, although, as has been seen, the number of Examiners appointed by the Court of Common Pleas, has fluctuated. The act of 1825 provided for the appointment of three Examiners for the term of one year, and enumerated as the branches of study in common schools, "Reading, Writing, Arithmetic, and other necessary branches of a common education." The act of February 10, 1829, directed the appointment by the *Clerk* of Common Pleas, of a suitable number of persons, not less than five, nor more than the number of townships in the county, to be called Examiners of Common Schools, and to serve for two years. In 1830, the Court resumed the appointment—otherwise the provision was as last above. In 1834, the number of Examiners was limited to five; but it was made the duty of the Board of County Examiners to appoint one School Examiner in each township, to examine female teachers only;

and in no case was a certificate to be given, unless the candidate was qualified to teach Reading, Writing, and Arithmetic, and sustained a good moral character.

The act of 1836 directed the election of three Examiners in each township; and on failure to elect, the Court of Common Pleas might appoint; but in 1838 the appointment of three county Examiners, for the term of three years, was again conferred upon the Court of Common Pleas.

The act of 1853 only differs from the law of 1838 in the standard of qualifications. Every candidate must be found qualified to teach "Orthography, Reading, Writing, Arithmetic, Geography, and English Grammar." The appointment of Examiners is by the Probate Judge.

COUNTY SUPERINTENDENTS.

Although county Auditors were and are, *ex officio*, county Superintendents, yet reference is here made to an act, passed February 8, 1847, which authorized county Commissioners to create the separate office of Superintendent of Common Schools within their jurisdiction. In that event, the Clerks of the school districts in the county, were constituted a body of electors, and might select said Superintendent, whose duties were as follows: To act as *ex officio* Chairman of the Board of School Examiners, his signature being made necessary to the validity of every certificate; to renew, at his discretion, the certificates of teachers who had been personally examined by the Board, and with the concurrence of one of the said Board of School Examiners, to annul the certificate of any teacher who might prove incompetent in respect to learning, ability to teach, or moral character; to visit and examine all the schools in the county, and keep a full record of such visits and examinations; to meet and address the people in the several school districts and townships, on the subject of education; to encourage the formation of township and county educational societies, and teachers' associations; and to transmit to the State Superintendent, at Columbus, an abstract of his transactions, and a statistical report, similar to that required from the county Auditor. His compensation was at the option of the county Commissioners. The law, at first local, was afterward extended over the whole State; but only one county, Ashtabula, established the office in question. That single experiment was eminently successful.

SPECIAL SCHOOL DISTRICTS.

The necessity for some special organization of schools in populous towns and villages, was early apparent. Cincinnati first illustrated this necessity and secured the requisite legislation. Since 1830–1, the public schools of that city have been managed by three bodies having distinct functions, to-wit: a Board of Trustees, a Board of Examiners, and a corps of teachers.

1. The Board of Trustees are elected by the people at the annual municipal elections, two for each ward, and have charge exclusively of what may be termed the business arrangements of the schools. Their duties are to make the necessary appropriations of money; to furnish, repair, and arrange the buildings; to appoint teachers, and make rules for their government, with all such powers as are incidental to the immediate government of the schools.

2. The Board of Examiners are appointed by the city Council, are seven in number, and their duties are to *examine* the teachers in respect to their qualifications. Without their certificate, no teacher can be appointed. To perform this duty with due regard to the various capacities of the teachers, the Board of Examiners have divided their certificates into, first, that he is qualified as *male principal;* second, that he is qualified as *male assistant;* third, that she is qualified as *female principal;* and fourth, that she is qualified as *female assistant.*

3. The body of teachers were two hundred and twenty-three in number—one hundred and sixty-eight females, fifty-five males—during the year ending June 30, 1855.

The officers of the Board of Trustees consist of a President, Vice-President, Corresponding Secretary, Superintendent of

Instruction, and Clerk and Librarian. Connected with the system, are two high schools—founded upon the Hughes and Woodward endowments—which are under the special charge of the Union Board of High Schools, composed of seven Hughes and Woodward Trustees, and six delegates from the General Board. Next below is an intermediate school, while the primary department consists of twenty district, sub-district, and asylum schools, and seven night schools. The report for 1855 exhibits 38,446 white youth of school age, by the census, of whom 17,444 are enrolled in the schools; 10,537 in average attendance; 8,920 in actual daily attendance, and 1,617, average daily absence. During the same year, the expenditure for the maintenance of all the schools, exclusive of expenditure for real estate and buildings, was $120,878.29 for an average attendance of 10,537 pupils, or at the rate of $11.47 per pupil. The cost of the high schools was $13,077.77 for an average attendance of* three hundred and thirty-two pupils, or at the rate of $39.39 per pupil.

The example of Cincinnati was contagious, and the act of February 8, 1847, "for the support and regulation of common schools, in the town of Akron," became the model for much subsequent legislation. It authorized the electors of Akron, to elect a Board of Education, consisting of six Directors, two of them retiring annually, and their places supplied at the spring election for the term of three years, and until their successors were elected and qualified. This Board were clothed with the usual school jurisdiction; their officers were a President, Secretary, and Treasurer, chosen from their own number; four constituted a quorum; special meetings might be called by the President, or by any two members of the Board, or giving two days' notice of time and place, but at no special meeting, unless all the Directors were present, could any resolution in relation to sites for school-houses, or any financial resolution or order, be passed, without two days'

---

* See Appendix, "School Laws in Force," chapter XXI, for the Cincinnati School Act.

notice, announcing the subject or subjects proposed to be acted upon; they were required to establish within the corporate limits of Akron, (which was constituted one school district,) six or more primary schools for teaching the rudiments of an English education, and also a central Grammar school, the latter being open to pupils who should pass a prescribed examination and were guilty of no misconduct; and they were directed, within thirty days after their organization, to report to the town Council the necessary expense of building suitable houses, and supporting schools therein for a year, and annually thereafter, in the report of their transactions, also required by the act, to specify "the amount of money necessary to be raised by taxation, to defray the expenses of said school system for the current year." No discretion was vested in the town Council, except to make the levy accordingly; although an act, passed in 1848, limited the amount of tax "to defray the expense of the school system" to four mills on the dollar, in any one year.*

The town Council were required to appoint three School Examiners, for a term of three years, who, in giving certificates, were instructed to name the branches a candidate was qualified to teach. The Examiners were made Inspectors and Visitors of schools, and were directed to report semi-annually to the town Council, and the Board of Education.

In 1848, any incorporated town or city was authorized to adopt the provisions of the Akron Law, on the petition of two-thirds of the electors; and in 1849, an act was passed, for the better regulation of the public schools in cities, towns, etc., which adopted the leading provisions of the Akron act, except that all questions of expenditure for school-house construction were submitted to a majority vote in town meeting; and School Examiners were appointed by the Board of Education. Under the act last named, it was the duty of the

---

* See Appendix, "School Laws in Force," chapter VIII, for the power in the authorities of any "municipal corporation" to borrow money for school-house purposes, passed March 11, 1853.

Board to provide, by taxation, the means of supporting schools not less than thirty-six, nor more than forty-four weeks in a year; but no tax for that purpose could exceed four mills on the dollar. Rate-bills, if other means of supporting schools the prescribed period proved insufficient, might be collected; but no scholar could be excluded from school for inability to pay the same. Provision was made for submitting the question, whether the Special School District system should be adopted, to a vote of the people of any town or city, in which six resident freeholders summoned a public meeting, pursuant to the act; and if the same was adopted, the Board of Education thereby created, were not limited to the organization of primary schools and a Grammar school, but might grade the schools at their discretion.

In the following year, March 13, 1850, the act last above recited was extended to incorporated townships, which should adopt the same by popular vote, provided the population of said township exceeded five hundred.

These acts are expressly continued in force by section sixty-seven of the school law of 1853, and constitute a most important department of the school administration of the State. Any city, town, or incorporated village, organized under any of these acts, may, however, conform to similar provisions in the act of 1853, (sections thirty-two to thirty-five,) for the organization of special school districts. *

GERMAN AND ENGLISH SCHOOLS.

By the act of March 16, 1839, amended in 1842, pupils might attend a German school, if taught by a teacher duly qualified, and be entitled to receive from the local Directors an order for a proportionate share of the school money. This was the first encouragement of such schools, and by the act of 1853, Boards of Education "may provide for German schools for the instruction of such youth as may desire to

* See Appendix, "School Acts in Force," chapters II to IX inclusive, for acts establishing and regulating special school districts.

study the German language, or the German and English languages together." The School Report of the Cincinnati Trustees, for 1855, observes that the German schools of that city work advantageously, and in entire harmony and unison with other parts of the general system. They are of two grades, junior and senior. The State School Commissioner reports fifty-five schools of this character in the State.

SCHOOLS FOR COLORED CHILDREN.

Prior to 1849, no provision was made for the education of this class of youth, unless an exemption from taxation for school purposes can be so regarded. But by the acts of February 24, 1848, and February 10, 1849, township Trustees, or the school authorities of cities, etc., were authorized to establish separate school districts for colored persons, within which adult male colored tax-payers might meet and choose Directors, in whom was vested the customary school jurisdiction. The property of colored tax-payers was alone chargeable for the support of these schools; but the powers and duties of township, county, and State officers extended equally to schools for colored children, as to other schools.

By the act of 1853, the foregoing provision was repealed. Colored youth are required to be annually enumerated, but returned separately. The property of colored tax-payers is no longer exempt from taxation; and section thirty-one provides that Boards of Education are authorized and required to establish, within their respective jurisdictions, one or more separate schools for colored children, when the whole enumeration exceeds thirty; so as to afford them, as far as practicable under all the circumstances, the advantages and privileges of a common school education. But in case the average number of colored children in attendance shall be less than fifteen for any one month, the school is to be discontinued for any period not exceeding six months; but if the number is less than fifteen, then the money raised on the number of colored children shall be applied in the best discretion of the township Board, for the education of such colored children.

Mr. Commissioner Barney reported eighty-eight schools for colored youth, in the year 1855.*

UNITED STATES SURPLUS REVENUE FUND.

Although this fund has ceased to be a resource for schools, yet the fact that such was the case for several years, would suggest a review of that appropriation, and its subsequent diversion to other purposes.

Congress, in 1836, passed an act directing the deposit with the States, in proportion to their respective representations in the Senate and House of Representatives, of the revenue which might be in the treasury of the United States on the first day of January, 1837, reserving the sum of five millions of dollars. The sum appropriated to Ohio, upon the terms and conditions contained in the act, was $2,007,260.34, and at the legislative session of 1836–7, an act was passed, providing for its deposit and investment in the counties according to their population of "white male inhabitants over the age of twenty-one years," and that "the net annual income thereof should be applied to the support and encouragement of common schools within the State," and for other purposes designated in the act. A Board of Fund Commissioners, appointed by the county Commissioners, were authorized to make loans at six per cent. in certain cases, to the county or State, and to individuals, on real estate securities, at an interest not exceeding seven, or less than six per cent., returning the income of these loans annually to the county Treasurer, who was required by section sixteen, to "pay over to or account with the State Treasurer, as for so much money received for his proper county for school purposes, such sum as would be equal to five per cent. on the amount received by such county." Section seventeen directed that the funds thus received should be paid out of the State treasury to the counties entitled to receive the same, as other

---

* See Appendix, "School Acts in Force," chapter XXI, section 17, for provisions for the above schools in Cincinnati.

school money was paid to the respective counties. By another act, passed March 19, 1838, the Fund Commissioners were authorized to retain whatever income should exist, after making the annual payment of five per cent. to the State school fund, and invest the same in profitable stocks or mortgages, and to fund annually the dividends and interests of the investment so made to accumulate, as a permanent fund for the support of schools, or for the promotion of internal improvements, or for the building of academies in their counties. The fund last named, so far as permanently invested by the counties, may now be appropriated (see acts of February 8, 1847, and February 16, 1849, *Swan's Revised Statutes*, p. 963, note *a*) to the encouragement of Teachers' Institutes.

Such an application of the United States revenue deposit corresponded not only with the recommendation of Governor Lucas, in his message of December 6, 1836, but with the legislation of all the States distinguished for systems of public instruction. New York, Michigan, Wisconsin, and other States, have not disturbed these provisions, but Ohio, by the act of March 13, 1843, pledged and appropriated the amount of surplus revenue received from the United States, and the proceeds of canal lands not otherwise pledged, for the redemption of the principal, after the year 1851, of a loan of one million five hundred thousand dollars, thereby authorized and applied to the payment of all sums due to the contractors on the public works of the State. By the act of 1843, and subsequent statutes, provision was made for the collection from the counties before 1850 (or at the utmost, 1852,) of the surplus revenue, although section 11 postponed the diversion of the income of five per cent. from the school fund until 1850. After the 1st of January, 1850, however, in the language of the fifth section, the surplus revenue was "held and appropriated to the redemption of the bonds issued under the provisions of this act, that were unredeemed at the time."

The original dedication of this fund to the encouragement and support of schools, was only modified by the obligation to redeem the principal of the seven per cent. stock issued in 1843, and redeemable in 1851; and even that obligation was shared in some degree by the lands which the General Government had donated to aid the public works of the State. This fact was recognized by the General Assembly, when, in the revision of the school law in 1851, the balance of the surplus revenue, after payment of the loan of 1843, was directed to be invested in the stocks of the State, and the proceeds appropriated to the State common school fund of $300,000, for which that act provided, in addition to a peremptory county tax of one mill; but two years thereafter, or simultaneously with the passage of the present school law, an act was passed creating a sinking fund for the payment of the principal and interest of the public debt of Ohio, which (beside the constitutional appropriation and some other resources,) devotes "*the principal and proceeds of surplus revenue loans to counties*," to the sinking fund. This disposition of the surplus revenue fund yet continues.

TEACHERS' INSTITUTES.

These voluntary associations of teachers for the purpose of mutual instruction, have been productive of great benefits to the school interests of the State; but hitherto have been very slightly encouraged by legislation.

Soon after the first introduction of Teachers' Institutes, the General Assembly became satisfied of the beneficial influence of such sessions, and a law was passed for their encouragement—at first, in a few northern counties, but now made general in its provisions—which authorizes appropriations by the county authorities in certain cases. The fund first specified for these aids, was that portion of the interest from the surplus revenue, which the counties were allowed to retain and invest permanently for certain local uses, namely: the difference, after payment of expenses, between the five per cent. required to be remitted to the State treasury, and the six or seven per cent. which was reserved on the loans—an average of at least one per cent., and which was, in some instances, so judiciously invested as to yield a good income.

The following is a brief synopsis of the legislation on this subject: By the statutes of February 8, 1847, February 24, 1848, and February 16, 1849, it is provided, that on the application of forty teachers, resident in a county, and proposing to organize a Teachers' Institute, county Commissioners *may* ("it shall be lawful for," etc.,) appropriate the avails of the fund last mentioned, or any part thereof, "for the purposes of such association." Section 2, of the act of 1847, provides that "the moneys so appropriated shall, upon the order of the county Auditor, be paid over and expended by the Board of School Examiners of the proper county; the one-half thereof, at least, to the payment of suitable persons as instructors and lecturers to such associations, and the balance thereof (in the language of the amendatory act of Feb. 24, 1848,) to the purchase and support of suitable common school libraries, for the several common school districts in the several counties in this State, that may be in the possession of the fund named in the first section of said act." The act of 1849 authorizes the county Commissioners to appropriate $100, when the special fund above named is insufficient, or does not exist, provided the county Examiners concur in the petition of the prescribed number of teachers, and the "said teachers shall have first raised and paid over, or secured to be paid over, to said Board of School Examiners, for the purposes and benefit of such association, at least one-half of the sum for which they shall so petition the county Auditor, and which payment, or security for payment, as aforesaid, shall be made known to said Auditor, by the receipt, or certificate, in writing, of said Board of School Examiners."

A recognition of the utility of Teachers' Institutes occurs in the act of 1853, which enjoins upon the State Commissioner of Common Schools the duty of "superintending and encouraging Teachers' Institutes," and requires his annual report to contain "a statement of the number of Teachers' Institutes, and the number of teachers attending them."

A SYNOPSIS OF INCIDENTAL SCHOOL REVENUES, FINES, SWAMP LANDS, ETC.

The State Commissioner compiled, in 1854, the numerous legislative provisions imposing fines to be paid for the use of schools. If an account of these was rendered in the different counties and townships, as the Commissioner well remarked, a considerable amount of arrearages might be ascertained:

"The following is a list of the fines, which the different acts, whose dates are given, direct to be paid into the county treasuries for the use of schools:

"1. One dollar for the importation or sale of salt, without legal inspection at Cincinnati, Portsmouth, or Cleveland—February 3, 1840. 2. Not exceeding five hundred dollars for procuring abortion—February 27, 1834. 3. One hundred dollars by county Treasurer for failing to make annual settlement with State Treasurer—January 3, 1843. 4. Not exceeding one hundred dollars for wantonly or maliciously opening enclosures—February 28, 1846. 5. Five dollars for every hundred pounds of fish, except shad, mackerel, or herring, sold without inspection—March 9, 1831. 6. Five to fifty dollars for failing to bury or burn the offal of fish, taken in the waters of this State, to the amount of one or more barrels—March 9, 1831. 7. Five hundred dollars for keeping gambling instruments, aiding in gambling, or becoming a common gambler—January 17, 1846. 8. Not exceeding fifty dollars by county Inspectors for receiving more than their prescribed fees, or buying condemned articles—March 9, 1821. 9. Not exceeding ten dollars for obstructing the navigation of the Muskingum river—March 1, 1834. 10. Not exceeding ten thousand dollars by any officer or corporation, who is in contempt for disregarding orders of court in *quo warranto* procedure—March 17, 1838. 11. Fifty cents by manufacturers of salt for each barrel not drained and packed according to law—April 30, 1852. 12. One-half of amount received by county Auditors (the other half applied to agricultural fund by act of February 8, 1847) for licenses of 'any traveling show'—(further defined as 'any natural or artificial curiosity or exhibition of horsemanship, in a circus or otherwise, for any price, gain, or reward')—at not less than twenty nor more than fifty dollars; also, one-half of fines of one hundred dollars for exhibiting without such license; Auditor to apportion the above proceeds to the respective school districts (now the townships and special districts) according to the number of youth therein—February 28, 1831, amended by act of February 8, 1847. 13. The amount of any debt or demand upon which any bank shall have taken illegal interest, less the per centage of the Prosecuting Attorney, provided the debtor has not commenced proceedings within six months from the transaction—March 19, 1850.

"The fines payable to township Treasurers for the use of schools, are as follows:

"1. Five to fifty dollars for unauthorized traffic near camp meetings—March 26, 1841. 2. Ten dollars for allowing Canada thistles to mature on defendant's land, and twenty dollars for knowingly vending any grass or other seed, in which there is any seed of the Canada thistle—March 6, 1844. 3. Divers penalties under the act to restrain immoral practices, passed February 17, 1834, namely: one to five dollars for Sabbath breaking; five dollars for selling spiritous liquors on Sunday; not exceeding twenty dollars for disturbing religious meetings; twenty-five cents to one dollar for each offense, 'if any person of the age of fourteen years or upward shall profanely curse or damn, or profanely swear by the name of God, Jesus Christ, or the Holy Ghost;' fifty cents to five dollars for exciting disturbance at a public meeting; fifty cents to five dollars for playing bullets, running horses, or shooting at a target in towns or villages; ten to one hundred dollars by any keeper of a public house, or retailer of spiritous liquors, who is connected with a nine-pin alley; ten dollars 'if any persons shall exhibit any puppet show, wire-dancing, or tumbling, jugglery, or sleight of hand, within this State, and shall ask and receive any money or other property for exhibiting the same;' ten dollars for defacing any advertisement set up by authority of law; not exceeding one hundred dollars for bull or bear-baiting and other torture of animals; not exceeding twenty dollars for any agency in 'the game commonly called cock-fighting;' one to five dollars 'if two or more persons shall run a match horse race or races, in any public road in common use, for the purpose of trying the speed of their horses; and if any Justice of the Peace fail to pay over the above fines for immoral practices, he shall forfeit double amounts. 4. Five to fifty dollars for firing cannon or exploding more than five ounces avoirdupois of gunpowder on public streets or highways, except in certain cases—February 10, 1845. 5. One dollar for each muskrat killed between May 1 and October 15, 'provided that nothing in this act contained shall be construed to prevent any person from destroying muskrats where the same shall be injurious to works of a public or private nature'—'an act to protect the fur trade,' passed January 18, 1830. 6. Fifty dollars for unlicensed peddling—February 7, 1848. 7. Five to fifty dollars by manufacturers who compel any women or children under eighteen years of age, or permit any child under fourteen years, to labor more than ten hours in any one day—March 19, 1852. 8. Twenty-five cents to one dollar by owner of 'habitually breachy or unruly animals, after due notice by township Trustees, payable to 'the treasury of the school district in which defendant resides' (now the township treasury)—January 17, 1840. 9. Five to twenty-five dollars by any tavern-keeper, grocery-keeper, or other person, for harboring any intoxicated Indian or Indians, 'for the use of the school district'—March 20, 1840.

"By act of March 14, 1853, personal property escheated to the State is appropriated to common schools.

"In respect to the swamp lands granted by the General Government to the Western States, by the act of September 28, 1850, the allotment to Ohio was only $25{,}720\frac{7}{100}$ acres, while Indiana receives $1{,}286{,}827\frac{44}{100}$ acres. This contrast proves the extent to which Ohio lands are susceptible of cultivation, or that the designation of "swamp lands" has not been applied with much precision, or governed by a uniform rule.

"The legislation by the State of Ohio assumes that these lands are in a condition unsuitable for tillage, and deleterious to health, and the acts of March 2, 1853, and April 25, 1854, offer inducements for promptly reclaiming them. The Auditors of the counties in which they are situated, are required to advertise for proposals to drain and reclaim such lands, and award the contract of drainage and reclamation to the lowest responsible bidder. A previous section provides for the appraisement of the lands *before they have been drained and reclaimed*, and the only means set apart by the act to pay for such drainage consists of 'said lands lying in said county at the appraised value thereof.' The first eight sections of the act of 1853 contemplate that, after the lands are reclaimed, they may be taken at the appraised value before reclamation to the amount of the contractor's bid; and then section nine adds, 'that if after the said swamp or overflowed lands of this State, lying within any county, be drained or reclaimed as herein provided, there shall remain any of the said lands undisposed of, it shall be the duty of the county Commissioners of such county to appraise the same, and make returns of such appraisal as aforesaid; upon the filing of such returns in his office, the county Auditor is hereby authorized to sell the said lands at the appraised value thereof to any applicant therefor, who will make an oath or affirmation that it is his intention to improve the same and make the same a permanent residence, or that the same adjoin to and are necessary to the proper improvement of lands then owned and improved by such applicant, which said oath or affirmation the said county Auditor is hereby authorized to administer; and in all cases of sales, as prescribed in this section, the said county Auditor shall receipt to the purchaser for the amount of money received, and describe therein the lands sold, which said receipt, upon presentation and delivery to the Governor, shall entitle the purchaser to a patent for such land: *Provided*, that such of said swamp or overflowed lands as are capable of being drained or reclaimed, may be sold without the oath or affirmation hereinbefore required.'

"Two years is the period fixed for the performance of these contracts of drainage, and when companies have been formed for the purpose, the work done by them may be estimated in money, and lands conveyed at the appraised value. Section ten finally provides 'that all moneys received by said county Auditor upon all sales as aforesaid, shall be paid into the county Treasury of the county in which the lands sold are situated, to reimburse the county for the expenditures of draining and reclaiming said swamp or overflowed lands, *and the residue, if any there be, shall be paid by said county Treasurers into the State treasury for the use of schools.*' Under these circumstances, it would be unreasonable to expect any material addition to the resources of schools from a reversionary interest so contingent."

CHAPTER XV.

CONSTITUTIONAL CONVENTION OF 1850–51.

Early in the session of the Ohio Constitutional Convention, which assembled in Columbus May 6, 1850, and closed its deliberations, after an adjournment to Cincinnati, on the 10th of March, 1851, the subject of education was entrusted to a Standing Committee, composed of the following delegates: Harmon Stidger, of Stark; Otway Curry, of Union; Samuel Quigley, of Columbiana; James W. Taylor, of Erie; Jacob J. Greene, of Defiance; A. G. Brown, of Athens; and John A. Smith, of Highland.

The attention of the Convention had been previously invited, by Mr. Stidger, to the consideration of the following resolutions:

"*Resolved*, That the Auditor of State be and is hereby requested to furnish for the use of this Convention, in addition to his report to the General Assembly of March 13, 1850, on the subject of the surplus revenue, full and distinct answers to the following questions:

"1. What per centum of the interest on sums originally deposited with the several counties, was applied to the use of common schools, and what was the aggregate amount of the school fund derived from that source?

"2. What amount of the surplus revenue, (if any,) has been repaid into the State treasury, since the date of the report referred to, and how much is now due from the counties severally?

"3. In what manner and to what purposes has the amount of the principal of surplus revenue, repaid to the State by the several counties, been applied?

"4. Whether the repayment of the principal of surplus revenue to the State, has in any wise diminished the common school fund? if so, how much?

"5. If a diminution of the school fund has been occasioned by the causes referred to, from what sources is it contemplated to raise means to preserve and keep up the amount of the school fund heretofore derived from the interest on surplus revenues?"

The resolution, when introduced, elicited a statement from Mr. Hawkins, as an additional point proper for inquiry, that $335,000 of surplus revenue recalled by the State, had been disbursed in the redemption of turnpike bonds, while, by the law of 1843, the fund was only pledged for the redemption of the seven per cent. bonds falling due in 1851, which were authorized by that law. No general discussion then followed, and the resolution was laid on the table, and ordered to be printed.

Subsequently the resolution was considered in Committee of the Whole, and the Convention declined to entertain it, the majority deeming the subject of the inquiry a matter of ordinary legislation, and not necessary to the proper adjustment of the article upon education. A permanent constitutional provision, in regard to the surplus revenue deposit, which, by its terms, might be withdrawn at any moment by the federal Government, although reported by the Committee on Education, did not receive the concurrence of the Convention.

On the 5th of July, (the fiftieth day of the Columbus session,) the following report was presented from the Standing Committee upon Education:

"SECTION 1. The General Assembly shall provide for the election, by the people, of a Superintendent of Common Schools, whose term of office, duties, and compensation, shall be prescribed by law; and shall provide for the election or appointment of such assistants, or other officers as may be found necessary, prescribe their duty, term of office, and compensation.

"SEC. 2. The General Assembly shall encourage, by suitable means, the promotion of moral, intellectual, scientific, and agricultural improvement.

"The proceeds of the sales of lands, that have been, or may hereafter be granted by the United States, for educational purposes, and all lands or other property given by individuals, for like purposes, together with the surplus revenue, deposited with this State by the United States, (until reclaimed,) shall be, and forever remain a permanent, irreducible fund; the interest and income therefrom shall be faithfully applied to the specific objects of the original grant, gift, or appropriation.

"SEC. 3. The General Assembly shall make such provision by taxation, and other means, (in addition to the income arising from the irreducible fund,) as will secure a thorough and efficient system of common schools, free to all the children in the State.

"SEC. 4. No religious sect, or party, shall ever have exclusive right to, or control of, any part of the common school funds of this State.

HARMON STIDGER,
SAMUEL QUIGLEY,
JAMES W. TAYLOR,
JACOB J. GREENE,
A. G. BROWN.

Mr. Curry submitted the following minority report:

"SECTION 1. Religion, morality, and knowledge, being essentially necessary to good government and the happiness of mankind, schools and the means of instruction shall forever be encouraged by legislative provision not inconsistent with the rights of conscience.

"SEC. 2. It shall be the duty of the General Assembly to provide, by law, that the principal of all funds arising from the sale of lands heretofore or hereafter granted or donated, from any quarter, for educational purposes, together with the principal which may be realized from donations of personal property and money for like purposes, and the surplus revenue deposited with this State by the United States, (until reclaimed,) shall be preserved inviolate and undiminished; and that the interest and income arising from such funds shall be faithfully applied to the object of the original gift or grant: *Provided*, the General Assembly may at their discretion, appropriate all or only a part of the proceeds of the surplus revenue to educational purposes.

"SEC. 3. The General Assembly shall provide for the election of a Superintendent of Schools and Seminaries of learning, under the care and patronage of the State. They may also provide for the election or appointment of such assistant Superintendents or other officers as may be necessary to carry into effect a thorough and uniform system of common school education; and they shall prescribe by law the terms of office, compensation, powers, and duties, of all officers elected or appointed under the authority of this section.

"SEC. 4. The General Assembly shall provide by law a system of common schools, and permanent means for the support thereof, by which a school shall be kept up in each school district in this State not less than six months in each year, and which shall be open to youth of all classes, under such regulations as may be prescribed by law: *Provided*, that black and mulatto youth shall not attend the schools for white youth, unless by common consent.

"SEC. 5. Provision shall be made by law for the establishment and support of as many normal institutes as the General Assembly may find to be necessary for the thorough instruction of professional teachers of the common schools of this State; and all persons applying to any of said institutes for admission and instruction, shall be required, before admission, to give such assurance as may be specified by law of their intention to devote themselves to teaching as a profession.

"SEC. 6. No religious sect or party shall ever have exclusive right to, or control of, any part of the common school fund, or of any of the schools, seminaries, or institutions of learning, under the care and patronage of this State.

OTWAY CURRY.

At the Cincinnati session the foregoing reports were fully discussed. Upon the various amendments offered, the following points were elicited, indicative of the temper of the body.

1. That it was inexpedient to limit the educational bounty of the State to white children, by any terms of direct exclusion; but how far colored children should be entitled to public instruction, was made a subject of unrestricted legislative cognizance.

2. Propositions to augment the State school fund to a sum which would produce a revenue of about a million of dollars, and to enjoin a minimum of six months' instruction, were not adopted—some apprehending that the people would not sustain such forward movements, while others believed that the Ohio school system would be even more progressive than its

most sanguine advocates in the Convention anticipated. The experience of a few years has fully vindicated the latter view.

3. An amendment, directing the organization of normal institutes, was lost by twenty to fifty-seven.

4. Even the clause establishing, in express terms, the office of Superintendent of Common Schools, was not retained in the final action of the Convention—the precise methods of superintendence being left to legislative discretion.

ARTICLE VI of the Constitution—upon "Education"—stands, therefore, in that instrument as follows:

"SECTION 1. The principal of all funds arising from the sale or other disposition of lands, or other property granted or intrusted to this State for educational and religious purposes, shall forever be preserved inviolate, and undiminished; and, the income arising therefrom, shall be faithfully applied to the specific objects of the original grants or appropriations.

"SEC. 2. The General Assembly shall make such provisions by taxation, or otherwise, as with the income arising from the school trust fund, will secure a thorough and efficient system of common schools throughout the State, but no religious or other sect or sects shall ever have any exclusive right to, or control of, any part of the school funds of this State."

The foregoing guaranties, indefinite as they are, have proved ample; and the legislative history of the State, since 1851, fully justifies the confidence of the Convention in the representatives of the people of Ohio.

CHAPTER XVI.

ORIGIN, PROGRESS, AND PROVISIONS OF THE ACT OF MARCH 14, 1853.

IT devolved upon the Senate of Ohio, at the first session of the General Assembly, to initiate the very important measure which is the topic of present consideration. The Standing

Committee of that legislative branch to which the subject of "common schools and school lands" was committed, consisted of Harvey Rice, of Cuyahoga, George Rex, of Wayne, and Alonzo Cushing, of Gallia. On the the 29th of March, 1852, they reported the Senate bill, No. 94, "to provide for the re-organization, supervision, and maintenance, of common schools." It reached its second reading, April 1st, after which it was committed to the Committee of the Whole, and made the order for the same day; but it was not reached in Committee until the 13th of April. Its discussion continued until the 15th, when the Committee rose, and the bill, with various amendments, was tabled for the residue of the session.

Its consideration was resumed almost immediately upon the re-assemblage of the Senate, at the adjourned session of 1852–3. After another elaborate discussion, in Committee of the Whole, from November 18th to December 6th, almost continuously, the bill was re-committed, with pending amendments, to the Standing Committee on Schools and School lands. The Committee were also instructed to state in the bill which they should report, "the school funds therein contemplated for the number of months enjoined to be taught annually." The Committee reported on the 12th of January, 1853; another discussion in Committee of the Whole occupied the Senate for three days, when the Senate proceeded to vote upon the numerous amendments which had accumulated during this protracted debate, upon every portion of the bill. The most important of these in which the Senate concurred, was the organization of every township as a single district, under the general supervision of a Board of Education, and a division of the district so established, as a school corporation, into sub-districts, each under the local administration of three local Directors, one of whom, when appointed Clerk, was thereby qualified and authorized to represent the sub-district in the central Board of Education.

The following propositions did not command a majority: 1. To pass the act contingently upon its approval, by a popular vote; 2. To require the establishment of schools for colored youth in all cases, when that class were denied admission to the schools; 3. To give a corporate character, with the capacity of suing and being sued, and holding the title of school property, to the local Directors in each sub-district; 4. And to limit the aggregate of State taxes levied and assessed under the provisions of the bill, to two mills on the dollar. The bill was ordered to be engrossed for its third reading four days thereafter, on January 20th, and on the 24th passed the Senate with but two dissenting voices—yeas 22; nays 2.

The House Committee upon Common Schools and School Lands, to whom the Senate bill was committed, after a brief consideration in Committee of the Whole, consisted of S. Plumb, of Ashtabula, C. K. Ward, of Crawford, B. H. Alexander, of Preble, John McClahanan, of Brown, and A. C. Ramage, of Belmont. They reported on the 28th of February, and on the 7th of March, the discussion of the various amendments proposed, commenced with great earnestness. On the suggestion of the Standing Committee, the following important features of the present act were proposed: 1. The last clause of section 1, securing the special school organization of cities or incorporated villages, from the operation of the section; 2. The body of section 8, directing the October enumeration of youth of school age—all of the section, indeed, except the last clause, which requires the township Clerk to transmit an abstract thereof, within twenty days, to the county Auditor; 3. That portion of section 16 which authorizes the formation of a joint sub-district from "parts of two or more townships;" 4. The provision, as it now stands in sections 20 and 21, for the establishment of central or high schools; 5. Section 22, or the manner in which the assessments for school purposes, by Boards of Education, are effected; 6. Section 24, or the rule for the disbursement of school funds by township Treasurer; 7. Section 32, or the authority to organize cities and incorporated villages, when the latter has a population of three hundred, into a special district; 8. Section 68, enabling Boards of Education to receive and hold in trust, any grant, devise, donation, etc., for the use of any school in their jurisdiction; 9. That portion of section 54 which directs the State Commissioner of Common Schools to re-distribute the laws relating to schools and Teachers' Institutes, whenever any material change is made in their provisions; 10. The last clause of section 58, which forbids the purchase for school libraries of books of a sectarian or denominational character, besides many verbal amendments.

Prior to the third reading of the bill, the following amendments were offered, and rejected by the House: 1. Imposing a fine upon parents or guardians whose children or wards, between the ages of eight and fourteen, do not attend school, at least three months in the year—yeas 30, nays 41; 2. To strike out the sections establishing the office of School Commissioner—yeas 27, nays 47; 3. To strike out the provisions for school district libraries—yeas 31, nays 42; 4. "To re-commit the bill, with instructions so to amend the same, as to provide for the classification of the enumerated youth of the State, in such manner that all may be enabled to participate in the advantages of the schools, without any interference with religious belief, which was lost without a division; 5. To strike out the provision for high schools—yeas 23, nays 52.

The bill was read the third time on the 5th of March, and while the question of its passage was pending, further amendments were offered. One, adding to the last section an extension of the powers and duties of school officers then in existence, until the local Directors, provided for in the bill, should be elected and qualified, was agreed to; another, directing a submission of the bill to a popular vote, was rejected—yeas 17, nays 50; and a third, requiring the Treasurer of cities and incorporated villages to give bond for the security of all school funds coming into his possession, was agreed to without a division. The bill passed the House, by a vote of 56 yeas to 20 nays.

On the 8th of March, the Senate Committee upon common schools and school lands, to whom the bill, as returned from the House, had been committed, reported in favor of the bulk of House amendments, and proposing only two material amendments—one, which is now the last clause of section 8, directing the township Clerk to return an abstract of the October enumeration of youth to the county Auditor; and another, now section 47, prescribing the term of office and manner of election of the State Commissioner of Common Schools.

The report of the Committee was concurred in. During the discussion, Mr. Finck moved to add to section 24, providing the manner of disbursing the funds applicable to the payment of teachers, the following proviso:

"Provided, that whenever any person having a certificate authorizing him to teach school in any county in this State, shall present and exhibit to the Board of School Directors of any township of the proper county, a certificate signed by the local Directors of any of the districts of any such township of having taught any number of scholars resident in said township, not less than twenty, who have not attended any of the other common schools or other schools named in this act, of the township during the year, and who have been enumerated for school purposes, stating the number of scholars so taught and the time they were in attendance, the said township Board shall draw the proper order for the pro rata amount to which such person shall be entitled for such services from the school fund, taking into consideration the number of scholars so taught, and the time employed by such teacher, and the same shall be paid from the school fund, as in other cases; and for the purpose of ascertaining such pro rata sum, the said Board shall ascertain the total amount of school fund for the proper township applicable to each youth entitled thereto for the year, and shall allow such teacher upon the principles above named."

The motion to amend was lost—yeas 8, nays 18.

The original Senate bill provided for the purchase of Webster's Unabridged Dictionary for the use of schools. The House of Representatives struck out this clause by their forty-sixth amendment. On motion of Mr. Rice, the Senate retained the provision. The subject was referred to a Committee of Conference, and the Senate finally receded from its disagreement, and the Dictionary clause was omitted. A full concurrence of both bodies having thus been attained, the bill became a law on the 14th of March, 1853. Its consideration had been marked by all the requisites of full deliberation. The interval between the regular and adjourned sessions of the General Assembly had been improved by Mr. Rice, the author of the bill, for a thorough canvass of public opinion; the most experienced teachers and careful legislators of the State had been furnished with copies, and their suggestions invited; and probably no similar measure ever engrossed more anxious attention than did the well-known "Senate bill, No. 94," from the beginning to the close of the session of 1852–3. The repealing clause displaced a bulk of enactments ten times greater than the provisions of the bill, although the latter reached sixty-nine sections. It was with a decided sensation of relief that the public learned of the existence of a single enactment constituting a school code, and a determination universally prevailed to submit to much inconvenience, rather than involve the school interests of the State in the uncertainty which had almost reached the extremity of Cimmerian darkness, during the preceding ten years. Of course, no one was so sanguine as to expect entire satisfaction with the new system. It embodies some important changes, though these were less numerous and important than many have been led to suppose. Probably two-thirds of its provisions were a compilation of existing legislation; while the new features of the act of March 14, 1853, may be briefly presented under the following heads:

A STATE SCHOOL TAX.

This, in itself, was no innovation. A State common school fund, partly raised by taxation, had been long in existence, and as recently as March 24, 1851, an act was passed providing a revenue for an annual distribution of $300,000. The same act required the county Commissioners to levy, in addition to the above provision, a county school tax of not less than one mill on the dollar. The act of 1853, in lieu of this mixed State and county taxation, provided for "the annual levy and assessment of two mills on the dollar valuation, (since reduced to a mill and a half,) on the grand list of the taxable property of the State," and directed the amount so collected to be "annually distributed to the several counties of the State, in proportion to the enumeration of scholars, and applied exclusively to the support of common schools."

This change in the method of distribution has led to much dissatisfaction in the cities of the State, where the aggregate of wealth is disproportionate to the enumeration of youth: Hamilton county, for instance, contributing to the State school fund about twice the amount which the enumeration of youth warrants the county to receive. This feature of the law is elsewhere sustained with great earnestness, and it is not pertinent to the object of these pages to determine the merits of the controversy. As a *practical* illustration of the operation of the provision in question, it may be well, however, to quote from the report of the School Commissioner for 1855, the following tabular statement:

LIST OF COUNTIES WHICH RECEIVED, IN 1855, MORE THAN THEY CONTRIBUTED TO THE STATE COMMON SCHOOL FUND, WITH THE AMOUNTS ANNEXED.

COUNTIES.	AMOUNT.	COUNTIES.	AMOUNT.	COUNTIES.	AMOUNT.
Adams - - -	$5,071 85	Hardin - - - -	$1,385 20	Paulding - - -	$1,030 06
Allen - - - -	4,854 13	Henry - - - -	2,151 38	Perry - - - - -	4,308 42
Ashland - -	2,219 03	Hocking - - -	5,944 37	Pike - - - - -	2,160 76
Ashtabula -	2,444 82	Holmes - - - -	7,273 92	Putnam - - -	2,994 70
Athens - - -	6,685 37	Jackson - - -	4,400 98	Richland - - -	1,832 39
Auglaize - -	3,556 27	Jefferson - - -	550 64	Sandusky - -	3,259 47
Belmont - -	2,836 31	Knox - - - - -	491 83	Scioto - - - -	2,341 40
Brown - - -	3,522 96	Lake - - - - -	255 74	Seneca - - - -	3,007 13
Carroll - - -	2,644 98	Lawrence - -	3,563 43	Shelby - - - -	2,182 48
Clermont -	1,762 88	Logan - - - -	1,333 62	Stark - - - - -	21 65
Columbiana	3,038 38	Lorain - - - -	2,122 60	Trumbull - -	537 93
Coshocton -	2,576 59	Lucas - - - -	972 81	Tuscarawas -	3,775 23
Crawford - -	1,746 01	Medina - - - -	1,308 82	Union - - - -	2,172 43
Darke - - - -	3,125 51	Meigs - - - -	5,906 39	Van Wert - -	2,180 28
Defiance - -	2,945 36	Mercer - - - -	3,586 97	Vinton - - - -	3,289 02
Delaware - -	2,296 01	Monroe - - -	9,212 56	Washington -	7,421 20
Fulton - - -	4,899 10	Morgan - - -	5,017 87	Wayne - - - -	625 38
Gallia - - - -	5,138 09	Morrow - - -	2,089 87	Williams - - -	4,728 51
Geauga - - -	727 26	Noble - - - -	6,510 34	Wood - - - -	3,522 66
Guernsey -	5,452 91	Ottawa - - - -	403 97	Wyandott - -	863 02
Hancock - -	4,548 35				

LIST OF COUNTIES WHICH CONTRIBUTED, IN 1855, TO THE STATE COMMON SCHOOL FUND MORE THAN THEY RECEIVED, WITH THE AMOUNTS ANNEXED.

COUNTIES.	AMOUNT.	COUNTIES.	AMOUNT.	COUNTIES.	AMOUNT.
Butler - - -	$9,467 00	Greene - - - -	$6,739 38	Miami - - - -	$1,914 49
Champaign	3,502 18	Hamilton - -	65,179 33	Montgomery	11,135 51
Clark - - - -	5,709 20	Harrison - - -	695 57	Muskingum -	584 27
Clinton - - -	1,469 77	Highland - -	246 00	Pickaway - -	8,650 05
Cuyahoga -	15,272 65	Huron - - - -	984 03	Portage - - -	2,786 63
Erie - - - -	1,540 41	Licking - - -	3,428 38	Preble - - - -	2,974 10
Fairfield - -	2,382 72	Madison - - -	6,417 32	Ross - - - - - -	6,270 42
Fayette - -	3,345 89	Mahoning - -	627 08	Summit - - -	851 01
Franklin - -	7,112 92	Marion - - - -	2,383 37	Warren - - -	5,698 73

The aggregate of the apportionment, above exemplified, was $1,208,283.84.

TOWNSHIP BOARDS OF EDUCATION.

Under the former system, the township Trustees were vested with power to establish and alter sub-districts; so the clause conferring this important and difficult function upon a central Board is not without precedent. The township Board of Education established by the act, is a representative body, consisting of that local Director in each sub-district who has been chosen Clerk for the current year; and the law seeks to confer upon the Board such a *general* jurisdiction as may secure uniformity and efficiency to the school system of the township, and yet leave to the local Directors the direct administration of the sub-district. Here is a divided jurisdiction; and in some instances a jar of the machinery is unavoidable; but the experience of a few years has removed this inconvenience in a great measure. In the State of Indiana, even in the rural districts, the whole administration of schools is confided to a township Committee of three, without any intervention whatever by local Directors; but our system has become too rigid in its present form to be so readily displaced. Still it is in the power of any township to adopt the provisions of the Special District System established by the act of February 21, 1849, (Swan's Revised Statutes, 858, 862,) and a very proper amendment of the act of 1853, would be to allow every township, as well as cities and incorporated villages, to extend over itself the single district organization provided for by sections 32–36.

An analysis of different parts of the school law presents the following powers and duties of Boards of Education:

1. Section 11 defines so explicitly the corporate character of Boards of Education, that it is given without paraphrase: "The said township Board of Education in each township of the State, and their successors in office, shall be a body politic and corporate in law, and as such may contract and be contracted with, sue and be sued, plead and be impleaded, in any court of law or equity in this State, and may receive any gift, grant, donation, or devise, made for the use of any school or schools within their jurisdiction; and, moreover, they shall be and hereby are invested in their corporate capacity with the title, care, and custody of all school-houses, school-house sites, school libraries, apparatus, or other property belonging to the school districts as now organized, or which may hereafter be organized, within the limits of their jurisdiction, with full power to control the same in such manner as they may think will best subserve the interests of common schools and the cause of education; and when, in the opinion of the Board, any school-house or school-house site has become unnecessary, they may sell and convey the same in the name of the township Board of Education of the proper township; such conveyance to be executed by the Chairman and Clerk of said Board, and shall pay the avails over to the township Treasurer of the proper township, for the benefit of schools, and all conveyances of real estate which may be made to said Board, shall be to said Board in their corporate name, and to their successors in office."

2. The regular sessions of the Board are on the third Monday of April and October, with power to adjourn from time to time, and to hold special meetings. At each meeting, a Chairman from their number must be appointed, and also a Clerk, *pro tempore*, if the township Clerk is absent. Sec. 12.

3. They have the exclusive control of central or high

schools, when the people of a township, in the manner prescribed by section 21, have authorized the same; and also of sub-district schools, when the local Directors shall neglect to discharge their duties; it is their duty to prescribe rules and regulations for the government of all the common schools within their jurisdiction; they determine a course of study, select suitable text-books, and have the complete charge of the library, with the title of the books, and the appointment of Librarian; and upon them is devolved the necessity of making the annual return of school statistics to the county Auditor. Sections 13, 17 19, 21.

4. The adjustment of sub-districts within their township, the formation of joint sub-districts from a part of their township, and part or parts adjacent, the distribution of pupils to schools of different grades, and a general discipline of the schools, are devolved upon Boards of Education, by sections 14, 15, and 16.

5. They are required to establish a school in each sub-district of the township of such grade as the public good, in their opinion, requires, and can be compelled to sustain the same seven months of the year, by a levy not exceeding two mills on the dollar valuation of the taxable property of the township. That assessment can not be exceeded for the purpose of tuition and sustaining central or high schools; but to that limit the Board can be required to go, if necessary to prolong the schools seven months in the year. On this point the law is imperative, the last clause of section 24 reading as follows: "Each township Board *shall* make the necessary provisions for continuing the schools in operation in their respective townships for at least seven months in each year." See sections 14, 22, 24.

6. The subject of school-house construction is the peculiar province of Boards of Education. The title of all school property is vested in them; they are the only school organization legally responsible; their power of taxation for the purpose of building school-houses, or, in the language of the act, "for school purposes other than for the payment of

teachers," is unlimited; and on their estimate and certificate, the Auditor of the county must make the required assessments. Ordinarily this taxation for school-house construction is collected from the whole township; but section 23 recognizes a discretion in the Board to authorize a special levy on a sub-district of "a just and equitable *portion* of the amount requisite to build a school-house, when the inhabitants have not heretofore borne a reasonable share of taxation for such purpose, in comparison with other sub-districts of the township." There is ground to apprehend that the exception here recognized too often becomes the rule. See sections 22 and 23.

7. They are authorized to provide German schools for the instruction of such youths as may desire to study the German language, or the German and English languages together, (section 13,) while schools for colored children are provided for by section 31, which is as follows:

"The township Boards of Education in this State, in their respective townships, and the several other Boards of Education, and the Trustees, Visitors, and Directors of Schools, or other officers having authority in the premises, of each city or incorporated village, shall be and they are hereby authorized and required to establish within their respective jurisdictions, one or more separate schools for colored children, when the whole number by enumeration exceeds thirty, so as to afford them, as far as practicable under all circumstances, the advantages and privileges of a common school education; and all such schools so established for colored children shall be under the control and management of the Board of Education, or other school officers who have in charge the educational interests of the other schools; but in case the average number of colored children in attendance shall be less than fifteen for any one month, it shall be the duty of said Board of Education, or other school officers, to discontinue said school or schools for any period not exceeding six months at any one time; and if the number of colored children shall be less than fifteen, the Directors shall reserve the money raised on the number of said colored children, and the money so reserved shall be appropriated for the education of such colored children under the direction of the township Board."

8. A very important provision is contained in section 13,

which authorizes a Board of Education to appoint one of their number the Acting Manager of Schools for the township, with such duties as the Board may prescribe in relation to the management and supervision of the different schools, and the educational interests of the township. He may be allowed a reasonable compensation for his services, but for the usual services of members of a Board of Education, the law provides no compensation.

A satisfactory method of determining the powers and duties of local Directors, is to study carefully the foregoing provisions, and assume that whatever school jurisdiction has been customary in this State, which is not expressly granted to Boards of Education, remains vested in the local Directors. More than this: In the absence of such rules and regulations as a Board of Education might establish, local Directors would unquestionably be recognized as the agents of the Board for the transaction of whatever may seem to be for the interest of the schools. It is in the power of a Board, at any time, to resume their functions; but as long as they tacitly abdicate them, great indulgence should be extended to the action of the Directors.

FREEDOM OF THE SCHOOL SYSTEM.

This expression is somewhat indefinite; but it is intended to express the fact, that the act of 1853 proposes, as the object of the taxation and organization thereby authorized, to afford "the advantages of a free education to all the youth of this State," and accordingly sweeps from the statute book every enactment imposing a rate-bill upon the parents or guardians of the children in attendance. While gifts, grants, devises, donations, etc., in aid of the munificent provision by legislation, are welcomed as sacred trusts, yet it is the crowning glory of the Ohio system, that in all her schools, education, like justice, is unsold—never denied. To accomplish such a result without convulsion, and with the universal acclamation of her people, is a proud record in the annals of the commonwealth.

SCHOOL DISTRICT LIBRARIES.

Another new feature of the school act has long been known, and favorably known, to the systems of other States, namely: the provision for school district libraries.

"The law devotes one-tenth of a mill upon the dollar valuation, on the grand list of property taxable for State purposes, as an annual fund 'for the purpose of furnishing school libraries and apparatus to all the common schools of the State,' and provides that 'every family in each district or sub-district, shall be entitled to the use of one volume at a time from the school library, although no member of such family attend any of the schools of the township.' The township Boards of Education are vested with the power to 'make and enforce such rules relative to the use and preservation of the school libraries and apparatus, as they may think advisable,' including the appointment and direction of Librarians. These libraries are 'deemed the property of said several Boards, or local school officers, to whom the same may have been delivered, and shall not be subject to execution, sale, or alienation, for any cause whatever.' Section 51 further provides that 'as soon as the revenue raised for the purpose of furnishing the common schools with libraries and apparatus, will admit, it shall be the duty of the State Commissioners of Common Schools to purchase the same, and the books and apparatus so purchased shall be distributed through the Auditor's office of each county, to the Board of Education in each township, city, or incorporated village, according to the enumeration of scholars.'

"Perhaps no single recommendation has been more frequently made by State officers charged with the superintendence of common schools, than some public provision for township or district libraries."

SUPERVISION OF THE SYSTEM.

In accordance with the example of all the States distinguished by their systems of public instruction, and the earnest recommendation of all who have ever had a practical acquaintance with the subject, the Legislature deemed their labor incomplete, until a separate school department was organized at the seat of Government, presided over by an officer, designated in the act as a State Commissioner of Common Schools. Sections 47 to 57 are occupied with the requisitions upon him. Elected for three years, with a salary of $1,500, he is required to execute a bond in the sum of $10,000, and take an oath of office; to spend annually, at least ten days in each of the nine judicial districts of the State, superintending and encouraging Teachers' Institutes, conferring with township Boards of Education, or other school officers, counseling teachers, visiting schools, and delivering lectures on topics calculated to subserve the interests of popular education; to purchase and distribute school district libraries; to exercise such supervision over the educational funds of the State as may be necessary to secure their safety and right application and distribution according to law; and, to that end, to require reports from all county municipal or school officers in the State; to prepare and circulate suitable forms and regulations for making all reports and conducting all necessary proceedings under the school act; to distribute copies of laws relating to schools and Teachers' Institutes, from time to time, with suitable forms and instructions; and to make an annual report, embracing full statistics of the public schools and school funds. He is also required to keep an office at the seat of Government, and attend the same, when not absent on public business.

Thus has been enumerated the distinctive features of the school legislation of 1853. For the rest of its provisions, they constitute a digest of pre-existing acts, modified slightly so as to conform to the new order of things.

Local Directors were a familiar organization. Their number was unaltered, but only one is elected annually, serving three years. This gives greater permanence to the body. It is devolved upon them to take the annual enumeration of youth in October; to manage and control the local interests and affairs of the sub-district; to employ teachers, certify the amount due them for services, and dismiss them on sufficient grounds; to visit the schools at least twice during each term, by one or more of their number; to negotiate and make, *under such rules and regulations as the township Board may prescribe*, all necessary contracts in relation to providing fuel for schools, repairing, building, or furnishing school-houses, purchasing or leasing school-house sites, renting school-rooms, and making all other provisions necessary for the convenience and prosperity of schools within their sub-district, provided such contracts do not exceed the sub-district share of school funds applicable to the above purposes, unless the Board of Education first approve of the same; and whatever contracts are made by the Directors are to be promptly reported to the township Board. In case of vacancy occurring, otherwise than by a failure to elect at a regular April meeting, the township Clerk appoints for the residue of the unexpired term; but in the exceptional case, the former incumbent continues in office, unless the electors summon a special meeting, as provided in section 4, and choose a successor.

The act also contains a system of special school districts, similar to the provisions of the Akron and similar enactments, the advantages of which are only available to cities and incorporated villages having a population of three hundred, when a majority of the electors have decided to assume the form of organization thus provided, in preference to the general system of the act. See sections 32 to 36.

The office of district Treasurer is abolished, and all the duties of that officer, as detailed in prior acts, are devolved upon the township Treasurer.

The township Clerk is, *ex officio*, Clerk of the Board of Education; he draws orders in favor of teachers upon the township Treasurer on the certificate of local Directors, or the order of the Board of Education. In case of neglect by the local Directors, he must take the October enumeration of youth, and return an abstract of the same to the county Auditor; he is Clerk of all meetings relating to high schools; and in case of forfeiture of the township Treasurer's bond, it is his duty to prosecute and collect the same for the use of the schools in the township.

The county Auditor is still, *ex officio*, county Superintendent of Common Schools; and is required to report the statistics returned to him, by Boards of Education, annually to the

State School Commissioner. The apportionment of school funds by the Auditor of State, to the different counties, and by the Auditors of counties to the school corporations, is thus regulated by the act:

"SEC. 37. The Auditor of State shall, annually, apportion the common school funds among the different counties, upon the enumeration and returns made to him by the State Commissioner of Common Schools, and certify the amount so apportioned to the county Auditor of each county, stating from what sources the same is derived, which said sum the several county Treasurers shall retain in their respective treasuries from the State funds; and the county Auditors shall, annually, and immediately after their annual settlement with the county Treasurer, apportion the school funds for their respective counties, according to the enumeration and returns in their respective offices; and no township or other district, city or village, which shall have failed to make and return such enumeration, shall be entitled to receive any portion of the common school funds. And in making such distribution, each county Auditor shall apportion all moneys collected on the tax duplicate of any township, for the use of schools, to such township; all moneys received from the State treasury, on account of interest on the money accruing from the sale of section sixteen, or other lands in lieu thereof, to the civil townships and parts of civil townships in the original surveyed township, or fractional township, to which such land belongs; all moneys received by the county Treasurer on account of the Virginia military school fund, United States Military District, and Connecticut Western Reserve, according to laws regulating the same; and all other moneys for the use of schools in the county, and not otherwise appropriated by law, to the proper township; and he shall, immediately after making said apportionment, enter the same into a book to be kept for that purpose, and shall furnish the township Treasurers and township Clerks, Treasurers, and Recorders of incorporated cities or villages, as the case may be, each with a copy of said appointment, and give an order on the county Treasurer to each township Treasurer, or to such Treasurer as may be entitled to receive the same, for the amount of money belonging to his respective township, city, or village, and take a receipt from such Treasurer for the amount thus received; and the said county Auditor shall collect, or cause to be collected, the fines and all other moneys for school purposes, in his county, and pay the same over to the county Treasurer; and he shall inspect all accounts of interest for section sixteen, or other school lands, whether the interest is paid by the State or by the debtors, and take all the proper measures to secure to each township its full amount of school funds.

"SEC. 38. When any original surveyed township in which section sixteen has been sold, shall lie in two or more counties, the Auditors of the respective counties shall certify to the Auditor of the county in which that portion of said township lies, containing said section sixteen, the enumeration of the scholars in that part of said township embraced within their respective counties; and the Auditor of said county in which said section sixteen is situate, shall apportion the fund derived from said section sixteen to the different portions of said township, according to said enumeration, and shall certify to the Auditors of the other counties the amount belonging to the parts of said township situate in their respective counties, and draw an order in favor of the Treasurers of the other counties on the Treasurer of his own county for the amount going to each; and the Auditors of the respective counties shall apportion the same, in their respective counties, to such portions or parts thereof as may be entitled thereto.

"SEC. 39. The interest on the purchase of any such section sixteen belonging to any such original surveyed township, so as aforesaid, lying in two or more counties, shall be paid over on the order of the Auditor of that county in which such section sixteen is embraced, to the Treasurer of the same county, to be apportioned as is pointed out in the preceding section."

The act is not unlike former legislation in the organization of a Board of School Examiners. They are appointed by the Probate Judge three in number, for the term of two years; and the indispensable branches for a candidate's certificate are, "Orthography, Reading, Writing, Arithmetic, Geography, and English Grammar." The compensation for Examiners is one dollar and fifty cents for every day necessarily engaged in official service, to be paid from the county treasury.

Among the miscellaneous provisions, school-houses with an inclosure not exceeding four acres, are exempted from sale on execution. Prior debts of school districts must be provided for by township Boards. The process against a township

Board is by summons, executed by leaving a copy thereof with the Clerk or Secretary of such Board, or other school officer, at least ten days before the return thereof; and it is the duty of the Prosecuting Attorney to attend to all suits for or against a Board. Provision is made for the adoption of the organization of the school act, by any municipality organized under a special law. The Akron law of February 8, 1847, and the acts amendatory thereto, the "act for the better regulation of schools in cities, towns, etc.," passed, February 21, 1849, and the acts amendatory thereto, besides other acts creating special school districts, were continued in force, except that the rules established for the compilation of statistics, and the apportionment of school funds, are in all cases to govern. Boards of Education may hold any grant or devise, gift, etc., for the use of public schools; and until the first officers elected under the law are qualified, all former school officers are recognized, and their acts made effective. The repealing clause, which was voluminous, protected all obligations, liabilities, and rights acquired under the acts repealed.

At the session of 1852, a law providing for the sale of section sixteen, was passed, (see Appendix, "School Laws in Force," chapter XVII,) and in 1853, an act regulating the schools of Cincinnati, (see Appendix, "School Laws in Force," chapter XXI.)

CHAPTER XVII.

RECENT EVENTS OF EDUCATIONAL INTEREST.

So far in advance of the expectations of the most sanguine advocates of the constitutional article upon education, was the legislative response of 1853 to the injunction in favor of "a thorough and efficient system of common schools throughout the State," that many apprehensions prevailed among the friends of education, that too much had been suddenly undertaken. But, although a reaction was apparent, yet it has been unable, as yet, to impair the foundations of the new and imposing structure. The State school tax, at the session of 1854, was reduced from two mills to a mill and a half; nevertheless, in the presence of a grand duplicate, much enlarged by the re-valuation of real estate in 1852–53, and the legislation pursuant to the new Constitution, the amount collected by the lesser rate was $1,208,283.84, against $1,118,089.02, which was the proceeds of the two mill levy of 1853.

Still the pressure upon the second General Assembly, under the Constitution of 1851, was very formidable. The Senate Committee upon Common Schools and School Lands, urged a further trial of the act which had so recently gone into operation, not only on the ground that its provisions had not been fairly tested, but the argument of their report did not rest here, and vindicated, with fullness and force, the leading provisions of the law. The House Committee conceded that the act of 1853 needed amendment, and reported a bill embracing the following modifications:

1. To extend the limits of a district so as to include all territory annexed to any of its sub-districts, in order to obviate the difficulties in managing and supporting a school at the expense of more than one corporate body.

2. To allow Boards of Education to modify the distribution of school funds, according to the local wants of sub-districts, and not peremptorily, according to enumeration, as the Supreme Court, in 1855, decided to be the true construction of the law.

3. Restricting Boards of Education in the exercise of the power of changing the boundaries of sub-districts, by a provision that such alteration be made at a regular session, after public notice of the proposed change, and in case of difficulty or disagreement, that a vote of the people should be decisive of the matter.

4. A proposition to reduce the State levy for schools, one-fourth, which was done.

5. A section giving the power to condemn private property for school-house sites. It is remarkable that no such power has been granted to school corporations, while so many private associations are clothed with it.

With the exception of the fourth point, none of the foregoing recommendations were agreed to. They were dictated by no hostile feeling, and will probably be revived at no distant day.

At the session of 1856, elaborate reports were presented to both branches of the Legislature. The Senate Committee upon Schools and School Lands, consisting of Herman Canfield, of Medina, Felix Marsh, of Preble, and M. D. Hardy, of Noble, reported adversely to memorials asking the Legislature to abolish the office of School Commissioner, and the system of district libraries; in favor of retaining the present method of examining teachers, and the mill and a half assessment for a State school fund; and against the expediency of erecting the office of county Superintendent, at the present juncture; but they reported a bill which proposed the following modifications of sections twenty-two and twenty-four, of the act of 1853:

1. To limit the power of taxation by township Boards of Education to one mill, for sustaining central or high schools, where established, one mill for prolonging sub-district schools after the State funds are exhausted, and one mill for school-house construction and other necessary expenditures. Another clause fixed the maximum of taxation at three mills, unless, at a special meeting called for the express purpose of determining the question, a majority should vote in favor of an increased rate of taxation.

2. Another amendment, suggested by a recent decision of the Supreme Court, allowed the Board of Education to vary from the ordinary rule, for distributing funds applicable to the payment of teachers, (according to the enumeration of youth,) so far as to prolong the schools at least six months in

the year, by an apportionment of the township fund raised for that purpose, according to the particular wants of each sub-district.

3. The minimum time in which Boards of Education are required to sustain schools, was proposed to be reduced from seven to six months.

The House Committee, consisting of James Monroe, of Lorain, W. Hendren, of Delaware, and C. Mendenhall, of Jefferson, reported very distinctly against any modification of the school act, except to limit the taxation for school-house and incidental purposes to a mill and a-half (unless a proposition for a higher rate was adopted in township meeting,) to reduce the minimum of instruction to six months, and suffer a distribution of the township tuition fund at the discretion of the Board of Education.

On the other hand, a formidable demonstration of hostility, especially to the office of State School Commissioner and the School District Libraries, was organized in the Legislature; and an amendment to the bill of the House Committee prevailed in that body, abolishing those features of the law. With this addition, the bill became obnoxious to its original friends, and the practical result occurred, that no change in the school law was able to command a majority of either branch of the General Assembly; although, by an omission to renew the levy of a tenth of a mill for library purposes, the distribution of books and apparatus was suspended for the current year.

Incidentally, however, to a revision of the law relating to the public printing, an important change in the administration was effected. A proviso to section six, of "an act providing for recording, and printing and distributing the journals of the General Assembly and the laws and public documents," passed April, 8, 1856, directs that "the school year shall begin on the 1st day of September annually, (instead of the 15th of November,) and close on the last day of the following August; and, that all school officers and township officers acting as such, who are or may be required to make annual reports to the county Auditor, shall make out the same and transmit them to the county Auditor on or before the 1st day of October following the school year; while the county Auditor must make his report to the State School Commissioner, by the 5th of November in each year. Hitherto the returns of Boards of Education were required to be made, within twenty days after the third Monday of October, ("at the same time when the return of the enumeration of youth is required to be made,") and the time limited for the report of the county Auditor was "on or before the twentieth day of December, annually." The report of the State School Commissioner, formerly postponed to the twentieth day of January, is now required to be made to the Governor on or before the twentieth of November previously.

On the 10th of April, 1856, an act was passed, legalizing all annexations or transfers of territory to or from the districts provided for in the act for the better regulation of public schools in cities, towns, etc., passed February 21, 1849, and the General School Act of March 14, 1853; and from abundant caution, authorizing the Boards of Education of any city or incorporated village, or union school district created by any law of this State, to transfer, by mutual agreement, territory to and from their respective districts, according to the general provisions of the act of March 14, 1853.

By another curative act, passed April 5, 1856, all sales of section sixteen, by the Trustees of civil townships, instead of the Trustees of the original surveyed or fractional townships, provided that the proceedings were otherwise in conformity with the provisions of the acts in force on that subject, when the sales occurred, were legalized in the possession of the purchasers, and their assignees, and heirs at law.*

Having thus closed a review of the general school legislation of the State, which, prior to 1851, has already been accompanied by full citations from Executive communications,

* The enactments above referred to are reprinted in Appendix, "School Laws in Force."

it is proposed to continue that transcript from the messages of those gentlemen who have held the gubernatorial chair under the present Constitution. These paragraphs afford an instructive commentary upon the legislative action of the government which they preceded and accompanied.

Governor Reuben Wood thus addressed the General Assembly of 1852, on the subject of education:

"The sixth article of the Constitution is imperative on the General Assembly to provide for an efficient system of common schools throughout the State. This is certainly one of the most interesting subjects which can occupy your consideration, or that of the American people. Under systems like ours, where the real sovereignty is with the citizen, and he rules himself: where government is upheld or put down by the opinions of the people, expressed through the 'self-renovating power of the ballot-box,' and not by violence, light, knowledge, intelligence, science, are essentially necessary to be widely spread among the masses of the community. A common English education is within the reach of all, and is, at least, indispensable to the happiness, safety, and prosperity of the State. Experience has shown that education, with the masses of the people, affords infinitely more protection to liberty, good morals, and more security to the rights of others, than all the criminal enactments that have ever been made, or prisons that have been built.

"If we desire the rising generation to be virtuous, lovers of freedom, and to cherish our institutions which we must soon leave behind; if civilization, intellectual enjoyment, substantial refinement, love of order, and prosperity, are to be leading characteristics with those who are to succeed us, the means must be provided, and an efficient common school system devised.

"The youth of the State must be educated and instructed in habits of useful and industrial pursuits; for habits formed in early life are likely to follow to its close.

"The Constitution has very wisely provided for the inviolability of the principal of the school funds, which now are, or hereafter shall be, under control of the General Assembly, and for the faithful application of the income to the purposes designed. It has also declared, that such sums shall be raised by taxation or otherwise, as, with the income of the school trust fund, will secure an efficient system of common schools throughout the State; and this Constitution the Representatives of the people have solemnly sworn to support.

"For the amount and condition of all moneys and grants for school purposes, the General Assembly is referred to the report of the Secretary of State.

"It is respectfully recommended that every school district should be required to have a school kept in it, from the first of December until the first of April in each and every year, and that parents or guardians, and all others intrusted with the custody of children, should be required to send them to some school, for at least three months of that time, unless for good cause excused by the Directors. It is likewise suggested, that some method should be provided, better suited than the one now in force, to prevent the employment of all but competent teachers, and those of unexceptionable moral character.

"I believe it to be true, that children in the habit of attending school become fond of it. The desire to learn increases. If the foundation be laid in youth, every one of either sex, as a general rule, and in any ordinary condition, may become possessed of a common English education, may be intelligent and intellectual. There is leisure sufficient from the employment of all, if the disposition exist.

"The General Assembly might do much to improve our common schools, and to promote the cause of education, by providing for suitable libraries in every school district, such as would be adapted to the capacities and tastes of youth.

"In Massachusetts, every school is furnished by the State with Webster's Dictionary, as the standard work of Orthography and Pronunciation. The same is recommended by a Committee of the New York Legislature for the Empire State.

"It is admitted to be the most valuable work of the kind extant, by the learned men both here and in Europe, and its general use in our schools would break down all provincialisms, so to speak, and produce uniformity and elegance in the use of our language. Words would then be used by every one in the same sense in which they are defined by that able lexicographer.

"Much might also be done by the General Assembly to encourage literary taste, by small aid from time to time, for the purchase of books, periodicals, and newspapers, for permanent literary associations, lyceums, and clubs, in our cities and towns.

"It would certainly have a tendency to prevent dissipation, by the desertion of places tending to immoralities, and cause young men to store their minds with useful knowledge, and elevate themselves in their own self-dignity and self-respect.

"Again, I would say, let the masses be educated. Send information and the means of instruction among all classes of our people unable to provide it, and jails will become tenantless, and your penitentiary greatly diminish in its occupants. The songs of riot and debauchery will be seldom heard in your streets, and your Executive will escape the constant annoyance of parents, wives, and children, for some ignorant and disgraced, but still cherished object, who has forfeited his liberty to satisfy the claims of justice.

"My predecessor, in his last annual message, among other things, recommended a thorough revision of the school laws. He remarks, 'The law which now professes to regulate this system has been in force for many years. It has undergone many alterations, is printed in many different volumes of the statutes, and is thus made difficult to be found and still more difficult to be understood, by the great majority of persons whose duty it professes to point out.'

"I fully concur with him in opinion, and the entire subject is earnestly and respectfully recommended to the early and deliberate consideration of the General Assembly, with the full conviction that the people of Ohio will cheerfully submit to any reasonable burdens that may be imposed in aid of the school fund, and which shall be faithfully applied to the purposes of common schools, believing, as they justly do, that it would relieve them from other burdens, in a measure, which are now levied to secure the faithful and prompt administration of penal laws."

Governor William Medill, at the second regular session of the General Assembly for 1854, thus expressed himself:

"Our common schools, from their universal diffusion, located as they are in every neighborhood, and distributing their healthful influence to every family, should always be regarded as among the very first objects of legislative care. They have not inaptly, at times, been styled 'the people's colleges,' and are certainly the palladium and most effectual defense of our free institutions.

"The new Constitution makes it imperative on the General Assembly, 'to make such provisions by taxation, or otherwise, as with the income arising from the school trust fund, will secure a thorough and efficient system of common schools throughout the State.'

"In accordance with this requirement of the Constitution,

the last General Assembly, with almost entire unanimity, passed a law re-constructing our educational system, elevating its standard, extending its usefulness, and imparting to it a greater degree of efficiency.

"It is claimed by the friends of the system thus created, that the new features engrafted upon it, are decided improvements — in perfect accordance with the educational progress of the age, and the educational demands of our rapidly increasing population.

"In a Republic like ours, founded as it is on the virtue and intelligence of the people at large, the thorough and efficient education of those who are soon to assume the duties and responsibilities of Government in all its departments, is essential to the healthful existence of the Government itself, and can not be neglected without danger to the vital interests of our free institutions.

"The new provisions of the present school law, involving changes radical in their character, must necessarily produce, for a time, much embarrassment and inconvenience, and in some instances it may be, actual oppression. But most of these being of a temporary nature, and incident to almost every innovation upon long established usage, they should not impel the General Assembly to hasty and inconsiderate legislation, lest the present law may be, in a short time, involved in the same complexity and confusion which, under the former laws, produced so much embarrassment.

"The annual assessment and levy of two mills upon the grand duplicate of the State, for school purposes, is regarded by many of the tax-payers as oppressive and unnecessary. This levy, however, is only half a mill greater than that authorized by the former law.

"Prior to the passage of the present law, the State levied half a mill, and county Commissioners were required to levy a mill, for school purposes; making a total school tax of one mill and a half. Under the new law, both levies have been united into one, and styled a State levy.

"Another tax which has borne very heavily upon the tax-payers the past year, is the one authorized to be assessed by township Boards of Education for the purchase of school-house sites, and the erection of school-houses. The amount that has been raised for these objects is very nearly as large as that levied by the State. It is a tax that will not require to be repeated, however, in the next fifteen or twenty years.

"In the establishment of all school systems, three objects should be constantly kept in view: brevity, simplicity, and the utmost degree of economy that is consistent with the proper education of the youth of the State. To attain these excellencies, however, much time and experience, and a careful observation of the working of the system, are necessarily required.

"The grand duplicate has been greatly increased by the re-valuation of the real estate. A levy of two mills, for the ensuing year, would produce one-fourth more revenue than was raised during the past year, under the same levy. No system can operate beneficially that bears too heavily on the people. I therefore recommend that the law be so modified in this particular, as not to require any increase, at least, of the amount now assessed by the State."

Again, in his annual message of January, 1856, Governor Medill observed:

"The State of Ohio is justly distinguished for a liberal and enlightened system of public instruction. Contemplated by the territorial legislation of Congress, it was undertaken by the people of the State, as soon as the exigencies of a frontier and the exposures of war would allow, and has encountered less obstruction and more encouragement from the public sentiment than has usually been observed in the progress of similar systems elsewhere. General education is recognized by the Constitution of 1851 as a duty of Government, no less than a parental obligation, and the law of March 14, 1853, not only furnished ample provision for schools of every grade, but will be memorable in our annals for establishing the principle that they are open to all—free or common schools—in the fullest sense of the term. Instead of a mixed State and county tax of a mill and a half for their support, the act in question directed a State school tax, and that its proceeds should be distributed from the State treasury in proportion to the enumeration of youth of school age within the respective counties. Every township was constituted a district, and intrusted to a Board of Education, consisting of a Representative from each sub-district, who are authorized to make or alter such sub-districts, to assess taxes for the construction of school-houses, and the extension of school terms; and to exercise whatever general supervision of educational interests may be consistent with the duties enjoined upon the local Directors in each sub-district. A fund of one-tenth of a mill yearly was appropriated 'for the purpose of furnishing school libraries and apparatus to all the common schools of the State,' and the supervision of the system was confided to a

State Commissioner, elected by the people. In other respects the present school law is a digest of previous legislation, and was intended to relieve the public mind from the confusion and uncertainty caused by frequent and inconsiderate amendment.

"A sufficient period has now elapsed for you to determine whether the people are generally satisfied with the present law, or in what respect it requires modification. There has been some complaint in the manner of distributing the State school fund. Those counties which include populous cities are assessed with greater amounts than the enumeration of youth entitle them to receive, and in one instance the amount received is only about one-half the sum contributed to the State fund. Still it is easy to see that if we consider the *child* as the object of public regard—as a ward of the State for a certain degree of instruction—that the direct application of the public bounty to the youth of the counties in proportion to the annual enumeration, is neither illogical nor inconsistent. It presents a fair subject, however, for the consideration of the General Assembly.

"The organization of township Boards of Education, which, to the extent of their powers and duties, reduce the authority of local Directors, was a centralizing measure, and has undoubtedly produced a greater degree of uniformity and efficiency; but it is a grave question whether the division of jurisdiction between those bodies has not led to disagreement and confusion, and whether the power of taxation, vested in Boards of Education, has not been injudiciously exercised.

"I deem it highly important that the school act should accurately define the powers and duties of these officers respectively; although it is quite possible that former uncertainty in this, and other respects, has been removed by the opinions and advice of the State Commissioner. The present system owes much to the habitual and judicious expositions of that officer.

"Boards of Education are required to furnish schools for seven months of the year, and they are authorized to direct assessments 'for school purposes other than for the payment of teachers,' under which head the item of school-house construction is included. They may also direct assessments not exceeding two mills on the dollar, for the support of central or high schools, when legally established, and for the purpose of prolonging, after the State funds have been exhausted, the terms of the several sub-districts or primary schools in the township. There does not seem to be any limitation of the power of taxation 'for school purposes, other than the payment of teachers.'

"The taxes assessed for local school purposes in 1854 amounted to $1,295,424, and in 1855 to $1,246,346, amounts almost equal to the State school tax of a mill and a half on the grand duplicate. The largest portion of these assessments were doubtless for school-house structures, and to prolong the schools beyond the period of seven months, and may be regarded as extraordinary expenditures. Why should not the proposition to incur them be submitted to the consideration of the people of the township? As the services of members of Boards of Education are gratuitous, those officers are usually ardent friends of education, and there is danger that their zeal in its behalf, however honorable to them, individually, may sometimes fail to be sustained by public opinion; a state of things certain to produce an injurious reaction, and to impair the usefulness of our school system. It would be better to distribute a certain degree of educational progress over several years, and be sure, meanwhile, of a cordial sentiment of public approval, than to precipitate the same results within a single year, and thereby alienate the sympathies of the community. The latter must accompany and sanction all our school movements, and no more serious error can be committed than to mistake the enthusiasm of a few for the conviction of the many. Let every step be carefully considered, and fully matured, and if unusual in its nature, ratified by a majority of the people of the district, at a meeting called for its discussion, and we may confidently dismiss our fears for the future prosperity and advancement of the cause of popular education."

Governor S. P. Chase, in his Inaugural Address of January, 1856, briefly alluded to the subject as follows:

"I need not commend to your judicious consideration the educational and benevolent institutions of the State. Universal education is our cheapest defense, and surest safeguard, and most enduring wealth. Our common schools, which secure to the people this great benefit, are firmly established in their affections, and will justly claim the fostering care of their Representatives."

Since February, 1854, the school department, re-organized so fully under the act of 1853, has been under the superintendence of Hon. H. H. Barney. Two reports have been made by him as State School Commissioner, from which very considerable compilation has been made in the progress of these pages. Much of their space has been occupied with historical details; but even a larger proportion has been devoted to practical dissertation upon the most effective methods for the external administration and internal management of schools.

From the last annual report of the State School Commissioner are compiled the following statistics, which are here presented as the highest evidence that the elaborate system, whose progress has been under consideration, is fruitful of benefit to the community which sustains it so munificently.

A general statement of the public expenditure for the purpose of education in Ohio, during the past year, embraces the following items:

Amount of State common school fund apportioned to the counties according to the enumeration of unmarried youth between the ages of five and twenty-one years, being at the rate of $1.48 per capita	$1,208,283 84.
Interest paid to the counties on school funds held by the State in trust	125,206 21.
Rents of Virginia Military school lands	2,903 54.
Local assessments for school-house construction, for teachers' wages in addition to State funds, fuel, and miscellaneous expenses	1,295,424 84.
Total	$2,631,818 40.

The number of school-houses reported by 1,198 Boards, is 7,830, valued at $2,229,911. The number in the whole State is probably 10,287, worth about $3,090,306. There were 740 school-houses built in 1855, at an aggregate cost of $438,602, or an average of $593. Of the school-houses heretofore erected and whose condition is stated in the reports, 4,592 are represented as "good," 1,515 as "bad," and 1,269 as "middling," while 464 are enumerated, but their condition is unreported.

From the mass of returns relating to the numbers engaged

in different studies, the following are selected as the most reliable:

Number of pupils		who can read			430,432.
do	do	who can write			362 497.
do	do	engaged in the study of the Alphabet			116,933.
do	do	do	do	Orthography	497,717.
do	do	do	do	Mental Arithmetic	233,756.
do	do	do	do	Written do	246,896.
do	do	do	do	Geography	115,839.
do	do	do	do	English Grammar	84,684.
do	do	do	do	History	55,948.
do	do	do	do	Algebra	16,502.
do	do	do	do	Geometry	15,328.
do	do	do	do	Nat. Philosophy	15,068
do	do	do	do	Chemistry	14 551.
do	do	do	do	Geology	24,721.

The special school tax levied by townships and districts, in 1854, for the expenditure of 1855, amounted to $1,295,424.84. The returns from all the counties in the State, except seven, will exhibit the nature of these expenditures, and indeed present intrinsic evidences of being very nearly accurate:

Purchasing school-house sites	$ 15,596 88.
Building and furnishing school-houses	455,027 07.
Hiring school-houses	1,726 41.
Repairing school-houses	47,688 31.
Fuel	34,418 61.
Cases for books and apparatus	775 06.
Other contingent school expenses	88,265 70.
Prolonging schools seven months	409,022 57.
Sustaining high schools	13,369 28.
Total	$1,065,759 89.

The reports of the county Auditors warrant the following statement of the amount paid for teachers' wages in 1855:

	MALES.	FEMALES.	TOTAL.
Common	$1,086,302 62	$600,116 04	$1,686,418 66.
High	50,904 18	20,848 01	71,752 19.
German and Eng.	7,965 68	1,072 15	9,037 83.
Colored	5,859 17	2,700 27	8,559 44.
Total	$1,151,031 65	$624,736 47	$1,775,768 12.

A satisfactory view is afforded by comparing the items as returned in 1854 and 1855 respectively:

	1854.	1855.
Total enumeration of youth of school age..	816,408	820,624.
Number enrolled in the schools..........	612,185	669,024.
Average daily attendance................	362,514	388,373.
Number of pupils in Orthography.........	385,912	497,717.
do do Arithmetic..........	226,289	246,898.
do do Grammar...........	61,027	84,684.
do do Geography..........	93,384	115,839.
do do Algebra.............	5,776	16,502.
do do Geometry...........	1,037	15,328.
do do Chemistry...........	1,033	14,551.
Male teachers in common schools.........	9,902	10,998.
Female do do	8,502	9,854.
Male do high do	71	115.
Female do do	63	81.
Wages per month of male teachers in common schools........................	$23 00	$25 02.
do do female do	13 00	14 20.
do do male do high	58 00	61 35.
do do female do do	28 50	30 60.
Total amount of teachers' wages........	$1,684,694	$1,775,768.
Special school tax levied...............	987,696	1,295,424.
Of this last item, amount levied for prolonging schools seven months........	404,378	409,022.
Number of Boards of Education........	1,514	1,574.
Number of sub-districts..............	11,365	10,000.
New school-houses erected............	770	740.
Cost of new school-houses..............	$346,944	$438,602.
Average cost of new school-houses.....	451	593.

This comparative statement, when it is considered that the interval covers a period in which the community sustained great depression by the unprecedented drouth of one year, and the extraordinary prevalence of sickness during its successor, justifies the belief that no step backward can be reasonably anticipated in the future career of the Ohio School System. Already has an opportunity been afforded to test the disposition of both the political parties of the State, under the responsibility of a legislative majority, and the fact that no mutation of State administration is likely to change the essential features of the existing provision for public instruction, in any essential feature, should be a subject of pride and congratulation to every citizen. These pages have indicated the gradual but sure development of that provision; and as the conclusion of the preceding review—contemplating the broad foundation and lofty proportions of the "thorough and efficient system of common schools" now firmly secured to the people of Ohio — no aspiration can be more appropriate than an enthusiastic Esto Perpetua—"May it live forever!"

SCHOOL LAWS IN FORCE.

SCHOOL LAWS IN FORCE.*

CHAPTER I.

GENERAL SCHOOL ACT.

An Act to provide for the reorganization and maintenance of Common Schools.

[*Passed March* 1, 1853, *LI vol. Stat.* 429.]

Townships compose districts: school districts are sub-districts.

Board of Education.

Local Directors.

Cities, etc.

SEC. 1. *Be it enacted by the General Assembly of the State of Ohio,* That hereafter each and every organized township in the State shall compose but one school district for all purposes connected with the general interests of education in the township, and shall be confined to the management and control of a Board of Education, and the several school districts and fractional parts thereof, which now are, or may hereafter be established in the several organized townships of the State, shall be regarded as sub-districts, and be confided to the management and control of local Directors, as hereinafter provided; but nothing contained in this act shall be so construed as to give to the township Board of Education, or to local Directors in sub-districts, jurisdiction over any territory in the township included within the limits of any city or incorporated village, with the territory annexed thereto for school purposes, which shall elect or appoint a Board of Education as hereinafter provided, or, which now is or may hereafter be governed, as to schools, by any special or other act, specified in the sixty-seventh section of this act.

* For the convenience of reference, the following acts are numbered as chapters.

ELECTION OF LOCAL DIRECTORS.

When, where, and how directors elected.

SEC. 2. On the second Monday of April, in the year eighteen hundred and fifty-three, there shall be held at the usual hour and place of holding district meetings in each of the sub-districts of the several townships of the State, a school meeting of the qualified voters resident within the sub-district, and having the qualifications of voters at the State and county elections, who, when assembled, shall organize by the appointment of a Chairman and Secretary, and proceed to elect by ballot, three School Directors for such sub-district; of those so elected, the person receiving the highest number of votes shall hold his office for three years; the person receiving the next highest number, shall hold the office for two years; and the person receiving the next highest number, shall hold the office for one year; and each shall continue in office until his successor is elected and qualified. In case two or more persons so elected have received an equal number of votes, the duration of their respective terms of office shall be determined by lot, in the presence of the Chairman and Secretary of the meeting; and annually thereafter, in the same manner, on the second Monday in April, there shall be elected in each sub-district of the proper township, one School Director for the term of three years; and the minutes of the proceedings of any such district meeting shall be signed by the Chairman and Secretary, and delivered to the Directors, who shall have been elected as aforesaid, to be recorded by the Clerk in the records of the sub-district, and the said Clerk of the sub-district shall forthwith certify to the township Clerk, the names of the local Directors so elected, specifying the term for which each was elected; if the Directors of any sub-district so elected shall deem it expedient, they may designate the specific hour of the day on which the annual election for such sub-district shall be held, and in such case, shall cause five days notice thereof, in writing, to be posted up in three of the most public places in such sub-district.

Term of office.

Minutes of the meeting.

Clerk to record.

Clerk to certify.

Hour of holding election. Who may designate. Five days' notice to be given.

Official oath.

SEC. 3. The said Directors, within five days after their election, shall take an oath or affirmation to support the Constitution of the United States, and of the State of Ohio, and faithfully and impartially to discharge the duties of their office; which said oath the Directors are authorized to administer to each other. And in case a vacancy shall occur in the office of Director, by death, resignation, refusal to serve, or

Vacancy, how filled.

otherwise, it shall be the duty of the township Clerk to fill such vacancy within ten days after being informed thereof, by appointment for the unexpired term.

Special meeting to elect directors.

SEC. 4. If the qualified voters of any sub-district shall fail to meet and elect School Directors, as prescribed in the second section of this act, it shall be lawful for any three qualified voters of such sub-district, to call a special meeting of the voters of such sub-district, for the purpose of electing directors, on first giving five days' notice, in writing, of the time and place of holding such meeting, by posting the same in three of the most public places in such sub-district; and the Directors, so elected at such special meeting, shall hold their offices for the same terms of time as if elected on the second Monday of April, as prescribed in said second section, except that their said terms of office shall be considered as having commenced on the second Monday of April next preceding the time of holding such special meeting.

Terms of office.

How Directors to organize, and their meetings.

SEC. 5. It shall be the duty of the Directors, any two of whom shall constitute a quorum, to meet as soon as practicable after having been elected and qualified, at such place as may be most convenient in the sub-district, and organize by appointing one of their number Clerk of the sub-district, who shall preside at the official meetings of the Directors, and record their proceedings in a book provided for the purpose, together with the minutes of the proceedings of the annual school meetings held in the sub-district, by the qualified voters thereof, which shall be a public record; and all such proceedings, when so recorded, shall be signed by the Clerk of the proper sub-district. The Directors may meet as frequently as they may think necessary for the transaction of business, and fill any vacancies in the office of Clerk which may occur in the sub-district; or, in case of his absence, either of the other Directors may officiate temporarily in his place.

Clerk of sub-districts; duties of.

DUTIES OF LOCAL DIRECTORS.

Their duties.

SEC. 6. It shall be the duty of the School Directors, in each sub-district, to take the management and control of its local interests and affairs, to employ teachers, to certify the amount due them for services to the township Clerk, who shall draw an order on the township Treasurer for the amount; and to dismiss any teacher, at any time, for such reasons as they may deem sufficient; and to visit the school or schools of the sub-district at least twice during each term, by one

Township Clerk to draw orders on treasury.

or more of their number, with such other person or persons competent to examine pupils in their studies, as they may choose to invite.

Duties of local Directors continued.

SEC. 7. It shall be the duty of the Directors, in their respective sub-districts, to negotiate and make, under such rules and regulations as the township Board of Education may prescribe, all necessary contracts in relation to providing fuel for schools, repairing, building, or furnishing school-houses, purchasing or leasing school-house sites, renting school-rooms, and making all other provisions necessary for the convenience and prosperity of schools within their sub-district; but no contracts shall be made by the Directors, under the provisions of this section, for the payment of money from the township school fund applicable to such purposes, which in any one year shall exceed the amount distributable to the sub-districts, in proportion to the enumeration of scholars resident therein, without first obtaining the consent or order of a majority of the township Board of Education; and all contracts made by the local Directors, under the provisions of this section, shall be reported to the said Board, at their next meeting after the making of such contracts; and said township Board of Education, in their corporate capacity, on the part of the sub-district, shall be held responsible for the performance thereof.

When consent of Board to be obtained.

Contracts to be reported to Board. Board responsible for performance of contracts.

Enumeration of youth.

SEC. 8. It shall be the duty of the Directors in each sub-district, to take, or cause to be taken, annually, between the first and third Monday of October, an enumeration of all the unmarried white and colored youth, noting them separately, between the ages of five and twenty-one years, resident within such sub-district, and not temporarily there, designating between male and female, and return a certified copy thereof to the township Clerk. And in case the Directors in any sub-districts shall fail to take and return the enumeration aforesaid, it shall be the duty of the township Clerk to employ a competent person to take the same, and allow him a reasonable compensation for his services, and shall proceed to recover the amount so paid, for such services, in a civil action, before any court having jurisdiction, in the name of the State of Ohio, against said Directors, in their individual capacity; and in such suits, said Clerk shall be a competent witness; and the money so collected shall be applied to the use of common schools in the proper township. The township Clerk shall make an abstract of the enumeration so returned to him, designating the number of youth in each sub-district, and transmit such abstract, duly certified, to the county Auditor, within twenty days after the return made to him by the Directors, or the person appointed to take such enumeration.

Abstract to be transmitted to Auditor.

SEC. 9. If any civil township, or part of a township, composing a sub-district, shall be partly situated in the Virginia Military District, the United States Military District, the Western Reserve, or in an original surveyed township, or fractional township, to which belongs any of section sixteen, or other lands in lieu thereof, or any other lands for the use of schools, or any interest in the proceeds of such school lands, the local Directors shall, in taking the enumeration of youth resident within their jurisdiction, return separately those residing in the Virginia Military District, or United States Military District, or Western Reserve, or original surveyed or fractional township, to which belong any school lands, or interest in the proceeds of school lands.

Different surveys to be noted separately.

TOWNSHIP BOARDS OF EDUCATION.

SEC. 10. That the township Board of Education shall consist of the township Clerk, and of the local Director from each sub-district of the township, who has been appointed Clerk in his sub-district, a majority of whom shall constitute a quorum for the transaction of business; and the Clerk of the township shall be Clerk of the Board, but shall not be entitled to a vote. It shall be the duty of said Clerk to be present at the meetings of the Board, and to record in a book, to be provided for the purpose, all their official proceedings, which shall be a public record, open to the inspection of any person interested therein; and all such proceedings, when so recorded, shall be signed by the Chairman and Clerk.

Of whom composed.

Quorum.

Township Clerk to be Clerk of Board.

SEC. 11. The said township Board of Education, in each township of the State, and their successors in office, shall be a body politic and corporate in law, and, as such, may contract and be contracted with, sue and be sued, plead and be impleaded, in any court of law or equity in this State, and may receive any gift, grant, donation, or devise, made for the use of any school or schools, within their jurisdiction; and, moreover, they shall be, and are hereby invested, in their corporate capacity, with the title, care, and custody of all school-houses, school-house sites, school libraries, apparatus, or other property belonging to the school district as now organized, or which may hereafter be organized, within the limits of their jurisdiction,

Powers and duties.

with full power to control the same in such manner as they may think will best subserve the interests of common schools, and the cause of education; and when, in the opinion of the Board, any school-house, or school-house site, has become unnecessary, they may sell and convey the same in the name of the township Board of Education of the proper township; such conveyance to be executed by the Chairman and Clerk of said Board, and shall pay the avails over to the township Treasurer of the proper township, for the benefit of schools; and all conveyances of real estate which may be made to said Board, shall be to said board in their corporate name, and to their successors in office.

Sessions of the Board, regular and adjourned.

SEC. 12. It shall be the duty of the township Board of Education to hold regular sessions on the third Monday of April, and on the third Monday of October in each year, in the usual place of holding township elections, or at any such place in the immediate neighborhood as may be convenient for the transaction of any business which may be necessary in relation to the subject of either the primary or graded schools of the township, with power to adjourn from time to time, or to hold special meetings at any other time or place within the proper township, as they may think desirable for the transaction of business as aforesaid, and at all such meetings shall appoint one of their number to the Chair, and in case of the absence of the township Clerk, may appoint one of their own number to serve temporarily as Clerk.

Management of central and high schools.

SEC. 13. The township Board of Education shall have the management and control of all the central and high schools of their proper township, which may be established therein under the authority of this act, with full power, in respect to such schools, to employ, pay, and dismiss teachers, to build, repair and furnish the necessary school-houses, purchase or lease sites therefor, or rent suitable school-rooms, and make all other necessary provisions relative to such schools as they may deem proper; and it shall also be the duty of said Board of Education, to exercise all the powers conferred on local Directors in respect to sub-district schools, whenever such local Directors shall neglect to discharge their duties in any sub-district, as required by this act; and it shall also be the further duty of said Board to prescribe rules and regulations for the government of all the common schools within their jurisdiction; said Board of Education may provide for German schools for the instruction of such youth as may desire to study

When to act as local Directors.

To prescribe rules, etc.

May provide for German schools.

the German language, or the German and English languages together, and if the Board shall deem it necessary, they may appoint one of their number the Acting Manager of Schools for the township, who shall do and perform all such duties as the Board may prescribe in relation to the management and supervision of the different schools, and the educational interests of the township, and may allow him a reasonable compensation for his services.

May appoint Acting Manager.

SEC. 14. The said Board shall prepare, or cause to be prepared, a map of their township, as often as they deem necessary, on which shall be designated the sub-districts of the township, which they may change or alter at any regular session, and the number of scholars assigned to each; but no sub-district shall contain within its limits, less than sixty resident scholars by enumeration, except in cases where, in the opinion of the Board, it is necessary to reduce the number; and it shall be the duty of the Board to establish a school in each sub-district of the township, of such grade as the public good, in their opinion, may require; and in the location of primary schools, or schools of higher grade, the Board shall have reference to population and neighborhood, paying due regard to any school-house already built, or site procured, as well as to all other circumstances proper to be considered, so as to promote the best interests of the schools.

Map of township.

Board may alter sub-districts.

Sub-districts not to contain less than sixty scholars, except.

School in each sub-district.

SEC. 15. The Board shall have power to assign such number of scholars to the several primary schools as they may think best; and when such assignment has been made, shall furnish the teacher a list of the scholars to be assigned; and the Board shall also have full power to regulate and control the admission of scholars to schools of a higher grade, according to age and attainments, and may admit scholars over twenty-one years of age, and may suspend, or authorize the local Directors to suspend, from the privileges of either of the schools, any pupil found guilty of disorderly conduct, which suspension shall not extend beyond the current session of the school.

Assignment of scholars to higher schools.

Disorderly scholars may be suspended.

SEC. 16. Whenever it shall happen that persons are so situated as to be better accommodated at the school of an adjoining township, or whenever it may be desirable to establish a school composed of parts of two or more townships, it shall be the duty of the respective Boards of the townships in which such persons reside, or in which such schools may be situated, or of the townships or parts of which the school is to be composed, to transfer such persons for educational purposes

Division of township for educational purposes.

17

Scholars may be transferred to another township.

to the township in which such school house is, or may be located; but the enumeration of scholars shall be taken in each township, as if no such transfer had been made, and such school, when so composed, shall be supported from the school funds of the respective townships from which the scholars may have been transferred; and the Board of that township in which the school-house is situated, shall have the control and management of such school, and the Board of the adjoining township or townships, so connected for school purposes, shall each make the proper estimates of their share of expenses of every kind necessary to sustain said school, and certify the same to the Auditor of their proper county, as part of their annual estimates for school purposes, and draw orders on their respective township Treasurers, for such sum as will be in proportion to the enumeration of scholars so transferred, in favor of the Board of that township in which such school is located, to be appropriated to the payment of teachers, and for other purposes connected with the establishment or maintenance of said school, as far as applicable.

Board to determine studies, books.

SEC. 17. The said Board shall have power to determine the studies to be pursued, and the school-books to be used in the several schools under their control, and shall make and enforce such rules and regulations relative to the use and preservation of the school libraries and apparatus as they may think advisable, and shall appoint, or authorize the local Directors to appoint a suitable person to act as Librarian, and to take charge of the school apparatus, resident at some convenient place in the neighborhood where the school is kept, and may require such Librarian to give bond for the faithful discharge of his duties, and allow him such compensation as they may think reasonable.

Librarian.

To give bond.

REPORT REQUIRED OF TEACHERS.

What report must show.

SEC. 18. It shall be the duty of the school-teacher to make out and file with the township Clerk, at the expiration of each term of the school, a full and complete report of the whole number of scholars admitted to the school during such term, distinguishing between male and female, the average attendance, the books used, the branches taught, the number of pupils engaged in the study of each of said branches, and such other statistics as he may be required to make by the township Board or local Directors, and until such report shall have been certified and filed by the said teacher as aforesaid, it shall not be lawful for said Board or local Directors to pay said teacher for his or her services.

STATEMENT REQUIRED OF DIRECTORS.

SEC. 19. The Board of Education in each township shall prepare, or cause to be prepared, and forwarded to the county Auditor, *at the same time when the return of the enumeration of scholars is required to be made,** a statement exhibiting the number of children in the township between the ages of five and twenty-one years, distinguishing between male and female; the number of schools, specifying the different grades; the number of teachers, male and female; the number of children, male and female, who have attended school during the past year; the average attendance; the length of the terms of schools, compensation of teachers, male and female; the number and condition of the school-houses and furniture, and the estimated value thereof; the number and condition of the books in the school libraries; the number of libraries; the kind of school books used in the schools; the number and value of school apparatus, and a full account of the expenditures for school purposes, together with such other statistics and information in relation to schools, as the State Commissioner of Schools may require.

Board of Education to report to Auditor.

CENTRAL OR HIGH SCHOOLS.

SEC. 20. Each township Board of Education shall have power, as hereinafter provided, to establish in their respective townships such number of graded schools, or such modifications of them, as the public may require; and, in case of the establishment of such graded schools, it shall be the duty of the Board so to classify the children of the township as to secure to all, as far as practicable, an equitable participation in the advantages thereof; and the Board shall designate the sub-districts by numbering them, and schools of a higher grade than primary, shall be known by the appellation of central or high schools.

Establishment of, and classification of children in.

SEC. 21. Whenever, in the opinion of the Board of Education, it shall become necessary or desirable to provide one or more such central or high schools in their respective townships, the said Board shall estimate the probable cost thereof, and call a special meeting of

Vote to be taken in establishing such schools.

---

* Modified: see *post* chapter XIII. This report must be transmitted "on or before the first day of October."

the qualified voters of the township, and who are not residents of any of the territory or districts named in the first section of this act, over which the jurisdiction of the township and local Directors is excluded, at the usual place of holding elections, first giving twenty days' notice of the time and object of holding such meeting, by posting the same in some public place in each of the several sub-districts of the township, in which notice the amount or rate of tax as estimated by the Board shall be stated, and the electors, when convened in pursuance of such notice, shall decide, by vote, any questions which may be deemed important in relation to the cost or location of the building or buildings, or other provisions necessary for the establishment of any such school, and also the amount of township tax which may be levied for the purpose; and the Chairman and Clerk of the Board shall be the Chairman and Clerk of the meeting; and the Clerk shall record, in the records of the Board, the action of the meeting, and the Board shall be governed by the direction and vote of said meeting in relation to the subjects or matters so submitted.

Twenty days notice to be given.

Officers of meeting.

ANNUAL ESTIMATES TO BE CERTIFIED BY THE BOARD.

SEC. 22. It shall be the duty of the Board of Education, in any organized township of the State, annually to determine by estimate, as nearly as practicable, the entire amount of money necessary to be expended in the township for school purposes other than for the payment of teachers, and also such additional amount as the Board may think necessary, not exceeding two mills on the dollar valuation of the taxable property of the township, for the exclusive purpose of sustaining teachers in the central or high schools, or for the purpose of prolonging, after the State funds have been exhausted, the terms of the several sub-district or primary schools in the township, or for both purposes, as the Board may adjudge best, which several amounts of money so estimated, the Board shall make known by certificate in writing, on or before the first Monday in June in each year, including any tax which may have been voted by a special meeting of electors, as provided in the preceding section, to the Auditor of the proper county, who shall thereupon assess the entire amount of such estimates on all the taxable property of the township not included in any city, or incorporated village, or territory annexed thereto, forming any special district, to be entered by said Auditor on the tax dupli-

Auditor to assess the estimates on the taxable property of township.

cate of the county, and collected by the county Treasurer at the same time and in the same manner as State and county taxes are collected; and, when collected, shall be paid over to the Treasurer of the proper township, on the order of the county Auditor; and said county Treasurer shall be entitled to receive for collection, one per cent. on all the moneys by him collected for school purposes, and no more.

Funds to be paid to township Treasurer. His per centage.

SEC. 23. The township Board of Education shall have power, when in their opinion justice and equity require it, to estimate separately the cost of purchasing a school-house site, and erecting or repairing a school-house thereon, in any particular sub-district of the township wherein the inhabitants have not heretofore borne a reasonable share of the burden of taxation for such purpose in comparison with other sub-districts in the township, and certify such portion as they may deem just and equitable, of the amount of such estimate, to the county Auditor of the proper county, together with a map of the lands and names of the tax-payers in any such sub-district, which amount, so certified, shall be assessed by the Auditor on the property therein subject to taxation, and placed on the county duplicate, specially, and be collected and paid over in the same manner as other school taxes, and be applied for the specific purpose of providing a school-house in such sub-district.

When tax to be assessed on property in sub-district to purchase sites and school-houses.

DISBURSEMENT OF SCHOOL FUNDS.

SEC. 24. All school funds which may come into the hands of the township Treasurer, from whatever source, shall be paid out only on the order of the Clerk of the Board of Education, under the direction of the Board; except in paying teachers for their services, the said Clerk may, on such teachers presenting their certificates of qualification, and depositing with the Clerk true copies thereof, draw the requisite orders on the Treasurer for such amount as may have been certified to be due by any two of the local Directors of the proper sub-district, in which the teacher was employed; and so much of the school moneys coming into the hands of the Treasurer as may be derived from the State tax, or for any township tax levied for the continuation of schools after the State fund has been exhausted, shall be applicable only to the payment of teachers in the proper township, and shall be drawn for no other purpose whatever; and all school funds made applicable to the payment of teachers only, shall be distributed to the several sub-districts, and

Funds to be paid out on order of Clerk, except teachers.

How teachers paid.

Disbursement of funds.

fractional parts thereof, in the township, in proportion to the enumeration of scholars, with the exception of so much of the township tax as may have been levied and reserved by the Board for sustaining teachers in the central or high schools; and such school funds as arise from the sale or rents of section sixteen, or other lands in lieu thereof, shall be distributed to the localities to which such funds belong. All other school funds of the township, not raised for the central or high schools, nor made applicable to the payment of teachers, as aforesaid, shall be applied, under the direction of the Board, in repairing, building, or furnishing school-houses, in procuring school-house sites, and in making such other provisions for schools in the sub-districts of the proper township, as may, in the opinion of the Board, be necessary; and each township Board shall make the necessary provisions for continuing the schools in operation in their respective townships for at least seven months in each year.

To provide for seven months' school in each sub-district.

DIVISION OF DUTIES, AND LIABILITY OF CLERK.

Duties of Clerk, etc.

SEC. 25. The Clerk of the Board of Education, or any one or more of the Board designated for that purpose, or the Acting Manager of Schools of the township, may do and perform all such duties and services connected with the interests of schools, as the Board may direct, and report the same to the Board for their action and approval; and it shall be the duty of the Clerk of the Board to keep a full record thereof, in connection with the records of the other official proceedings of the Board; and, in case of failure to keep such record, or other records required by this act, the Clerk of the Board shall be liable in a civil action for all loss or damages that may ensue to any person or persons, or to the school district, in the name of such person or persons, or Board of School Directors, as the case may be, and shall, moreover, be liable, on complaint filed in the name of the State of Ohio, before any Justice of the Peace, or other court having jurisdiction, to a fine, not exceeding one hundred dollars, which, when collected, shall be paid over to the Treasurer of the proper township, for the benefit of schools.

SETTLEMENT WITH TREASURER.

Board to settle with township Treasurer.

SEC. 26. It shall be the duty of the Board of Education to make settlement with the township Treasurer at their regular session in April, annually; but if, for want of time, or other reason, a settlement can not be made at said session, then it shall be the duty of the Board to appoint a Committee composed of one or more of their own members, to make such settlement as soon as practicable, and report the result to the Clerk of the Board, who shall record an abstract thereof in the records of the Board.

TREASURER, AND HIS DUTIES.

Duties of township Treasurer; to give bond; its condition, etc.

SEC. 27. The township Treasurer, in each township, shall be the treasurer of all school funds for school purposes, belonging to the township, arising from whatever sources; and on his election, and before entering upon the duties of his office, he shall give bond, with sufficient security, in double the probable amount of money that shall come into his hands, payable to the State of Ohio, to be approved by the Trustees of the township, conditioned for the faithful disbursement, according to law, of all such funds as shall, from time to time, come into his hands, and, on the forfeiture of such bond, it shall be the duty of the township Clerk to prosecute and collect the same for the use of the schools in the township; if such township Clerk shall neglect, or refuse to so prosecute, then any freeholder may cause such prosecution to be instituted.

When township Clerks to prosecute.

Certificate to be furnished Auditor.

SEC. 28. Before the county Auditor shall issue to the township Treasurer any order on the county Treasurer for the payment of any school funds belonging to the township, such township Treasurer shall furnish the Auditor with a certificate from the township Clerk, that such Treasurer has executed and filed with him a bond, as provided for in the foregoing section, and also stating the amount of said bond; and the Auditor shall in no case permit the township Treasurer to have in his hands, at any one time, an amount of school funds over one-half the amount of the penalty in such bond; and the township Trustees shall allow the township Treasurer a compensation equal to one per cent. on all school funds disbursed by him, to be paid on the order of the Trustees, out of the township treasury.

Settlement of Auditor and Treasurer.

SEC. 29. The township Treasurer shall, annually, between the first and twentieth of February, settle with the county Auditor, and account to him for all moneys received, from whom and on what account, and the amount paid out for school purposes in his township; the Auditor shall examine the vouchers for such payments, and, if satisfied with the correctness

Auditor's certificate.

thereof, shall certify the same, which certificate shall be *prima facie* a discharge of such Treasurer; and at the expiration of his term of service, said Treasurer shall deliver over to his successor in office, all books and papers, with all moneys, or other property, in his hands, belonging to said township, or the schools therein, and also all orders he may have redeemed since his last annual settlement with the county Auditor, and take the receipt of his successor therefor, which he shall deposit with the township Clerk within ten days thereafter; and for making such annual settlement, he shall be entitled to receive the sum of one dollar, to be paid out of the county treasury, on the order of the county Auditor.

Treasurer to deliver over books, papers, etc.

Treasurer's receipt, etc.

Penalty against township Treasurer.

SEC. 30. In case the township Treasurer shall fail to make such annual settlement within the time as prescribed in the preceding section, he shall be liable to pay a fine of fifty dollars, to be recovered in a civil action in the name of the State of Ohio, and when collected, to be applied to the use of common schools in the proper township; and it is hereby made the duty of the county Auditor to proceed forthwith, in case of such failure, by suit, against such Treasurer, before any Justice of the Peace of his county, to recover the penalty aforesaid; but when it shall appear, on trial, to the satisfaction of said Justice, that said Treasurer was prevented from making such settlement within the time prescribed, by sickness, or unavoidable absence from home, and that such settlement has since been actually made, it shall be lawful for the Justice to discharge such Treasurer on the payment of costs.

SCHOOLS FOR COLORED CHILDREN.

Schools for colored children.

SEC 31. The township Boards of Education in this State, in their respective townships, and the several other Boards of Education, and the Trustees, Visitors, and Directors of Schools, or other officers having authority in the premises, of each city or incorporated village, shall be, and they are hereby authorized and required to establish within their respective jurisdictions, one or more separate schools for colored children, when the whole number, by enumeration, exceeds thirty, so as to afford them, as far as practicable under all the circumstances, the advantages and privileges of a common school education; and all such schools, so established for colored children, shall be under the control and management of the Board of Education, or other school officers who have in charge the educational interests of the other schools; but in case the average number of colored children in attendance shall be less than fifteen for any one month, it shall be the duty of said Board of Education, or other school officers, to discontinue said school or schools, for any period not exceeding six months at any one time; and if the number of colored children shall be less than fifteen, the Directors shall reserve the money raised on the number of said colored children, and the money so reserved shall be appropriated for the education of such colored children, under the direction of the township Board.

CITIES AND VILLAGES.

What cities and villages are school districts.

SEC. 32. Each city or incorporated village, including the territory annexed to the same for school purposes, not otherwise specially regulated by charter, or governed as to schools by laws as specified in the sixty-seventh section of this act, and which, with the territory annexed, contains not less than three hundred inhabitants, shall be, and hereby is created a separate school district; and the qualified voters of such city or village, with the territory annexed, shall, at the same time, and in the same manner, that local Directors of the sub-districts of the township are elected by the provisions of this act, proceed to elect three persons who shall constitute a Board of Education for such city or village, with the territory so annexed, and such Board shall have the same powers, perform the same duties, and be subject to the same penalties as township Boards of Education: provided, that by agreement between the Board of Education of the township in which such city or village, with the territory annexed, may be situated, and the Board of Education of such city or village, transfers of territory not within the limits of such corporation, may be made to or from the districts provided for in this section.

Power of Board in cities and towns.

SEC. 33. That said Board of Education, in any city or incorporated village, shall be authorized, when they think it advisable, to divide such city or village into sub-districts; and they may establish schools of different grades, and ordain such rules and regulations for the government and discipline of such schools as they may think conducive to the public good; and it shall be lawful for the township Board of Education, in any township in which such city or incorporated village is situate, by and with the consent of the Board of Education of any such city or incorporated village, to transfer thereto for educational purposes the scholars of such parts of their respective townships as lie adjacent thereto, and all such transfers shall be controlled, and such schools supported in the same manner, and on the same principles, as in case of like transfers for the convenience of schools where two or more townships adjoin, as provided in this act.

Clerk of the Board—his duties.

SEC. 34. In all such cities or incorporated villages, the Clerk or Recorder of such incorporated body shall be the Clerk of the Board of Education, and he shall do and perform all the duties required of the Clerk of a township Board of Education, and such other duties as the Board of Education may, from time to time, prescribe; and all orders of the Board of Education for the payment of money shall be countersigned by the Clerk or Recorder of said corporation, and it shall be the duty of the Treasurer of any such city or incorporated village, to receive and disburse the school funds of any such city or village, in the same manner as is required of the township Treasurers in their respective townships, and for his services shall be entitled to the same compensation: Provided, that the Board of Education shall require the Treasurer to enter into a bond, as required of township Treasurers, and that the said Treasurer shall furnish the Auditor a certificate from the Clerk or Recorder of such city or incorporated village, that such Treasurer has executed and deposited such bond, stating also the amount, as is required of township Treasurers in similar cases.

Duty of Treasurer of city or town.

To give bond.

Clerk or Recorder's receipt.

Further powers of the Board.

SEC. 35. The Board of Education of any city or incorporated village, shall have, and may exercise all the powers which are by this act conferred upon the township Boards of Education, and shall do and perform the like duties, in all respects, so far as applicable, and the school funds shall be divided among the sub-districts, so as to make the distribution as nearly equitable as possible. All taxes for building, purchasing, repairing, or furnishing school-houses and lots, shall be equally assessed on all the property subject to taxation in such city or incorporated village, and the Board of Education, in expending the same, shall make the necessary provisions for the sub-districts.

Ev'ing schools.

SEC. 36. In any district or sub-district, composed, in whole or in part, of any city or incorporated village, the Board of Education may, at their discretion, provide a suitable number of evening schools, for the instruction of such youth over twelve years of age as are prevented, by their daily avocation, from attending day schools, subject to such regulations as said Board, from time to time, may adopt for the government thereof.

APPORTIONMENT OF SCHOOL FUNDS.

State Auditor to apportion funds and certify apportionment.

SEC. 37. The Auditor of State shall, annually, apportion the common school funds among the different counties, upon the enumeration and returns made to him by the State Commissioner of Common Schools, and certify the amount so apportioned to the county Auditor of each county, stating from what sources the same is derived, which said sum the several county Treasurers shall retain in their respective treasuries from the State funds; and the county Auditors shall, annually, and immediately after their annual settlement with the county Treasurer, apportion the school funds for their respective counties, according to the enumeration and returns in their respective offices; and no township, or other district, city, or village, which shall have failed to make and return such enumeration, shall be entitled to receive any portion of the common school funds. And, in making such distribution, each county Auditor shall apportion all moneys collected on the tax duplicate of any township, for the use of schools, to such township; all moneys received from the State treasury, on account of interest on the money accruing from the sale of section sixteen, or other lands in lieu thereof, to the civil townships and parts of civil townships in the original surveyed township, or fractional township, to which such land belongs; all moneys received by the county Treasurer on account of the Virginia Military school fund, United States Military District, and Connecticut Western Reserve, according to laws regulating the same; and all other moneys for the use of schools in the county, and not otherwise appropriated by law, to the proper township; and he shall, immediately after making said apportionment, enter the same into a book, to be kept for that purpose, and shall furnish the township Treasurers and township Clerks, Treasurers, and Recorders of incorporated cities or villages, as the case may be, each with a copy of said apportionment, and give an order on the county Treasurer to each township Treasurer, or to such Treasurer as may be entitled to receive the same, for the amount of money belonging to his respective township, city, or village, and take a receipt from such Treasurer for the amount thus received; and the said county Auditor shall collect, or cause to be collected, the fines, and all other moneys for school purposes, in his county, and pay the same

County Auditor to make apportionment in county and how.

over to the county Treasurer; and he shall inspect all accounts of interest for section sixteen, or other school lands, whether the interest is paid by the State or by the debtors, and take all the proper measures to secure to each township its full amount of school funds.

Where part of section 16 lies in two counties.

SEC. 38. When any original surveyed township in which section sixteen has been sold, shall lie in two or more counties, the Auditors of the respective counties shall certify to the Auditor of the county in which that portion of said township lies containing said section sixteen, the enumeration of the scholars in that part of said township embraced within their respective counties; and the Auditor of said county in which said section sixteen is situate shall apportion the fund derived from said section sixteen, to the different portions of said township according to said enumeration, and shall certify to the Auditors of the other counties the amount belonging to the parts of said township situate in their respective counties, and draw an order in favor of the Treasurers of the other counties on the Treasurer of his own county for the amount going to each; and the Auditors of the respective counties shall apportion the same, in their respective counties, to such portions or parts thereof as may be entitled thereto.

Interest on section.

SEC. 39. The interest on the purchase of any such section sixteen belonging to any such original surveyed township, so as aforesaid lying in two or more counties, shall be paid over on the order of the Auditor of that county in which such section sixteen is embraced, to the Treasurer of the same county, to be apportioned as is pointed out in the preceding section.

RETURN OF ABSTRACT TO STATE COMMISSIONER.

Duty of county Auditor as to returns to State Commissioner, etc.

SEC. 40. The Auditor of each and every county shall, *on or before the twentieth day of December*,* annually, make out and transmit to the Commissioner of Common Schools, at Columbus, an abstract of all the returns of school statistics made to him from the several townships in his county, according to the form that may be prescribed by the State Commissioner; and he shall cause to be distributed all such circulars, blanks, and other papers, including school laws and documents, in the several townships in the county, as said Commissioner shall lawfully require. In case the county Auditor

---

* Modified: See chapter XIII. This report must be transmitted on or before the fifth day of November.

shall fail, from any cause, to make return of the abstract as aforesaid, it shall be the duty of the county Commissioners to deduct for every such failure, from the annual salary or allowance made to the Auditor for his services, the sum of fifty dollars.

Penalty against county Auditor.

SEC. 41. The county Commissioners of each county in this State shall make the same allowance to the county Auditors, out of their respective county treasuries, for services performed and expenses incurred under this act, as is allowed for other services of like nature.

Compensation to county Auditor.

SEC. 42. The township Clerks and county Auditors shall be responsible for all losses sustained by any township or county, by reason of any failure on their respective parts to make and return the enumerations and abstracts thereof as herein provided, and shall each be liable for the same, in a civil action, at the suit of the State of Ohio; and the amounts so recovered shall be apportioned, in the same manner as the school funds would have been, to the respective counties or townships, as the case may be.

Liability of the Clerk and county Auditor for loss.

SCHOOL-HOUSES EXEMPT FROM SALE ON EXECUTION.

SEC. 43. Each and every lot or parcel of land which heretofore has been, or hereafter shall be appropriated for the use of common schools in this State, on which there has been or shall be a school-house erected, and which has been or shall be occupied for the purpose of accommodating a common school of whatever grade, in the usual manner, from time to time, howsoever or by whomsoever the legal title to the same may be held and vested, shall be and the same is hereby exempted from sale, on any execution, or other writ, or order in the nature of an execution: Provided, that the lot of land so exempted, shall not exceed four acres, and if there be any excess, that portion most convenient for school purposes shall remain exempt as aforesaid, to be determined by the proper School Directors, or other officers having charge of schools.

What school property exempt from execution.

APPOINTMENT OF SCHOOL EXAMINERS, AND THEIR DUTIES.

SEC. 44. It shall be the duty of the Probate Judge, in the several counties of this State, as soon after the election of school officers under the provisions of this act as practicable, to appoint a county Board of School Examiners, to consist of three competent persons, resident in the county, who shall hold their office for the

Probate Judge to appoint board of examiners.

term of two years, and until their successors are appointed; and all vacancies in said Board which may thereafter occur, whether from expiration of the term of office, refusal to serve, or otherwise, shall be filled by like appointment by said Judge.

Powers and duties of Board.

SEC. 45. It shall be the duty of the Examiners to fix upon the time of holding meetings for the examination of teachers, in such places in their respective counties as will, in their opinion, best accommodate the greatest number of candidates for examination; notice of all such meetings having been published in some newspaper of general circulation in their respective counties; and at such meetings, any two of said Board shall be competent to examine applicants and grant certificates; but no fee or charge shall be made for a certificate. No certificate of qualification shall be valid in any county except that in which the examination took place, nor for a longer period than two years, and if at any time the recipient of the certificate shall be found incompetent or negligent, the Examiners, or any two of them, may revoke the same, and require such teachers to be dismissed; but such teachers shall be entitled to receive payment for services only up to the time of such dismissal; and no person shall be employed as a teacher in any primary common school, unless such person shall have first obtained from said Examiners, or any two of them, a certificate of good moral character, and that he or she is qualified to teach Orthography, Reading, Writing, Arithmetic, Geography, and English Grammar; and, in case such person intends to teach in any common school of higher grade, he or she shall first obtain a certificate of the requisite qualifications in addition to the branches aforesaid.

Notice of meetings.

To grant certificates to teachers.

May revoke the same.

Clerk of Board.

SEC. 46. The said Board of Examiners shall appoint one of their number to serve as Clerk, who shall keep a record of their proceedings, noting the number and date of each certificate given, to whom, for what term of time, and for what branches of studies; and the said Board may make all needful rules and regulations for the proper discharge of their duties. The members of the Board shall be entitled to receive each one dollar and fifty cents for every day necessarily engaged in official service, to be paid out of the county treasury, on the order of the county Auditor, exclusive of blank books and stationery, which the county Auditor shall furnish; and the county Auditor may require the accounts, when presented, to be substantiated on oath, which said officer may administer and file in his office.

Rules of Board; their fees.

Stationery.

STATE COMMISSIONER.

SEC. 47. There shall be elected by the qualified electors of this State, at the next annual election for State and county officers, and every three years thereafter, a State Commissioner of Common Schools, who shall hold his office for the term of three years, and until his successor is elected and qualified. The election of said Commissioner, and the returns thereof, shall be the same, in all respects, as is provided for the election of Judges of the Supreme Court; and in case a vacancy shall happen in said office by death, resignation, or otherwise, the Governor shall fill the same by appointment, for the unexpired term. *When Commissioner elected. Term of office. Vacancy, how filled.*

SEC. 48. Before entering upon the discharge of his official duties, the said Commissioner shall give bond, in the penal sum of ten thousand dollars, to the State of Ohio, with two or more sureties, to the acceptance of the Secretary of State, conditioned that he will truly account for and apply all moneys, or other property, which may come into his hands in his official capacity, for the use and benefit of common schools, and that he will faithfully perform the duties enjoined upon him according to law; and he shall also take and subscribe an oath or affirmation to support the Constitution of the United States and of the State of Ohio, and diligently and faithfully to discharge the duties of his office, as prescribed by law, which bond, with the certificate of his oath indorsed thereon, shall be filed with the Treasurer of State. *His official bond and oath.*

SEC. 49. The books and papers of his department shall be kept at the seat of Government, where a suitable office shall be furnished by the State, at which he shall give attendance when not absent on public business; and the State Librarian shall, in addition to the duties of his office, discharge the duties of Secretary to the Commissioner of Common Schools, under his direction. *Office, etc., at seat of Government. His Secretary.*

SEC. 50. It shall be the duty of the Commissioner to spend, annually, on an average, at least ten days in each judicial district of the State, superintending and encouraging Teachers' Institutes, conferring with township Boards of Education, or other school officers, counseling teachers, visiting schools, and delivering lectures on topics calculated to subserve the interests of popular education. *His duties in visiting the several judicial districts,*

SEC. 51. As soon as the revenues, to be raised as hereinafter provided, for the purpose of furnishing the *and in purchasing books and apparatus.*

schools with libraries and apparatus, will admit, it shall be the duty of the said Commissioner, to purchase the same, and the books and apparatus so purchased shall be distributed through the Auditor's office of each county to the Board of Education in each township, city or incorporated village, according to the enumeration of scholars.

His supervision over school funds.

SEC. 52. He shall also exercise such supervision over the educational funds of the State as may be necessary to secure their safety, and right application, and distribution according to law. He shall have power to require of county Auditors, township Boards of Education, or other local school officers, Clerks and Treasurers of townships, county Treasurers and Clerks, Recorders and Treasurers of cities and villages, copies of all reports by them required to be made, and all such other information in relation to the funds and condition of schools, and the management thereof, as he may deem important.

May require reports from certain officers.

To prepare forms, etc.

SEC. 53. He shall prescribe suitable forms and regulations for making all reports and conducting all necessary proceedings under this act, and shall cause the same, with such instructions as he shall deem necessary and proper for the organization and government of schools, to be transmitted to the local school officers, who shall be governed in accordance therewith.

Duties as to distribution of school laws, etc.

SEC. 54. He shall cause as many copies of the laws relating to schools and Teachers' Institutes, with an appendix of appropriate forms and instructions for carrying into execution all such laws, to be printed in a separate volume, and distributed to each county with the laws, journals, and other documents for the use of the school officers therein, as often after the first distribution as any change in said laws may be made, of sufficient importance, in the opinion of the Commissioner, to require a republication and distribution thereof.

His annual report.

SEC. 55. It shall be the duty of said Commissioner of Common Schools to make an annual report, *on or before the twentieth day of January, in each and every year*,* to the General Assembly, when the body shall be in session any such year; and when not in session in any one year, then the report shall be made to the Governor, who shall cause the same to be published, and shall also communicate a copy thereof to the next General Assembly.

---

* Modified: see chapter XIII. This report must be made "on or before the twentieth day of November."

SEC. 56. The State Commissioner, in the annual report of his labors and observations, shall present a statement of the condition and amount of all funds and property appropriated to purposes of education; a statement of the number of common schools in the State, the number of scholars attending such schools, their sex, and the branches taught; a statement of the number of private or select schools in the State, so far as the same can be ascertained, and the number of scholars attending such schools, their sex, and the branches taught; a statement of the number of Teachers' Institutes, and the number of teachers attending them; a statement of the estimates and accounts of the expenditures of the public school funds of every description; a statement of plans for the management and improvement of common schools, and such other information relative to the educational interests of the State as he may think of importance.

What it shall present.

SEC. 57. The said Commissioner shall be entitled to receive for his services the sum of fifteen hundred dollars annually, payable quarterly, out of the State treasury, on the warrant of the Auditor of State.

Salary of Commissioner.

SCHOOL LIBRARIES.*

SEC. 58. For the purpose of furnishing school libraries and apparatus, to all the common schools in the State, and for the further purpose of sustaining and increasing such libraries, and keeping up a supply of school apparatus in the schools, as aforesaid, from time to time, as may be considered necessary, in order to afford equal facilities to the said schools in this respect, as nearly as practicable, there shall hereafter be assessed, collected, and paid annually, in the same manner as the State and county revenues are assessed, collected and paid on the grand list of property taxable for State purposes, a State tax of one-tenth of one mill on the dollar valuation, to be applied exclusively for the purposes aforesaid, and the attendant expenses, under the direction of the Commissioner of Common Schools. In purchasing the libraries for the common schools, no books of sectarian or denominational character shall be purchased for said libraries.

One-tenth of a mill to be assessed for libraries;

SEC. 59. The amount of said tax, when collected, shall be paid over by the county Treasurers to the

which is to be paid to State Treasurer.

* The General Assembly, having omitted at the session of 1856, to appropriate for this purpose, the operation of sections 58-62 is suspended.

State Treasurer, at the time of making their annual settlement, and shall be paid out by that officer for the purposes aforesaid, upon the warrant of the State Auditor.

Distribution of books and apparatus.

SEC. 60. It shall be the duty of the county Auditor, when the said libraries or apparatus shall be received, to distribute the same to the Clerks of the township Boards of Education, or other local school officers, in their respective counties, having in charge the interests of common schools; and the books and apparatus so furnished, shall be deemed the property of said several Boards, or local school officers, to whom the same may have been delivered, and shall not be subject to execution, sale or alienation, for any cause whatever.

Who accountable for same.

SEC. 61. The local Boards of Education, or other school officers having charge of common schools shall be held accountable for the preservation of said libraries and apparatus; and they shall have power to prescribe the time of taking and the periods of returning the books belonging to the libraries, and also to assess and collect the damages which may be done to the books by persons entitled to their use; and also to provide for the safe keeping of the school apparatus.

Who to appoint Librarian, etc.

SEC. 62. It shall be the duty of the local School Boards, or other school officers having charge of schools, to appoint the Librarians and determine the places where the libraries shall be deposited, selecting such central points as will best accommodate the schools and families of the districts or sub-districts, as hereinafter provided; and every family in each district or sub-district shall be entitled to the use of one volume at a time from the school library, although no member of such family attends any of the schools of the township; and the library shall be open, under the inspection of the Librarian, at stated periods throughout the year, to be prescribed by the Board of Education, or other proper school officers, without regard to the sessions of the schools.

Families entitled to books.

STATE SCHOOL FUNDS.

Two mills on the dollar to be assessed for school purposes, and collected and distributed.

SEC. 63. For the purpose of affording the advantages of a free education to all the youth of this State, the State common school fund shall hereafter consist of such sum as will be produced by the annual levy and assessment of *two mills** upon the dollar valuation,

* By act of May 1, 1854, a tax of "one and one-half mill" was substituted for the above rates: and this section, with that change, re-enacted.

on the grand list of the taxable property of the State; and there is hereby levied and assessed annually, in addition to the revenues required for general purposes, the said *two mills** upon the dollar valuation, as aforesaid; and the amount so levied and assessed, shall be collected in the same manner as other State taxes, and when collected, shall be annually distributed to the several counties of the State, in proportion to the enumeration of scholars, and be applied exclusively to the support of common schools.

Debts of districts to be provided for.

SEC. 64. The debts which have heretofore been contracted by any school district for school purposes, shall be provided for by the estimates of the proper School Boards created under the provisions of this act.

Process against school officers.

SEC. 65. The process, in all suits against any township Board of Education, or other local officers having charge of any of the public schools under the provisions of this act, shall be by summons, and shall be executed by leaving a copy thereof with the Clerk or Secretary of such Board, or other school officers, at least ten days before the return day thereof. And any suit either in favor of or against any such Board, or other school officers, shall be prosecuted or defended, as the case may be, by the Prosecuting Attorney of the proper county, as a part of his official duties.

Duty of Prosecuting Attorney.

How schools governed under other laws may accept this act.

SEC. 66. The local Board of Education, or other local officers having charge of schools in any city, township, or village, in which common schools have been organized under the act for the better regulation of public schools in cities, towns, etc., or under any special act, shall be, and are hereby authorized, whenever they may deem it expedient, to call a meeting of the qualified voters of any such city, township or village, on giving thirty days public notice thereof, to determine by vote whether the common schools of such city, township or village, shall be conducted and managed in accordance with the provisions of this act; and if a majority of the voters are found to be in favor of the change, then said local Board, or other local school officers, shall thereafter proceed, in accordance with the provisions of this act, until their successors shall be elected and qualified; and such city or village may provide by ordinance for the election or appointment of a Board of Education, prescribing their number and terms of office; and such Board, when so elected or appointed and qualified, shall, together with

* By act of May 1, 1854, a tax of "one and one-half mill" was substituted for the above rate: and this section, with that change, reenacted.

the Clerk or Recorder of such city or village, possess the same powers and discharge the same duties, within the limits of their jurisdiction, as local Directors and Boards of Education in townships.

Certain acts not repealed by this act.

SEC. 67. This act shall not be so construed as to repeal, change, or modify in any respect, the several provisions of the "act for the support and better regulation of common schools in the town of Akron," passed February 8, 1847, and the acts amendatory thereto; or the "act for the better regulation of schools in cities, towns, etc.," passed February 21, 1849, and the acts amendatory thereto, nor the several acts creating special school districts, or any other special acts in relation to schools, except that it is hereby made the duty of the several Boards of Education, or other school officers acting under the provisions of any of the acts to which reference has been made in this section, to make similar reports of school statistics annually, as required of school officers by this act; nor shall it be lawful for any county Treasurer to pay over any portion of the school fund to any local Treasurer, Board of Education, or other school officers of any city, township, or village, organized as to schools either under a general or a special law, except on the order of the Auditor of the proper county; and no such order shall be drawn by the county Auditor, unless the local Treasurer, Clerk, Recorder, or Secretary of such Board, or other school officer, shall first deposit with said Auditor annually, an abstract of the enumeration of scholars and other statistics relative to the schools under their charge, as required by this act, of teachers, local Directors, and Boards of Education in townships.

But such acts affected, and how.

Power of Board to hold real estate.

SEC. 68. The respective township Boards of Education, and their successors in office, shall have power to take and hold in trust, for the use and benefit of any central or high school, or sub-district school in the township, any grant or devise of land, and any donation or bequest of money or other personal property, to be applied by the Board to the maintenance and support of any such school or schools, according to the intention of the grant or donation.

ACTS REPEALED.

Repealing section.

Swan, 824.

SEC. 69. That "an act for the support and better regulation of common schools, and to create permanently the office of Superintendent," passed March seventh, one thousand eight hundred and thirty-eight;

an act to amend an act entitled "an act for the support and better regulation of common schools, and to create permanently the office of Superintendent," passed March sixteenth, one thousand eight hundred and thirty-nine; an "act to abolish the office of Superintendent of Common Schools," passed March twenty-third, one thouand eight hundred and forty; an act to amend the act entitled "an act for the support and better regulation of common schools, and to create permanently the office of Superintendent," of March seventh, one thousand eight hundred and thirty-eight, and the act amendatory thereto, passed March twenty-ninth, one thousand eight hundred and forty-one; an act to amend the act entitled "an act for the support and better regulation of common schools, and to create permanently the office of Superintendent," passed March seventh, one thousand eight hundred and forty-two; an act further to amend the act entitled "an act for the support and better regulation of common schools, and to create permanently the office of Superintendent," passed March eleventh, one thousand eight hundred and forty-three; an act to amend the act entitled "an act for the support and better regulation of common schools, and to create permanently the office of Superintendent," passed March twelfth, one thousand eight hundred and forty-four; an "act to amend the sixth section of an act for the support and better regulation of common schools, and to create permanently the office of Superintendent," passed March twelfth, one thousand eight hundred and forty-five; an act to amend the act entitled "an act to amend an act for the support and better regulation of common schools, and to create permanently the office of Superintendent," passed March twelfth, one thousand eight hundred and forty-five; "an act authorizing School Directors to establish libraries for the use of common schools," passed February twenty-eighth, one thousand eight hundred and forty-six; an act to amend an act, passed March eleventh, one thousand eight hundred and forty-three, entitled an act further to amend the act entitled "an act for the support and better regulation of common schools, and to create permanently the office of Superintendent," passed March second, one thousand eight hundred and forty-six; "an act to provide for the appointment of county Superintendents of Common Schools, and defining their duties in certain counties therein named," passed February eighth, one thousand eight hundred and forty-seven; an act further to amend the act entitled "an act to amend an act entitled an act

Swan, 840.

Swan, 844.

Swan, 844.

40 R. Stat. 49.

41 R. Stat. 59.

42 R. Stat. 48,

43 R. Stat. 98.

43 R. Stat. 132.

44 R. Stat. 81.

44 R. Stat. 114.

45 R. Stat. 33.

for the support and better regulation of common
schools, and to create permanently the office of Superintendent," passed February eighth, one thousand eight
hundred and forty-seven; an act to amend an act enti-
45 R. Stat. 26. tled "an act for the support and better regulation of
common schools, and to create permanently the office
of Superintendent," passed March seventh, one thousand eight hundred and thirty-eight, and the acts
amendatory thereto, passed February twenty-fourth,
46 R. Stat. 83. one thousand eight hundred and forty-eight; "an act
to secure the returns of the statistics of common
schools," passed January twenty-first, one thousand
46 R. Stat. 28. eight hundred and forty-eight; an act to provide for
the establishment of common schools, for the education of the children of black and mulatto persons, and
to amend the act entitled "an act for the support and
better regulation of common schools, and to create permanently the office of Superintendent," passed March
seventh, one thousand eight hundred and thirty-eight,
and the acts amendatory thereto, passed February
twenty-fourth, one thousand eight hundred and forty-
46 R. Stat. 81. eight; an act to amend the act entitled "an act for the
support and better regulation of common schools, and
to create permanently the office of Superintendent,"
passed March seventh, one thousand eight hundred and
thirty-eight, and the acts amendatory thereto, passed
February twenty-fourth, one thousand eight hundred
46 R. Stat. 83. and forty-eight; an act to amend the eighteenth section
of the school law of March seventh, one thousand eight
hundred and thirty-eight, passed February fourteenth,
46 R. Stat. 51. one thousand eight hundred and forty-eight; "an act
to authorize the establishment of separate schools for
the education of colored children, and for other purposes," passed February tenth, one thousand eight
47 R. Stat. 17. hundred and forty-nine; an act to amend an act, passed
February twenty-fourth, one thousand eight hundred
and forty-eight, entitled "an act to amend the act entitled an act for the support and better regulation of common schools, and to create permanently the office of
Superintendent," passed March seventh, one thousand
eight hundred and thirty-eight; and the acts amendatory thereto, passed March sixth, one thousand eight
hundred and forty-nine; an act to amend an act enti-
47 R. Stat. 39. tled "an act for the support and better regulation of
common schools, and to create permanently the office
of Superintendent," passed March twelfth, one thousand eight hundred and forty-nine; an act to amend an
47 R. Stat. 43. act entitled "an act for the support and better regulation of common schools, and to create permanently the

office of Superintendent," passed March seventh, one thousand eight hundred and thirty-eight, and the acts amendatory thereto, passed March twenty-fourth, one thousand eight hundred and forty-nine; an act in relation to school district tax, providing for the annual school district meetings, and requiring maps of school districts, passed March seventh, one thousand eight hundred and fifty; an act for the appointment of a State Board of Public Instruction, passed March twenty-second, one thousand eight hundred and fifty; an act supplementary to the act for the appointment of a State Board of Public Instruction, passed March twenty-third, one thousand eight hundred and fifty; an "act providing for school districts, and school district meetings, prescribing the duties of district officers and Clerks and Treasurers of townships, and increasing the State and county common school funds," passed March twenty-fourth, one thousand eight hundred and fifty-one—be, and the same are hereby repealed: Provided, that the obligations or liabilities incurred, and the rights acquired under the provisions of any of the acts hereby repealed, shall remain, and be in no wise altered or affected, but may be enforced, as if this act had not been passed; and the school officers in the several school districts of the State, as now organized, shall hold their respective offices, and perform their respective duties, until the local Directors herein provided for, shall have been elected and qualified.

47 R. Stat. 52.

48 R. Stat. 41.

48 R. Stat. 44.

48 R. Stat. 47.

490 R. Stat. 27

Liabilities incurred, and rights acquired, not affected.

JAMES C. JOHNSON,
Speaker of the House of Representatives.
GEORGE REX,
President of the Senate, pro tempore.

CHAPTER II.

THE AKRON SCHOOL LAWS.

An Act for the support and better regulation of Common Schools in the town of Akron.

[*Passed February* 8, 1847, XLVI *vol. Stat.* 105.]

Six Directors shall be elected.

SEC. 1. *Be it enacted by the General Assembly of the State of Ohio,* That the electors in the town of Akron, in the county of Summit, qualified to vote for members of the town Council, shall, at the time and place of holding the annual election for said members of the town Council, in the year one thousand eight hundred and forty-seven, meet and elect six Directors of the Common School for said town of Akron; two of whom shall serve for one year, two for two years, and two for three years; the order of seniority to be determined by lot, by such Directors, after the election, and annually thereafter, at the time and place above specified; there shall, in like manner, be two Directors elected, who shall serve for three years, and until their successors are elected and qualified. All vacancies which may occur, shall be filled by the town Council.

Board of Education, officers, powers, etc.

SEC. 2. The said Directors, within ten days after their first appointment as aforesaid, shall meet and organize, by choosing from their number a President, Secretary, and Treasurer; and such Treasurer, before he enters on the duties of his said office, shall give bond and security, to be approved by the town Council, and filed in the office of the Mayor of said town, conditioned for the faithful disbursement of all moneys that shall come into his hands as such Treasurer, which bond shall be made payable to the State of Ohio; and when such bond shall be forfeited, it shall be the duty of the town Council to sue and collect the same, for the use of the common schools in said town; and the said Directors, so organized and qualified, and their successors in office, shall be a body politic and corporate in law, by the name of "The Board of Education of the town of Akron," and, as such, and by such name, shall be authorized to receive all moneys accruing to said town, or any part thereof, for the use and benefit of the common schools in said town; and the said Board shall be capable of contracting and being contracted with, suing and being sued, pleading and being impleaded, in any court of law or equity in this State; and shall also be capable of receiving any gift, grant, donation, or devise, made for the use of the common schools in said town; and said Board, by resolution, shall direct the payment of all moneys that shall come into the hands of said Treasurer; and no money shall be paid out of the treasury, except in pursuance of such resolution, and on the written order of the President, countersigned by the Secretary.

Meetings of the Board.

SEC. 3. That said Board shall hold their meetings at such time and place as they may think proper; that any four of said Board shall constitute a quorum; that special meetings may be called by the President, or by any two members of the Board, on giving two days' notice of the time and place of holding such meetings; but at no special meeting, except all the Directors be present, shall any resolution in relation to sites for school-houses, or financial resolution, or order be passed, unless the two days' notice, as aforesaid, be given, and the subject or subjects to be acted on, be specified in the notice, and a quorum of at least four members be present.

Shall have control of common schools, etc., in Akron.

SEC. 4. That said Board of Education shall have the entire management and control of all the common schools in said town of Akron, and of all the houses, lands, and appurtenances already provided and set apart for common school purposes, as well as those hereafter to be provided for the same purposes; and the said town of Akron, from and after the first Tuesday in June next, after the passage of this act, shall constitute, in law, but one school district; and all moneys accruing to said district for school purposes, under any law of the State, shall be paid over to the Treasurer for said Board of Education.

Number and grade of schools —admission of pupils, etc.

SEC. 5. It shall be the duty of said Board of Education, so soon as they may realize sufficient funds for the purpose, to establish within the bounds of the town corporate of Akron, six or more primary schools, to be located in different parts of the town, so as best to accommodate the inhabitants, in which the rudiments of an English education shall be taught. It shall be the further duty of said Board to establish a central Grammar school in said town, where instruction shall be given in "the various studies and parts of study" not provided for in the primary school, and yet requisite to a respectable English education. To each school in this system there shall be gratuitous admission for the children, wards, and apprentices of all residents of the town corporate of Akron, and such other persons in the immediate vicinity as may own property, charged with a school tax in said town corporate of Akron, with the following restrictions, namely: No pupil shall be admitted to the Grammar school who fails to sustain a thorough examination in the studies of the primary school; and the teacher shall have power, in either school, with the advice and direction of the Board of Education, to exclude for misconduct, in extreme cases, and to classify the pupils as the best good of the school shall seem to require: Provided, however, that said Board of Education shall not make any rules which will exclude from said primary schools any scholar who, by the general laws of this State, would be entitled to admission into the common schools, within said town, and said Board shall not so appropriate the school fund, which, by the provisions of this act, shall come under their control, as to reduce the amount applicable to the support of said primary schools, below the sum to which, under the general laws of this State, the common schools within said town would be entitled.

Power of Board.

SEC. 6. The said Board of Education shall have power to make and enforce all necessary rules and regulations for the government of teachers and pupils in said schools, to employ teachers, male and female, and pay them a suitable compensation, to purchase all necessary books and apparatus, to select sites for school-houses, and superintend the building of the same upon their own plan, and to pay for the lands, and houses, and furniture, as well as other expenses of said school system, from the public moneys in the hands of the Treasurer.

Town Council to levy taxes for school purposes.

SEC. 7. The said Board of Education, within thirty days after their organization, shall report to the town Council of Akron the number and description of buildings necessary for the purposes of the common schools in said town, which report shall be in writing, and shall specify the amount of money necessary to be raised to meet the expense of erecting such buildings; and such Board shall also specify, in said report, the amount of money necessary to be raised in addition to the money accruing to said town under the general school laws of the State, to defray all the other expenses of said school system during the current year; and thereupon the said town Council shall proceed to levy a tax sufficient to meet such expenses of buildings and repairing school-houses, and the expenses attendant upon the maintenance of said free schools in Akron, during the whole year, customary vacations only excepted; said tax to be levied and collected as other taxes of said town are or may be collected. And it shall be the duty of said Board, on or before the first Monday in April, in every year thereafter, to make report in writing to the town Council, of all moneys received, how and for what purpose expended, with the proper vouchers, and such other information in relation to said schools as they may deem important, specifying in said annual report the amount of money necessary to be raised by taxation, to defray the expenses of said school system for the current year; and said town Council shall, annually, upon the coming in of such report, and within thirty days thereafter, proceed to levy a tax sufficient to meet such expenses, to be levied and collected as other taxes of said town. And the town Council shall cause all such reports of the Board of Education to be published, or so much thereof as they may deem necessary, the reports themselves to be left with the Mayor of the town, open to public inspection.

Reports of Board.

SEC. 8. All legal titles to lands and houses, and other property used for common school purposes in said town of Akron, shall vest in the town Council of Akron at the taking effect of this act, and all titles acquired thereafter shall be in the name of said town Council; and said town Council shall have power to sell, lease, and convey, any and all of the lands and tenements held under and by virtue of this act, and to purchase other lands and tenements in more eligible positions, by and with the advice of said Board of Education, but not otherwise.

Titles to Board, etc.

SEC. 9. The town Council shall, immediately after the appointment of Directors, as hereinbefore provided, appoint three competent persons to serve as School Examiners of said town, all of whom shall be citizens of Akron; one to serve until the first Tuesday in June, one thousand eight hundred and forty-eight; one until the first Tuesday in June, one thousand eight hundred and forty-nine; and one until the first Tuesday in June, one thousand eight hundred and fifty, and until their successors are qualified; and annually, at the first

Examiners of teachers and schools.

regular meeting of the town Council, after the annual election for members of that body, they shall appoint one person for Examiner, to serve for three years, and until his successor is qualified; and the Council shall fill all vacancies that may occur by death, removal, or otherwise. The Examiners, or any two of them, shall examine such persons as may apply for that purpose; and if they find the applicant qualified, they shall give him a certificate, naming the branches he is qualified to teach, that they have carefully inquired into his character, and believe it to be moral and good, and that they believe him to be well qualified to govern and teach; they shall, also, in every case where two of their number concur, have power to annul any certificate previously given, and the person holding the same shall be discharged from the public schools in said town;* they shall, also, separately or otherwise, together with such other persons as may be appointed by the Mayor, visit said schools at least as often as once in every quarter, observe the discipline, mode of instruction, progress of the scholars, and such other circumstances as they may deem of interest; and, semi-annually, at such times as the Board of Education shall [appoint,] they shall report their proceedings to the town Council, and also to the Board of Education, with such suggestions as they may think proper, the publication of which shall be in the discretion of the town Council.

Reports.

Public examination of schools.

SEC. 10. Annually, at such time as the Board shall appoint, public examinations of all the schools shall be had, under the direction of the Mayor, Council, the Board of Education, and the Examiners.

Repealing clause.

SEC. 11. So much of the general school law, and so much of any and all other laws of this State, general or local, as may be inconsistent with this act, or any of its provisions, is hereby repealed as to said town of Akron.

Extended to Dayton.

SEC. 12. The power conferred upon the Board of Education of the town of Akron, in the fifth section of this act, is hereby conferred upon the Managers of the common schools of the city of Dayton.

Right of repeal.

SEC. 13. Any future Legislature may alter, amend, or repeal this act.

WILLIAM P. CUTLER,
Speaker of the House of Representatives.
EDSON B. OLDS,
Speaker of the Senate.

Modified: see section 3 of the act of June 28, 1848, chapter III. Tax not to exceed four mills on the dollar: see section 1 of same act.

CHAPTER III.

An Act to amend the act entitled "An Act for the support and better regulation of Common Schools in the town of Akron," passed February 8, 1847.

[*Passed January* 28, 1848, XLVI *vol. Stat.* 110.]

Amount of tax.

SEC. 1. *Be it enacted by the General Assembly of the State of Ohio*, That the amount of tax heretofore to be assessed to defray the expense of the school system, introduced into said town by virtue of the act to which this is an amendment, shall not exceed, in any one year, four mills on the dollar of the taxable property in said town.

Powers of the Board of Education.

SEC. 2. The Board of Education of the town of Akron shall have full power and authority to determine what branches of education shall be taught in any and all of said schools under their management and control; and said Board shall also have power, at their discretion, to restrict the right of admission into any and all of said schools, to the children, wards, and apprentices of actual residents, within the limits of the town corporate of Akron, with power to admit scholars from abroad, upon such terms and conditions as said Board shall see fit to prescribe.

Duties of Auditor and Treasurer.

SEC. 3. That on or before the first Monday of June, in each year, it shall be the duty of the said Board of Education to make known to the Auditor of the county of Summit, the amount of tax which they may want levied for school purposes during the current year; and thereupon it shall be the duty of said county Auditor to assess the taxable property in said town of Akron, as the same appears upon the grand list; and the said tax shall be collected by the county Treasurer at the same time with the State and county taxes, and in the same manner; and, when collected, the amount shall be paid over to the Treasurer of said Board of Education.

SEC. 4. That so much of the act to which this is an

Repealing Clause.

amendment as conflicts with the provisions of this act, be, and the same is hereby repealed.

JOSEPH S. HAWKINS,
Speaker of the House of Representatives.
CHARLES B. GODDARD,
Speaker of the Senate.

CHAPTER IV.

An Act to provide for extending the provisions of an act entitled "An Act for the support and better regulation of Common Schools in the town of Akron," and the amendatory acts thereto, to the cities and incorporated towns of this State.

[*Passed February* 14, 1848, XLVI *vol. Stat.* 48.]

All incorporated towns may organize under preceding acts, and how.

SEC. 1. *Be it enacted by the General Assembly of the State of Ohio,* That every incorporated town or city in this State, shall have the provisions of the act entitled "an act for the support and better regulation of common schools in the town of Akron," and the amendatory act thereto, passed by the forty-sixth General Assembly of this State, extended to all or any of the said incorporated towns or cities, wherever two-thirds of the qualified voters thereof shall petition the town or city Council in favor of having the provisions of said acts so extended.

Election of Directors.

SEC. 2. That whenever two-thirds of the qualified voters of any city or incorporated town shall petition the town or city Council in favor of having the provisions of said acts extended to said city or incorporated town, the electors qualified to vote for members of the town or city Council, shall assemble at the time and place within said town or city, of which at least ten days' previous notice shall be given by the city or town Council, by posting written or printed notices in at least three of the most public places in said city or incorporated town, and then and there proceed to the election of six Directors, by ballot, who shall serve, and in all respects be governed by the provisions of the act entitled "an act for the support and better regulation of common schools in the town of Akron," and the act amendatory thereto; and the common schools in said city or incorporated town shall, in all respects, be governed and organized according to the provisions of said acts.

How number of voters ascertained.

SEC. 3. That the last preceding election in said city or incorporated town, shall be the basis upon which to determine the number of qualified voters.

Repealing clause.

SEC. 4. That all acts, or parts thereof, inconsistent with the provisions of this act, are hereby repealed: *Provided*, that this act shall not extend to, nor be in force in the city of Cincinnati.

JOSEPH S. HAWKINS,
Speaker of the House of Representatives.
CHARLES B. GODDARD,
Speaker of the Senate.

CHAPTER V.

An Act to amend an act entitled "An Act for the support and better regulation of Common Schools in the town of Akron," passed February 8, 1847, and the acts amendatory thereto.

[*Passed March* 15, 1849, XLVII *vol. Stat.* 45.]

Boards of Education may adopt certain laws.

SEC. 1. *Be it enacted by the General Assembly of the State of Ohio,* That the Board of Education in any city, town, or village, which has adopted the act entitled "an act for the support and better regulation of common schools in the town of Akron," passed February 8, 1847, and the acts amendatory thereto, may adopt the eleventh, twelfth, and fifteenth sections of the act entitled "an act for the better organization of the public schools in cities, towns," etc., passed February 15, 1849, whenever, in the opinion of said Board of Education, the educational interests of such city, town, or village, may require it.

SEC. 2. All acts, or parts thereof, inconsistent with the provisions of this act, are hereby repealed.

JOHN G. BRESLIN,
Speaker of the House of Representatives.
BREWSTER RANDALL,
Speaker of the Senate.

CHAPTER VI.

GENERAL ACT FOR SCHOOLS IN CITIES, TOWNS, ETC.

An Act for the better regulation of the Public Schools in cities, towns, etc.

[*Passed February* 21, 1849, XLVII *vol. Stat.* 22.]

Towns of 200 inhabitants may be single school districts.

SEC. 1. *Be it enacted by the General Assembly of the State of Ohio,* That any incorporated city or town in this State, or any incorporated town or village, except such city, town, or village, as is now, in whole or in part, governed as to schools by some special law heretofore passed, containing within the town or village plot, as laid out and recorded, two hundred inhabitants or more, with the territory attached, or hereafter to be attached to said city, town, or village, for school purposes, may be organized into and established as a single school district, in the manner and with the powers hereinafter specified; but the provisions of this act shall not apply to any city, town, or village, or any part thereof, which is now governed as to schools by any special law.

Qualified voters to vote for or against the adoption of this act.

SEC. 2. That, in order to such organization, written notices shall be posted up in three or more of the most public places in said contemplated district, signed at least by six resident freeholders of the same, requesting the qualified electors in said district to assemble upon a day, and at some suitable place in said district, to be named in said notices, then and there to vote, by ballot, for or against the adoption of this act, which notice shall be so posted up at least ten days next prior to said meeting.

Manner of casting such vote.

SEC. 3. That the electors assembled at said time and place shall proceed to appoint a Chairman, Assistant Chairman, and Clerk, who shall be Judges of said election. That the electors in favor of the adoption of this act for said district, shall write upon their ballots, "School law," and those opposed thereto shall write upon their ballots, "No school law;" the adoption or rejection of this act to be determined by a majority of the votes to be cast in manner aforesaid.

Directors to be chosen.

SEC. 4. That in case a majority of votes shall have been cast for said law, the electors of said districts shall assemble at the place last aforesaid, within twenty days from the time of the adoption of said act, of which at least ten days' previous notice shall be given by said Chairman and Clerk, in the manner aforesaid, and shall then choose, by ballot, six Directors of the public schools of said district, two of whom shall serve for one year, two for two years, and two for three years, the time that each shall serve to be designated on the ballots; and annually thereafter, there shall be chosen, in the same manner, two Directors, each of whom shall serve for three years, and until their successors shall be elected and qualified; such intermediate vacancies as may occur to be filled by the acting Directors until the next annual election, when such vacancies shall be filled by the electors.

Directors to organize.

SEC. 5. That said Directors, within ten days after their appointment as aforesaid, shall meet, and organize by choosing from their number a President, Secretary, and Treasurer; that said Treasurer, before he enters upon the duties of his office, shall give bond payable to the State of Ohio, with security, to be approved by said Board, and to be by them kept, conditioned for the faithful discharge of his duties as such Treasurer.

Their powers and duties.

SEC. 6. The said Directors, and their successors in office, shall be a body corporate, by the name of the Board of Education of said city, town, or village, and, as such, and by such name, shall receive all moneys, and other property, belonging or accruing to said district, or to said city, town, or village, or any part of the same, for the use or benefit of the public schools therein; and the said Board shall be capable of contracting and being contracted with, suing and being sued, pleading and being impleaded, in any court of law or equity; and also shall be capable of receiving any gift, grant, bequest, or devise, made for the use of the public schools in said city, town, or district, and all moneys accruing to said city, town, or district, for school purposes, under any law of this State, shall be paid over to the Treasurer of said Board of Education.

Meetings of the Board.

SEC. 7. Said Board of Education may hold stated meetings at such times and places in said district as they may appoint, four members of said Board, at all meetings thereof, constituting a quorum for business; that special meetings thereof may be called by the President, or by any two members, on giving one day's notice of the time and place of the same; and said Board, by resolution, shall direct the payment of all moneys that shall come into the hands of the Treasurer, and no money shall be paid out of the treasury except in pursuance of such resolution, and on the written order of the President, countersigned by the Secretary.

Money, how paid out.

School-houses, how built.

SEC. 8. That whenever said Board shall deem it necessary to purchase or erect a school-house, or school-houses for said district, or to purchase sites for the same, they shall call a meeting of the legal voters in said district, by giving at least ten days' notice of the time, and place, and object of said meeting, in some newspaper printed in, and in general circulation in such district, if any such there be; and if there be no such newspaper, then by posting up written or printed notices thereof, at five or more of the most public places in said district, and the President of said Board, and in his absence one of the other Directors, shall act as Chairman of said meeting, and said meeting may determine, by a majority vote, upon the erection of a school-house or school-houses, and the purchase of a site or sites therefor, and the amount of money to be raised for the purpose aforesaid, and the time, or times when the same shall be paid, which money, so voted, shall be thereupon certified by the Board of Education, by its Chairman and Secretary, to the Auditor of the county, and shall be assessed in said district, collected and paid over to the Treasurer of said district, in the same manner as the tax hereinafter provided for in the twelfth section of this act.

Board to establish primary schools.

SEC. 9. It shall be the duty of said Board, so soon as the means for that purpose can be provided, to establish in said district an adequate number of primary schools; to be so located as best to accommodate the inhabitants thereof, and in which the rudiments of education shall be taught, and it shall be the further duty of said Board, to establish in said district, a suitable number of other schools of a higher grade or grades, wherein instruction shall be given in such studies as may not be provided for in the primary schools, the number of schools, and also of the different grades thereof, to be determined by said Board; and it shall be the further duty of said Board to decide what branches shall be taught in each and all of said schools, provided that no other language than the English or German shall be taught therein, except with the concurrence of two-thirds of said Board.

High schools.

Branches to be taught.

SEC. 10. Admission to said schools shall be gratuitous to the children, wards and apprentices of all actual residents in said district, who may be entitled to the privileges of the public schools, under the general laws of this State, provided that said Board shall have power to admit to said schools other pupils, upon such terms, or upon the payment of such tuition, as they may prescribe.

What scholars admitted.

SEC. 11. Said Board shall have power to make all necessary regulations for said schools, to prescribe and enforce rules for the admission of pupils into the same, not inconsistent with the preceding section, and the examination that pupils must pass preparatory to admission into the schools of higher grades than the primary; to subdivide said school district, if they shall think proper; to select sites for school-houses; to superintend the building of the same, and to pay therefor, their appurtenances, furniture, and apparatus, to borrow money for the erection of school-houses, upon a majority vote of said district therefor, and to incur all other expenses of said school system, and pay the same from the public moneys of said district.

General powers of the Board.

SEC. 12. It shall be the duty of said Board to keep said schools in operation not less than thirty-six, nor more than forty-four weeks of each year, to determine the amount of the annual tax to be raised for the purpose aforesaid, including all the necessary expenses of said schools, except for the erection of school-houses and the purchase of sites; and on or before the first day of July, of each year, to make known the amount of such tax to the Auditor of the county in which said district is situate; and thereupon it shall be the duty of said Auditor to assess the same upon the taxable property of the said district as the same appears on the grand list in his office, and the said tax shall be collected by the county Treasurer, in the same manner, and at the same time, with the State and county taxes, and when collected shall be paid over to the Treasurer

How long schools to be kept in each year.

School tax, how levied and collected.

Not to exceed four mills on the dollar.

of said Board:* Provided, however, that the tax to be assessed under this section shall not exceed four mills on the dollar upon the taxable property of said district, as the same appears upon the grand list; provided further, that in case the amount so authorized to be raised, together with the other school moneys of said district, shall be insufficient to support said schools for the portion of the year mentioned in this section, that said Board of Education may require such sum as may be necessary to support the same for the residue of said time, to be charged at the discretion of said Board upon the tuition of the pupils attending such schools; Provided, however, that the children of indigent parents, or orphans, who are unable to pay such charges, shall not be excluded from said schools for the non-payment of the same; and it shall be the further duty of said Board to keep an accurate account of their proceeding, and of their receipts and disbursements for school purposes, and at the annual meeting for the choice of Directors in said district to make report of such receipts, and the sources from which the same were derived, and of said disbursements, and the objects to which the same were applied, and they shall also make report at the same time of such other matters relating to said schools, as they may deem the interests of the same to require.

Board shall report to annual meeting.

Board shall appoint School Examiners.

SEC. 13. That said Board of Education, within twenty days after their election, shall appoint three competent persons, citizens of said district, to serve as School Examiners of the public schools therein, one to serve for one year, one for two years, and one for three years from the time of their appointment, and until their successors shall be appointed, and annually thereafter said Board shall appoint one Examiner to serve for three years, and until his successor is appointed and qualified; and said Board shall fill all vacancies that may occur from death, removal, or otherwise. Said

---

* The following law is probably still in force:

An Act to regulate the fees of county Treasurers in certain cases.

[*Passed December* 21, 1852, LI *vol. Stat.* 288.]

Treasurers to collect school taxes under certain acts.

SEC. 1. *Be it enacted by the General Assembly of the State of Ohio*, That the county Treasurers of this State shall be allowed, for collecting and paying over school taxes assessed under the act of February 21, 1849, and an act amendatory thereto, passed March 13, 1850, for the better regulation of common schools in cities and towns, the sum of one per cent. on all moneys by them collected and paid over under the provisions of said acts.

JAMES C. JOHNSON,
Speaker of the House of Representatives.
WILLIAM MEDILL,
President of the Senate.

Examiners, or any two of them, shall examine any person that may apply for that purpose, with the intention of becoming teachers in any of the schools in said district; and if they find the applicant, in their opinion, qualified to teach in any of said schools, and to govern the same, and of good moral character, they shall give said applicant a certificate naming the branches in which the holder of said certificate was found qualified to teach—and no person shall be permitted to teach in said schools without such certificate—and said Examiners may, in all cases where two of their number concur, have power to annul such certificate, and, when so annulled, the person holding the same shall be discharged as a teacher of said schools; said Examiners shall also, separately or otherwise, together with said Board of Education, or any of them, or such person as they may appoint, or invite, visit said schools as often as once in every term, and observe the discipline, mode of teaching, progress of the pupils, and such other matters as they may deem of interest, and make such suggestions, and report thereupon to said Board, as they may think proper, which report may be published at the discretion of said Board. Duty of Examiners.

SEC. 14. Upon the adoption of this act in the manner herein provided, by any city, town, village, or district, all laws now in force therein, inconsistent herewith, are hereby repealed. Acts repealed

SEC. 15. That said Board of Education, or the Treasurer thereof, shall have power to collect any charge or account for tuition, in the same manner as the Treasurer of any common school district in this State, is now, or may hereafter be, authorized to collect any such charge or account. Treasurer may collect charges for tuition.

JOHN G. BRESLIN,
Speaker of the House of Representatives.
BREWSTER RANDALL,
Speaker of the Senate.

CHAPTER VII.

An Act to amend the act entitled "An Act to provide for the organization of cities and incorporated villages," passed May 3, 1852.

[*Passed March* 11, 1853, LI *vol. Stat.* 364.]

Certain appropriations not authorized.

SEC. 12. That the ninety-eighth section of said act be, and the same is hereby so amended as to read as follows: That the Council of any municipal corporation shall not authorize any loan or appropriation not predicated on the revenues of the corporation for the current fiscal year, and shall not authorize any order or appropriation of money, when there is not, in the city treasury, money unappropriated sufficient to pay such appropriation; and any appropriation otherwise made or authorized, shall be held and deemed utterly void and of no effect as against said corporation: *Provided*, however, that for the purpose of purchasing necessary grounds, and erecting suitable school buildings for the use of public schools, the Council of any such corporation may, at the request of the Board of Education of said corporation, make sufficient appropriation therefor, and shall have power to borrow money upon the credit of such corporation, sufficient for the aforesaid purposes, at such rates of interest as said Council may deem proper; and, for the purpose of effecting such loan, the said Council shall have power to pledge the faith of said corporation for the payment of both principal and interest, including the power to levy a tax for the payment of the same, whenever the same may become due, and to make and execute such bonds, or other evidences of debt, and payable at such times and places as shall be agreed upon by the parties so contracting, which said bonds, or other evidences of debt, may be made transferable and redeemable in such form, and at such times and places, as may be therein designated; and the necessary grounds shall be procured, and the said school buildings hereby authorized

Council may borrow money for school purposes.

Loan how perfected.

shall be constructed under the direction of, and in accordance with, a plan, or plans, furnished by the Board of Education of said corporation. * * * School Buildings, how constructed.

CHAPTER VIII.

An Act to amend the "Act for the better regulation of the Public Schools in cities, towns, etc.," passed February 21, 1849.

[*Passed March* 13, 1850, XLVIII *vol. Stat.* 40.]

Extending act in reference to public schools.

SEC. 1. *Be it enacted by the General Assembly of the State of Ohio,* That the act for the better regulation of the public schools in cities, towns, etc., passed February 21, 1849, be, and the same is hereby extended to incorporated townships, and to school districts, now or hereafter to be organized, which shall adopt the same in the manner specified in the second and third sections of said act: Provided, however, that said act shall not be so extended to any township or school district, containing less than five hundred inhabitants, unless said school district consists, in whole or in part, of an incorporated town or village.

Single school districts.

SEC. 2. Township and school districts to which said act may be extended in the manner aforesaid, shall thereafter be known and recognized in law as single school districts, with all the powers, rights, and franchises which, for educational purposes, are, or may be conferred upon incorporated cities, towns, and villages, in virtue of the act aforesaid; and the Board of Education of such townships and school districts, shall be elected and organized in the same manner as is provided in the fourth and fifth sections of said act, and shall have like powers, rights, and privileges, and perform like duties as Boards of Education of cities, towns, etc., under the act aforesaid.

Board of Education.

Title to real estate to vest in Board.

SEC. 3. The title to all real estate, and other property belonging, for school purposes, to any city, town, village, township, or district, or to any part of the same, which is or may be organized into a single school district, in accordance with this act, or the act to which this is an amendment, shall be regarded in law as vested in the Board of Education thereof, for the support and use of the public schools therein, and said Board may dispose of, sell, and convey said real estate, or any part of the same, by deed, to be executed by the President of said Board, upon a majority vote for such sale at any regular meeting of the Electors of said district.

Board to have power to exclude children under six years of age.

SEC. 4. The Board of Education of any city, town, village, township, or school district, organized for the support of schools under this act, or the act to which this is amendatory, or the act for the support and better regulation of common schools in the town of Akron, and the acts amendatory thereto, or under any special local act, shall have authority to exclude from the public schools, in such city, etc., all children under the age of six years.

BENJAMIN F. LEITER,
Speaker of the House of Representatives.
CHARLES C. CONVERS,
Speaker of the Senate.

CHAPTER IX.

AMENDMENTS OF THE GENERAL SCHOOL ACT OF 1853.

An Act to amend an act entitled "An Act to provide for the organization, supervision, and maintenance of Common Schools," passed March 14, 1853.

[*Passed March* 1, 1854, LII *vol. Stat.* 110.]

Tax levied for school purposes 2½ mills on the dollar valuation

SEC. 1. *Be it enacted by the General Assembly of the State of Ohio,* That section sixty-three of the act entitled, "an act to provide for the re-organization, supervision, and maintenance of common schools," passed March 14, 1853, be, and hereby is so amended as to read as follows: Section 63. For the purpose of affording the advantages of a free education to all the youth of this State, the State common school fund shall hereafter consist of such sum as will be produced by the annual levy and assessment of one and one-half mills on the dollar valuation, on the grand list of the taxable property of the State; and there is hereby levied and assessed annually, in addition to the revenues required for general purposes, the said one and one-half mills upon the dollar valuation as aforesaid, and the amount so levied and assessed, shall be collected in the same manner as other State taxes; and when collected, shall be annually distributed to the several counties of the State, in proportion to the enumeration of scholars, and be applied exclusively to the support of common schools.

Section repealed.

SEC. 2. That section sixty-three of the act to which this is amendatory, be, and the same is hereby repealed.

F. C. LEBLOND,
Speaker of the House of Representatives.
ROBERT LEE,
President of the Senate, pro tem.

CHAPTER X.

An Act to provide for the completion of certain contracts heretofore made by School Directors.

[*Passed February* 6, 1854, LII *vol. Stat.* 17.]

To empower township Boards of Education to complete certain contracts.

SEC. 1. *Be it enacted by the General Assembly of the State of Ohio*, That in all cases where pursuant to law, contracts have been made or entered into for the sale of school-house sites or lands, the property of any school district heretofore existing in this State, and the sale remains to be perfected by conveyance, the township Board of Education, in the township where such property may be situate, shall be authorized to complete the same by executing a conveyance in the manner prescribed in section eleven of the act entitled an act to provided for the re-organization, supervision, and maintenance of common schools, passed March 14, 1853, on full compliance therewith by the purchaser or purchasers.

F. C. LeBlond,
Speaker of the House of Representatives.
Robert J. Atkinson,
President of the Senate, pro tem.

CHAPTER XI.

An Act relating to Common Schools

[*Passed April* 10, 1856, LVIII *vol. Stat.* —.]

Preamble.

Whereas, certain Boards of Education, organized under an act for the better regulation of public schools in cities, towns, etc, passed February 21, 1849; and certain Boards of Education organized under an act to provide for the reorganization, supervision and maintenance of common schools, passed March 14, 1853, acting under said acts have by agreement between said Boards, under the act passed February 21, 1849, and the Boards, under the act passed March 14, 1853, made annexations and transfers of territory to and from the districts provided for in said acts respectively for the promotion of education, according to the true intent and meaning of said acts; and whereas, doubts exist as to the legality of such annexations and transfers of territory, therefore,

Transfers made valid.

Sec. 1. *Be it enacted by the General Assembly of the State of Ohio,* That all annexations or transfers of territory to or from the districts provided for in the said act passed February 21, 1849, and in the said act passed March 14, 1853, made pursuant to said acts respectively, and the agreement of the Boards of Education organized under said acts respectively, heretofore made or agreed upon, or which shall hereafter be thus made or agreed upon, shall be held to be as valid as if the same had been specially and more particularly provided for in said acts, or the acts amendatory thereto.

Sec. 2. *Be it further enacted,* That the Boards of Education of any city, or incorporated village, or union school district created by any law of this State, shall have power according to the general provisions of said act passed March 14, 1853 by mutual agreement between the township Board and the city or village Board to transfer territory to or from the respective districts under the control of said respective Boards.

SEC. 3. That this act shall be in force from and after its passage.

N. H. VAN VORHES,
Speaker of the House of Representatives.
THOMAS H. FORD,
President of the Senate.

CHAPTER XII.

An Act providing for recording, printing, and distributing the Journals of the General Assembly, and the laws and public documents.

[*Passed April* 8, 1856, LIII *vol. Stat.* —.]

SEC. 6. All county, township, city and village officers, and all officers and Boards of officers, of all State institutions and buildings, and all officers connected with the public works of the State, and all corporations (except such as by their characters are required to make their reports at some other specified time) which are now, or may hereafter be required by law, to make annual reports for any purpose to any State officer or officers, shall make out the same on or before the fifth day of November of each year, and forthwith transmit the same to the proper officer or officers. For the purpose of making out all such reports as come within the provisions of this section, the year shall begin on the first day of November of each year, and end on the last day of October of the succeeding year: Provided, that the school year shall begin on the first day of September annually, and close on the last day of the following August; and all school officers and township officers acting as such, who are or may be required to make annual reports to the county Auditor;

When official reports to be made.

School year.

shall make out the same and transmit them to the county Auditor on or before the first day of October following the expiration of the school year.

Reports of State officers.

SEC. 7. All State officers, and Boards of officers, and the officers of all such institutions and buildings, as are now, or may hereafter be required to make annual reports to the General Assembly, or to the Governor, shall hereafter make such reports to the Governor on or before the twenthieth day of November of each year, and the Governor shall cause the same to be printed as soon thereafter as practicable, by the printer having the contract for this branch of the public printing, and the Governor shall lay before the General Assembly all such reports, in printed form, at the same time that he lays before it his regular message. But nothing in this section, or in this act, shall be held to modify, in any respect, the existing laws in relation to the annual report of the State Board of Agriculture.

CHAPTER XIII.

TEACHERS' INSTITUTES.

An Act to encourage Teachers' Institutes.

[*Passed February* 8, 1847, XLV *vol. Stat.* 67.]

Preamble.

WHEREAS, it is represented that, in several counties, associations of teachers of common schools, called Teachers' Institutes, have been formed, for the purpose of mutual improvement and advancement in their profession, which, it is represented, have already accomplished much to elevate the standard of common school instruction in their respective counties; therefore, in order to encourage such associations, and thus promote the cause of popular education,

SEC. 1. *Be it enacted by the General Assembly of the State of Ohio,* That in the several counties mentioned in the fifth section, in which such associations now exist, or in which such associations shall be hereafter formed, it shall be lawful for the county Commissioners of said counties to appropriate the annual avails, or any part thereof, of the fund provided for in the third section of the act passed March 19, 1848, entitled "an act declaratory of, and amendatory to, an act entitled 'an act providing for the distribution and investment of this State's proportion of the surplus revenue,'" passed March 28, 1837, for the purposes of such associations.

County Commissioners may appropriate annual proceeds of surplus revenue.

SEC. 2. The moneys so appropriated shall, upon the order of the county Auditor, be paid over to, and expended by the Board of School Examiners of the proper county; the one-half thereof, at least, to the payment of suitable persons as instructors and lecturers to such associations, and the balance to the purchase and support of a suitable common school library, for the use of such associations.

Moneys to be paid to lecturers, and for library.

SEC. 3. Every teacher of common schools of the county, and every person of the county intending to become a teacher of common schools within the next twelve months, shall have the right, without charge for instruction, to attend the meetings of such associations, and enjoy all their benefits.

Who shall have a right to attend the meetings of associations.

SEC. 4. It shall be the duty of all the county Boards of School Examiners, in the several counties mentioned in the fifth section, to report, annually, to the Secretary of State, during the month of December, the number of male and female teachers examined by them during the year, the number of certificates given, how many authorized the teaching of Reading, Writing, and Arithmetic only; and when moneys shall have been received by virtue of this act, they shall also report how it has been expended, and with what results.

County Boards of Examiners to report to Secretary of State.

SEC. 5. This act shall be in force only in the counties of Ashtabula, Lake, Geauga, Cuyahoga, Erie, Lorain, Medina, Trumbull, Portage, Summit, Delaware.

WILLIAM P. CUTLER,
Speaker of the House of Representatives.
EDSON B. OLDS,
Speaker of the Senate.

CHAPTER XIV.

An Act to amend an act to encourage Teachers' Institutes, and to extend the provisions of the acts providing for Teachers' Institutes, and county Superintendents, to the several counties of this State.

[*Passed February* 24, 1848, XLVI *vol. Stat.* 86.]

Former law made general.

SEC. 1. That the provisions of the act entitled "an act to encourage Teacher's Institutes," and the act entitled "an act to provide for the appointment of county Superintendents of Common Schools, and defining their duties in certain counties therein named," passed February, 1847, be, and the same are hereby extended to all the counties in this State.

Former act in reference to libraries amended.

SEC. 2. That the second section of the act entitled "an act to encourage Teachers' Institutes," passed February 8, 1847, is hereby so amended that all money used under the provisions of said section, in purchasing libraries, shall be used in purchasing and supporting suitable common school libraries, for the several common school districts in the several counties in this State that may be in possession of the funds named in the first section of this act.

JOSEPH S. HAWKINS,
Speaker of the House of Representatives.
CHARLES B. GODDARD,
Speaker of the Senate.

CHAPTER XV.

An Act to amend an act entitled "An Act to encourage Teachers' Institutes, passed February 8, 1847.

[*Passed February* 16, 1819, XLVII *vol. Stat.* 19.]

Sec. 1. *Be it enacted by the General Assembly of the State of Ohio,* That the county Commissioners of the several counties mentioned in the act to which this is an amendment, shall be, and they are hereby authorized, at their June session, in each year, whenever, for any cause, the sum of one hundred dollars shall not arise from the means and source as provided in the first section of the aforesaid act, to appropriate such sum as shall be sufficient to make up said sum of one hundred dollars, from any moneys in the county treasury not otherwise appropriated.

County Commissioners may appropriate $100.

Sec. 2. That in case there are no moneys at the disposal of the said county Commissioners, they are hereby authorized to levy a tax (in the usual manner) for the purposes named in the preceding section.

May levy a tax.

Sec. 3. That no part of the money appropriated by virtue of this act, or of the act to which this is an amendment, shall be ordered by the county Auditor to be paid over, except upon the petition of at least forty practical teachers, who shall therein declare their *bona fide* intention to attend such association within their respective counties, and who shall also, at the time of so petitioning as aforesaid, be permanent residents of the county in which application shall be made; and which payment and appropriation shall also be approved and recommended in writing, indorsed upon said petition by the Board of School Examiners of such county.

Money, how and for what appropriated.

Sec. 4. That said sum of one hundred dollars, or any part thereof, shall not be ordered by the county Auditor to be paid over as aforesaid, until said teachers shall have first raised and paid over, or secured to be paid over, to said Board of School Examiners, for the

Not to be paid over until teachers raise half the amount asked for.

purposes and benefit of such association, at least one-half of the sum for which they shall so petition said county Auditor, and which payment, or security for payment, as aforesaid, shall be made known to said Auditor by the receipt, or certificate in writing of said Board of School Examiners.

JOHN G. BRESLIN,
Speaker of the House of Representatives.
BREWSTER RANDALL,
Speaker of the Senate.

CHAPTER XVI.

SALE OF SECTION SIXTEEN.

An Act to regulate the sale of School Lands and the surrender of permanent leases thereto.

[*Passed April* 16, 1852, L *vol. Stat.* 168.]

Section Sixteen school lands may be sold.

SEC. 1. *Be it enacted by the General Assembly of the State of Ohio*, That all those lands granted by the Congress of the United States for school purposes, known as section sixteen, together with all such as have been granted in lieu of said section sixteen, may be sold, and such sale shall be regulated by, and conducted according to the provisions of this act.

How vote of the citizens shall be taken.

SEC. 2. In case there has been no vote taken for the sale of any such lands, the Trustees of any original surveyed township, to which such lands may belong, shall, at least thirty days prior to taking of any such vote, cause not less than eight notices to be posted up in as many of the most public places of such township, notifying the legal voters resident therein, to meet at some convenient place and time therein specified, and then and there cast their ballots, for or against the sale of any such lands belonging to such township.

Same subject.

SEC. 3. The Trustees of the township shall preside

at the taking of such ballots, and shall appoint two Clerks, who shall keep two poll books, containing the names of the voters and the result of the ballot, which poll books shall be signed by the Trustees and Clerks; and, in case such ballot shall result in favor of a sale, the Trustees shall, within ten days after such election, deposit one of said poll books with the Auditor of the county, within which such lands (or the greater portion thereof) may be situated, with a copy of the notice given, and the affidavit of one or more of the Trustees, stating the manner of giving said notices, and the time and place of putting up the same; which notices, affidavit, and poll book, shall be, by said Auditor, copied into a book for that purpose to be provided; and when so recorded, such record shall be proof of the facts therein stated.

SEC. 4. When such record has been made, the Trustees of such township to which said lands belong, shall file a petition in the Court of Common Pleas of the county within which said lands (or the greater portion of them) may be situate, setting forth the giving of said notice, the taking of said ballot, the result of the same, the filing and recording of the aforesaid papers in the office of the Auditor of the proper county, and asking the Court to appoint three disinterested freeholders, not resident of the township in which the land may be situated, to divide and value the same in money. Trustees to petition Court of Common Pleas.

SEC. 5. If such Court shall be satisfied that the statements made in the petition are true, the Court shall appoint three persons to divide and appraise the same, according to the prayer of such petition; and said appraisers, after being first duly sworn before some officer authorized to administer oaths, and taking to their aid, if they think necessary, the county Surveyor, shall proceed to divide said lands into such parcels or tracts as, in their opinion, will be best for the sale thereof, and return in writing such divisions, suitably numbered and described, to the said Court, with a just valuation of each separate division, in money. Court to appoint appraisers.

SEC. 6. The Court, on such return being made, and having been by said Court examined, and found in all things regular, just and fair, shall certify the same, and order the same to be entered of record, together with the petition, and all the proceedings therein had; a copy of which the Trustees shall cause to be filed in the office of the Auditor of the proper county, who shall copy the same into a book containing the notice, affidavit, and poll book aforesaid, and immediately following the same. Returns, etc., to be recorded.

County Auditor to advertise sale.

SEC. 7. The Auditor of the county, on the recording of said proceedings, shall forthwith cause a notice to be published in some newspaper of general circulation in said county, for six consecutive weeks before the day of sale; and, at the same time, by posting up copies of such notice in six of the most public places in said county, two of which shall be in the township where the lands are situate, and one at the court-house, containing a description of the lots or lands to be sold, the valuation thereof, and the time when said land shall be offered at public auction, by said Auditor, at the door of the court-house, at not less than the appraised value thereof; one-twelfth of the purchase money to be paid at the time of sale, and the balance in eleven annual installments, of equal amount, with annual interest thereon; and said Auditor shall, at such time and place, proceed to offer the same to the highest bidder, at or over the appraisement, and on the terms stated in said notice.

Same.

SEC. 8. In case said lands, or any part thereof, shall not be sold as aforesaid, the Auditor may continue to offer the same on the application, in writing, of the Trustees of the township to which said lands may belong, at any future time or times, until they shall be sold, having first given the like notices herein provided, to be given on the first sale thereof: Provided, that no sale shall be had on any valuation made more than two years prior to the day of the sale.

Reappraisement.

SEC. 9. The Court of Common Pleas aforesaid is hereby required, on the petition of the Trustees aforesaid, setting forth the former appraisement, and the subsequent proceedings thereto, and that two years have elapsed, and the land remaining unsold, to direct a new valuation of the same to be made in the manner hereinbefore directed, unless said Court, on testimony, shall be satisfied that the former appraisement is a just and fair valuation of said lands; in that case, the Court shall make an entry of the fact, which entry shall be certified to, and recorded by the Auditor, in manner aforesaid, and shall have the same effect as a new appraisement.

In cases of permanent leases, etc.

SEC. 10. In case said lands are held under permanent leases, or leases for ninety-nine years, the legal or equitable holder of any such lease, wishing to surrender the same, and to purchase the fee of the premises so held by lease, may, with the consent of the Trustees of the original township to which such lands belong, file his petition in the court of Common Pleas of the county in which the largest portion of such lands are situate, setting forth a description of the premises so held, the state of his lease, or his title thereto, that he is desirous of surrendering such lease and becoming the owner of the premises in fee, and asking the Court to appoint three disinterested freeholders of the county, and not resident of the township wherein such lands are situate, to value the same; and the Court, on being satisfied of the truth of the facts set forth in such petition, shall appoint such appraisers, who shall proceed, under oath, to make a just valuation of the premises in money, without reference to the improvements made thereon, under and by reason of said lease, and shall return such valuation, in writing, to said Court; and the said Court, if it shall be satisfied that said valuation is just, shall confirm the same, and order it, with the petition and other proceedings therein, to be recorded: Provided, that before the Trustees of any original surveyed township shall consent to the surrender of any lease, as provided in this act, they shall cause the proposition to be submitted to the electors of said township, at an election to be held and conducted in conformity to the provisions of the second section of this act; and if, at such election, a majority of the electors shall vote to such surrender, then, and not otherwise, said Trustees shall consent to the surrender, in manner and form as herein provided.

Same subject.

SEC. 11. Any such lessee, on producing to the Auditor of the proper county, within one year after the making of the same, a certified copy of such petition and appraisement, and confirmation, shall be permitted, by endorsement thereon, attested by the Auditor, to release to the State of Ohio all his interest, title, and claim in and to such lease, for the benefit of the township to which the same may belong; which certified copy of said record and said release, shall be recorded in a book for that purpose to be provided.

Payments to county Treasurers, etc.

SEC. 12. The purchaser of any such lands, at any Auditor's sale, or the lessee of any such land held under such lease, on executing his release, as aforesaid, shall each, forthwith, pay to the Treasurer of the county one-twelfth of the purchase money in the first case, and one-twelfth of the valuation in the second, and take the Treasurer's receipt therefor; and the Auditor, on receiving the Treasurer's receipt for said first installment, shall give to said purchaser or lessee a certificate, containing the name of the purchaser or lessee, a description of the premises, the number, amount, and time of payment of the subsequent installments, and that said purchaser or lessee, their heirs or assigns, on the punctual payment of the sums still due, with annual interest up to the time of payment, shall be entitled to receive a final certificate from such Auditor: Provided, that such lessee shall produce to the Auditor the certificate of the proper officer, that all rents due on such premises have been paid up to the time of surrendering said lease.

Same subject.

SEC. 13. Any person wishing to pay any money under the provisions of this act, in part or full payment of any such lands, shall first obtain the certificate of the Auditor, of the amount due, or to be paid; and on the presentation of the same, the Treasurer is authorized to receive the amount therein specified, and shall give to the person paying the same a certificate, directed to the Auditor, of the payment of said sum of money; and the Auditor, on the presentation of said certificate, shall give to such person a receipt therefor, credit him with the amount in his books, and charge the Treasurer therewith.

County Auditor to report sales to Auditor of State.

SEC. 14. The county Auditor shall keep an account with the county Treasurer, of all sales made, and leases surrendered, and moneys paid thereon, by each purchaser or lessee, and report the same to the Auditor of State, on the first day of February, May, August, and November, in each and every year; and, from the time of such report, the State shall be liable to pay interest on all such sums so reported as paid; and the Treasurer of State, on receiving a certified copy of the account from the Auditor of State, shall be authorized immediately to draw said money from the county Treasurers.

In case of failure of purchaser to pay, lands to be re-sold, for cash.

SEC. 15. If any such purchaser or lessee shall fail to make any payment on any tract of land, for the space of twelve months after the time the same shall become due and payable, the Auditor of the proper county shall forthwith proceed to sell such tract or tracts of land, with all the improvements thereon, at the door of the court-house, to the highest and best bidder therefor, in cash, having first given notice of the time and place of such sale, containing a description of the lands, and the money due and to become due thereon, by publishing the same in some newspaper of general circulation in said county, for six consecutive weeks before the day of sale; and on such sale, no bid shall be entertained for a sum which will not be sufficient to pay all the purchase money due the State, and all expenses incident to such sale; and in case said premises can not be sold for that amount, they shall revert to the State, in trust for said township, and be sold in the manner hereinbefore provided for the sale of such lands not under permanent leases, or leases for ninety-nine years.

Purchaser to receive certificate.

SEC. 16. When said lands sell as aforesaid, the purchaser shall pay to the Treasurer of the county the amount so bid for the said premises; and on producing to the Auditor the Treasurer's receipt for such payment, the Auditor shall give him a final certificate, stating the fact of such sale, the name of the purchaser, the description of the lands sold, the amount for which sold, the payment of the same, and that the purchaser is entitled to receive, from the State of Ohio, a deed in fee simple for the same, on producing to the proper officer this certificate.

Final certificate.

SEC. 17. When any purchaser or lessee, their heirs or assignees, shall have made payment in full, the Auditor shall give to such person a final certificate, containing, in addition to the former one, the fact of the payment in full, and that said person is entitled to receive from the State of Ohio, a deed in fee simple for said premises, on the presentation of this certificate to the proper officer or officers.

Deed from the State.

SEC. 18. The Auditor of State, upon the filing of any such final certificate in his office, shall make out the draft for a deed therefor, and deliver the same, with such final certificate, to the Governor of the State, who shall sign said deed, and cause the same to be sealed with the great seal of the State, and countersigned and recorded by the Secretary of State, and by him delivered to the grantee, on demand.

Excess of money, how disposed of.

SEC. 19. All excess of moneys made on any sale of delinquent lands as aforesaid, after paying all sums due, interest and costs, shall be paid, on demand, to such delinquent owner, his heirs or assigns, from the county treasury, on the order of the Auditor, if such demand be made within one year from the time of such sale; and if not so demanded, it shall be paid into the State treasury; and, unless the same shall be demanded within one year after the same shall have been paid into the State treasury, it shall be applied for the same uses as the lands are subject to.

Fees.

SEC. 20. The fees for services under this act shall be as follows: The Court shall tax such fees on any petition filed in the same, as are allowed for similar services on proceedings in chancery. The county Auditor to be allowed one dollar and fifty cents on each sale made by him; for each certificate, fifty cents; for each receipt, six cents, to be paid by the purchaser, and the same fees for recording as is allowed to county Recorders, to be paid out of the first moneys paid in as interest or rents, on such sale or surrender. All printers' fees for advertising, shall be paid out of the county treasury, on the order of the Auditor, and refunded out of the first moneys received on such sale, as interest or rents. The cost in Court shall, in case of a petition by the Trustees, be paid out of the county treasury, on the order of the county Auditor, and refunded out of the first moneys received from the sale, as interest or rents; in case of a lessee being petitioner, all costs shall be paid by him.

Acts repealed. SEC. 21. The act entitled "an act to provide for the
sale of section sixteen, granted by Congress for the use
of schools," passed January 29, 1827; the act entitled
Chase, 1552. "an act to extend the time of payment to purchasers
of school lands in this State," passed January 3, 1843;
41 v. Stat. 4. the act entitled "an act to regulate the sale of ministerial and school lands, and the surrender of permanent
leases thereto," passed February 2, 1843; the act enti-
41 v. Stat. 20. tled "an act to amend an act entitled an act to extend
the time of payment to purchasers of school lands in
this State," passed March 6, 1844; the act entitled
42 v. Stat. 39. "an act to amend the act to regulate the sale of ministerial and school lands, and the surrender of perma-
nent leases thereto, passed February 2, 1843," passed
42 v. Stat. 43. March 12, 1844; the act entitled "an act to fix the
minimum price of the sales of school lands," passed
43 v. Stat. 58. March 4, 1845; and the act entitled "an act to amend
an act entitled an act to extend the time of payment to
purchasers of school lands in this State, and an act
amendatory thereto," passed February 1, 1847, be,
45 v. Stat. 21. and the same are hereby repealed: *Provided*, such
repeal shall not impair, or in any manner affect any
rights or interests acquired under any of said acts.*

JAMES C. JOHNSON,
Speaker of the House of Representatives.
WILLIAM MEDILL,
President of the Senate.

---

*An act to provide for the appointment of Register of the Virginia Military School Lands, was passed February 23, 1852, 50 v. Stat. 108. As to the sale of Western Reserve School Lands, see 46 v. Stat, 38; 47 v. Local Laws, 232; 48 v. Stat 53.

CHAPTER XVII.

An Act to confirm sales made by the Trustees of the civil townships of section sixteen, and other lands granted by Congress in lieu thereof, to purchasers.

[*Passed April* 5, 1856, LIII *vol. Stat.* —.]

Preamble.

WHEREAS, in many counties of the State of Ohio, through misapprehension of an act entitled "an act to regulate the sale of ministerial and school lands, and the surrender of permanent leases thereto," passed February 2, 1843; also of an act entitled "an act to regulate the sale of school lands and the surrender of permanent leases thereto," passed April 16, 1852, the Trustees of the civil townships have sold section sixteen to various purchasers, who have purchased said lands in good faith, have paid the purchase money and taken possession of said lands, and in many instances made large improvements on the same; therefore, in order to cure the defects in the titles of such purchasers to such lands, and to quiet them in the possession thereof,

Title confirmed.

SEC. 1. *Be it enacted by the General Assembly of the State of Ohio,* That such sales of section sixteen in the original surveyed townships or fractional townships, and all sales of land granted by the Congress of the United States in lieu of said section sixteen, which have been made otherwise in conformity with the provisions of the acts recited in the foregoing preamble be, and the same are hereby confirmed; and such purchasers and their assignees and heirs at law shall hold the purchases so by them made, by a title as good and valid as though the proceedings for such sale had been instituted by the Trustees of the original surveyed or fractional townships.

N. H. VAN VORHES,
Speaker of the House of Representatives.
THOMAS H. FORD,
President of the Senate.

CHAPTER XVIII.

SCHOOL FUNDS.

An Act to establish a fund for the support of common schools.

[*Passed March* 2, 1831. *Took effect, June* 1, 1831. XXIX *vol. Stat.* 423.]

Fund established, etc.

SEC. 1. *Be it enacted by the General Assembly of the State of Ohio,* That there is hereby constituted and established a fund, to be designated by the name of "the common school fund;" the income of which shall be appropriated to the support of common schools in the State of Ohio, in such manner as shall be pointed out by law; of which fund the Auditor of State shall be the Superintendent, until otherwise directed by law.

Auditor of State the Superintendent;

—And how to keep account of funds from sale of school lands;

SEC. 2. That whenever, and so often, as any moneys shall be paid into the State treasury, arising from the sale of any lands which heretofore have been, or hereafter may be, appropriated by Congress, for the use or support of schools in any original surveyed township, or other district of country, in this State, the Auditor of State shall forthwith open an account, in a book or books to be provided for that purpose, and shall pass the said moneys to the credit of such township, or other district of country; which said money shall constitute an irreducible fund, the proceeds accruing from which shall be paid over and appropriated, in the manner which shall be pointed out by law, for the support of common schools within the township, or other district of country, to and for no other use or purpose whatever.

—Irreducible;

—Rate of interest and account thereof;

SEC. 3. That all moneys paid into the State treasury as aforesaid, shall bear an annual interest of six per centum; which interest shall be cast from the time of the payment of any principal sum, up to the first day of January, next succeeding such payment, and on the first day of January, annually, thereafter; and where the same has not been done, the Auditor of State shall, in a book or books to be provided for that purpose, open an interest account with every township, or other district of country, to which a credit in the irreducible fund aforesaid shall have been passed; and he shall, in such book or books, keep accurate accounts of the accrual and disbursement of all interest accruing from such fund, so as aforesaid belonging to any township or district of country; and the faith of the State of Ohio is hereby pledged for the annual payment of the interest aforesaid, to the person who, and in the manner which, shall be pointed out by law; which said interest shall be appropriated and expended for the support and maintenance of common schools within the township, or other district of country, entitled as aforesaid to the same.

—Pledge for its payment;

—Its appropriation;

Sec. 4. That for the payment of any interest that shall have accrued, and be payable to and for any township, or other district of country as aforesaid, the county Auditor of the proper county shall, annually, on or after the first day of January, draw an order on the Treasurer of State, in favor of the Treasurer of the proper county, for the interest which shall be payable in such county; and upon such order being presented to the Auditor of State, he shall thereupon certify an abstract of the amount of interest payable to each township, or other district of country, in such county; and thereupon, on presentation of said order, the Treasurer of State shall pay the amount of interest appearing by said abstract to be due; and the said county Treasurer, or the person presenting said order for him, shall indorse on said order a receipt for so much as shall be paid thereon, and shall also sign a duplicate receipt, which shall be lodged with the Auditor of State, who shall credit the State Treasurer therewith, and charge the several items constituting the aggregate of such abstract, to the proper township, or other district of country; and the money so drawn, shall be paid out by the county Treasurer, on the order of the county Auditor, in the proportions established by law, to the proper person or persons in each school district authorized to receive the same. And in all cases in which a county line shall divide any original surveyed township, or fractional part thereof, the interest, payable in such township; shall be received and disbursed in manner aforesaid, by the Treasurer of the county wherein the greatest quantity of land belonging to

—Order therefor and payment;

—Receipt, etc.

—Distribution.

such township shall be situate; but if it be uncertain in which county the greatest quantity of land in such township be situate, then the said interest shall be received and disbursed by the Treasurer of the oldest county in which any part of such township shall be situate.

Donations and bequests to vest in common school funds, etc.

SEC. 5. That whenever any donation or devise shall be made, by gift, grant, last will and testament, or in any other manner whatever, of any estate, either real, personal, or mixed, to the State of Ohio, or to any person, or otherwise, in trust for the said common school fund, by any individual, body politic or corporate, the same shall be vested in said common school fund; and whenever the moneys arising from such gift, grant, or devise, shall be paid into the State treasury, the proper accounts thereof shall be kept, and the interest accruing therefrom shall be appropriated according to the intent and design of such donor, grantor, or devisor.

General fund established.

SEC. 6. That there shall be constituted a fund for the support of common schools, which shall belong, in common, to the people of this State; which shall consist of the net amount of the money which heretofore has been, or hereafter may be, paid into the State treasury, from the sales of the lands commonly called the salt lands, and such donations, legacies and devises, as may be made to such fund, or to any person or persons, in trust for the same. And the State of Ohio is hereby pledged to pay the interest, annually, on any and all sums of money which shall have been, or may hereafter be, paid into such treasury, from the passage of this act, or the receipt of such money into the treasury aforesaid; and the interest arising as aforesaid, shall be funded annually, until the first day of January, in the year eighteen hundred and thirty-five; after which time the said interest shall be annually distributed to the several counties in this State, in proportion to the number of white male inhabitants above the age of twenty-one years, as by law shall be ascertained, for the apportionment of Representatives; and the proportion of interest, due to each and every such county, shall be distributed for the support of common schools, in the respective counties, in the manner prescribed in the act to provide for the support and better regulation of common schools.

Of what to consist.

State pledged for the interest.

Interest funded until 1835.

How distributed afterward.

[The balance of the chapter is probably superseded by the act organizing the sinking fund. The provisions are retained in Swan's Revised Statutes.

It it also questionable whether the State common school fund, organized in section 6, is in existence. If so, the act of March 6, 1844, adds to it "all moneys arising from licenses to peddlers, all moneys arising from auction duties, or licenses to auctioneers, except in the county of Hamilton; and all fines and penalties collected under the laws relating to each of said funds;" but the same act limits the fund, however derived, to $200,000.

The doubt grows out of the language of section 63 of the General School Act, (chapter I, *ante,*) namely: "The State common school fund *shall hereafter consist* of such sum as will be produced by the annual levy and assessment of one mill and one-half mill on the grand list of taxable property," etc. The late revisors, Swan and Curwen, regard those provisions as yet in force, and the repeal is exclusively by implication. The following act stands on the same footing:*]

CHAPTER XIX.

An Act to increase the general fund for the support of common schools, established by the sixth section of the act to establish a fund for the support of common schools, passed March 2, 1851, by the appropriation of the proceeds of the swamp lands to that fund.

[*Passed March* 24, 1849, XLIX *vol. Stat.* 40.]

Proceeds of sales of swamp lands to be added to the common school fund.

SEC. 1. *Be it enacted by the General Assembly of the State of Ohio,* That the net proceeds which may hereafter be paid into the State treasury, from the sales of swamp lands granted to the State of Ohio, by act of Congress, passed Sept. 28th, 1850, be, and the same is hereby appropriated to the general fund for the support of common schools; and the State of Ohio is hereby pledged to pay the interest, annually, on any and all sums of money which may be paid into the

---

* See Swan's Revised Statutes, 853-4.

State treasury, from the sales of said lands, from the receipt of such money into the treasury aforesaid; and the interest arising as aforesaid, shall be funded annually, until the first day of January, in the year eighteen hundred and fifty-five; after which time the said interest shall be annually distributed to the several counties in this State, in proportion to the number of white male inhabitants above the age of twenty-one, as by law shall be ascertained, for the apportionment of Representatives; and the proportion of interest due to each and every such county, shall be distributed for the support of common schools in the respective counties, in the manner prescribed in the "act to provide for the support and better regulation of Common Schools."

JOHN F. MORSE,
Speaker of the House of Representatives.
CHARLES C. CONVERS,
Speaker of the Senate.

CHAPTER XX.

An Act to provide for the maintenance and better regulation of common schools in the city of Cincinnati.

[*Passed January* 27, 1853, LI *vol. Stat.* 503.]

Corporate authorities of Cincinnati to provide for common schools.

SEC. 1. *Be it enacted by the General Assembly of the State of Ohio,* That the corporate authorities of the city of Cincinnati are hereby authorized and required, at the expense of said city, to provide for the support and regulation of the common schools of said city, in the manner prescribed by the provisions of this act.

A Board of Trustees and Visitors of Common Schools to be elected.

SEC. 2. At every annual election of city officers, there shall be elected in each ward of said city, by the qualified electors thereof, one judicious and competent person to serve as Trustee and Visitor of Common Schools of said city, for the term of two years from the first Tuesday in July succeeding his election, and until his successors shall be elected and qualified; and the person so elected, together with the Trustees and Visitors of the several wards of said city, already elected for two years, and whose term of office will not expire at the close of the present school year, shall constitute a Board of Education for said city, to be denominated the Board of Fund Trustees and Visitors of Common Schools.

Board to appoint officers and fill vacancies.

SEC. 3. The said Board of Trustees and Visitors shall take an oath of office, and, at their first meeting in July, choose a President, Vice-President, and Corresponding Secretary; the said Board may appoint and fix the salaries of a Superintendent, Clerk, and Messenger, and prescribe their duties; they shall meet once in every week, at such time and place as to them may be convenient, a majority of whom shall constitute a quorum; they shall have power to fill all vacancies in their own body, and if any Trustee shall absent himself from the regular meetings of said Board for six consecutive weeks, unless by reason of sickness, or by consent of the Board, such non-attendance shall be considered a virtual resignation on his part, and the Board, upon entering such fact upon its minutes, shall proceed to fill such vacancy. They shall also have power to make such by-laws, rules, and regulations for their own government, not inconsistent with this act, and the laws of the State, as they may deem proper and expedient, and they shall cause a record of their proceedings to be kept in books provided for that purpose.

Board to fix the amount of school taxes.

SEC. 4. That the said Trustees and Visitors shall, on or before the second Monday of May, annually, cause to be certified to the city Council of Cincinnati, an estimate of the amount necessary to be raised in said city, for school purposes, not exceeding two mills on the dollar, upon all property in said city valued or appraised, and liable and subject to taxation for State and county purposes, corporation, school-house, and school taxes; and the city Council shall certify the said amount so to be raised to the county Auditor, who is hereby authorized and directed to place the same on the duplicate of taxes for said county, in the same manner as township taxes now by law are placed on such duplicate, which said school taxes shall be collected by the county Treasurer of said county, and be by him paid into the city treasury on the first day of January, annually.

Court may alter or make new school districts.

SEC. 5. That the said Board shall have power to alter the boundaries of the school districts of said city, and to form new districts when the public convenience requires it.

SEC. 6. That the said Trustees and Visitors shall

Their power as to the purchase of land, and building school-houses.

have authority to purchase, in fee simple, (subject to the confirmation of the Council,) or receive as a donation for the use of said city, such additional lots of land, or sites for school-houses, as may be required for the several districts in said city, and shall, by concurrence of the city Council, cause to be erected thereon good and substantial school-houses, of such dimensions and capacity as shall be requisite and convenient for the use of common schools of said city; the purchase-money of said lots, and the expense of erecting buildings thereon, shall be paid out of the common school funds provided for in the fourth section of this act; and all property so purchased, and all other property heretofore purchased for school purposes, shall be held exempt from the general debts of said city, and only liable for debts contracted for common school purposes.

Interest on bonds, how paid.

SEC. 7. That the said Trustees and Visitors shall cause to be paid out of the school funds made subject to their control by this act, the interest accruing on the bonds given by the city for common school purposes,

Payment of bonds to be provided for.

and shall provide, by a sinking fund, or otherwise, for the final redemption and payment of said bonds, as the

Funds to be applied to school purposes exclusively.

same shall become due. And all other funds made subject to the control of said Board by this act, shall be exclusively applied to the maintenance and support of the schools hereby provided for, and for no other purpose whatever.

Board to have control of school fund.

SEC. 8. That all moneys heretofore collected for the use of common or colored schools, remaining on hand and unexpended, in the city treasury, shall be held by the city Treasurer, subject to the order of said Board, for the payment of bills for school purposes, by them allowed, and to be paid out by said Treasurer on the check of the city Auditor, and shall be kept on deposit where other city funds are deposited; and all such moneys, and all other moneys belonging to the common school fund, or appropriated in any manner for the purpose of public education, paid into the city treasury, shall be kept by said Treasurer as a separate and distinct fund, and the same shall not be applied, paid over, or pledged, under any pretense whatever, to any other use than that for which it was levied and collected, and paid into the city treasury, nor upon any other order or authority than that of the Board of Trustees and Visitors, as certified by their clerk: *Provided*, that no money shall be paid out of the city treasury for school purposes, except on a vote of a majority of the members of said Board.

SEC. 9. That the said Trustees and Visitors shall have superintendence of all the schools in said city, organized and established under this act, and from time to time shall make such regulations for the government and instruction of the children therein as to them shall appear proper and expedient. They shall appoint and employ all teachers and instructors for the same, and fix their salaries. They shall, at least every third year, during the month of October, cause to be taken an enumeration of all children between four and twenty-one years of age, residing in the several school districts, distinguishing, in such enumeration, the white from the colored children; and on or before the fifteenth day of November following, through their Clerks, certify the same to the Auditor of Hamilton county; and such enumeration shall, until another be taken, form the basis of the city portion, in the annual distribution of the State school fund. And the said Board of Trustees and Visitors shall fix, by resolution, the school year of said schools, and determine the times and duration of all the vacations thereof; they shall provide for an annual examination of all said schools, and, at the close of every school year, make and publish, for the information of the citizens, a report on the condition of the schools under their charge, as well as the fiscal and other concerns in relation thereto, and a particular account of the administration thereof, and generally do and perform all matters and things pertaining to the duties of their said office, which may be necessary and proper to promote the education, morals, and good conduct of the children instructed in said schools.

To superintend schools; to make all rules and regulations.

To employ teachers, and every three years make an enumeration of all children between 4 and 21 years of age.

To make a report at the close of the school year.

SEC. 10. That the said Trustees and Visitors, for the purpose of better organizing and classifying the schools under their supervision, shall have power to establish and maintain, out of any fund under their control, such grades of schools, other than those already provided for, as may to them seem necessary and expedient for the above-named purposes, and are hereby authorized to cause to be taught therein, such other studies in addition to those taught in their district schools, and under such regulations as said Trustees and Visitors may from time to time prescribe: *Provided*, however, that said funds shall not be appropriated toward the establishment and maintenance of such other grade of schools so as in any wise to impair the efficiency and permanency of the common district schools of said city.

To establish such grades of schools as they may think proper.

SEC. 11. That it shall be the duty of said Board of

Their power in relation to German schools.

Trustees and Visitors of Common Schools to provide a suitable number of German schools for the instruction of such youth as may desire to study the German language, or the German and English languages together. The said Board may, when, in their opinion, the same shall be necessary, establish one or more German-English senior or principal departments, the transfers to which shall be made irrespective of the districts established for English schools, and the schools provided for in this section shall be subject to such regulations as said Board may adopt for the government thereof, and also subject to the proviso contained in the tenth section of this act.

Schools equally free and accessible to all white children.

SEC. 12. That the common schools in the several districts of the city, and all other grades of schools authorized, or established and maintained, in whole or in part, from the school funds of said city, shall, at all times, be equally free and accessible to all white children not less than six years of age, who may reside in said city, and subject only to such regulations for their admission, government, and instruction, as the Trustees and Visitors may from time to time provide: *Provided*, that nothing in this act shall be construed so as to interfere with or interrupt the public high schools in said city as now established and organized.

Board may establish evening schools.

SEC. 13. The said Trustees and Visitors may provide a suitable number of evening schools, during the fall and winter months, for the instruction of such youth, over ten years of age, as are prevented, by their daily avocations, from attending day schools, which schools shall be subject to such regulations as said Board may, from time to time, adopt.

Board of Examiners.

SEC. 14. There shall be a Board of Examiners, composed of seven members; and, at the expiration of the respective terms of those now in office, the said Board of Trustees and Visitors shall appoint, for the term of three years, suitable persons, residents and citizens of said city, of competent learning and abilities, as Examiners of said schools, and of the qualification of teachers thereof, which Examiners, when organized by the election of a President, shall constitute and be denominated the "Board of Examiners" of common schools in Cincinnati, and all vacancies which may occur in said Board shall be filled by said Trustees and Visitors. It shall be the duty of said Board of Examiners to meet at least once in every month, to examine the qualifications, competency, and moral character of all persons desirous of becoming teachers and instructors in said schools, as well with reference to their methods of instruction and mode of government as literary attainments; and any four members of said Board shall have power to grant certificates thereof to such persons as, in their opinion, shall be entitled to receive the same; and no person shall be employed and paid, directly or indirectly, as teacher or instructor in any of said schools, until he or she shall have obtained from said Board of Examiners a certificate of qualifications as to his or her competency and moral character.

How Trustees and Visitors may sell school property.

SEC. 15. And the said Board of Trustees and Visitors shall have power to contract for the sale of any real estate held by said city for school purposes, which they may deem unsuitable for such purpose, and upon their certifying such fact to the city Council; and, if said city Council approve such sale, they shall direct the proper city officers to execute, on behalf of said city, a good and sufficient deed for the property so contracted to be sold, and the proceeds of such sale shall be placed to the credit of the school funds.

Certain fines, etc., expended for school purposes.

SEC. 16. All fines and penalties that may be received or collected under the provisions of any law levying a tax on sales at auction, and all fines collected under the city ordinances not appropriated by law, are hereby appropriated to the use, benefit, and support of the common schools in the city of Cincinnati; and it is hereby made the duty of the Treasurer of Hamilton county and the Mayor of said city, to pay the same into the city treasury, for school purposes.

SEC. 17.* [The property of all colored persons in said city shall be listed and taxed for school purposes

---

* Section 17, in the act of January 27, 1853, was as follows:

Schools for colored children.

"SEC. 17. The property of all colored persons in said city shall be listed and taxed for school purposes in the same manner as the property of other persons, and separate schools shall be established for the education of the colored children of said city, in such districts as the Board of Trustees and Visitors of Common Schools shall select for that purpose. The school so established shall be under the management and control of said Board, and so much of the school funds of said city as, upon an equal distribution of the same per capita, under any enumeration required by this act, would fall to the share of the colored children of said city, shall be appropriated as a fund, subject to the order of said Board, for the support of schools for colored children."

By an act, passed April 18, 1854, (LII vol. Stat. 49,) the section was amended to read as follows:

Colored schools to be separate.

"SEC. 17. The property of all colored persons in said city shall be listed and taxed for school purposes in the same manner as the property of other persons, and separate schools shall be established for the education of the colored children of said city, in such districts as the Board of Trustees and Visitors of Common Schools shall, from time to time, establish for that purpose; and the district schools so established, shall be conducted under the control and management of three Directors in each of said districts, who shall be elected annually, in the month of June, by the said Board of Trustees and Visitors of Common Schools, at a regular meeting, from among the colored people resident in such districts respectively, and who shall take an oath of office. Said Directors shall hold their office one year, or until their successors shall be elected and qualified, and vacancies in their number shall be filled by said Trus-

in the same manner as the property of other persons; and the separate schools now established for the education of colored children in said city, in such districts as the Board of Trustees and Visitors shall have established, shall continue until changed as hereinafter provided; and the district schools so established shall be conducted under the control and management of three Directors in each district, who shall be elected annually from among the residents in such districts respectively, by the adult colored males resident in such districts, at a meeting to be held in each district, on the last Monday in June of each year, of which public notice of time and place of election shall be given, by the Clerk of the Board, for at least one week previous to each election, by publication in a newspaper published in said city; and said Directors, when elected, shall take an oath of office, and shall hold their office one year, or until their successors shall be elected and qualified; and vacancies in their numbers shall be filled by said Directors; and they shall have the care and management of the schools and school property of their respective districts, appoint teachers, and regulate their salaries, regulate the course of studies and text-books, fix and determine the times and duration of such schools, and the vacations thereof, provide suitable accommodations, furniture, and fuel for their due maintenance, and perform all the duties necessary for keeping up such schools, and for the government and instruction of the colored children of their respective districts in

Directors of Colored Schools.

---

tees and Visitors, and said Directors shall have the care and management of the schools and school property of their respective districts, appoint teachers, and regulate their salaries, regulate the course of studies and text books, fix and determine the times and duration of such schools, and the vacations thereof, provide suitable accommodations, furniture, and fuel, etc., for their due maintenance, and perform all the duties necessary for keeping up such schools, and for the government and instruction of the colored children of their respective districts in such schools; said Directors shall cause a record of their proceedings to be fairly kept in books, which they shall provide for that purpose, and transmit to their successors; and said Directors shall render accounts monthly, in detail, of all their expenditures or liabilities, to the said Board of Trustees and Visitors of Common Schools, and, if approved by said Board, the same shall be paid, upon the order of said Board, out of the fund for colored schools provided by this act; and so much of the school funds of said city as, upon an equal distribution of the same *per capita* under any enumeration required by this act, would fall to the share of the colored children of said city, as ascertained by any such enumeration, shall be appropriated as a fund, subject to the order of said Board of Trustees and Visitors, for the support of said schools for colored children: *Provided*, that no person shall be employed or paid, directly or indirectly, as teacher or instructor, in any of said schools, until he or she shall first have obtained from the Board of Examiners created by this act, a certificate of qualification, as to his or her competency and moral character."

Duty of Directors.

Board of Trustees and Visitors to control school funds. Proviso.

By an act passed April 8, 1856, this section was again revised, and is printed above as now in force. Section two of this last amendment defined the words "colored persons" and "colored children" to mean those who are reputed to be, in whole or in part, of African descent.

said schools. Said Directors shall cause a record of their proceedings to be fairly kept, in books which they shall provide for that purpose, and transmit to their successors; and all powers and duties conferred or imposed upon the Board of Trustees and Visitors of Common Schools in said city by sections five, six, seven, eight, nine, ten, thirteen, and fifteen, of the act entitled "an act to provide for the better regulation of common schools in the city of Cincinnati," passed January 14, 1853, be and the same is hereby conferred and imposed upon said Board of Colored Directors, so far as the same are applicable to colored schools; and so much of the school funds of said city, as, upon an equal distribution of the same *per capita*, under any enumeration required by this act, as would fall to the share of the colored children of said city, as ascertained by any such enumeration, shall be appropriated as a fund, subject to the order of said Board of Directors, for the support of said schools for colored children: *Provided*, that no person shall be employed or paid, directly or indirectly, as a teacher or instructor in any of said schools, until he or she shall first have obtained from the Board of Examiners, created by this act, a certificate of qualification as to his or her competency and moral character. The said Board of Directors for Colored Schools shall, on or before the second Monday of May, annually cause to be certified to the Board of Trustees and Visitors of the Common Schools of the city of Cincinnati, an estimate of the amount necessary for the support of the schools under the control of the Board of Directors for colored schools; and said Board of Trustees and Visitors shall include said estimate, or so much of it as they shall deem necessary, in their annual certificate to the city Council of the city of Cincinnati, of the amount necessary to be raised for school purposes in said city.

Duties of Colored Directors.

Fund for Colored Schools.

SEC. 18. That the act entitled "an act supplementary to an act to increase the number of Trustees and Visitors of Common Schools in the city of Cincinnati, and for other purposes," passed March 7, 1837, passed March 12, 1845; the act entitled "an act to authorize the city Council of Cincinnati to levy taxes for school purposes," passed February 8, 1847; the act entitled "an act to authorize the appointment of a Superintendant of Common Schools in Cincinnati, and for other purposes," passed March 23, 1850; section one of the act entitled "an act for the better organization and classification of the common schools of Cincinnati and Dayton, and for other purposes," passed

Acts repealed.

February 11, 1845, so far as the same relates to the common schools of the city of Cincinnati; and the act entitled "an act to authorize the establishment of separate schools for the education of colored children, and for other purposes," passed February 10, 1849, so far as the same relates to schools for colored children in the city of Cincinnati, be, and they are hereby repealed.*

When act to take effect.

SEC. 19. That this act shall take effect, and be in force from and after the 15th day of March, A. D. 1853.

JAMES C. JOHNSON,
Speaker of the House of Representatives.
WILLIAM MEDILL,
President of the Senate.

---

* The act for the organization of the schools of Cincinnati, is deemed of sufficient importance for insertion among the general acts now in force. See the laws organizing the following special school districts. Columbus, XLVI vol. stat. 151; XLIX vol. 579; Zanesville, XLVI vol. 54, XLIX vol. 570; Lancaster, XLVI vol. 199, XLVIII vol. 647; Cleveland, XLVI vol. 151.

AN HISTORICAL REVIEW

OF

POPULAR EFFORTS

FOR

FREE EDUCATION IN OHIO;

WITH

SKETCHES OF THE CONDITION OF COMMON SCHOOLS
AT DIFFERENT PERIODS.

By WILLIAM T. COGGESHALL.

POPULAR MOVEMENTS.

CHAPTER I.

FIRST POPULAR MOVEMENTS—EFFORTS OF EPHRAIM CUTLER, CALEB ATWATER, AND NATHAN GUILFORD.

Legislation in Ohio, for Common Schools, has been the result, mainly, of local influences, which created a demand, more or less general, for the support or advancement of Public Education.

A complete representation of the development of the common school system of our State must, therefore, necessarily include a fair record of the labors and sacrifices of far-seeing men, who awakened public sentiment and directed public opinion.

Republican legislation, to be enduring, must answer public demand. It may be somewhat contemplative, but if in too large a degree, it is unsafe. To be efficient, it need not express the indefinite wish of a majority, but it must represent the intelligent will of an influential minority, and be based upon principles conducive to public good.

Though steadily opposed and often overruled by prejudice and selfishness, the legitimate necessity of free education for all the children of our commonwealth, gradually gained recognition in Ohio laws, and has now executive fulfillment, because no legislative step-forward has been taken, without pressing demand, grown out of liberal foresight and well-directed energy on the part of a few wisely reflective men.

The purpose of this article is to sketch the history of the popular movements which they led, and indicate the effect of those movements upon the legislation elsewhere described in this book.

The school history of our State is distinguished by four periods:

FIRST. Until 1821, when the first General Law was passed.

SECOND. Until 1825, when a School Fund by taxation was authorized.

THIRD. Until 1838, when a State School Fund was created, and the law of 1825 revised.

FOURTH. Until 1853, when a State Tax was authorized, and the doctrine practically recognized that the property of the State should educate the children of the State.

The settlement of Ohio was by men who had witnessed the advantages of common schools. In their local government they provided for public instruction. Their influence was prominent in the Territorial Legislature, and in 1802, when a constitutional Convention for Ohio had been called, Ephraim Cutler, son of one of the original founders of the Marietta colony, was chiefly instrumental in securing a clause in the organic law of our State, which required legislative encouragement of the means of education.

The first public allusion to education in Ohio, is found in an oration by Solomon Drown, at Marietta, in 1789.*

The first memorial on behalf of the general interest of public schools, read in our Legislature, was proposed in 1816, by Rev. Samuel P. Robbins, then president of Marietta College. It was referred to a committee of three, in the Senate, but was not otherwise acted upon.

In 1817, a committee of the House reported a bill in favor

---

* See page 72.

of so disposing of lands in the Virginia Military District, as to erect a building for, and support, a public seminary. It failed to become a law on account of opposition in the Senate.

Between 1802 and 1820, petitions and memorials respecting School Lands were urged upon every Legislature , and a variety of legislation for their management and disposal was had; but there was no general sentiment upon public schools, and there was no general legislation.

From the days of the Territory, when Arthur St. Clair exercised authority in the executive office, up to the period just mentioned (1820), our governors, in view of growing common school interests in other States, and a few local movements in their own, strengthened their messages with recommendations for the promotion of public education; but having less regard for gubernatorial suggestions than for the clamors of men who were interested in diverting the proceeds of school lands from their legitimate purpose, no practical attention was given to the constitutional requirement, by our General Assembly.

As early as 1816, influences in behalf of general education proceeded from Cincinnati. They were received with favor and were extended by gentlemen in Cleveland and other northern towns. Nathan Guilford was their leading spirit. He had then a bookstore in Cincinnati. For the purpose of advertising his business, and of advocating a few favorite theories, he published an almanac. It was edited by "Solomon Thrifty," and was to the West as important a publication as the almanac of "Poor Richard" had been to the East. During the seven years in which it was circulated by Mr. Guilford, the course of popular education was presented to the public in all its practical bearings. Every page on which a paragraph, a table of statistics, a scrap of poetry, a line of satire, or an argument for the increase of knowledge could appear, was crowded with matter well calculated to advance the common school cause.

This almanac was not only sold, but was circulated gratuitously, wherever it was known that it would reach inquiring readers. Supported by private correspondence, and occasionally by a liberal newspaper, it contributed largely to the awakening of a public sentiment to which the General Assembly of 1821–2 deemed a response due.* That body not only passed the first law, making provision for the encouragement of schools, but it charged a committee of five of its members with the duty of considering and reporting upon school wants.

The little circle of friends of popular education in southern Ohio, actively urged its correspondents to secure an expression of public sentiment; and numerous petitions were sent to the General Assembly, asking for a liberal school system. After considering these petitions, the committee of five recommended a committee of seven Commissioners, to be appointed by the Governor, who should be instructed to acquaint themselves with the school systems of other States, and report one for Ohio. This recommendation was accepted in January, 1822, and the Governor appointed a Board of Commissioners, in which Caleb Atwater, Rev. James Hoge and Rev. John Collins, were the active men. Atwater was directed to prepare a series of pamphlets, urging the need of increased facilities in the State, for the encouragement of education — setting forth a plan for the accomplishment of the desired purpose, and arguing the advantages of its adoption. These pamphlets were accordingly published, and 1500 copies of each were circulated. Mr. Atwater devoted his whole time, for the greater portion of a year, to the purposes of his commission, and was never adequately rewarded. It did not happen that the system agreed upon by the Commissioners was adopted, but Atwater, Hoge and Collins are entitled to grateful remembrance for what they did toward awakening an interest, upon which more was accomplished than they deemed it advisable to recommend. Their system was based upon that of New York, and made no provision for a general school revenue, other than might arise from judicious management of the school lands.

* See page 122. † See page 131.

Nathan Guilford, who had been appointed one of the commissioners because of his well known interest in, and knowledge of, common schools, refused to co-operate with the Board. He deemed their plan inadequate, and addressed a letter to the Commissioners, in which he presented the first argument ever made at length in Ohio, for a general tax to support common schools. This letter was reported to the Legislature, and was published by its order. It contended ably that the income arising from lands could not be adequate to the support of schools; that the schools should be free, and that to render them free a tax *ad valorem* upon the property of the counties was required.

The following is a significant paragraph, which should be remembered in Mr. Guilford's honor.

"The funds arising from school lands will not be sufficient to educate properly one child in ten. It is unnecessary to dilate upon the importance and necessity of education in a free State. That the mass of the people should be well informed, and enabled to understand their rights and the policy of the government under which they live, is universally acknowledged by all enlightened and reflecting men. Public intelligence and public morals ought to be the peculiar care of every Republic, and as every man is interested and benefited, either directly or indirectly, in the political safety, good morals, good order, intelligence and social happiness of the community of which he is a member, he ought to contribute freely to their promotion and support. And the Legislature, as the public guardian, has an unquestioned right to compel every individual, by a tax, to bear his proportionable share of the expense. And if the means are not otherwise provided, it becomes the duty of the Legislature to exercise that right, and to make such provision that every child of the Republic, whether rich or poor, should have an opportunity of receiving a common, decent education."

The Legislature of 1823–4 was timid. The members were not convinced that public sentiment demanded taxation for school purposes, and nothing was done to promote public instruction. The friends of education determined to press the question upon the people. In the campaign of 1824, the cause of education was discussed, and several well known friends of free schools were elected—Nathan Guilford was chosen a senator from Hamilton county, and Ephraim Cutler was elected a senator from Washington. These men devoted themselves earnestly to the work of convincing a majority of the members that liberal legislation for common schools was required. They succeeded in securing a committee,* which agreed to a report and a bill, from the pen of Mr. Guilford. The bill was in fulfillment of the views Mr. Guilford had expressed in his letter of the year previous, and it passed the Senate by a vote of twenty-eight to eight, and was accepted by the House, without amendment, in a vote of forty-six to twenty-four.

Mr. Guilford and Mr. Cutler had worked against bitter opposition, with private tact rather than public display, and when the final vote was taken in the House, they stood side by side, intensely anxious concerning the result. They were not confident of the support of several of the members, and when the Speaker announced that the bill had a majority of twenty-two votes, Mr. Cutler turned to Mr. Guilford, and with an impressive manner, in subdued tones, said, in the language of the Prophet Simeon,

"—Now, Lord! lettest thou thy servant depart in peace, according to thy word, for mine eyes have seen thy salvation."

When we remember that Mr. Cutler had been the friend of education in the Constitutional Convention, and that Mr. Guilford had been the foremost advocate of free schools for seven or eight years, we recognize a significance in the scene which renders it worthy the pencil of a great painter. †

For eleven years after the passage of the Act of February, 1825, no adequate measures were taken to make it generally efficient, though almost every Legislature amended or modified it. ‡ In Cincinnati, by means chiefly of zealous efforts on the part of Nathan Guilford, free schools of good character were established. Improvement was secured in the schools of Cleveland, Dayton, and one or two other large towns,

---

* See page 141.

† For the law, see page 142.

‡ See, from page 146 to 158.

as well as in some of the second class villages, but free schools were enjoyed nowhere outside of Cincinnati.

Among the men deserving particular regard in the memories of the recipients of the benefits of common schools in Ohio—whose names have not appeared in these pages—are, Thomas Morris, of Clermont county, for twenty-four years a legislator, and during one term a United States' senator, and Charles Hammond, from 1816 to 1821 a legislator, and afterward editor of the Cincinnati *Gazette.*

In 1828, Mr. Morris, during a speech in the Senate, said:

"To provide means for the instruction of every citizen, is a duty that devolves on those who are called to administer the government. This is not only necessary to the safety and correct administration of the government, but for the happiness of the people. * * * * Let us not either overlook female education. * * * * * The instruction and cultivation which woman receives, has always been justly viewed as evidence of the improved state of society, where it exists. * * * * * Where female virtue, knowledge and intelligence abound, man can never be degraded or a slave."

In 1829, an institution called the "Academic Institute," held regular meetings in Cincinnati for the discussion of questions involving the best interests of public education. These discussions were led by Albert Picket and Alexander Kinmont, both teachers and benefactors. The objects of the institute were regarded with so much favor that its leaders were induced to call a general convention of the friends of education in the Mississippi valley in June, 1831. At this Convention, discussions and addresses were given which commanded public attention, and an association was formed called "The Western College of Teachers." The proceedings of the first meeting were published in the "Academic Pioneer," edited by Albert Picket, the first educational journal in the North West—begun in 1831 and continued about ten years.

The purpose of the College of Teachers was announced to be the promotion, by every laudable means, of the diffusion of knowledge in regard to education, and especially by aiming to elevate the character and profession of Teachers to their just intellectual and moral influence on the community.

Albert Picket, Alexander Kinmont, Samuel Lewis, Milo G. Williams, Daniel Drake, Edward D. Mansfield, Calvin E. Stowe, W. H. McGuffee and John L. Talbott, were the most active men of the College, but a large number of the leading men of the Mississippi valley were its supporters. Addresses were delivered, between 1831 and 1845, not only by those whose names have been mentioned, but by T. S. Grimke, O. M. Mitchell, Rev. J. L. Wilson, John P. Foote, Joseph Ray, James H. Perkins, T. M. Post and others, upon subjects embracing the general as well as the special relations of education. These addresses were published in six annual volumes. They have given the College of Teachers a place in the educational history of the West, to which thinking men gratefully look, regretting that, as early as 1840, the institution should have been suffered to languish, and five years thereafter cease to exist.

Upon the popular educational movement of Ohio, the College of Teachers left abiding influence. Under its auspices educational associations were formed in different parts of the State, and directly and indirectly, from its influence, was awakened a popular interest which very distinctly demanded more general and more efficient execution of the law of 1825, as it had been amended in 1827–'29 and '31.*

The Legislature of 1835–6, in view of increasing popular interest in the cause of education, passed a resolution, introduced by Liecester King, senator from Trumbull county, on behalf of the Committee on Schools and Colleges, to whom had been referred a communication from Calvin E. Stowe (then a Professor in Lane Seminary at Cincinnati, about to visit Europe), authorizing him to inquire into, and report upon, the most forward School Systems of the old World.

The thirty-fifth Legislature (1836–7), understood more nearly

---

* See, from page 149 to 159.

what leading school-men required, and what the School System of the State needed, than some of its immediate predecessors, and appointed a State School Superintendent.

CHAPTER II.

LABORS OF SAMUEL LEWIS, AND THEIR RESULTS.

ALFRED KELLY, representative of Franklin county, introduced a resolution instructing the Standing Committee on Schools and School Lands, to inquire into the expediency of creating the office of Superintendent of Common Schools. William B. Van Hook, of Butler county, who was chairman of that committee, reported on the 27th of January, 1837, in favor of the office, and presented a bill defining the duties of the officer. On the 10th of February it passed the House by one majority, and on the 22d of March was adopted in the Senate. Senator Price, of Hamilton county, proposed Samuel Lewis as the State School officer, and on the 30th of March his proposition was accepted by the Senate. The following day it passed the House, and Samuel Lewis became the first Superintendent of Common Schools in Ohio, for one year, with a salary of $500 per annum.

A law, authorizing taxation for school purposes, and providing for the local management of schools, had been in operation eleven years. From 1832, a School Fund had been accumulating from the sale of section sixteen;* it was increased in 1835 by the income of salt lands;† and in 1837 was farther increased by the interest on the surplus revenue of the United States;‡ and yet, in 1837, there were no free

---

* See page 154. † See page 191. ‡ See page 203.

schools in Ohio, outside of Cincinnati; and, excepting in the larger towns, where private teachers were encouraged, but a few schools afforded, even for three or four months in a year, instruction in reading, writing and arithmetic. Professional teachers, who would accept common schools, could be found only in the cities.

The children of a greater portion of the State, were under the instruction, for one, two, three, four or five months in a year, of young men who had neither education, experience nor pride, adequate to the proper conduct of a primary school.

The Legislature of 1835–6, in order to gain direct knowledge of the schools of the State, required County Auditors to report to the State Auditor the number of school children in each county, with such other information, in reference to schools, as might be useful. Only thirty-three Auditors responded to that law, and their returns were so meager and unreliable as to be altogether unsatisfactory.

In view of these facts, Mr. Lewis hesitated to accept the office of Superintendent, but he was pressingly urged, and his reluctance was overcome. He entered upon the discharge of his duties with zeal and steady purpose; and spent the spring, summer, and part of the fall of 1837, sending circulars to County Auditors, traveling on horseback from county to county, delivering addresses, talking with school officers, visiting schools, and encouraging teachers. He traveled over twelve hundred miles, and visited three hundred schools. His first report was made in December, 1837. By a resolution of the General Assembly, Mr. Lewis read it to the members at two evening sessions. It was a clear picture of the deplorable condition of schools; an emphatic presentation of public sentiment in favor of free education; an exposition of the abuse of school lands, and an earnest appeal in behalf of more liberal legislation than had been witnessed in Ohio.

Mr. Lewis recommended:

School Libraries;

A State School Fund, of $200,000;

Township High Schools;

Town Boards of Education;

Evening Schools in towns and cities;

County Superintendents;

A School Journal, to be distributed to school officers gratuitously;

Encouragement for the formation of Teachers' Associations;

Authority for districts to borrow money to erect school-houses;

The employment of women as teachers;

Full reports from teachers and school officers.

In support of these recommendations, Mr. Lewis had spoken throughout the State with rare eloquence, and as the result of his observations, he said to the Legislature:

"The thousands with whom I have conversed, of all classes and in all departments of life, are unanimous, and they represent their neighbors as unanimous, in favor of efficient and active measures, on the part of the Legislature, for the promotion of Common Schools. I have heard of persons and of neighborhoods, that were said to be opposed to such a course; but on visiting such persons and places, the objections were found to be not against proper legal provision for these schools, but against particular details in the law. Complaints against defects are often erroneously put down by lookers on, as opposition to the law, when in fact the complainers are its most ardent friends, and in favor of the most active measures. It is one way of making a friend of reform odious, by representing his complaints as opposition. I have not found an individual that, for himself, objected to the expense, provided the schools are made good." * * * * *

"Whatever I may be compelled to say of the present condition of schools, they are certainly improving everywhere in the State. In many counties, associations are formed of teachers and friends of learning, to promote this object; and the education of the masses is a marked feature in all discussions and reports. Nothing will rally the people more readily than the discussion of subjects connected with education. Still, leaving Cincinnati for the present out of the question, there are but very few places in the State where common school instruction proper is furnished approaching near the grade we have supposed; that is, where the means of proper instruction *are free to all*, *rich and poor*, *on equal terms*. The city of Cleveland has, within a few months, commenced

22

organizing her free schools on principles which, if carried out to the extent demanded in that flourishing place, will distinguish her on the list of free school cities; but even there the provision is not half enough, and the schools have from fifty to eighty children to the teacher." * * * *

"In towns and large villages, the *common* schools are poorer than in the country. In the latter, neighborhoods depend more on them, and of course take a deeper interest in their control; while in the former there is too frequently but little attention paid to these schools, by persons able to provide other means of instruction. Private schools are considered the best, and being patronized by the wealthy, create a distinction that is ruinous. I am unwilling to repeat the remarks, in reference to this point, that I have often heard made; it may be sufficient to say, that in many instances the whole tendency is to bring the schools into disrepute, if not positive disgrace." * * * * *

"The result is, that so far as common schools proper extend, though there are many good schools and good teachers, and a great amount of money expended, yet for want of a proper system by which the educational labors of the State may be concentrated, so as to unite economy with efficiency, nothing like proper means of instruction are afforded; and there is left a class, by no means small, who either get no learning at all, or get so little and in so defective a manner and under so many forbidding circumstances, that it does but little if any good." * * * * *

"Where the schools are kept free in this State, they flourish best. In Cincinnati they have marched steadily forward, overcoming every difficulty, and the people look upon them as the most valuable of their privileges." * * "From my knowledge of public opinion in this State, and especially of practical men, I have no doubt that four-fifths are in favor of this kind of schools, and will heartily approve such measures as may be required to establish and sustain them. These schools must be made good, we repeat, as well as free. Reason on theories as we may, they will never controvert facts and experience. These prove that the only way to make free or common schools useful, is to make those who support them interested therein. The people say, they expect efficient measures. They think it a favorable time to revise, improve and render permanent the system; and they desire that early and efficient measures may be taken to give general circulation to the law, so that they can be early made acquainted with its provisions, and conform their action thereto; and though they do not expect perfection, they say they can gradually overcome the difficulties better than to have frequently to change their mode of proceeding."

The General Assembly to which the School Superintendent thus addressed himself, was composed chiefly of good men. Among its members were several prominent individuals who have since been the public servants of our people in the highest places for which our Constitution provides. In the Senate were Benjamin F. Wade, David A. Starkweather, and Leicester King; in the House, Seabury Ford, William Medill, Nelson Barrere, Alfred Kelly, Otway Curry, James J. Farran, William B. Thrall, W. Trevitt, and John A. Foote.

A disposition to accept the recommendations of Mr. Lewis was evident early in the session. His report was favorably received by the people, and its characteristics were commended by leading newspapers.

W. B. Van Hook was chairman of the school committee of the House of Representatives. He was a personal friend of Mr. Lewis, as well as a public friend of public education; and accepting Mr. Lewis's views as those of a wise and well informed man, he reported to the committee a bill embodying nearly all of his recommendations. That bill was introduced to the House on the 5th of February, 1838. It was discussed with earnestness and bitterly opposed, but on the 17th of February, passed by a vote of 46 yeas to 20 nays.

When it went to the Senate, important questions were raised upon the manner of providing a State School Fund of $200,000. The Finance Committee was instructed to report upon it, and John H. James of Champaign county, chairman of that committee, reported that it must be raised from the following sources:

Interest on the U. S. Deposit Fund,	$100,350
" " Fund from Salt Lands,	2,100
Tax on Banks, etc.,	48,000
	150,450
To be provided for by general property tax,	50,000
	$200,450

This, it was reported, as the bill then stood, would make the school tax

In Counties,	2 mills,
For State,	1 "
	3 mills,

Making the burden of taxation, in the aggregate, 8½ mills, independent of local taxation.

This presented a formidable obstacle to the passage of the bill, but after slight amendment it passed the Senate on the 3d of March, by a vote of 21 yeas to 13 nays. The House concurred in the Senate amendments, and on the 7th of April, 1838, the law was in force.*

The salary of the Superintendent had been increased to $1,200, and his term extended to five years, for which Mr. Lewis was elected. Mr. Lewis was Superintendent of Schools during the years 1837, 1838 and 1839.

In 1838 he published six numbers of an official journal called "The Ohio School Director," visited a majority of the counties of the State, delivered public addresses in nearly every county town and in most of the cities, and to the General Assembly reported not only upon the condition of the schools of the State and their needs, but made an elaborate report in answer to resolutions of the previous Legislature, asking information upon the propriety, costs, etc., of establishing a State Seminary for Teachers at Columbus. These resolutions were offered by Mr. Van Hook, of Butler. It passed on the 19th of March, 1838.

The following extracts from Mr. Lewis's Second Annual Report, give a sketch of his labors in 1838, and a just picture of the schools in that year, as well as a clear representation

* On page 158, a paragraph fails to do justice to this law. It ought to have been there published. It was not a mere revision of previous laws, but comprised important new features, as the statement of Mr. Lewis's recommendations, which were adopted, shows. It would be published here in full, but from the fact, that the chapter on the laws, from 1831 to 1851, beginning page 187, contains its chief points.

of what he conceived to be the public sentiment respecting free education.

"As the law was in some of its provisions entirely new, and many inquiries were made on the subject, it was generally desired that public addresses should be delivered, which was done in most of the counties through which I passed. Opportunity was afforded me of conversing with different school officers and citizens, as well as visiting a great number of schools, where I could not only observe what was doing, and upon what principles, but also the general state of education throughout our country. * * * * * * These labors, with the various other duties of the department, have occupied all my time, and have enabled me, I think, to understand the condition of schools in the several counties, and what further is required to supply the demand, and comply with the wishes of the people. * * * * * * * * * * From all the information thus derived, I have no doubt that a large majority of the people are in favor of, and comparatively but few opposed to, the present law. But time enough has not elapsed to enable the warmest friends to have witnessed the full operation of the present system; it is new, and aims at reducing to order, harmony and usefulness, a department admitted by all to have had neither order nor harmony, and comparatively but little usefulness. It was with two-thirds of those who were active, a new work, and in many places an arduous one; the duties, in many cases, being left to be performed by officers elected for other purposes. Though the law was in force from the first of April, yet, as it continued the former directors in office, they were almost uniformly governed by the old law, and were so in fact from necessity, as in four-fifths of the districts they had no funds to allow any more than ordinary arrangements to be made." * * * *

"Hitherto the burdens of the law only have been known, and yet, we can not shut our eyes to the facts that meet us everywhere, proving beyond cavil, that the year 1838 has witnessed a more rapid and extensive development of public enterprise and effective action for common schools, than has been known at any former period. Letters from county auditors and other officers, in different parts of the State, furnish the most encouraging information and abundant evidence that the work is progressing as rapidly as its most ardent friends could have expected." * * * * *

"Every possible variety is found in the character of the teachers, and the kind and manner of instruction. There is this encouragement, however, the people are very generally convinced of present defects, and seem determined to remedy the evils. There are but few places where a teacher can be employed, who does not pretty well understand English grammar and geography, in addition to reading, writing and arithmetic. One error still prevails to a ruinous extent; namely, the neglect of cultivating and developing the powers of the mind, while every thing is attempted to be done by taxing memory with the weight of names and abstractions, allowing no play for thought, and exciting no interest whatever in the child's mind." * * * * * *

"It may be said with truth, that Ohio does not (except in a few cases) furnish instruction for females, at all adapted to their sphere in life, or such as will be likely to elevate their views, refine their taste, and cultivate that delicacy of sentiment and propriety of conduct, which the good of the country, no less than their own happiness, requires."

* * * * * * * *

"In a large part of our county towns, votes have, within a few months, been taken to raise from $3,000 to $6,000 for school-houses, and in other places measures are in progress to determine on the proper plan preparatory to action. In the country districts, too, this work is progressing. In many places where efforts have been made for years, heretofore unsuccessfully, votes, this year, have been taken with great unanimity. Nothing is hazarded in saying, that at least one thousand school-houses have been built, and are now building, under the new law; mostly brick or frame, and many of them of a superior kind, exhibiting good taste and ample accommodation.

"Individuals are sometimes loud in their opposition, but when the questions are tested by popular votes the measures are carried by overwhelming majorities."

* * * * * * * *

"It is proper to notice particularly the school system adopted in Cincinnati. That city is laid out into districts containing a large number of children in each; houses are built in the several districts large enough to contain three hundred scholars and upward: there are male and female teachers in each house, and classing is adopted to a considerable extent. All the English branches are taught that are usual in our best English schools, and without drawing invidious distinctions, it may be said that, as a class of schools, they are good. The rich and poor send their children, and though there are many private schools in the city, they create no division of feeling or interest. The officers are very careful in their supervision, as, indeed, the public require them to be. The increase of funds provided last winter enables them to extend their labors, and every year increases the interest felt by the people in these institutions; they are, in fact, the peculiar favorites of the whole community. Cleveland has, during the last year, extended her system as nearly on the same plan as she can without large buildings. Steubenville, Warren, Newark, Portsmouth, Dayton, Chillicothe, Lebanon, and many other towns, have already voted the money for erecting houses of the same kind, and some even more commodious. Some towns are peculiary situated, and should have special regulations for their government, among which is Zanesville." * * * * * *

"For the first time in our State has the law required the schools to be free, or furnished the means to defray the expense, and even yet, the directors are hardly willing to risk the employment of teachers, because they do not know the amount coming to them; and yet it is a principle so entirely new, that, while they almost unanimously approve of it, they are doubtful of the result. The year 1839 will, I am confident, dissipate their doubts, and thenceforth they will never suffer the support of these schools to be withdrawn. The direct benefits of the present law have not yet begun to be felt." * * * * * *

"There are some townships that have the means and a desire of establishing central township schools or academies, and in most of our townships the youth over twelve years of age could with convenience attend such a school. The number of townships now prepared for this measure is small but will be increasing." * * * * *

"The people have not heretofore followed any particular system. The directors of each district have done that which was right in their own eyes, and generally adopted, as far as they could, the particular system of the State from whence they came. There was not enough energy in the law to create much action or interest; and, what the law was, did not so much concern them, nor was it scanned critically by any one, or at least, but by few. Now every man is interested, and every man is more or less active in examining the law with scrutiny. They are but just beginning the work under it. Actual experience proves, that it has roused the whole State on the subject of education, and has produced, and is producing, inquiry and action on the part of the people a hundred fold beyond any former period. The pleasing and encouraging part of this activity is, that it is all progressive, it nowhere goes back; it is in extension of popular rights and privileges; the people, in the exercise of the powers conferred on them, build school-houses and sustain all other measures required, in full expectation that they are now to have free schools provided by the law for the education of all their children. * * * * * *

"It is the almost unanimous wish of the people that no amendment should be made affecting any essential principle or practice. Stability is now greatly needed, and to introduce material changes, would be going back and beginning anew."

Mr. Lewis's report on a State University, contained much that is of interest to all who desire to form a conception of what our schools have been. We subjoin several extracts. It answered the first action in the General Assembly, which contemplated a State School for the practical instruction of those designing to teach; and Mr. Lewis not only argued with force the need of schools to teach the art of teaching, but he suggested Teachers' Institutes, and stating what common schools ought to be, very nearly described the graded schools now popular in the towns and cities of Ohio.

"The general representation of persons in every county, proves that there is not a sufficient number of teachers to answer the demand of the twelve thousand schools required to be taught; and we include now all that teach or desire to teach, good and bad; if the examiners could see any prospect of procuring good teachers, they would reject one-third of the number that now receive certificates, but they are compelled to give men and women certificates of qualification against their own judgment, because, if they are rigid, the districts must go without schools. Directors, too, are compelled to employ teachers having the lowest class of certificates, because they can not get such as they wish.

"There are in this State a large number of teachers, both male and female, that are well qualified. In general, the females are better qualified than the males; but the number of those of either sex that are well qualified, bears no proportion to the number required. If reliance can be placed on the accounts we receive (and there can not, it is believed, be any doubt of their correctness), not more than one half of those engaged in teaching are even tolerably qualified for the business. On this point a great variety of evidence could be produced, but the statement will be admitted, because almost every man, from his own observation, knows it to be true. At the present time, incompetent teachers are doing more harm to the cause of education, and more effectually hindering the introduction of good schools, on a good system, than all other influences put together. It is not uncommon to find teachers complaining of a law that requires them to keep records and make quarterly reports, simply because they have not sufficient business knowledge to perform the work. Those who despair of perfecting our school system, urge the defective character of teachers, as the strongest evidence to sustain their views, alleging that we have no sufficient mode of securing a better class of teachers, without which the character and usefulness of the schools can not be elevated to the rank that the majority of the community aspire to." * * *

"Poor teachers, and penurious men, are ever averse to raising the standard of education; and they labor hard to create an impression that the rights of the people are infringed by requiring teachers to possess certain qualifications before they can draw public money, for services in this department."

Arrangements had been made by the Directory of the College of Teachers for a State Educational Convention at Columbus in 1837, but the first convention, at which the different sections of the State were represented, was held under the auspices of the College in December, 1838. Mr. Lewis, in his addresses, had urged upon teachers and school officers the necessity of attending the convention, and had published earnest appeals for it in the *School Director*. Between eighty and ninety delegates were present. Wilson Shannon, then Governor, was elected President, and Milo G. Williams first Vice President. Addresses were delivered by D. Pearce, then President of Western Reserve College; W. H. McGuffey (who had accompanied Mr. Lewis, during the autumn of 1838, and delivered lectures in several northern counties), and Calvin E. Stowe. Discussions were had upon important resolutions, in which leading educational men from different parts of the State engaged. These resolutions, vigorously indorsed Mr. Lewis as State Superintendent, recommended Normal Schools, urged the cultivation of Music in the common schools, and appealed to the people for earnest support of the school law.

The Convention, conducted as it was by the men of most

prominence at that time, in colleges and schools, had decided influence, but the election for the General Assembly had already taken place, and several men of known hostility to the school law had been chosen. Early in the session of 1838–9, efforts were made to destroy, in a considerable degree, the efficiency of the school system.

A semi-monthly paper, entitled the *Pestalozzian*, by E. L. Sawtell and H. K. Smith, started in April, 1838, at Akron, Summit county, had ably supported Mr. Lewis and the school system. Conventions had been held in a number of counties, which resolved against any decided change, and under those influences, men had been elected who did not fear to declare a determination to resist any measures which would retard school progress. Mr. Lewis knew that there was to be a warm contest, and he devoted himself night and day to the task of saving the law.

The School Committee consisted, in the House, of J. E. Hanna of Morgan, Erastus Chester of Ashtabula, Leverett Johnson of Cuyahoga, Elisha Garrett of Portage, Israel Brown of Hamilton; in the Senate, of Simeon Fuller of Cuyahoga, Aaron Harlan of Green, and Benjamin F. Wade of Ashtabula.

On the 12th of December, 1838, Mr. Johnson, representative of Stark, offered a resolution to abolish the office of Superintendent, reduce the county tax to one mill, and make the duties of School Directors less onerous. The resolution was laid on the table.

Petitions to repeal the law, forwarded from a small number of counties, had been referred to the Standing committee in the House. Mr. Hanna, from that committee, reported against the prayer of the petitioners; argued that education should be furnished by the State; that a Superintendent was indispensable, and hoped the law would only be amended so as to give German pupils an opportunity to attend schools taught in their own language.

Mr. Spangler, senator from Fairfield and Hocking, moved to abolish the office of Superintendent. John H. James of

Champaign, moved to lay the resolution on the table; which was lost, and the question on the motion to abolish it, was lost, nays 24, yeas 8.

In the House, a motion to abolish the office of Superintendent, was lost by a vote of 29 yeas to 34 nays. A motion by Mr. Milliken of Butler, to destroy the State School Fund, was lost by a large majority; and the vote, on a motion by John Brough of Fairfield, to release township superintendents, failed, 33 to 37. A motion by Mr. Johnson of Stark, to make the Auditor of State, School Superintendent, was lost by a vote of 33 to 36; but a motion by the same gentleman to reduce the county tax to one mill, was carried in the House, 43 to 19. Attempts were made repeatedly to postpone all further action, but the friends of the school system were firm, and when the General Assembly adjourned, the school law stood as passed the year previous, excepting, that the School Director was suspended; County Commissioners were allowed to reduce the county tax to one mill, and were authorized to excuse township clerks from acting as school superintendents; but evening schools in towns were provided for; equal privileges secured to all white youth, and the borrowing money for the building of school-houses, ordered to be paid by taxation.

The law of 1838, as amended in 1839, contained all of the important recommendations urged by Mr. Lewis, excepting township libraries and county superintendents.

The Superintendent's health had been impaired by severe exposure and arduous labor, and he was obliged to announce that he could not canvass the State in 1839 as he had in 1838. He immediately addressed circulars to county auditors, announcing the changes in the school law, and appealed to county commissioners not to reduce the tax.

During 1839, he delivered not more than half a dozen public addresses, but he discussed important questions bearing upon the practical advantages of education, and the means by which they were to be secured, in a series of model circulars, which were widely published in the city and county newspapers. His arguments in defense of the school law were clear and cogent; and his appeals to the people, based upon interests which they could see and appreciate, had permanent influence.

A monthly paper called the "Common School Advocate," was published at Cincinnati. More educational conventions were held in the different counties than had been before known, and the number of educational associations was largely increased.

A State Convention, called by the College of Teachers in December, 1839, was more numerously attended than any previous one, and was more interesting than any of its predecessors. Mr. Lewis delivered an address upon the history of common schools and their effects upon pecuniary interest. W. H. McGuffey lectured upon the influence of private opinion on common schools; Warren Jenkins, upon the school laws of Ohio; and Milo G. Williams, upon "Cabinets of natural science in common schools."

Governor Shannon, appreciating what was being done for common schools, deprecated any radical change in the law,* but the opposition which had been manifested in the Legislature of the previous winter, had accumulated during the summer and fall, notwithstanding increased school interest in many counties. This opposition, as Mr. Lewis said in one of his circulars, sprang, for the most part, from men who had not read the law, or who had studied it in order to misrepresent its features. But it had opponents also among school officers who were unwilling to discharge the duties imposed upon them, and among school teachers who were incompetent to meet its requirements. The General Assembly had in it a majority which represented opposition to important features of the school system.

Mr. Lewis presented his third annual report, on the 24th of December, and resigned his office. It was not as elaborate as either of the previous documents from the school department, but was able and interesting.

---

* See page 168.

So much of it as relates to the labors of the Superintendent, and the condition and prospects of the schools, is subjoined:

"It has heretofore been a reproach to our State, that sufficient provision was not made for the education of the poor, and it was, as late as last winter, declared, that such provision was not even then made." * * * *

"In a considerable part of the State, the funds allow a free school to be taught, for all the youth, from four to nine months in the year, and where there is a deficiency, it is paid by those who are able." * * * * *

"Whatever we may find to cause regret to the patriot or Christian, by reason of deficiency in quantity and quality of education, or whatever difficulties may exist in particular cases, there is nothing more evident than that a general increase and improvement exist in this department. This is not confined to any one class of schools, but extends to all; there is more attention paid to the character and competency of the teacher—more disposition to encourage good teachers, by allowing reasonable salaries; the number of schools is increased, and they are kept open longer than formerly. The standard of education is raised for common schools, in almost every county of the State, and where opposition is rife, attention is awakened and improvement goes on in the most important work of education among the people. This is producing its natural consequences. Academies are coming forward, of an improved character, both in morals and literature, and beyond them still, all our colleges are in a more prosperous condition than at any former period." * * *

"There are occasionally two or more teachers in the same school, and sometimes one teacher teaches the district school in two districts at different periods, so that the number of teachers often varies from the number of schools for these different reasons. The number of male teachers, in the aggregate, exceeds that of the females. In the northern counties, the schools, to say the least, are as good as in any counties in the State; and their practice is, to employ females for teaching the small children." * * * * *

"In 691 townships, 731 school-houses have been built, this year, at a cost of $148,959, being $504 each; and if we suppose that as many have been erected in the non-reporting townships, it will present evidence of public sentiment and public educational enterprise that has no parallel out of Ohio, and it proves more than any thing else, what the public feeling is on this subject. It is true, some of these houses have cost but little, but we should take into view, that it is harder, in some districts, to expend $20 for a school-house, than in others to expend $10,000; beside, in many districts, half the land is still held by the State or national governments, and bears no part of this tax; and in other places, much of the land actually taken up has been entered within five years, and is not subject to taxation." * * * *

"I am informed that a large number of school-houses have been voted for, the present year, in addition to those reported." * * * * * *

"The number of directors reported by the township clerks, shows, in some counties, much neglect in holding annual school elections. This evil, however, was less in 1839 than in 1838.

"The returns show that the school tax has been reduced, in ten counties, one mill, and, in three counties, a half mill, leaving the other counties with the tax as fixed by general law. In thirty-three counties, one or more townships have voted additional school tax." * * * *

"The average wages of the teachers, per month, is $13 43. But more than two-fifths of the teachers are females, who do not receive an average of over $10 per month (though some females receive much more). This would leave to the male teachers an average pay of $16 per month."

Opposition was made, in the Legislature, to printing the School Report; but it was overcome, and five thousand copies were ordered. Of the second Report, ten thousand copies had been printed.

The Standing committee on Schools, in the House, consisted of J. S. Rogers of Ashtabula, W. B. Lloyd of Cuyahoga, Elihu Johnson of Jackson, J. Purviance of Darke, and W. B. Miller of Gallia and Lawrence. In the Senate, of John Hough of Ross, Pike the Jackson, Richard Lord of Cuyahoga, and William Scott of Guernsey and Monroe counties.

Henry West of Belmont moved that the Standing committee on Schools in the House, be instructed to inquire into the expediency of abolishing the office of Superintendent. This motion was agreed to on the 19th of December. The committee reported adversely to the resolution of Mr. West, and against the petitions to the same purpose, which had been referred.

T. W. Bartley of Richland, on the 21st of January, moved to appoint a Select committee of three to report a bill reorganizing or abolishing the office of School Superintendent. The motion prevailed, and a committee, of which Mr. Bartley was chairman, was appointed. That committee did not report.

A bill from A. L. Perrill of Pickaway, to accomplish the object of Bartley's resolution, was afterward referred to a select committee, from which two reports were made. The active men on this committee were Mr. Perrill and A. A. Bliss of Lorain. Perrill reported favorably, and Mr. Bliss adversely. Mr. Perrill's bill was stubbornly discussed and indefinitely postponed. The question then turned on Mr. Bliss's bill. It was evaded by a variety of parliamentary maneuvers; motions to indefinitely postpone, to reduce the salary to $500, to make it $800, and to reduce it to $1,000, were lost. At length, on the 10th of March, it passed, giving the Superintendent $800 and a clerk, in the Auditor's office, by a vote of 45 to 17.

When the bill was sent to the Senate, the Standing committee, on motion of David Tod of Trumbull, was instructed so to amend it as to make the Auditor of State, School Superintendent. On the 17th of March, the bill, amended according to instructions, was reported back. Mr. Scott, of the Standing committee, moved its indefinite postponement; which motion was lost, 22 to 8. Mr. McLaughlin of Richland, moved to refer the bill to the Judiciary Committee, with instruction to abolish the office of superintendent, and vest the power he held in township Trustees. That motion was lost, 20 to 10. Mr. Vance of Clark, moved that $400 be allowed the Auditor for a clerk, which prevailed; when Mr. Green of Pickaway and Licking, moved to strike out Auditor of State and insert Secretary of State. The vote on this motion stood, 20 yeas to 11 nays.

On the 18th of March, 1840, the bill as amended passed the Senate. The House refused to concur in the Senate amendments, and committees of conference were appointed. They could not agree, and a second conference was held; meantime

Scott of Monroe and Guernsey, moved that Caleb J. McNulty, then Clerk of the Senate, be elected School Superintendent. This motion passed the Senate on the 23d of March, by a vote of 19 to 9.

The House refused to act upon the resolution appointing McNulty, but accepted the report of the Committee of Conference, confirming the action of the Senate, and on the 23d of March, the last day of the session, the Secretary of State was made School Superintendent, and was voted $400, for the purpose of employing a clerk. In all other respects the school law was unchanged.*

Mr. Lewis retired from his office, with the best wishes of the friends of education in all parts of the State. For his three years' labor he had received no more money than was sufficient to defray his expenses, while absent from home, but he had saved, by his exposure of abuses in the lease and sale of school lands, many thousands of dollars. Because by his zealous efforts and judicious advice he had largely advanced the educational interests of the State, he was not then denied grateful thanks, and as long as common schools are encouraged in Ohio, his memory will be kindly cherished.

The following statements of the relative importance of the Public Schools, during the three years of his superintendentship, exhibit progress of which he had good reason to be justly proud.

---

* The names of the men who opposed and actively defended the school law in 1838–9 and 1839–40, and the names of the counties they represented, have been given, because they indicate where liberal school sentiment was most wanting at that time.

STATEMENT

OF THE RELATIVE IMPORTANCE OF COMMON SCHOOLS WHILE SAMUEL LEWIS WAS SUPERINTENDENT:

AS REPORTED TO THE SUPERINTENDENT.

Dates........	No. of Counties	No. of Counties Reported....	No. of Whole Districts	No. of Fractional Districts..	No. of Common Schools	No. of Scholars Enrolled.			Average Attendance.			Tot. No. School Youth.....	No. of Teachers.			Amount paid Teachers.			No. of Months Tau't,			No. of School Houses built.	Cost of School Houses built.
						Male.	Fem'l.	Total.	Male.	Fem'l.	Total.		Male.	Fem'l.	Total.	Male.	Fem'l.	Total.	Male.	Fem'l.	Total.		
1837	75	62	7,033	....	4,336	76,975	69,465	146,440	......	......	......	468,812	4,757	3,205	7,962	....	....	$286,757	......	......	22,168	4,378	$513,973
1838	76	54	4,882	....	4,030	57,539	51,467	109,006	40,179	33,126	73,305	588,590	2,677	1,728	4,403	$154,284	$46,272	200,556	10,683	6,113	16,796	393	65,732
1839	76	65	5,442	....	7,295	......	......	254,612	......	......	......	....	......	......	7,288	....	....	392,091	......	......	29,199	731	148,959

AS ESTIMATED BY THE SUPERINTENDENT.

Dates.	No. of Districts.	No. of Common Schools	No. of Scholars Enrolled.			Tot. No. School Youth......	No. of Teachers.			Amount paid Teachers.			No. of School Houses built.	Cost of School Houses built.
			Male.	Female.	Total.		Male.	Female.	Total.	Male.	Female.	Total.		
1837	7,748	....	....	....	173,440	492,837	....	....	....	....	....	$317,730	4,378	513,973
1838	8,334	6,880	98,238	87,852	186,090	588,590	4,569	2,946	7,515	$263,379	$78,975	342,354	571	112,203
1839	....	13,049	....	....	455,427	....	....	....	12,860	....	....	701,338	1,308	206,445

CHAPTER III.

CONTINUED POPULAR ACTION, EDUCATIONAL JOURNALS AND TEACHERS' INSTITUTES.

From the year 1840 to 1845, the common school interests of Ohio were but slightly advanced. Compared with 1839, educational enterprise in 1840, was neither active nor wide spread, and in 1842 and 1843 there was less accomplished than in 1840. Reports from the County Auditors to the Secretary of State were meager and unsatisfactory. The Secretaries did not fail, as State Superintendents, to represent the condition of Schools to the General Assembly, and they recommended several valuable measures for their improvement;* but having no personal relations with school officers, nor immediate intercourse with teachers or the friends of education, they were unable to keep alive the interest which had been awakened by the personal exertions of the Superintendent in 1839.

Educational societies, in a few counties, were kept up, and opposition to the school law was in a great degree removed in others, by the encouragement of schools in which German teachers were employed, but there was no pervading pride in, or effort for, educational progress.

The following tabular statement, exhibits more clearly than any form of words, the general decline of school interest, if thoughtfully compared with the statements that have been given for the three years, during which Samuel Lewis, with persuasive eloquence, appealed to the people for vital interest in free schools.

---

* See page 189.

STATEMENT

OF THE RELATIVE CONDITION OF COMMON SCHOOLS, FROM 1840 TO 1845,

AS REPORTED TO SUPERINTENDENTS.

Dates........	No. of Counties	No. of Counties Reported....	No. of Whole Districts	No. of Fractional Districts..	No. of Common Schools	No. of Scholars Enrolled.			Average Attendance.			Tot. No. School Youth.....	No. of Teachers.			Amount paid Teachers.			No. of Months Tau't,			No. of School Houses built.	Cost of School Houses built.
						Male.	Fem'l.	Total.	Male.	Fem'l.	Total.		Male.	Fem'l.	Total.	Male.	Fem'l.	Total.	Male.	Fem'l.	Total.		
1840	79	14	......	....	......	......	......	......	......	......	......	618,746	......	......	......	......	......	......	......	......	......	......	......
1841	79	45	4,018	472	3,181	76,047	61,823	137,870	29,593	21,921	51,514	....	1,746	1,400	3,146	$94,627	$29,809	$124,436	.6,525	4,186	10,711	123	$21,722
1842	79	53	5,430	714	4,627	5,544	3,967	9,511	36,213	25,217	61,430	....	5,409	1,461	6,870	301,200	30,460	331,660	7,764	4,472	12,236	153	25,831
1843	79	45	4,813	606	4,284	24,239	20,503	44,742	44,226	30,581	74,807	....	2,693	1,573	4,266	144,631	31,890	176,521	9,034	4,540	13,574	125	14,930
1844	79	45	4,870	656	3,321	25,698	23,172	48,870	33,518	22,999	56,517	....	2,210	1,179	3,389	112,220	24,482	136,702	7,357	3,753	11,110	115	17,217

These figures show clearly and forcibly, in view of what Samuel Lewis accomplished, the wisdom of those who created the office of School Superintendent, and consequently the want of foresight displayed by those under whose influence it was abolished. Every Secretary of State complained of the extra task imposed upon his department, and no one had been able to give it due attention. Mr. Galloway, who made the school department his special care in 1844 and '45, declared his inability to bestow upon it the study and labor which its importance demanded.*

A few local efforts were put forth, with good effect in, 1844, to re-awaken public interest, but no general movements were had, until the fall and winter of 1845. Early in that year, the school apathy, apparent in a greater portion of the State, became the subject of newspaper paragraphs, and Samuel Galloway, then Secretary of State, recognizing the need of a school revival, determined to employ all the legitimate agencies of his office in its accomplishment. He was ably seconded by influential men, in various parts of the State, and was most creditably successful. He conducted a wide-spread correspondence, attended educational meetings, delivered public addresses, sent circulars to County Auditors and other local school officers, and reported to the Legislature, for 1845, a more prosperous and promising condition of the public schools than had been exhibited in any previous year, excepting 1839, and yet he was compelled to make bitter complaints. In his School Report for 1845, he said:

"During the past year the Superintendent has, by correspondence with the friends of education, by personal consultation, by issuing circulars, and by addressing the people in some parts of the State, endeavored to inspire and concentrate sentiment in favor of some immediate action by which the prostrate cause might be restored, and vigor and prosperity crown its existence. The result of the effort has been to strengthen the conviction that the people are ready to receive

---

* For legislation, between 1840 and 1845, see chapter xiv, from page 187.

and consummate decided legislative action, that the common school cause may be resuscitated."

* * * * * * * *

"The auspicious omens which appear, and urge us onward are, that in the cities of Cincinnati, Cleveland, and other important points, common schools, under the kind influence of philanthropy, and an enlightened public spirit, are exhibiting those rich fruits which alike show the practicability of the scheme, and excite others to a participation in similar benefits. Teachers' Institutes and Associations are springing up in many sections, enlisting the zeal and activity of men of all grades and professions; greater success in elections favorable to a school tax; more enthusiasm exhibited for the advancement of the cause by County Superintendents, as will appear in the fuller and more interesting communications received this year; and more satisfactory statistics than in any previous year since 1839." * * * * *

"Not the least cause of grievance, as represented by many of the most influential friends of education, is, that the directors in many districts, availing themselves of their prerogative under the law, prohibit any branches being taught, except reading, writing and arithmetic." * * *

"It is gratifying to record the fact, that in many portions of our State, these unfailing indications of the advance of education (Teachers' Associations), are in successful operation. Within the past year, in some of our Western Reserve counties, a decided impulse, with encouraging results, has been given to the movement. It is easy to anticipate the beneficial influence of such measures upon teachers, schools and public sentiment." * * * * * *

"The reports of several County Superintendents, which are herewith transmitted, exhibit unequivocal evidence of efficient exertions on their part, in the performance of the responsible duties assigned them by law, and by the instructions of this department. To their efforts is to be attributed, to a very great extent, the revolution in public sentiment, by which the district school, from being the object of general aversion and reproach, begins to attract the attention and regard of all."

In 1838, Rev. Nelson Slater opened a Teachers' Seminary at Kirtland, Lake county. The following year it was conducted by A. D. Lord, and between 1840 and 1845, sent out into the schools of Northern Ohio, several men who have since become prominent educators. These men, seconded with vigor the efforts made in 1845, in other parts of the State, and contributed largely to the awakening of a sentiment which, from that period, has been maturing and extending with great advantage to the general prosperity of the people of Ohio.

Information that Conventions for the instruction of teachers had done good work in the State of New York, was spreading in Ohio, when Rev. L. Howe of Sandusky, invited Salem Town, who was popular as a lecturer at the New York Conventions, to visit our State. Mr. Town accepted the invitation. Notice was given of his expected visit; A. D. Lord of Kirtland, was engaged to assist at the Convention, and in September, 1845, the first Teachers' Institute, ever held in the Western country, was conducted at Sandusky by Salem Town, A. D. Lord, and M. F. Cowdery (then a teacher in the Kirtland Seminary); Rev. Mr. Howe, Ebenezer Lane, and other men of influence, took part in the exercises. The Institute was successful in establishing faith in the usefulness of such Conventions. It was attended by about one hundred pupils. Encouraged by their success at Sandusky, Lord and Cowdery, assisted by M. D. Leggett, held a second Institute at Chardon, Geauga county, in October. It was attended by one hundred and forty teachers, and was regarded with distinguished favor by the leading citizens of the county.

Thus was auspiciously commenced a series of Teachers' meetings for mutual improvement, and the elevation of the profession of teaching, which have become a feature of educational movements in Ohio, so important, that the county which, during any year, is without one, depreciates in the regard of all who have observing interest in common schools.

Educational men, in all parts of the State, were encouraged by the events of 1845, and taking advantage of opportunities then opened to them, signally advanced the common school cause in Ohio, during the four succeeding years.

In July, 1846, A. D. Lord published, at Kirtland, the first number of the *Ohio School Journal.* It was a thin duodecimo magazine, advertised to appear monthly. It was conducted with spirit, advocated Teachers' Institutes, and argued the general need of a State Educational Society. There had then been no State Educational Convention for six or seven years, and the want of a concert of action among the friends of education was everywhere felt. Making progressive measures the special objects of its articles, and urging upon teachers the necessity of elevating their profession, the *Journal*, though not liberally supported, was recognized as a valuable organ of educational sentiment.

Henry D. Barnard, well known as Superintendent of Schools in Connecticut, was invited to visit Ohio, and in the autumn of 1846, spent several weeks in our State. He lectured at Cleveland, Cincinnati, and other prominent cities and towns, and was warmly welcomed in all. Arrangements had been made, early in 1846, for Teachers' Institutes, and during that year nine were held, in northern counties, with increasing success and widening interest, as their purposes and advantages became known.

The first Institute held in the southern part of the State, was at Cincinnati, in February, 1847.

The first one held in middle Ohio, was at Newark, Licking county, in March, 1848.

In November, 1846, the *Free School Clarion*, by William Bowen, at Massillon, Starke county, appeared as a coadjutor of the *School Journal*. It was issued semi-monthly. It republished the calls which had been put forth for a State Teachers' Association, and added arguments of its own in favor of such an organization.

But a few numbers of the *Clarion* had been issued, when a third school paper attracted attention. It was the *Common School Friend*, published monthly, at Cincinnati, by Winthrop B. Smith & Co. With January, 1847, came a fourth periodical—representing the growing educational sentiment of the State—the *Western School Journal*, published monthly, at Cincinnati, by W. H. Moore & Co. Lord's *School Journal* had been removed to Columbus, in December, 1846.

By means of Educational Associations, Teachers' Institutes, and County Conventions, a public opinion was developed in

1847 and 1848, which demanded more liberal legislation than had characterized 1844, 1845 or 1846. Teachers' Institutes were encouraged, county Superintendents were authorized, and a step taken toward the establishment of School Libraries: provision was made for the better regulation of schools in towns and villages, and taxation for the support of schools was rendered sure.*

The law to encourage Institutes was in answer to petitions from the counties in which they had been held, suggested by resolutions adopted at Sandusky and Chardon, in 1845, recommending to the friends of education the importance of memorializing the Legislature in favor of endowing Institutes and making them a part of the school system of Ohio. And the act authorizing counties to elect Superintendents, was a response to petitions that had been industriously circulated in northern and middle counties. The counties in which Commissioners were authorized, upon a vote of the people, to set apart a sum of money for the support of county Superintendents, were Lake, Geauga, Cuyahoga, Medina, Delaware, Knox, Muskingum, Lorain, Portage, Holmes, Gallia, Lawrence, Champaign, Trumbull, Mahoning, Franklin, Madison, Clark, Hancock, Licking, Seneca, Sandusky, Crawford and Wyandot.

Those in which Teachers' Institutes were encouraged by the appropriation of money from the income of the surplus revenue, were Ashtabula, Lake, Geauga, Cuyahoga, Erie, Lorain, Medina, Trumbull, Summit, Portage and Delaware.

The Commissioners of Delaware county appropriated $200 for an Institute; Geauga county gave $200 for a Superintendent; Medina, for an Institute, $300; and Ashtabula, for a Superintendent, $350. Sandusky and Ashtabula were the only counties in which Superintendents were elected.

In 1847, thirteen Institutes were held in the State. A revival, begun in Cincinnati, spread over Southern Ohio, and very decided improvements were made in the cities of Cincinnati, Cleveland, Dayton and Portsmouth, and in the towns

---

* See pages 197, 205-6.

of Akron, Sandusky, Delaware, Massillon and Lebanon, by the establishment of High Schools.

The following extracts from Samuel Galloway's Report to the General Assembly, for 1847, are of interest, as the opinion of a man who, with favorable opportunities, closely watched the indications of school progress:

"The only full report which has been presented, for many years, is that transmitted this year by A. H. Bailey, Superintendent of Schools for Ashtabula county. His letter indicates the efficient action which he has adopted, and the report shows that, if a general law were passed, creating the office of County Superintendent, and other counties would imitate the example of Ashtabula, the school system of Ohio would soon fulfill the expectations of its founders, and its friends. The only other returns, which even approximate accuracy, are those of the counties of Athens, Meigs, Knox, Morgan, Licking and Summit. For these, we are principally indebted to the active exertions of the Auditors, and it may here be appropriate to remark, that the Auditor of Licking county has especially distinguished himself by diligence in obtaining statistics."

* * * * * * * *

"As evidence of the improvement which may by appropriate exertions be realized, and as deservedly complimentary to those who have conducted and sustained the laudable enterprise, it may be stated, that an intelligent citizen of this State, who recently visited the public schools (which have not been one year in existence) of this city (Columbus), remarked that their organization, mode of instruction, and advantages, were superior to those which he had seen, or in which he had been educated, in his native New England State. It is probable that the schools of Cincinnati, Cleveland, Dayton, and other prominent points, possess even a higher reputation than those specified, as they have for a number of years, been in successful operation. Within the last year, in many of our larger towns, measures have been adopted for enlarging the means and advantages of common schools, and establishing them upon a basis similar to that upon which the schools in some of our cities are founded. These signs are auspicious, and betoken, though dimly, a better day." * * *

"The oral and printed discussions of the subject of education, the expressions of the press, the establishment of Teachers' Institutes, and the gradual but certain intellectual improvement of our people, have contributed to elevate the expectations of the people, and the standard of attainment for teachers.

The public mind is beginning fully to realize that there is an impropriety in the school-room being converted into *winter quarters* for exhausted energy, and a "city of refuge" for those who have been chased from other employments. Notwithstanding the advance which has taken place in public sentiment, a more extensive improvement is yet demanded. The cold indifference which is manifested by parents, and those having supervision of schools, would amaze us, if we had not become so familiarized to its contemplation."

* * * * * * * *

"Our system of education has had a feeble, uncertain existence; occasionally giving signs of a reviving life, and as frequently exhibiting symptoms of dissolution. It never has commanded watchful, affectionate protection, but, on the contrary, unblessed by the love of any, it has been left to the capricious charities of all.

"That spirit of enterprise and speculation which has given origin and impetus to physical improvement, has not been imbued with those loftier attributes with which it has been elsewhere characterized, and has not extensively embraced the moral and intellectual improvement of our people. Our wealthy men have not, as in older States, honored themselves by liberal benefactions for the endowment of schools and colleges. Donations for educational purposes, with us, are rare. In other States they have been frequent. Our population has been of a transitory character, and but little disposed to the pursuit or accomplishment of any object as much identified with general, as with individual, welfare. Our society has not assumed that harmonious and uniform character which would secure that unanimity so essential to successful educational effort. There has also operated, for many years, and during the greater part of the time since the re-organization of our school system, the depressing influence of a heavy State debt." * * * * * * *

"When the influence of these, and other difficulties which might be enumerated are contemplated, in connection with the deplorable apathy which has been exhibited by the professed friends of education, it is indeed strange that the system has not been crushed with obloquy and contempt. Its preservation can only be attributed to a deep-seated yet dormant attachment to general intelligence, and to that ineradicable love for human welfare, which all feel, and which but few effectively exhibit."

CHAPTER IV.

SUPERINTENDENCE OF THE STATE DEPARTMENT.

In 1847, the Secretary of State (Galloway), addressed circulars to prominent men, in different parts of the State, inviting reports upon common schools, and upon the general interest in popular education. The replies to his letters exhibited, in connection with the reports of Auditors and county Superintendents, a wide-spread determination, independent of government authority or influence, to extend and improve common school privileges.

A most gratifying feature of this general interest was, a growing public spirit among teachers. Institutes appeared to have aroused them to a new sense of their obligations. Wherever Institutes were held, the necessity of the elevation of teachers, of thorough school organization, in counties and for the State, and of the enlargement of the sphere of the common schools, were topics of discussion and illustration. Resolutions, embodying these doctrines, were often passed, and were published in the county papers.

At Institutes held in Ashland, Chardon and Akron, in the fall of 1847, M. F. Cowdery, Lorin Andrews, William Bowen, J. Hurty, A. D. Lord and M. D. Leggett, were appointed a committee to make arrangements for the organization of a State Educational Society.

They called a Convention at Akron, on the 31st of December, 1847, and a State Teachers' Association was there formed, with Samuel Galloway as President; T. W. Harvey of Geauga county, Recording Secretary; M. D. Leggett of Summit, as Corresponding Secretary; and William Bowen of Stark, as Treasurer.

An Executive Committee, consisting of M. F. Cowdery of Lake, Lorin Andrews of Ashland, M. D. Leggett of Summit, J. Nichols of Lake, J. Hurty of Richland, F. W. Tappan of Portage and H. K. Smith of Summit, was instructed to prepare a plan for the awakening of educational interest, and the elevation of the profession of teaching.

Eleven counties had been represented in the Convention, and the Executive Committee was encouraged to take energetic measures. An address to teachers and the friends of education was agreed upon, inviting co-operation, and urging interest in a meeting of the Association, to be holden in June, 1848. The Committee announced its intention to hold Institutes in forty counties of the State, and issued a circular, appealing for aid, and explaining the object to be attained.

These movements of the Executive Committee, and the objects generally of the State Teachers' Association, were approved by the newspapers of the State, and in all the educational journals earnest appeals were made in their behalf.

The year 1848 is distinguished in the School History of Ohio. The Secretary of State reported encouragingly to the General Assembly, and the legislation of the winter of 1848–9 was liberal.*

Mr. Galloway said:

"The legislation for schools, within the last three or four years, exhibits an improved and advancing state of public sentiment, which demands more enlarged views for educational action than that which exists. The recent amendments to the original laws are as "new cloth in an old garment," and although all may not have been made worse, yet the appearance, at least, manifests the necessity of an entirely new dress." * * * * * * *

"The cause of common school education is slowly, but certainly advancing, notwithstanding the many impediments which it has to encounter. The conviction is annually becoming stronger, that a common school system is adapted to our wants; that it is susceptible of immediate improvement, which will secure for it general confidence and patronage;

---

* See pages 191, 200 and 206.

that no other plan, securing general education, can be established; and that our social and political prosperity are intimately identified with success. Some who once denounced common schools, as an unworthy object of public benefactions, are now beginning to appreciate their advantages; many who have had no children to educate, but who have been uncomfortably taxed to support the cause, now perceive results which, at least, measurably compensate them for their imagined loss of funds; and a still larger number who have apprehended injury to the morals and manners of their children from association with the children of those occupying a different social and pecuniary position, are ascertaining, alike from facts and observation, that correct principles of faith and of conduct, and the decencies of life, can be as successfully taught and practiced in common, as in select schools." * * * *

"Another auspicious sign of improvement is to be found in our cities and some of our larger towns. Within the last four years, schools of the highest order have been established, rivaling in extent, efficiency and usefulness, those schools of New England and New York which have been reared under highly improved educational systems, and which have been liberally sustained by the patronage of funds, and of an enlightened public sentiment. The generosity and taste of the citizens in these points have been interestingly exemplified by the erection of many substantial and commodious buildings, and in the selection of teachers of the highest attainments and character."

It was a part of the duty of the Executive Committee of the State Teachers' Association to report to the State School Department. From the report of M. F. Cowdery, made in December, 1848, we quote:

"In assuming the responsibility of conducting the business affairs of the Association, twelve months since, the committee selected the following objects, as most worthy of their immediate attention: First, the elevation of the teachers of the State, through the agency of Teachers' Institutes, courses of lectures to teachers, educational conventions and associations, and a more conscientious adherence to the law relating to the qualifications of teachers on the part of county examiners. The second object of the committee was to encourage a reorganization of the schools in the cities and incorporated towns of the State. This was proposed to be accomplished by addressing citizens publicly, and stating the importance, practicability and *economy* of such a change in the common school organization as would give, to every child of a town or city, an education fitting him for his duties as a citizen; and lastly, it was the wish of the committee, as far and as fast as practicable, to prepare the public mind for a school system for our State, unparalleled for the liberality of its provisions, the wisdom of its measures, and the harmony and efficiency of its operations.

"During the past year these objects have been kept steadily in view." * * * * * *

"Early in January last the committee made conditional arrangements for holding Teachers' Institutes in one half the counties of the State in the spring following, and matured plans for holding others in the remaining counties of the State, during the succeeding autumn.

"Teachers of ability and experience were secured to visit these counties, and give a course of instruction, for one week, to the teachers of the county, provided the county examiners, teachers themselves, and friends of education, should co-operate in the measures proposed. Several hundred letters were written by the committee to public men and private citizens, in the counties designated, asking their influence and effort in behalf of the plans of the committee. The following counties accepted the propositions of the committee, and Institutes were held during the months of March and April last: Ashland, Richland, Huron, Licking, Seneca, Starke, Columbiana, Wayne and Washington. The number of teachers attending the Institutes, in the above counties, was between six and seven hundred.

"During the summer, proposals were issued by the committee for holding an Institute during the succeeding autumn, in any county of the State where teachers and friends would co-operate with the committee. The following counties accepted the proposals of the committee, and Institutes were held, during the past autumn, in Montgomery, Medina, Portage, Huron, Seneca, Miami, Sandusky, Champaign, Ashtabula and Washington.

"The number of teachers instructed at the Institutes during the fall, in the above counties, was above eight hundred, making in all about fifteen hundred, who have attended Institutes during the past year, in connection with the State Association.

"In January last, the committee issued proposals for a Course of Lectures to Teachers, on subjects immediately connected with their qualifications and duties, and the improvement of schools, to continue nine weeks, and be given in any county of the State where the friends of education would offer the most liberal inducements to the committee for the course. From all the propositions received, the offer from Huron county, pledging to the committee nearly $500, with a suitable building, was deemed best, and the course was accordingly given in that county. About one hundred and twenty persons attended the course." * * *

The following are selected from among the resolutions passed by the teachers, at the close of the course:

"*Resolved*, That, in our opinion, Normal Classes, and Teachers' Institutes, as conducted by our State Teachers' Association, are among the most efficient auxiliaries for promoting the improvement of teachers, and the consequent elevation of our common school system.

"*Resolved*, That we heartily approve of the manner in which the first Normal Class has been conducted by M. F. Cowdery, chairman of the Executive Committee of the Ohio State Teachers' Association, and that we have been extremely gratified with the choice of gentlemen to lecture on the various subjects before us.

"*Resolved*, That Messrs. M. F. Cowdery, L. Andrews, H. Benton, Professor S. St. John, G. W. Winchester, J. B. Howard, J. Hurty, T. W. Harvey, Professor H. Mandeville, Professor I. J. Allen and M. D. Leggett, are entitled to our cordial gratitude for the untiring zeal of their efforts, and for the very able and interesting manner in which they have addressed us on the subjects assigned them." * * *

"During the summer, proposals were issued by the committee for another course, similar to the one in Huron county, to be given where the best offer should be made. The offer from Summit county was deemed best, and the course was given in that county during the months of September and October. The class numbered about sixty. Similar resolutions were presented by this class, and similar expressions of approval were given by citizens and the press.

"Gentlemen who have been employed to conduct Teachers' Institutes, have invariably presented the subject of Union Schools in all the counties they have visited; and it is believed, that important results have already grown out of their labors. Several towns have already adopted the plan of classifying the pupils, and bringing all the schools under one uniform and connected system, while others are making the preliminary arrangements to introduce the same general method.

"It is believed that there is a strong and growing public sentiment in favor of all practicable improvement in the system of education in our State. The committee have been sustained and encouraged in the various efforts they have made the past year, by private citizens, teachers and others, far beyond their expectations. In many sections of the State, it only needs to be known that a measure is really an improvement, and that it is practicable, and the means for introducing it are speedily provided." * * * *

The Lectures complimented in the Resolutions above quoted, were by Professor St. John on Geology; by H. Benton on the English Language; by Lorin Andrews on Arithmetic; by M. F. Cowdery on Geography and Vegetable Physiology; by J. B. Howard on Linear Drawing; by J. Hurty on Civil Government; by T. W. Harvey on American History; by Professor Mandeville on Elocution; by G. W. Winchester on Book-keeping; by I. J. Allen on Natural Philosophy; by M. D. Leggett on Human Physiology; and on Music by Mr. Andrews and Mr. Howard.

Active interest for Normal Schools, was manifested in 1848. The educational journals pressed their value, and Mr. Galloway urged the Legislature to encourage the establishment of one or more. Another feature of the movement of that year, under the auspices of the State Teachers' Association, was Union Schools.

A Committee of the Association, consisting of A. D. Lord, S. S. Rickey, and H. H. Barney, made the encouragement of Union Schools a speciality, and reported to the State School Department, lively encouragement. Some paragraphs from that report will be found of decided interest, as a part of the history of the educational progress of the year.

The Committee arguing the advantage of thorough system, and presenting the advantages of Union and Graded Schools, said:

"It is a well known fact, that in most of the towns and villages of this State, where classified public schools have not been established, there are few, if any, good school-houses; that the teachers employed are generally poorly paid, and often entirely incompetent; that the scholars attend irregularly, and derive but little benefit from their attendance; that school officers and citizens take but little interest in the schools, and that the better class of families, including nearly all who are able to provide for the education of their children elsewhere, and most, if not all, of those who value the manners and morals of their children, feel compelled to stand entirely aloof from these schools, and secure their education by sending them abroad, or by sustaining private schools near home, at a heavy expense." * * * * *

"After a trial of this plan for years, the opinion has become almost universal in the Eastern States, and in many parts of our own State, that the only means of providing a respectable education for the great mass of the youth of a town, and that the best and cheapest plan for securing the same for those who are able to provide it at their own expense, is by establishing well regulated public schools, sustained during at least ten months in the year, and supported by a tax on the property of the town or district. These schools are divisible into two classes; Union schools for moderate-sized towns and villages and the more densely populated country districts, and properly classified or Graded public schools for larger towns and cities."

* * * * * * * *

"In country districts, a house containing three rooms can, probably, be built and furnished for $1,000 or $1,500. The cost of the Union school in Perrysburg, intended for three hundred scholars was $3,000. The cost of each of the three public school-houses in Columbus, containing six rooms, and intended for three hundred pupils, was not far from $3,000, exclusive of the expense for site. The expense of the Union school-house in Lancaster, which is fifty-six by eighty feet on the ground, two stories in hight, and contains eight school rooms for fifty scholars each, was $6,000; for site (two lots), $800; for building and furniture, $5,200. The Union school house in Massillon, ninety by sixty feet, and three stories in hight, cost about $7,000, exclusive of the site, which was a donation." * * * * * *

"The salaries now paid to female teachers in different places in Ohio, where Union schools or well regulated public schools have been established, range from two to seven dollars per week. In the schools of Cleveland, they are paid from two to five dollars per week; in Columbus, primary teachers receive $160 per year, and secondary teachers $200; in Cincinnati the different grades of teachers receive from $192 to $336; and in Massillon, from $200 to $400 per year. The salary of the teachers of the Senior or Grammar schools in Columbus is $400; in Cleveland, $440; in Cincinnati, $600. The salary of the Principal of the High School in Cleveland, and of the Superintendent of Schools in Akron is $500; that of the Principal of the Union School in Perrysburg, and of the Principal of the Boy's School in Zanesville $600; of the Superintendent of the Public Schools of Sandusky City, $700; of the Principal of the Massillon Union School, and the Superintendent of Schools in Columbus, $800; and the present salary of the Principal of the Central School in Cincinnati is $1,500." * * * * * * *

"The average price of tuition in the several schools of Cleveland, for the last year, was $3.96; in the schools of Columbus, $5.25; in those of Cincinnati, $7.00; in the Union school of Massillon it is not far from $6.00; in the Public schools of Philadelphia, employing six hundred and thirty-one teachers, instructing more than forty thousand different scholars, and an average of about thirty-five thousand, the average cost of education, including tuition, books and stationery, was $6.49, and including the interest on $750,343 (the amount which the city and county has invested in real estate for school purposes), the cost was $7.15 per scholar."

* * * * * * * *

"Of eleven teachers in the schools of Akron, ten are females; of twenty-one in Cleveland, only five are males; of twenty in Columbus, six are males; of one hundred and twenty-seven in Cincinnati, thirty-five, or a little more than one-fourth, are males; of an aggregate of more than fifteen hundred, in the twenty cities before named, only one-fourth are males; and of six hundred and thirty-one, employed in Philadelphia, eighty, or a little more than one-eighth, are male teachers."

* * * * * * * *

"The sum levied, for the last year, in Columbus, was four-fifths of one mill; in Akron and Cincinnati, two mills on the dollar."

There were then not more than twenty Union Schools in Ohio; Cincinnati had led the movement by good example, and her schools were of wider range and higher sphere than any others in the State; but Cleveland, Columbus, Dayton, Zanesville, Sandusky, Portsmouth, Mansfield, Massillon, and a few other towns, were then, as they are now, forward competitors for common school distinction.

The State Teachers' Association, at the period which we are now considering, as it did for at least five years after 1848, and as it does in a great measure yet, discharged important duties which properly belong to a State Department of Public Schools. There had been from 1839, growing demand for a State School Department. Despairing of success in petitioning the Legislature, without an active increase of public interest, a few leading teachers had determined to show in how far the interests of schools might be advanced by co-operation, independent of State patronage. They succeeded better than they had reason to anticipate, but did not at any time lose sight of what they believed to be the obligations of government. They resolved, at the semi-annual meeting of the Association in Dayton, June 1848, that a State Superintendent of Schools ought to be appointed, and as we have seen reported to the Secretary of State, at the end of the first year of their endeavors.

The first annual meeting of the State Teachers' Association was held in Columbus, December 27, 1848. Samuel Galloway delivered an address and was re-elected President. Asa D. Lord was chosen Chairman of the Executive Committee. The Convention discussed the necessity of a State Normal School, and of State and County Superintendents, and the best plans for schools in incorporated towns and cities.

In 1849, the cholera visited Ohio. On account of it, the semi-annual meeting of the Teachers' Association, which was to have been held at Springfield in June, was postponed. There was very general depression throughout the State in the summer of that year, and educational enterprise was consequently retarded, but very decided measures were taken in a large number of towns to secure Union schools, and in the second annual meeting of the State Teachers' Association, at Columbus, December, 1849, a majority of the counties of the State had representatives. Samuel Galloway was again elected President, and Asa D. Lord was continued as Chairman of the Executive Committee.

Addresses were delivered by the President on the importance of Universal Education, and by S. Hanbury Smith on the Animal Kingdom. Reports were presented upon a variety of topics affecting practically the prosperity and efficiency of the public schools. A series of resolutions, presented by Lorin Andrews, demanding a Board of School Commissioners, and an educational paper, under State authority, were discussed and adopted.

Mr. Galloway included these resolutions, in his report for 1849; to the General Assembly—his last report as Secretary of State. The plan for the State superintendence of schools they provided, was diligently urged upon the Legislature.

A committee to memorialize the General Assembly, consisting of A. D. Lord, H. H. Barney and Milo G. Williams, had been appointed by the State Teachers' Association, and that committee did not fail to discharge its duty. Educational journals supported the resolutions, and from several counties, influential petitions were sent in praying for the commission.

W. B. Fairchild, representative from Greene county, presented a bill, embodying the plan recommended by the Teachers' Association, in its main features, and that bill became a law, but so late in the session that no appointments were made under it, and consequently it failed to go into operation.*

Perhaps in summing up the results of the labors of educationalists in Ohio, during the period of four years previous to 1849, no better idea of the effect of those labors can be given than may be afforded in the fact that then Grammar and Geography were, for the first time, required to be taught in public schools.

That the statistics of common schools, as reported to the State Department, may be compared with those given in previous chapters—from 1837 to 1845—we present the following:

---

* See page 189, for an abstract of the law.

STATEMENT

OF THE RELATIVE CONDITION OF COMMON SCHOOLS, FROM 1845 TO 1850,

AS REPORTED TO SUPERINTENDENTS.

Dates........	No. of Counties	No. Cos. Rep'd	No. of Whole Districts	No. of Fractional Districts..	No. of Common Schools	No. of Scholars Enrolled.			Average Attendance.			Tot. No. School Youth	No. of Teachers.			Amount paid Teachers.			No. of Months Tau't,			No. of School Houses built.	Cost of School Houses built.
						Male.	Fem'l.	Total.	Male.	Fem'l.	Total.		Male.	Fem'l.	Total.	Male.	Fem'l.	Total.	Male.	Fem'l.	Total.		
1845	81	52	5,661	797	5,385	10,794	8,520	19,314	49,166	35,310	84,476	....	3,224	2,095	5,319	$158,792	$45,616	$204,408	10,543	6,464	17,007	194	$42,126
1846	83	55	5,676	954	4,362	19,834	15,029	34,863	43,714	35,036	78,750	728,638	2,581	1,988	4,569	138,237	55.504	193,741	8,966	6,361	15,327	164	27,325
1847	83	56	6,156	876	4,882	33,232	30,626	63,858	44,257	34,605	78,862	754,193	2,829	2,577	5,406	160,102	62,736	222,838	19,120	8,039	27,159	175	35,866
1848	85	57	6,826	951	5.062	50,211	44,419	94,630	50,442	40,253	90,695	....	2,799	2,412	5,211	141,967	44,814	186,781	8,816	6,928	15,744	153	39,727
1849	85	80	9,711	1,392	11,075	213,738	153,870	357,608	173,240	145,316	318,556	....	8,005	4,374	12,379	435,807	113,302	549,109	28,318	11,972	40,290	158	36,442

AS ESTIMATED BY SUPERINTENDENTS.

Dates.	No. of Districts.	No. of Common Schools	No. of Scholars Enrolled.			Tot. No. School Youth	No. of Teachers.			Amount paid Teachers.			No. of School Houses built.	Cost of School Houses built.
			Male.	Female.	Total.		Male.	Female.	Total.	Male.	Female.	Total.		
1844	7,000	13,000	....	....	460,000	....	....	....	13,000	....	....	....	....	....
1845	9,000	....	....	....	....	....	....	....	12,000	....	....	....	250	$60,000
1846	10,000	21,000	....	....	500,000	720,638	12,000	11,000	23,000	$395,000	$155,000	$550,000	550	70,500
1849	10,211	12,000	....	....	500,000	....	....	....	14,000	....	....	....	....	....

CHAPTER V.

ACTION UNDER THE NEW CONSTITUTION.

In 1850, a Convention for the formation of a new State Constitution was a topic of public discussion. It had been authorized by the Legislature of 1849–50, and the election for members having been held in the spring of 1850, educational men, expecting from it a revision of the School System of the State, circulated petitions, and made zealous efforts to keep up the interest in public schools which had been productive of so much good in 1848 and 1849.

A. D. Lord's *Journal of Education* had been united, at the commencement of the year 1850, with Smith's *Western School Friend*, at Cincinnati. M. Hazen White, who had edited the *Friend* for several years, retired, and A. D. Lord, H. H. Barney, C. Knowlton and Joseph Ray, were employed to conduct it. It was an interesting and efficient organ of school reform.

Samuel Galloway had been succeeded in the Secretary of States' office by Henry W. King, an active friend of the common school cause.

During 1850, Educational Societies and Teachers' Institutes were maintained in a larger number of counties than had received the benefits of them during any previous year, and to the Legislature for 1850–1, Mr. King, as School Superintendent, reported favorably. He gave a clear revision of the School Laws of the State, and recommended such legislation, as would embrace in one act, the good features of those in force. Mr. Galloway, in 1849, received school reports from all the counties in the State, except Adams, Brown, Hardin,

Miami and Pickaway, but complained (as had all his predecessors) of the general imperfection of the reports. Mr. King received reports, in 1850, from all the counties, except eight. He repeated Mr. Galloway's complaint, upon the imperfection of reports, and, without exception, his successors reiterated it. The counties from which no reports at all were received in 1850, were Guernsey, Jefferson, Pickaway, Scioto, Vinton and Williams. Returns for Marion and Miami came after the Secretary's Report had been prepared. In reference to reports, Mr. King said:

"No report has been received from Miami county, for the last five years. Prior to the present year, no report has been received from Brown county for five years; and prior to 1849, no report has been received for four years from the counties of Carroll, Coshocton, Hocking, Montgomery, Perry, Portage, Stark and Wyandot, severally; while, for the same four years, but one report each had been received from the counties of Crawford, Darke, Paulding and Wayne. It is, however, a matter of much encouragement, and proves, very conclusively, the wholesome influence which the law of 1848 has exerted, that, for the last two years, during which that law has been in operation, very good reports have been received from all the twelve counties last named, excepting Perry and Paulding. From Perry the report for 1849 was quite defective, while from Paulding the reports of both years have been merely nominal. The salutary influence of this law is also shown by a comparison of the number of counties which were delinquent, prior to the passage of the law, with the number at this time. The number of counties from which no reports whatever were received at this office, is as follows: in 1846, 28; in 1847, 27; in 1848, 28; in 1849, 5; in 1850, 8; including the new county of Vinton, whose recent organization may have been a sufficient reason why none should be expected from it. Again, some ground for the belief that this subject is receiving an increased attention, may be drawn from the fact, that complete returns of the enumeration of youth have been received this year, for the first time, from every county in the State. On the other hand, it is a matter of regret that since the law of 1848 has been in operation, a few counties seem to have been less prompt than heretofore. For instance, from the county of Pickaway no reports have been made for the last two years, while for many years previous they were regularly received. So, too, Guernsey and Marion counties have, this year, failed to report, for the only time in six years." * * * * * *

"The reports which have been returned to this office during the present season, evince a deep and abiding interest in the cause, on the part of very many of the County Auditors throughout the State. Some twenty-two of the Auditors have made full reports, many of them have bestowed great labor in the preparation of their reports, as well as in the collection of materials therefor. Foremost among them, it is no more than justice to mention those of the counties of Hamilton, Hardin, Holmes, Licking, Meigs and Wyandot."

In 1849, the Auditor of State, John Woods, in obedience to frequent inquiries, whether the State School Fund might not be increased, suggested that the State could, without inconvenience, make the Fund $300,000. Mr. King pressed this suggestion upon the Legislature, and the fund was increased to the sum named.*

The State Teachers' Association, held both its semi-annual and its annual meeting in 1850. The summer meeting was at Springfield, and that in winter at Columbus.

At Springfield, the number of members of the Associations was one hundred and sixty. Addresses were delivered by Rev. D. Shephardson, and J. C. Zachos of Cincinnati. Reports upon important subjects were presented by experienced Teachers, and the Association resolved, that the Constitution of the State ought to provide for a Normal School, and for a State Superintendent.

A resolution taht each Clergyman of the State be requested to deliver a Sermon, in October, on the advantages of Common Schools, was passed without opposition. At the next meeting of the Teachers, there was no report of the number of ministers who responded to the resolution, and it can not be exactly ascertained, but in several towns and cities sermons were preached, which contributed materially to a proper understanding of common schools, and their bearings upon the morals of community.

* See page 191.

The annual meeting of the Teachers was the most important one held, up to that period, by the Association. Samuel Galloway again delivered the opening address. Ira Mayhew, Superintendent of Schools in Michigan, gave a public lecture upon Popular Education, and very important discussions were had upon a variety of resolutions. The most important of the resolutions adopted were, that the School Laws should be revised; that the law authorizing a Board of School Commissioners should be put in force, and that the new Constitution should recognize Public Education for all the youth of the State.

The resolution on the Board of Commissioners, was discussed at greater length than any other resolution had ever been in the Association, and was adopted by a vote of sixty-one to thirty-one. On motion of H. H. Barney, it was then recommended that none but enlightened educators ought to be appointed to office in the Board.

In view of what the Constitutional Convention did, and of the law of 1853 framed under it, the following resolution, adopted by a large majority, is interesting:

"That it is the opinion of this Convention, that the organic law of every State should guarantee a free education to all the youth of the State, and provide for the establishment of schools in which the same shall be communicated."

Isaac Sams of Highland county, was elected President of the Association, and Lorin Andrews was chosen Chairman of the Executive Committee.

Mr. Andrews was then Principal of the Massillon High School. He resigned his post, and voluntarily became a Common School Missionary, without assurance of any reward but that which springs from the consciousness of well doing. He issued circulars, appealing for the interest and support of Teachers' Institutes, and immediately began a thorough canvass of the State.

At the July meeting of the Teachers' Association in Cleveland, an interesting and influential meeting, his disinterested labors were most cordially approved, and a resolution to sustain him pecuniarily, unanimously adopted. At the same meeting, resolutions were adopted, declaring that girls and boys ought to sit in the same room; that phonotypy was to be encouraged, as a means of teaching children to read; and that the Legislature ought to establish one or more Houses of Reformation for juvenile offenders.

Supported by the action of the Teachers' Association, and encouraged by the favorable manner in which the people had received his labors, Mr. Andrews devoted himself with renewed vigor, during the fall of 1851. The annual meeting of the Association at Columbus, in December of that year, exhibited the value of his efforts, in the number of its members, and the character of their action.

It was determined to continue Mr. Andrews as State Agent; to establish a monthly Educational Journal; and to petition the Legislature for District School Libraries, and for a State Superintendent.

Rev. W. C. Anderson, President of Miami College, was elected President of the Association. Addresses were delivered by Joseph Ray of Cincinnati, I. W. Andrews of Marietta, and George Willey of Cleveland. The Convention adjourned to meet at Sandusky in July, 1852.

In his report to the Legislature for 1851, the Secretary of State acknowledged, in handsome terms, the good influence of the State Teachers' Association, by its semi-annual meetings, through the labors of its agent, and by means of county Institutes and Associations.

"The teachers of the State have shown a noble zeal and energy in their efforts to sustain the agent of the Association. They have voluntarily contributed for that purpose, about one thousand dollars, during the past year, and have pledged themselves, from different parts of the State, to raise a still larger sum for the ensuing year. The heroic purposes exhibited by this self-sacrificing action, on the part of the teachers of Ohio, is without a parallel in any other State in the Union, and certainly augurs well for the educational interests of this State. With such a corps of teachers in Ohio, no fears need be entertained of the ultimate success of common school education, if any considerable portion of their generosity can be made to characterize the legislation of the State.

"Were no other end proposed by the State Teachers' Association, the effect of the semi-annual meetings, held by the teachers, could not be otherwise than salutary. The opportunities thus afforded of consulting upon topics which interest the profession throughout the State, of interchanging sentiments upon proposed improvements in modes of teaching or managing schools, would be of great service in harmonizing and concentrating the views of the entire body of teachers, while it would stimulate the less advanced to aim at higher attainments in their profession."

In discussing the condition of schools in the State, and urging Legislative reform, in several respects, Mr. King said, in the report from which the above extract is taken:

"While in many of our towns and cities, schools of a high order have been, for years past, sustained and fostered by the municipal governments under which they exist; while such schools are, in most instances, cheerfully supported and cherished by the tax-paying community, who reap from them no other advantages than such as are common also to those who pay nothing for their support, thus proving, abundantly, that our people are willing to be taxed for the support of free schools, provided only they are good, it is yet lamentably true, that in many portions of the State, and probably in a majority of the counties, the common schools are in a languishing condition." * * * * * *

"No one doubts that our school system has already accomplished, and is accomplishing, a vast amount of good to the population of the State. No one doubts that we have, in certain portions of the State, and particularly in many of its towns and cities, public schools equal, perhaps, to the best that can be found elsewhere. No one doubts that a greatly improved public sentiment prevails throughout the State on the whole subject of education; and no one can surely do otherwise than derive great hope and sincere pleasure from these admitted truths. But, upon the other hand, it is equally apparent that the present school system has its defects, more or less radical; that further advances can be made; and that renewed health, and a more vigorous life can be imparted to it. All must admit, that our schools do not, as yet, answer the purpose for which they were designed." * * *

"Abstracts of the returns made to county Superintendents have been received from all the counties in the State, excepting Brown, Fulton, Henry, Lucas, Pickaway, Williams and Wood." * * * * * * *

"An examination of the table of abstracts, furnishes evidence that an improvement is gradually taking place in respect to the employment of female teachers. The relative number of female teachers employed is increasing, though not as rapidly as is desirable. Out of 14,056, the whole number reported for the State, 5,706 are females, being about forty per cent. In 1849, the whole number reported was 12,379, of whom 4,374 were females, being about thirty-five per cent. In the following counties the number of female teachers exceeds the males, viz: Ashtabula, Athens, Cuyahoga, Defiance, Delaware, Erie, Geauga, Huron, Lake, Lorain, Mahoning, Medina, Meigs, Ottawa, Portage, Trumbull, Union, Washington."

* * * * * * * *

"A larger sum is raised by a tax of one mill upon the dollar, now, than was yielded by a tax of two mills in 1838. The total amount of taxable property upon the tax duplicates of the different counties in the State, in 1838, was $106,953,018, while the amount now is $452,652,708. A tax of one mill upon the dollar will therefore raise over $450,000; a sum larger, by one-half, than the increased amount of $300,000 proposed hereafter to be distributed by the State.

When these provisions are carried out, and the amounts thus required by law are furnished by the State, and by the counties respectively, as will be the case in 1853, if no changes are made in the law, the whole amount of public funds (including special and trust funds), distributed by the State, and contributed by the several counties, will be but little, if any, less than one million of dollars. Meantime the provision, so far as the counties are concerned, will be made available next season, and our schools will then begin to realize the effect of an increased expenditure in their behalf."

To these extracts from the Secretary's report, may be added some paragraphs of interest from the report of Lorin Andrews, as the agent of the State Teachers' Association. They will show that the agent of the teachers had nearer relations to the school interests of the State, and weightier influence for their advancement, than the official Superintendent:

"The committee commenced its labors with three principal objects in view: First, to grow up a strong public sentiment, which will be satisfied with nothing less than an educational system, which will afford to every child in the State, a proper physical, intellectual, and moral development; second, to recommend to the towns and cities of the State, the adoption of the Union School system; and third, to improve teachers and elevate the profession of teaching.

"It is hoped that something has been done during the past year to advance each one of these important objects. The committee has secured the delivery of more than two hundred practical educational addresses, to large assemblies of citizens in various parts of the State. The minds and hearts of not less than sixty thousand citizens of Ohio, have been appealed to and influenced by the truths presented and illustrated in these evening lectures. In addition to this, three thousand teachers, who have been assembled in the Institutes during the past year, and whose love for their profession has been thereby increased, and their zeal for the improvement of our common schools has been quickened, have gone out as efficient, intelligent missionaries, into three thousand distinct fields of labor, better qualified, not only to *teach*, but also to *preach* school. Through these instrumentalities, it is hoped much has been done, and that much more will be done, for the education and elevation of a strong public sentiment, which will demand 'a school system for our State, unparalleled for the liberality of its provisions, the wisdom of its measures, and the harmony and efficiency of its operations.'

"About seventy of the towns and cities of the State, have established Free Graded schools, and of these, more than fifty have been organized within the past three years, and by the adoption of the law of 1849 'for the better regulation of Public Schools in cities, towns, etc.' Although the unparalleled success which has attended the establishment of Union Schools in Ohio, is very encouraging to the friends of education, yet it should be remembered that there are at least one hundred and fifty remaining towns in the State whose educational interests imperatively demand the immediate organization of Free Graded schools.

"During the past year, thirty towns have been visited, and their citizens have been publicly addressed upon the advantages and economy of the Union School system. Some of these towns have already organized Union schools; and several others, it is believed, will soon follow their good example." * * * * * * *

"In order to elevate the profession of teaching, the committee has principally relied upon the holding of Teachers

Institutes. Probably no instrumentality in so short a time, and at so little expense, can effect so great and extensive a work for the improvement of teachers, as well-conducted Institutes. In the outset of its labors, the committee found the great obstacle in the way of holding Institutes, was the impossibility of securing the services of a sufficient number of competent and experienced Lecturers to take charge of them. The most of the teachers in the State, who could thus be profitably employed, were constantly and necessarily engaged in their own local fields of labor. In order to supply, in some small measure, this deficiency, the chairman of the Executive Committee felt it to be his duty to leave his 'pleasant school' and generous patrons, and devote himself wholly to this work. In February, a circular was issued to teachers and friends of education, calling for aid in the Institutes proposed to be held in the spring, and a like call was made during the summer, in order to secure help for the fall Institutes. In both instances, the appeal of the committee was heartily and generously responded to by a noble band of men and women, who, at a great sacrifice of time and money, threw themselves resolutely into the work. During the year, application was made to the committee for aid, for forty-five Institutes; but it was found utterly impossible to supply all with the desired assistance, at such times as would be convenient; and hence, to the great detriment of the cause of education, several of the proposed Institutes could not be held. Several counties, such as Stark, Mahoning, Crawford, Seneca, Ashtabula, and Huron and Erie, were unaided by the committee with Lecturers from a distance, because it was well known that they contained within themselves, teachers who, from their experience and qualifications, could successfully instruct in their Institutes. Nor were the committee disappointed in the result, for in no counties have more spirited Institutes been held." * * *

"There is a wide-spread, hopeful anticipation, extensively prevalent in our State at this time, of efficient action in favor of education by the next General Assembly, the first to convene under the new Constitution. Should the Legislature fail to satisfy these just expectations, a strong public sentiment will be grievously outraged.

"In a large number of Institutes, resolutions were unanimously passed in favor of a more thorough supervision of educational interests, by the appointment of a State Superintendent and four or more District Superintendents. It is the undoubted opinion of the great mass of teachers and friends of education in our State, that one Superintendent can not do the great work which ought to be done." * * *

"An *absolutely necessary prerequisite* to the permanent and proper improvement of the country schools, is *an enlargement of the school districts.* In brief, some of the many advantages of an enlargement of school districts, would be a better classification of pupils; a less frequent change of teachers and text-books, more system and skill in the methods of teaching and governing; a much less expenditure of money for the same amount of instruction; longer sessions of the schools; thus teaching would become a permanent employment; teachers would be better qualified, and pupils at fourteen years of age would be made better scholars than now at twenty."

The educational questions before the people of Ohio at the beginning of the year 1852, were the importance of Union schools—the necessity of Normal schools—the need of a State Superintendent—the advantage of School Libraries, and the full recognition, by statute, of the doctrine that the property of the State should educate the children of the State.

In his report for 1851, the Secretary of State argued with spirit the justice of the claims made by the friends of Universal Education for these measures. In reference to the encouragement of Union schools, he made suggestions which deserve to be remembered. He said:

"In a large portion of the State, the townships are laid off in a square form, and in sizes varying from five to six squares. They are usually intersected by roads running across them, at convenient distances, and have one or more settlements, more often occurring near the middle of the township than at any other point. Now, if one or more schools of a higher grade, corresponding to the Central or High School of the Union school system, could be established at suitable points in the township—say at the points where the thickest settlements have been made—adapted to scholars of greater age and better attainments in their studies, it would unquestionably be an advantage—an inestimable advantage—to all the schools, and to all the youth in such township." * * *

"It may indeed be doubted, whether a single well-conducted High School, in many of the townships of the State, would not do more to *educate* the youth of the township, than all schools now taught therein. Witness the salutary influence which a single academy will often exert upon the community in which it is taught. Witness the influence often exerted by a single pupil of such an academy, in the family circle to which he or she may belong; and especially upon the younger members of the family. But the Union High School can easily be made as good as the best of academies, and many, if not all the townships of the State, can be supplied with one or more such schools. Nothing is required to accomplish this desirable result, but proper energy on the part of parents and guardians, and a moderate increase of funds now expended upon schools of comparatively little value."

In his views the Secretary was supported by the Governor,* and both these officers were sustained by the Agent of the State Teachers' Association, and by the leading newspapers throughout the State.

The need of a State Educational journal, under the auspices of the Association, as well as the necessity of a Normal school, had been regular topics of private and public discourse, before the Association was two years old. The Association did not feel strong enough, however, to undertake even the desired journal, until 1852.

A monthly journal, called the *Ohio Teacher*, was started by Thomas Rainey, in 1851, which was encouraged by many leading educators; but it did not represent generally the sentiment of the State Teachers' Association, and was inefficient and short-lived.

At the annual meeting for 1851, as before stated, a monthly organ was determined upon, and Asa D. Lord was elected resident editor, with H. H. Barney of Cincinnati, M. F. Cowdery of Sandusky, J. W. Andrews of Marietta, J. C. Zachos of Dayton, and Andrew Freese of Cleveland, associate editors. Members of the Association pledged a list of twelve hundred subscribers, and the *Journal* was commenced with spirit. It supported with vigor the action of the Association, and had weighty influence in the educational movements of 1852 and 1853.

---

* See page 237.

The action of the Constitutional Convention, and of the first General Assembly under it, by which the common school system of Ohio was revised, is so well sketched in another part of this work,* that it is proper here to pass immediately to the events which directly preceded the official career of the first State Commissioner of Common Schools.

But it is not improper to remind the reader, that the new law was, in the main, a consolidation of statutes in force; and that in its new features, no great educational needs were recognized, which had not been discussed and plead for by Ohio educators during twenty years.

As described by H. H. Barney, the prominent provisions which were new—improvements in the estimation of those who advocated and enacted the law—may be stated as follows:

1. A State school tax was substituted for the county tax.

2. A township Board of Education, consisting of a representative from each district (or sub-district, in the language of the act), succeed to the power, previously vested in the township trustees, of making or altering districts, and are intrusted with the general administration of schools in the township, the assessment of taxes requisite for the construction and repair of school-houses, the selection of their sites, the title, care, and preservation of all school property, and kindred duties not inconsistent with those enjoined upon the local directors in each sub-district.

3. "Free education to all the youth in the State," and the abolition of rate bills.

4. A fund of one-tenth of a mill yearly, "for the purpose of furnishing school libraries and apparatus to all the common schools in the State."

5. The supervision of the system by a State Commissioner of common schools.

No words are here necessary to show any one who has read the foregoing pages attentively, that the law of 1853 was not in advance of the general educational sentiments, or of the practical ability of the State.

---

* See pages 211 to 244.

CHAPTER VI.

ACTION UNDER THE NEW CONSTITUTION CONTINUED.

William Trevitt, elected Secretary of State under the new Constitution, succeeded Henry W. King in 1852. In his report on the condition of common schools for that year, to an adjourned Session of the Legislature, Mr. Trevitt confined himself mainly to a presentation of statistics, but repeated with zeal the argument of his predecessor, in favor of a revision of the school system.

At the semi-annual meeting of the Teachers' Association, in Sandusky, the school bill, reported by the Senate committee the winter previous, was indorsed by three hundred teachers, representing the interests of education in forty-three counties of the State.

At the time of this semi-annual meeting in Sandusky, an Association was formed for the promotion of Female education. There had been, from time to time for ten years, active interest in different localities for that purpose, but the movement of July, 1852, was the first one, general in its scope.

P. B. Wilber of Cincinnati, was elected President, and A. D. Lord Secretary; J. C. Zachos of Dayton was chosen chairman of the Executive Committee. Questions of importance were discussed, and gentlemen of experience were appointed to report upon them, at Columbus, in December following.

At the annual meeting of the Teachers' Association, M. F. Cowdery delivered an address, in which, speaking of what he knew from observation, he said:

"Those who are acquainted with the recent history of our State, are aware, that five years since, the cities and larger towns of Ohio, with two or three exceptions, perhaps, were entirely destitute of a system of classified public schools,—generally, nearly or quite destitute of school buildings of any value, and as might well be expected, destitute of proper discipline, as well as properly digested systematic courses of instruction.

"Nurseries of confusion instead of order, of coarseness and obscenity instead of refinement and delicacy, they had sunk so low in public estimation, that many a good citizen had felt the conviction, that the common school system could never prove a suitable and reliable agency for educating the children of the State. The duty which public authorities had assumed, of providing wholesome instruction for the young, had, for a series of years, either been so unfaithfully met, or the whole system had within it such intrinsic elements of weakness and decay, that all expenditures of talent and money upon it seemed to promise but slight returns of beneficial results to society. Private tutors, private institutions, private and special instruction in some form, seemed to be the only alternative to the parent deeply anxious for a suitable education for his offspring. In the country school districts, better confidence prevailed, scarcely better buildings and no better classification.

"We have the rich and rare pleasure, now, of witnessing important changes in the educational condition of our State. Great interests that seemed in imminent peril, through the neglect or indifference of their proper guardians, have received some attention, some thought, some sympathy. In three-fourths of the towns of Ohio, with a population of one thousand inhabitants and upward, substantial school buildings have been erected by the free contributions of the people; the schools themselves have been more or less accurately classified, thus preparing the way in the best possible manner for all other practicable improvements; and lastly, the confidence of the public in the capacity of the common school system to afford a suitable education to all, has been almost immeasurably increased."

The teachers who heard these words, elected Joseph Ray of Cincinnati, as the president of the Association for 1853, and determined to continue Lorin Andrews as chairman of the Executive committee, and as State agent. Fifteen hundred dollars a year were guaranteed Mr. Andrews, as a salary; and he was encouraged to go on, as he had begun, in the strongest language which could be summoned by the committee on resolutions.

Mr. Andrews reported to the Association, that thirty-one Institutes had been held in 1852—that the *Journal of Education* had proved self-supporting, with an edition of three thousand copies; and that Union schools were being liberally encouraged. Reviewing the past, and hoping for the future, he said:

"There are about eighty Union schools in operation in the State. Their statistics indicate that the school-houses, including the grounds attached, are worth about $750,000; that the total annual expenditures for the support of these schools, including the cost of fuel and the interest on the value of school buildings amount to about $325,000; and that the average length of the school year is over ten months. The above figures are clearly indicative of a readiness on the part of the people of Ohio, to adopt *liberal* measures for the improvement of public schools." * * * *

"Gratifying evidences of an increased and increasing educational spirit, present themselves in every portion of our great State. During the last five years, many school buildings have been erected in Ohio, which, by the amplitude of their structure, the commodiousness of their plan and the beauty of their finish, would do honor to the wealth and liberality of older States, more than one million of dollars has been raised to endow higher institutions of learning; at least eight thousand teachers have been assembled in Institutes, and have thus been better prepared to act efficiently as missionaries in the great work of education, the professional teachers of the State, by their untiring efforts, their self-sacrificing spirit, and the bold comprehensiveness of their plans, have not only done themselves lasting honor, but they have set an example worthy of imitation by the teachers of other States; from a condition of great indifference on the subject of education, the great mass of the people have become friends and advocates of free schools, and now, more than one-half of the five hundred millions of property in the great State of Ohio, by the voluntary votes of its possessors, is taxed to support schools which afford the advantages of intellectual and moral culture, as free as the air of heaven to the children of the State, and in addition to these evidences of progress, we now have, what we have not very frequently had—a General Assembly, the members of which seem anxiously to desire to advance the interests of education by prudent and proper legislative action."

The Teachers' Association expressed sympathy with the movement for Female education, and at a meeting of the friends who had organized at Sandusky, Mr. Wilber was re-elected President, and Dr. Lord Secretary of the Association for the Education of Women.

The year 1853, opened under auspices favorable to education; auspices more favorable than had ever crowned the opening of a year in Ohio. The *Journal of Education*, in a salutatory for its second volume, congratulated the Teachers of Ohio, and the friends of education, as follows:

"In no other country, in no State of our Union, has a body of Teachers attempted what has been undertaken here. Teachers have generally been content to follow the lead of Boards of Education, to go forward in the work of improving themselves, and elevating their schools as fast, and as far as the requisitions or the demands of public sentiment required. In the absence of correct views of the importance of providing the means of educating all the youth of the State, and of efficient legislation for the promotion of this object, our Association has undertaken to disseminate, as widely as possible, by the aid of the press, and the living speaker, such information as will lead to the formation of correct opinions on this whole subject, impress upon the minds of all an abiding conviction of the magnitude of the interest involved, and as soon as possible secure from the Legislature a School System, which, in the comprehensiveness of its policy, the liberality of its provisions, and the efficiency of its administration shall be worthy of the State, and the age in which we live."

These words were true and well deserved. The fifth semi-annual meeting of the Association at Dayton, in July, 1853, added additional significance to them. Rev. E. V. Gerheart delivered an address upon "Government in its Relations to Education," and Chauncey N. Olds spoke upon "The Bible as a Basis of Education;" Benn Pitman addressed the Teachers upon Phonetic Reform, and discussions were had and resolutions were adopted, showing that the Teachers of the Association were well prepared for the increased advantages to them and to their pupils, promised under the law of the March previous.

A new force was added to the educational instrumentalities of the State, by the appointment, at Dayton, of C. S. Royce, as Agent of the State Phonetic Society, which had been organized in January, 1853, with Elias Longley of Cincinnati, as President.

Mr. Royce issued circulars to the friends of education and to educational societies, offering his services as a lecturer; and from that time up to the present, has been a self-sacrificing laborer for the promotion of the general interests of education as well as for the furtherance of Phonetic sentiment, and the imparting of Phonetic instruction.

The new law abolished the official relations of the Secretary of State to the common schools, but made no provision for supplying the deficiency, consequently a State School Department was wanting, until February, 1854, and the act went into operation under great disadvantages. It was sustained, however, with vigor by the Agent of the Teachers' Association, and by nearly all the teachers of every county; yet, lacking an official exponent and defender, met opposition, which, under other circumstances, might not have been arrayed against it. The Secretary of State gave it attention whenever called upon; but, having no authority, except that which grew out of the prestige of his office in the past, his influence was not weighty.

Lorin Andrews, and H. H. Barney, were the candidates for the office of School Commissioner, created by the law of 1853. Mr. Barney was elected. To the Legislature of 1853–4, in response to a Senate resolution, he reported a series of answers to questions on the School Law, but his first regular report was made for the year 1854.

His communication to the Senate was published with a report from the Secretary of State, of what statistics had been sent him, and a report upon petitions respecting the School Law, from a Senate Committee, consisting of G. W. Stokes, Heslip Williams and Ira Norris. This committee was in favor of the School System, established by the new law. Commending a few minor amendments, they presented a sketch of the opposition, which can best be understood in their own words:

"The whole number of petitions, praying for the repeal or alteration of the present school law, is forty-one; twenty-five of these are from the counties of Ashtabula and Richland, and the balance from Fairfield, Ashland, Morrow, Montgomery, Crawford, Holmes and Cuyahoga, seventy-nine counties having sent up no petitions, requesting either the repeal or alteration of the school law.

"The entire number of petitioners is, one thousand seven hundred and thirty-three; of these, nine hundred and fifty-seven reside in Ashtabula and Richland counties, and four-fifths of the whole number reside in the five counties of Ashtabula, Richland, Fairfield, Morrow and Ashland.

"More than one-half of the petitioners, virtually pray for the repeal of the entire law; and nearly all desire the abolition of the office of State Commissioner of common schools, and the repeal of the provisions of the law, creating Township Boards of Education, and authorizing a State tax of one-tenth of one mill on the dollar valuation, for the purpose of furnishing school apparatus and libraries to all the common schools of the State.

"A large number of the petitioners pray for a reduction of the State levy, and assessment of two mills on the dollar, which was created for the express purpose of affording the advantages of a free education to all the youth of this State; also for the restoration of the old independent district system; also for the election of school examiners at the annual township meetings; also for vesting in the local directors the right to employ teachers without certificates of qualification, and to keep their schools in session such length of time as may be agreed on by the inhabitants of the district.

"Inasmuch as the great bulk of the petitions and memorials have come from less than one-twentieth of the counties in the State, the others having solicited no changes directly or indirectly; and inasmuch as the prayers of these petitioners are exceedingly diverse, and the reasons assigned for them are still more diverse, the committee can not derive from them any satisfactory indication of what the petitioners themselves most desire; and much less the general wish of the great body of the people." * * * * *

"It is believed that the law is in perfect accordance with

the educational spirit and tendency of the age, and of the grand idea that the great end of public instruction is not merely to have schools, but to have good schools, having all the means and appliances calculated to arouse thought, discipline mind, form good mental habits and tastes, and cultivate good principles."

The committee, except upon the tax clause, agreed in reporting against material changes in the law. Mr. Norris dissented on this point, contending that one and a half mills levy was sufficient.

Mr. Barney published an able pamphlet, in answer to the petitions, which, with the report just quoted from, and the active personal exertions of friends of education, was sufficient to prevent the Legislature from impairing the efficiency of the law.*

At the annual meeting of the teachers in 1853, Horace Mann delivered an address on the "Motives of Teachers," and Rev. Dr. Thompson lectured upon "The Moral Influence of the Teacher."

Lorin Andrews resigned his agency and his post as Chairman of the Executive Committee. He reported a still growing interest in schools, and gave statistics of thirty-eight Institutes for 1853. He said there were about one hundred Graded Schools in the State, and was confident that rural districts were to be benefited by the new law. A. D. Lord was elected Chairman of the Executive Committee and Agent of the Association, and Mr. Andrews was unanimously chosen President.

For several years the teachers had discussed the need of a State Normal School, and in 1853 it was determined that the Association should take the initiatory steps for the establishment of such a school.

This determination was realized in the summer of 1855, when Cyrus McNeely of Hopedale, Harrison county, presented the Association with land and buildings, valued at

---

* See page 233.

$11,000, and the teachers accepted the gift, pledging themselves to contribute $10,000 for the support of the Institution; a pledge they have nobly fulfilled.

Before sketching Mr. Barney's official relations to the common schools of Ohio, we may take notice that the Teachers' Association held regularly, during 1854, '55 and '56, its semi-annual and annual meetings. Growing each year in interest and solid character, it must continue to exert upon educational movements directly, and upon schools indirectly, influences which cannot be too highly regarded by those who have pride and hope in our common school system.

Andrew J. Rickoff of Cincinnati, succeeded Lorin Andrews as President, and he was succeeded in 1856 by Rev. Anson Smyth of Toledo, who had been chosen editor of the *Journal of Education*, at the resignation of A. D. Lord, in 1855. John Hancock of Cincinnati, succeeded Dr. Lord, as Chairman of the Executive Committee, and he now holds that place. M. F. Cowdery, who through all the trials of the Association, has been chairman of the Finance Committee, is likely to guard its pecuniary interest during life.

The Association was addressed, during the three years, about which we now write, by I. W. Andrews, on "The Teachers' Calling," and James W. Taylor on "The History of Ohio," at Zanesville, in July, 1854; by Rufus King of Cincinnati, on "The Responsibilities of Teachers," and Jehu Brainard of Cleveland, on "Natural Sciences," at Cincinnati, in December, 1854; by J. M. Root of Sandusky, and Rev. J. A. Thome at Cleveland, in July, 1855; by Rev. D. S. Burnett, on the "Life and Character of Joseph Ray," and Melvin Clark of Marietta, on "Popular Education as an Element of Republicanism," in December, 1855; by Rev. J. B. Bittenger of Cleveland, on "The Will, as an Educational Power," and Rev. Dr. Hitchcock of Western Reserve College, on "Intellectual Life," at Mansfield, in July, 1856; by Rev. W. S. Kennedy of Sandusky, on "What Common Schools should be;" by W. T. Coggeshall, on "The History of Common School Movements in Ohio;" and by Rev. J. B. Walker of

Mansfield, on "Faith, as a Basis of Moral and Intellectual Life," at Columbus, in December, 1856.

Without explicit acknowledgment of the good accomplished by the State Teachers' Association, it would be unfair to close this chapter. In his first report (for 1854) as Agent of the Association, Dr. Lord gave a summary of what had been accomplished since its organization, which can be here fitly quoted:

"During the year 1847, in which our society was formed, the whole sum appropriated by the State for education of 754,193 children and youth of school age, was $288,660 55, or a little more than thirty-eight cents per scholar. How many were benefited by the schools of that year is not known, as the number of scholars enrolled was reported from only ten counties, and the average attendance from only forty-six of the eighty-three counties. Judging from those reported, about 500,000 were enrolled, and the average attendance was about 140,000. During the past year, the number of children enumerated was 811,957; the whole sum appropriated by the State was $1,233,276 26, or $1.51 for each youth between five and twenty-one years; the number enrolled in the schools was 612,185, and the average daily attendance, 367,594. So that the State paid $2.01 for each child instructed, and $3.35 for each one in actual daily attendance.

"At the commencement of 1847, there was not a single well organized Public High School in the State; now there are more than forty, in which a thorough Academic education is given, beside nearly an equal number in which instruction is given in some of the higher branches. Then, no city or town in the State, except Cincinnati, had a system of regularly classified Public Schools, now about one hundred towns are enjoying the benefits of such schools. But the interest felt in the cause of education, and the appreciation of its benefits may perhaps be judged more correctly by the salaries paid to teachers than by any other standard. At that time the highest salary paid to any teacher of common schools was $600, and it is believed that no teacher, out of Cincinnati, received a salary of more than $540. During the past year, at least, four superintendents and principals have received a salary of $1,500; some five or six have been paid $1,200; some twenty have received $1,000 or more; and a larger number have been paid $600 or more. A similar increase of the compensation of females, and of teachers of every grade has been made, though it is not possible to determine the average salaries paid to teachers of district schools, in 1847, for the wants of the statistics.

"This increase of compensation to teachers, and the change of public sentiment, which has caused people in a large number of districts to pay $100, or more, per quarter for the services of a teacher (when several years since they were less willing to pay $45 or $50, for the same length of time), may be attributed mainly to the efforts of our Association for the professional improvement of Teachers; since, even to the present time, the State has done next to nothing to encourage this work. Previous to 1847, only eleven Teachers' Institutes had been attended, in which 1,270 teachers had been instructed; during that year, thirteen were held, which were attended by 1,200 teachers. Since that time, an average of more than 3,000 have been instructed in these schools each year. The expense of attending these sessions of one week is not less than an average of $5.00 to each teacher; multiplying this, by the number who have attended them, we have $15,000, as the lowest estimate of the sum which has yearly been expended in this manner by teachers for their professional improvement."

The subjoined statement of the number of Teachers' Institutes, held in the State for ten years, and the number of pupils attending them, may be appropriately considered in connection with the claims made for the Teachers' Association by its Agent.

STATISTICS OF TEACHERS' INSTITUTES IN OHIO FOR TEN YEARS.

Dates.	No. Institutes.	No. Pupils.
1845	2	240
1846	9	997
1847	13	569
1848	19	1500
1849	20	1600
1850	25	2000
1851	41	3251
1852	31	2824
1853	38	3738
1854	41	2198
Total.	239	18917

CHAPTER XII.

LABORS OF COMMISSIONER BARNEY.

THE popular Educational forces of the State, when H. H. Barney entered upon the discharge of his duties as Commissioner of Common Schools, were: the State Teachers' Association—a Phonetic Society—a Society for the Improvement of the Education of Girls—County Educational Societies, Teachers' Institutes, and Normal Classes.

His labors, varied and novel, were, in many respects, rendered lighter by these auxiliaries, but they served him rather in the awakening of popular interest than in the administration of the law; of which he was necessarily the expounder, and for which he was officially the advocate.

His first report, for the year 1854, was confined chiefly to the statistics of Schools as reported; to a historical outline of school progress, and to arguments for the new law, upon the measures in which it differed from, or reached farther than, the statutes it had repealed.

The important facts of the report have been given already in this work, in contrast with the principal items of school interest for 1855,* and we may here quote from Mr. Barney's second report, a paragraph expressing what he considered the phrase, "Common Schools," to imply.

"A thorough and efficient system of common schools throughout the State," is the object proposed by the sixth article of the constitution; and it is an inquiry of particular interest, what construction we shall give to the term 'common schools.' In the infancy of public provision for this object, perhaps a limitation of the course of study to a few elementary branches, might have satisfied public opinion; but in the progress of popular instruction, the welfare of the State

* See page 246.

has long since suggested a different construction. We now think and speak of common schools as lawyers are accustomed to mention the common law—not as limited or insignificant in scope or importance—but as the 'birthright' of the youth of the commonwealth, free to all and denied to none. It has become the laudable purpose, both of government and people, to supply to the rising generation from infancy to majority—or from the ages of five to twenty-one—the *opportunity* for mental improvement and the acquisition of useful knowledge: nor, of course, with such an aim, can the schools of the people be suffered to fall behind the cotemporary standard of instruction.

"There is another sense in which our public schools are common. The constitution prescribes that 'no religious or other sect or sects shall ever have an exclusive right to, or control of, any part of the school fund in this State.' Such a prohibition is made necessary by the separation of church and state, which is so vital an element of our Republican system. If government is properly restrained from any interference with the religious opinions of the citizen, neither can the teacher, who is the agent of government for the instruction of youth, exercise any rightful control of that nature over the pupil. There is a common ground of morals, where men of all creeds meet in harmony; the law requires every teacher to be a person of good moral character; and however difficult to determine where this universal agreement of good men begins or ends, yet no duty is clearer than that enjoined upon the authorities and teachers of public schools, under no circumstances to depart from a strict neutrality between religious sects."

Under these views Mr. Barney recommended the encouragement of Agricultural Schools, and the support of Normal Institutes. In relation to Institutions for the Instruction of Teachers, which had been established in the State, he expressed himself as follows:

"It affords me pleasure to add that Mr. Cyrus McNeely of Hopedale, Harrison county, has donated buildings admirably adapted for school purposes, and thus occupied, hitherto, to the endowment of Normal Schools. The gift includes spacious and beautiful grounds; has been appraised at $11,600, but is subject to the condition that the State Teachers' Association shall raise the additional sum of $10,000. An effort is now making to comply with this condition; and no worthier object for the aid of the State is likely to be presented for the consideration of the General Assembly.

"The McNeely Normal School was organized by the election of eleven trustees, who have appointed Cyrus McNeely President, Asa D. Lord Secretary, and George K. Jenkins Treasurer. The regular course will occupy two years, to enter upon which, with profit, the students should already be familiar with the branches usually taught in schools.

"The studies of the first year are, Reading, Orthography and Phonetic Analysis; Penmanship and the Elements of Drawing; Geography, History and the Constitution of the United States; English Grammar, and the Analysis of Words and Sentences; Arithmetic, Mental and Written, Elements of Algebra; Physiology and the Laws of Health; Natural History and Botany; Natural Philosophy and Astronomy, Elementary Geometry and Mensuration.

"The studies of the second year, are Language, its History and the Various Modes of Analysis; Physical Geography and Meteorology; Geology and Mineralogy; Chemistry, Geometry and Trigonometry; Universal History; Mental and Moral Philosophy; Natural Theology; Evidences of Christianity; Logic, Rhetoric, Elements of Criticism.

"An Academic Department will also be sustained; and arrangements are making for an Experimental School, in which the children of the village of Hopedale may be taught by the pupil-teachers. The school year of the Institution consists of forty weeks, and the price of tuition is $20 in the Academic, and $30 in the Normal Department.

"A similar enterprise has been undertaken at Lebanon, Warren county, under the designation of the 'Southwestern State Normal School.' Mr. Alfred Holbrook, with five assistants, are announced as teachers. The organization resulted from a general concert of action among those engaged in the instruction of youth, and is auxiliary to the Ohio State Teachers' Association—a very favorable location, and commodious buildings have been already secured—the first session has elapsed with seventy pupils in attendance, and all the indications of future usefulness are very satisfactory. The terms are so arranged that while some young persons can pursue a regular course of training, study and practice in an experimental school, others, already engaged as teachers, can, during the interims of their own schools, attend a session of eleven weeks, more or less, without interfering with those pursuing a regular course of study, the latter being not unlike what is prescribed at the McNeely Institution. This temporary arrangement gives opportunity for teachers permanently engaged, to adjust the terms of their own schools so as to attend a part or whole of a session of eleven weeks at the Normal School; while others, not permanently engaged, can enter the Normal School at any time that may suit their convenience, and, after devoting a reasonable period to special preparation, will doubtless find full compensation for the expense in the more ready demand for their services. The organization of the 'Southwestern State Normal School' seems to be well considered, and is entitled to the confidence of the public."

His appeals to the people and his arguments to the Legislature, Mr. Barney based upon the following propositions, which he claimed to be among the various means and plans, that had been fully tested and approved by enlightened Educationists, for rendering school systems efficient:

"1. Each city, town, incorporated village, and civil township, should compose but a single school district, and the schools thereof be confided to the management and control of a properly constituted Board of Education.

"2. Properly constructed school-houses, occupying eligible sites, and possessing ample play grounds.

"3. Well educated, efficient and devoted teachers.

"4. Great care and thoroughness in the examination of teachers.

"5. Normal Schools organized and conducted with reference to the sole and definite object of instructing in the art of teaching.

"6. Properly managed Teachers' Institutes, Teachers' Meetings, and the formation of Teachers' Associations.

"7. Competent visiting agents charged with the important duty of organizing and superintending Teachers' Institutes, delivering educational addresses, and suggesting to teachers, in their own schools, the best manner of instructing classes.

"8. A system of vigilant and thorough supervision.

"9. Teaching but few subjects at one time, and teaching them thoroughly.

"10. A judicious course of study and oral exercises for each class, department, and grade of the school.

"11. A uniform series of class or text-books, and a strict adherence to it for a reasonable length of time.

"12. Judicious efforts on the part of teachers, parents and school officers, to induce all the youth of suitable age, resident within the district, to attend the schools.

"13. Unremitting efforts to secure regularity of attendance.

"14. The active and zealous co-operation of parents and school officers.

"15. Maps, charts, diagrams, globes, and other illustrative apparatus, for common schools, and chemical and philosophical apparatus for high schools.

"16. School district, or township libraries.

"17. The introduction of the system of gradation to the greatest practicable extent.

"18. The establishment of high schools and high school departments.

"19. The education of youth at schools in their own neighborhood or township.

"20. The education of both sexes at the same school, provided they can board at home, while attending it."

These propositions the Commissioner explained and enforced so amply and clearly, that his report for 1855 must long be regarded, by educational men, as among the most valuable documents upon free schools, published by our own, or any other State

Neither in his First nor Second report, did Mr. Barney especially describe his own labors, nor record his observations; but in the report for 1856 we find the following:

"During the past school year I have visited forty counties, lectured before seventy-one educational meetings, and visited a large number of schools. From my school visits, conferences with county auditors and other school officers, and from my observations generally, I have seen abundant and unmistakable indications of the steadily increasing popularity of our present school system.

"The conviction seems to be gradually settling down upon the public mind, that our present school law, with a few slight changes and modifications, would compare favorably with the school law of any other State in the Union.

"Within the last six months I have visited schools in several of the States, and endeavored to make myself thoroughly acquainted with the general educational system adopted in them all. From these observations, as well as from the admissions made by a large number of the leading educationists of those States, I am fully convinced that not one of those systems, as a whole, is superior to our own. Indeed, it was often conceded that our system, taken as a theory, possessed many advantages over their own. Among these advantages, the provision for supplying the people with libraries and the schools with maps, charts, globes, and other illustrative apparatus; the making of each city, incorporated village and township a single district for all purposes connected with the general interests of education; the annual levy and assessment of one and a half mills upon the dollar valuation on the grand list of the taxable property of the State, and the distribution of the school funds thus raised, in such a manner as to afford the advantages of *free education* to all the youth of this State, were particularly referred to and commended. The flexibility of our school system was also spoken of as an admirable feature, and worthy of being introduced, as it has been, into the system of other States.

"This excellent feature in our system is too often overlooked, or not duly appreciated. Hence it sometimes happens, that the people in certain localities complain of a want of efficiency in the system, and that too, before they have availed themselves of the privileges and advantages which it offers. The fact is too frequently overlooked that, if the provisions of the general school law are not satisfactory, they possess ample power to become organized as to schools under the 'act for the support and better regulation of common schools in the town of Akron,' passed February 8, 1847, and the acts amendatory thereto; or the 'act for the better regulation of schools in cities, towns, etc.,' passed February 21, 1849, and the acts amendatory thereto. Again, if the people of any city, town or incorporated village, organize as to schools under either of the above acts, or under any other act creating a special school district, sec. 66 of the general school act, confers upon them the power of relinquishing their organization under those special acts, and of having their schools conducted and managed in accordance with the provisions of the general act.

"By the provisions contained in sections 14 and 15, the Board of Education of any township in the State may, if the best interests of education and the wishes of the people demand it, unite two or more populous sub-districts into one, and establish therein such number of primary schools, and a school of such higher grade, as the public good and the wants of the people may require; or the board may establish one high school for the entire township, whenever the qualified voters thereof shall so determine by their votes, at a meeting called for the purpose, as provided in section 21.

"The foregoing provisions, together with the power vested in the people, through their boards of education, to raise funds, by a township tax, for the purpose of prolonging their schools, would seem to afford all the educational privileges that could reasonably be desired.

"It is to be regretted that, in some cases, township boards of education have either misapprehended or disregarded their duties, and neglected to make the necessary provisions for continuing the schools in operation in their respective townships for the length of time which the law requires, and which the inhabitants of the sub-districts desired. But this neglect is not so much the fault of the law as that of the people, in failing to elect those who, with intelligence and zeal, would carry the law into full and effective operation. The best school law which human wisdom could devise, would require enlightened and earnest school officers to work it, otherwise it would not secure its full measure of benefit to the people. No law can work or execute itself, or raise up, as by magic, wise and discreet officers where none can be found, or where the electors fail to exercise reasonable discretion, or manifest an intelligent interest in the selection of those who are to administer the law. A good law can not effect a good work unless it be well executed.

"It is gratifying to be able to state that, wherever the people have been fortunate in the selection of competent school officers, and zealously co-operated with them in carrying the law into efficient operation, the schools have risen to a degree of excellence far above what they ever attained under any former school law. In all such localities the present law is highly popular; for a fair trial of its adaptation to the character, spirit and educational wants of the times, has fully disclosed its merits, and justified its claims for the support of all those who believe that a wisely matured and judiciously organized system of public instruction is, under a government like ours, an essential agent of civilization, and especially of that modern republican, democratic civilization which professes to aim at the greatest good of the greatest number; and who also believe that education, thorough, systematic and universal, is almost the only means by which all the rich and varied blessings of our free institutions can be preserved and perpetuated; and that it is only under the guidance of knowledge that man's intellectual and moral powers can be duly developed, wisely applied, and himself prepared for the full enjoyment of this improved civilization.

"It is also encouraging and cheering to the heart of every true patriot, every sincere philanthropist, to be able to assure the friends of free schools that it is fast becoming the universal public sentiment of the intelligent, reflecting, philanthropic portion of the people of this State that, to withhold from the children of the State that intellectual and moral training which would give them the full command of every faculty, both of body and mind, which would call into play their powers of observation and reflection, and give them objects of pursuit and habits of conduct favorable to their own happiness, would be to deny them access to a large proportion of the best and noblest influences supplied by Christianity—by science and the arts; that every child has the most undoubted right to demand at the hands of the State the establishment and maintenance of such a system of public schools as would give him a place where his mental and bodily powers, his manners and morals could be trained up to a healthful, vigorous and graceful activity, and the proper foundation be laid to make him a thinking, reasonable being, an enlightened, virtuous citizen; that it is the duty, as well as the noblest privilege of the legislature to establish a system of public schools on such a broad and liberal foundation that the same advantages, without being abridged or denied to the children of the rich, may be open at the same time to the children of the poorest and humblest parent; that select or private schools, on account of their expense, being accessible only to the children of the more wealthy, must, on that account, always cause invidious distinctions between the rich and the poor, which ought not to exist anywhere, and especially in our own country, because, destined as all are to meet on the broad field of competition, and, at the same time, to labor together for the common weal, it is unwise to separate them in early life, and to make our schools, which ought to be so many bonds of union, the occasions of jealousy and inequality of privileges.

"Indeed, it is rare to find a city, village, township, or even school district, in the State, in which the doctrine is not earnestly and intelligently advocated, 'that education is a concern of government; that government may of *right*, and is in *duty bound* to support it, and that the property of the State may be justly taxed for that support, on account of the protection which that property itself derives from the dissemination of intelligence through all classes of society.' The former theory, 'that the cost of education should be regarded as mainly a personal burden, which every man should bear for the education of his offspring, or else they should be doomed to go out into the world ignorant and degraded,' now finds very few advocates in any section of our State. The great mass of the people now believe that free common schools, occupying commodious, well furnished, warmed, and ventilated houses, supervised by a discreet, efficient board of school officers, and instructed by teachers of sound education, mature judgment and large experience, should be considered as the peculiar objects of legislative care.

"From their universality, reaching as they do every neighborhood, shedding their benign influence upon every family, and into every mind, expelling the primary causes of vice and crime, and erecting altars to patriotism and virtue, free schools ought to be cherished, supported, and defended, by every man who has property to be protected, or who would live in a peaceable neighborhood, or enjoy a quiet home.

"It affords me great satisfaction to bear testimony to the fact that, wherever I traveled, and wherever I visited schools, or lectured, whether in city, village, or rural district, I never failed to find earnest, faithful, enlightened, eloquent advocates for the noble cause of free popular education. Among statesmen, lawyers, physicians, clergymen, farmers, mechanics and merchants, there was no difficulty in finding those who were ready to proclaim from the house-tops and the hill-tops, in the eloquent language of an eminent jurist and statesman,—'The idea of universal, free education is the grand central idea of the age.' Upon this broad and comprehensive basis, all the experience of the past, all the crowding phenomena of the present, and all our hopes and aspirations for the future, must rest. Our forefathers have transmitted to us a noble inheritance of national, intellectual, moral and religious freedom. They have confided our destiny, as a people, to our own hands.

"Upon our individual and combined intelligence, virtue, and patriotism, rests the solution of the great problem of self-government. We should be untrue to ourselves, untrue to the memory of our statesmen and patriots, untrue to the cause of liberty, of civilization and humanity, if we neglected the assiduous cultivation of those means by which alone we can secure the realization of the hopes we have excited. Those means are the *universal education of our future citizens*, without discrimination or distinction. Wherever, in our midst, a human being exists, with capacities and faculties to be developed, improved, cultivated, and directed, the avenues of knowledge should be freely opened, and every facility afforded to their unrestricted entrance. Ignorance should no more be countenanced than vice and crime. The one leads almost inevitably to the other. Banish ignorance, and in its stead introduce intelligence, science, knowledge, and increasing wisdom and enlightenment, and you remove, in most cases, all those incentives to idleness, vice, and crime, which now produce such a frightful harvest of retribution, misery, and wretchedness. Educate every child, 'to the top of his faculties,' and you not only secure the community against the depredations of the ignorant and the criminal, but you bestow upon it, instead, productive artisans, good citizens, upright jurors and magistrates, enlightened statesmen, scientific discoverers and inventors, and dispensers of a pervading influence in favor of honesty, virtue, and true goodness. Educate every child physically, morally, and intellectually, from the age of four to twenty-one, and many of your prisons, penitentiaries, and almshouses, will be converted into schools of industry and temples of science; and the immense amount now contributed for their maintenance and support, will be diverted into far more profitable channels. Educate every child—not superficially—not partially—but thoroughly; develop equally and healthfully every faculty of his nature—every capability of his being—and you infuse a new and invigorating element into the very life-blood of civilization—an element which will diffuse itself throughout every vein and artery of the social and political system, purifying, strengthening and regenerating all its impulses, elevating its aspirations, and clothing it with a power equal to every demand upon its vast energies and resources.

"These are some of the results which must follow in the train of a wisely matured and judiciously organized system of universal education. They are not imaginary, but sober inductions from well authenticated facts—deliberate conclusions from established principles, sanctioned by the concurrent testimony of experienced educators and eminent statesmen and philanthropists. If names are needed to enforce the lesson they teach, those of Washington, and Franklin, and Hamilton, and Jefferson, and Clinton, with a long array of patriots and Statesmen, may be cited. If facts are required to illustrate the connection between ignorance and crime, let the official return of convictions in the several courts of the State for the last ten years be examined, and the instructive lesson be heeded. Out of nearly 28,000 persons convicted of crime, but 118 had enjoyed the benefits of a *good* common school education; 414 only had what the returning officers characterize as a 'tolerable' share of learning; and of the residue, about one-half only could either read or write. Let similar statistics be gathered from the wretched inmates of our poor-house establishments, and similar results would undoubtedly be developed. Is it not, therefore, incomparably better, as a mere prudential question of political economy, to provide ample means for the education of the whole community, and to bring those means within the reach of every child, than to impose a much larger tax for the protection of that community against the depredations of the ignorant, the idle, and the vicious, and for the support of the imbecile, the thoughtless, and intemperate?

"The plan of educating the youth of our State at public schools, open and free to all, without distinction between the rich and poor, the high and the low, the native and foreign, is most in keeping with our republican principles, and best adapted to promote the perpetuity of the happy form of government under which it is our good fortune to live. It also furnishes one of the best securities to the fortunate wealthy for the peaceable enjoyment of their possessions, while it extends the blessings of education to thousands who otherwise would be doomed to live in ignorance, perhaps in vice and crime.

"Every consideration, therefore, connected with the present and future welfare of the community — every dictate of enlightened humanity—every impulse of an enlarged and comprehensive spirit of philanthropy, combine in favor of the adoption of this great principle. Public sentiment is everywhere pronouncing in its favor. The new States which, within the past few years have been added to the confederacy, have adopted it as the basis of their system of public instruction; and the older States, as one by one they are reconstructing their fundamental laws and constitutions, are engrafting the same principles upon their institutions. Surely, then, in this noble enterprise of universal free education, Ohio should not retrace her steps, nor disappoint the high hopes which she has excited, by receding from the advanced position which she now occupies in the very van of the great educational movement of the age.

"The meritorious character of her present school system, its adaptation to supply the educational wants of the times, the numerous schools of high order now rapidly springing up in every quarter, the deep and abiding interest in the cause of popular education, everywhere manifested by her citizens, are the subjects of warm and frequent encomiums, even in those States which have been longest distinguished for the excellence of their schools, and for the hearty and enlightened zeal exhibited in so many commendable ways, in behalf of popular education. One can hardly visit a school or converse with a school officer, in any of the middle or eastern States, without having his ears greeted and his heart cheered with such declarations as the following, viz: 'Ohio is doing a noble work in the matter of free schools.' 'She is outstripping all her sister States in this beneficent enterprise.' 'Her statesmen, her teachers, and her friends of education generally, have performed a work which will forever illustrate the pride and the glory of her history.' 'The career of Ohio in all those elements which go to make up the essential wealth, prosperity and greatness of a people, has been one of wonderful progress, manifesting the enterprise and public spirit of her people, and the wisdom of her far-seeing statesmen.' 'The people of Ohio, acting upon the principle that knowledge is power, and that knowledge and wisdom are ultimately to be the stability of our times, are taking away from us our pre-eminence in this respect; and unless we redouble our diligence, zeal and efforts in the great work of educational improvement, we shall soon be obliged to say, 'farewell self-respect, farewell the rich rewards of large intelligence and well-cultured minds; the age will pass us by, and we, who have led the way, and who have still the first advantages for success, will be distanced in the race, stripped of our crown, and deprived of our true glory.'"

These encouraging paragraphs were succeeded by suggestions upon the workings of the School Law, with arguments in favor of a few modifications, chief among which were the introduction of Township, for District Libraries—the making of each Township a single District, and the establishment of a Board of School Library Commissioners, consisting of the Governor, State Auditor, Librarian, and Commissioner.

After quoting so liberally from the Commissioner's last report, it is unnecessary to add any general remarks upon the character of our School System, or the estimation in which it is held; and we at once invite a comparison of the statistics in the following statement, with those which, in tabular form, have preceded it.

STATEMENT

OF THE RELATIVE CONDITION OF COMMON SCHOOLS FROM 1850 TO 1857.

AS REPORTED TO THE SUPERINTENDENTS.

Dates	No. of Counties	No. of Co's. Reported ..	No. of Whole Districts ...	No. of Fractional Districts	No. of Com. Schools	No. of Scholars Enrolled.			Average Attendance.			To. No. Scho'l Youth	No. of Teachers.			Amount paid Teachers.			No. of Months Taught.			No. of School Houses b'lt.	Cost of School Houses b'lt.
						Male.	Feml.	Total.	Male.	Feml.	Total,		Male.	Feml.	Total.	Male.	Female.	Total.	Male.	Fem'l.	Total.		
1850	87	79	9,590	1,342	12,279	236,827	184,906	421,733	190,891	146,984	337,875	810,163	7,924	5,168	13,092	$493,691	$138,428	$632,119	28,009	15,077	43,086	248	$64,823
1851	88	81	9.783	1.519	12.664	238.571	207,426	445,997	203,487	159,760	363,247	828,583	8,350	5,706	14,056	510,503	175,590	686,093	29,041	16,022	55,063	300	109,303
1852	88	70	8,537	1.285	9,916	240,152	197,560	437,712	144,982	121,285	266,267	838,669	7,272	5,292	12,564	599,187	172,958	772,145	11,808	13,954	25,762	171	61,837
1853	88	70	9.026	136	5,894	....	....	....	....	....	....	806,782	....	....	....	....	....	....	....	....	....	....	....
1854	88	77	11.203	162	10,451	191,956	166.461	358.417	150,529	126,667	277,196	817,106	7,540	6,476	14,016	565,026	289,276	854,302	....	....	31,129	770	346,944
1855	88	81	8.313	709	12,246	294,888	257,051	551,939	170,545	145,306	315,851	820,624	9,091	7,683	16,764	923,280	469,941	1,393,222	....	....	....	740	438,602
1856	88	85	8.311	672	11,319	299,226	262,089	561,315	171,877	150,766	322,643	826,680	9,491	8,432	17,923	1,023,212	531,195	1,554,407	....	....	....	627	374,547

AS ESTIMATED BY SUPERINTENDENTS.

Date.	No. of Districts	No. of Com. Schools	No. of Scholars Enrolled.			To. No. Scho'l Youth	No. of Teachers.			Amount paid Teachers.		
			Male.	Female.	Total.		Male.	Female.	Total.	Male.	Female.	Total.
1854	....	13,914	327,962	284,223	612,185	....	9,902	8,502	18,404	$899,555	$464,875	$1,364,430
1355*	....	14,714	350,863	304,860	655,663	....	10,998	9,854	20,852	1,086,302	600,116	1,686,418

* For 1856 there was no estimate.

In addition to the foregoing statement, the following statistics, reported for 1856, from all but three counties of the State, Adams, Brown and Henry, are important and interesting, because they show the relative number, cost, etc. of the schools of different grades:

NUMBER OF SCHOOLS.

Common	11,076
High	97
German, or German and English	58
For colored youth	88
Total	11,319

NUMBER OF YOUTH ENROLLED IN THE SCHOOLS.

	Males.	Females.	Total.
In the common schools	290,784	254,078	544,862
" high "	4,225	4,329	8,554
" German, or Ger. and English	1,977	1,625	3,602
" schools for colored youth	2,240	2,057	4,297
Total	299,226	262,089	561,315

NUMBER OF YOUTH IN AVERAGE DAILY ATTENDANCE.

	Males.	Females.	Total.
In the common schools	166,675	145,686	312,361
" high "	3,012	3,183	6,195
" German and English	1,106	837	1,943
" colored	1,084	1,060	2,144
Total	171,877	150,766	322,643

AVERAGE LENGTH OF TIME THE SCHOOLS WERE KEPT OPEN.

Common schools	6 1-10th months.
High "	9 1-5th "
German, or German and English	6 1-10th "
Schools for colored youth	5 4-5ths "

NUMBER OF TEACHERS EMPLOYED.

	Males.	Females.	Total.
In the common schools	9,235	8,248	17,483
" high	102	78	180
" German and English	43	7	50
" colored schools	69	31	100
Total	9,449	8,364	17,813

AVERAGE WAGES, PER MONTH, PAID TEACHERS.

	Males.	Females.
In the common schools	$26.70	$15.63
" high "	57.30	30.63
" German and English schools	30.83	30.00
" colored schools	25.73	20.00

EXPENDITURES OF SCHOOL MONEY.

Amount of Taxes levied and collected in the townships, cities and incorporated villages, as stated in the reports of boards of education.

For purchasing school-house sites	$ 15,015 46
Building and furnishing school-houses	441,527 23
Hiring school-houses	8,954 77
Repairing school-houses	53,655 77
Providing fuel, etc.	44,235 69
Providing book and apparatus cases	2,706 78
Other contingent school expenses	93,983 18
Prolonging schools	394,453 48
Sustaining high schools	12,259 86
Total	1,066,762 22

Whole amount of money paid for teachers' wages, in the several cities, townships and incorporated villages, from which reports were received:

	Males.	Females.	Total.
In the common schools	$947,860 15	$503,190 36	$1,451,050 51
" high "	56,464 26	22,843 48	79,307 74
" German and English	7,958 93	1,794 80	9,753 73
" colored	10,928 95	3,366 31	14,295 26
Total	1,023,212 29	531,194 95	1,554,407 24

Whole amount of money received, during the year ending August 31st, 1856, by the Boards of Education of the several townships, cities, and incorporated villages in the State, as reported:

From the State school tax	$1,113,918 85
Rents or sale of "section 16"	124,208 42
Virginia Military School Fund	7,105 66
United States " "	6,507 88
Western Reserve School Fund	12,113 60
Taxes assessed for the purpose of prolonging schools, building, repairing and furnishing school-houses, and for other contingent school expenses	441,334 52
Peddlers' and auctioneers' licenses and auction duties	609 24
Fines and penalties	4,303 63
Exhibition licenses	715 86
Miscellaneous sources	70,198 41
Unappropriated funds of previous year	319,847 85
Total	$2,100,863 92
Whole number of school-houses in the State as reported 8,144	
Total value	$3,270,691 00

NUMBER OF SCHOLARS INSTRUCTED IN THE VARIOUS BRANCHES DURING THE YEAR.

In the Alphabet	42,448
Spelling	270,745
Reading	299,002
Penmanship	249,922
The principles of Orthography	277,339
Mental Arithmetic	82,640
Written "	166,665
Geography	90,784
English Grammar	63,414
Physiology	2,571
Map Drawing	9,023
Composition	15,201
Declamation	23,909
The Elements of Drawing	2,496
Vocal Music	26,070
History	5,824
Algebra	5,790
Goemetry	934
Natural Philosophy	1,167
Moral "	276

Mental Philosophy	212
Chemistry	514
Rhetoric	404
Astronomy	655
Geology	297
Zoology	155
Latin	675
Greek	113
German	903
French	180
Book Keeping	63
Botany	53
Uranography	40
Natural History	20
Butler's Analogy	10
Trigonometry	5
Surveying	1

LIBRARY FUND.

Library and apparatus fund apportioned * in	1854,	$55,903.45
" " "	1855,	80,573.75
" " "	1856,	83,811.18
Total,		$220,288.38
Value of books distributed in	1854 †,	$ 48,367.42
" " "	1855,	102,427.61
" " "	1856,	51,430.90
Total,		$202,225.93
Value of apparatus distributed in	1854,	$6,347.87
" " "	1855,	9,555.23
" " "	1856,	3,514.67
Total,		$19,417.77
Total number of volumes distributed in 1854-5-6		332,579
Total value of books and apparatus distributed in 1854-5-6,		$221,643.60

Adding together certain columns of the Tabular statements which have been given in these pages, produces the following:

* By the State Auditor. † By the Commissioner.

AGGREGATE OF SCHOOL ITEMS OF GENERAL INTEREST FOR TWENTY YEARS, AS REPORTED.

No. of Children enrolled	$4,098,437
No. of Teachers employed	158,623
Amount paid Teachers	$8,897,888
No. of School-houses built	9,718
Cost of " " "	$2,385,706

Comparing the school statistics as reported with the estimates by Superintendents, at different periods, it is fair to conclude that the aggregates above presented, might at least be doubled without doing violence to truth. Thus considered, they show, from the past, encouragement for the future.

The people of Ohio have just pride in, and active love for, their School System. With the instrumentalities for the awakening of Educational interest *—with the facilities for affording instruction to Teachers, which popular efforts have secured, and with the support given by the State to Common Schools †—a support which is in no respect more liberal, in no degree more ample, than the sentiment of the people demands and their highest interest requires—Ohio now occupies, and will maintain, a position which, the brief period of her history as a State considered, is not second, in an educational point of view, to that of any State of the Union.

---

* Among which the general support of the newspaper and periodical press is to be included, as well as the *Journal of Education*, continued under the auspices of the Teachers' Association, with John D. Caldwell as Editor.

† A prominent feature of which is the office of School Commissioner, now filled by Rev. Anson Smyth.

www.ingramcontent.com/pod-product-compliance
Lightning Source LLC
LaVergne TN
LVHW020101110826
845151LV00001B/44

* 9 7 8 1 4 2 5 5 4 5 1 6 1 *